Criminal Justice in Post-Mao China

Criminal Justice in Post–Mao China: Analysis and Documents

Shao-chuan Leng, with Hungdah Chiu

State University of New York Press
ALBANY

Published by
State University of New York Press, Albany

For information, address State University of New York
Press, State University Plaza, Albany, N.Y., 12246

Library of Congress Cataloging in Publication Data

Leng, Shao Chuan, 1921–
    Criminal justice in post-Mao China.

    Bibliography: p. 306
    Includes index.
    1. Criminal justice, Administration of—China. 2. Criminal
procedure—China. I. Chiu, Hungdah, 1936- . II. Title.
LAW   345.51'05   84–16362
ISBN 0–87395–950–7   345.1055
ISBN 0–87395–948–5 (pbk.)

10 9 8 7 6 5 4 3 2 1

Contents

II DOCUMENTS

Tables

Wade-Giles–Pinyin Conversion Table

Wade-Giles	Pinyin	Wade-Giles	Pinyin
A	a	chiao	jiao
ai	ai	ch'iao	qiao
an	an	chich	jie
ang	ang	ch'ieh	qie
ao	ao	chien	jian
		ch'ien	qian
CHA	zha	chih	zhi
ch'a	cha	ch'ih	chi
chai	zhai	chin	jin
ch'ai	chai	ch'in	qin
chan	zhan	ching	jing
ch'an	chan	ch'ing	qing
chang	zhang	chiu	jiu
ch'ang	chang	ch'iu	qiu
chao	zhao	chiung	jiong
ch'ao	chao	ch'iung	qiong
che	zhe	cho	zhuo
ch'e	che	ch'o	chuo
chei	zhei	chou	zhou
chen	zhen	ch'ou	chou
ch'an	chen	chu	zhu
cheng	zheng	ch'u	chu
ch'eng	cheng	chua	zhua
chi	ji	ch'ua	chua
ch'i	qi	chuai	zhuai
chia	jia	ch'uai	chuai
ch'ia	qia	chuan	zhuan
chaing	jiang	ch'uan	chuan
ch'iang	qiang	chuang	zhuang

ch'uang	chuang	hsing	xing
chui	zhui	hsiu	xiu
ch'ui	chui	hsiung	xiong
chun	zhun	hsu	xu
ch'un	chun	hsuan	xuan
chung	zhong	hsueh	xue
ch'ung	chong	hsun	xun
chü	ju	hu	hu
ch'ü	qu	hua	hua
chüan	juan	huai	huai
ch'üan	quan	huan	huan
chüch	jue	huang	huang
ch'üch	que	hui	hui
chün	jun	hun	hun
ch'ün	qun	hung	hong
		huo	huo
E, O	e		
en	en	I, YI	yi
eng	eng		
erh	er	JAN	ran
		jang	rang
FA	fa	jao	rao
fan	fan	je	re
fang	fang	jen	ren
fei	fei	jeng	reng
fen	fen	jih	ri
feng	feng	jo	ruo
fo	fo	jou	rou
fou	fou	ju	ru
fu	fu	juan	ruan
		jui	rui
HA	ha	jun	run
hai	hai	jung	rong
han	han		
hang	hang	KA	ga
hao	hao	k'a	ka
hei	hei	kai	gai
hen	hen	k'ai	kai
heng	heng	kan	gan
ho	he	k'an	kan
hou	hou	kang	gang
hsi	xi	k'ang	kang
hsia	xia	kao	gao
hsiang	xiang	k'ao	kao
hsiao	xiao	ke, ko	ge
hsich	xie	k'e, k'o	ke
hsich	xian	kei	gei
hsin	xin	ken	gen

k'en	ken	lung	long
keng	geng	lü	lu
k'eng	keng	lüan	luan
ko, ke	ge	lüeh	lue
k'o, k'e	ke		
kou	gou	MA	ma
k'ou	kou	mai	mai
ku	gu	man	man
k'u	ku	mang	mang
kua	gua	mao	mao
k'ua	kua	mei	mei
kuai	guai	men	men
k'uai	kuai	meng	meng
kuan	guan	mi	mi
k'uan	kuan	miao	miao
kuang	guang	mieh	mie
k'uang	kuang	mien	mian
kuei	gui	min	min
k'uei	kui	ming	ming
kun	gun	miu	miu
k'un	kun	mo	mo
kung	gong	mou	mou
k'ung	kong	mu	mu
kuo	guo		
k'uo	kuo	NA	na
		nai	nai
LA	la	nan	nan
lai	lai	nang	nang
lan	lan	nao	nao
lang	lang	nei	nei
lao	lao	nen	nen
le	le	neng	neng
lei	lei	ni	ni
leng	leng	niang	niang
li	li	niao	niao
lia	lia	nieh	nie
liang	liang	nien	nian
liao	liao	nin	nin
lieh	lie	ning	ning
lien	lian	niu	niu
lin	lin	no	no
ling	ling	nou	nou
liu	liu	nu	nu
lo	luo	nuan	nuan
lou	lou	nun	nun
lu	lu	nung	nong
luan	luan	nü	nu
lun, lün	lun		

nüeh	nue	sha	sha
		shai	shai
O, E	e	shan	shan
ou	ou	shang	shang
		shao	shao
PA	ba	she	she
p'a	pa	shei	shei
pai	bai	shen	shen
p'ai	pai	sheng	sheng
pan	ban	shih	shi
p'an	pan	shou	shou
pang	bang	shu	shu
p'ang	pang	shua	shua
pao	bao	shuai	shuai
p'ao	pao	shuan	shuan
pei	bei	shuang	shuang
p'ei	pei	shui	shui
pen	ben	shun	shun
p'en	pen	shuo	shuo
peng	beng	so	suo
p'eng	peng	suo	suo
pi	bi	ssu, szu	si
p'i	pi	su	su
piao	biao	suan	suan
p'iao	piao	sui	sui
pieh	bie	sun	sun
p'ieh	pie	sung	song
pien	bian	szu, ssu	si
p'ien	pian		
pin	bin	TA	da
p'in	pin	t'a	ta
ping	bing	tai	dai
p'ing	ping	t'ai	tai
po	bo	tan	dan
p'o	po	t'an	tan
pou	bou	tang	dang
p'ou	pou	t'ang	tang
pu	bu	tao	tau
p'u	pu	te	de
		t'e	te
SA	sa	tei	dei
sai	sai	teng	deng
san	san	t'eng	teng
sang	sang	ti	di
sao	sao	t'i	ti
se	se	tiao	diao
sen	sen	t'iao	tiao
seng	seng	tieh	die

Wade-Giles	Pinyin	Wade-Giles	Pinyin
t'ieh	tie	tsung	zong
tien	dian	ts'ung	cong
t'ien	tian	tu	du
ting	ding	t'u	tu
t'ing	ting	tuan	duan
tiu	diu	t'uan	tuan
to	duo	tui	dui
t'o	tuo	t'ui	tui
tou	dou	tun	dun
t'ou	tou	t'un	tun
tsa	za	tung	dong
ts'a	ca	t'ung	tong
tsai	zai	tzu	zi
ts'ai	cai	ts'u	ci
tsan	zan		
ts'an	can	WA	wa
tsang	zang	wai	wai
ts'ang	cang	wan	wan
tsao	zao	wang	wang
ts'ao	cao	wei	wei
tse	ze	wen	wen
ts'e	ce	weng	weng
tsei	zei	wo	wo
tsen	zen	wu	wu
ts'en	cen		
tseng	zeng	YA	ya
ts'eng	ceng	yai	yai
tso	zuo	yang	yang
ts'o	cuo	yao	yao
tsou	zou	yeh	ye
ts'ou	cou	yen	yan
tsu	zu	yi, i	yi
ts'u	cu	yin	yin
tsuan	zuan	ying	ying
ts'uan	cuan	yu	you
tsui	zui	yung	yong
ts'ui	cui	yu	yu
tsun	zun	yuan	yuan
ts'un	cun	yueh	yue
		yun	yun

Preface

This book is an introductory survey of the formal criminal justice system built by Mao ZeDong's successors as a part of the current far-reaching reforms in the People's Republic of China between 1977 and 1983. Hopefully it will shed light not only on the development of Chinese legal institutions, but also on the prospects of the PRC's drive for modernization under the post-Mao leadership of Deng Xioaping and his associates.

In preparing this book, we have received valuable assistance from the Committee on the People's Republic of China of the American Bar Association, the Fulbright-Hays Foundation, and the Woodrow Wilson International Center for Scholars. Between us we have made three research trips to China, Hong Kong, and Taiwan respectively in the last four years, and we are grateful to many people who provided valuable information to us during our trips.

We would also like to acknowledge our indebtedness to Professor Jerome Alan Cohen and the Harvard University Press for their permission to reproduce the following translations of Chinese documents appearing in Jerome Alan Cohen, *The Criminal Process in the People's Republic of China 1949–1963, An Introduction* (1968):

Act of the People's Republic of China for Punishment of Counterrevolutionaries (pp. 299–302)

Act of the People's Republic of China for Security Administration Punishment (pp. 215, 218–219, 224, 227, 228, 230, 231, 232, 233, 235, 237, 250)

Decision of the State Council Relating to Problems of Rehabilitation Through Labor (pp. 249–250)

Act of the People's Republic of China for Reform Through Labor (pp. 365–368, 374–375, 376–377, 589–595, 619–621, 634)

Provisional Measures for Dealing with the Release of Reform Through Labor Criminals at the Expiration of Their Term of Imprisonment and for Placing Them and Getting Them Employed (pp. 410–411)

Finally, we wish to thank William Eastman, Courtney Reid, and Nancy Sharlet of the State University of New York Press for their help in making the publication of this book possible, and to Nancy Hasler and Lu Ann Young Marshall for skillful typing of the manuscript.

The responsibility for all facts and opinions in this book rests, of course, solely with us and not with any institution or other individual.

Shao-chuan Leng
Hungdah Chiu

May, 1984

I

Text

CHAPTER ONE

Introduction

Legal development in the People's Republic of China (PRC) during the period between 1949 and 1977 was not only inconsistent but also subject to several radical fluctuations. With the exception of a brief period from 1954–1956 when the PRC seemed to develop a legal system based on the Soviet model, the trend of legal development was to play down the role of law in Chinese society. The PRC operated a criminal justice system unique among its fellow Communist countries, with neither a criminal code, a criminal procedure code, lawyers,[1] nor prosecutors.[2] For a while, it appeared that this "unique legal system" was going to continue: the PRC gave the impression that it had solved the crime problem besetting all capitalist and "revisionist" countries without the modern luxury of codes, prosecutors, and lawyers.[3]

Then, unexpectedly, beginning in early 1978, less than two years after the death of Mao Zedong, virtually all the media on the Chinese mainland, from official newspapers and publications to wall posters, the underground press and other sources, burst out with complaints about abuses under the existing criminal justice system, especially during the last ten years of Mao's rule. They called for the reform of the legal system, especially of criminal justice. The PRC government and the Communist Party of China also frankly acknowledged that the Chinese legal system was manifestly imperfect and badly in need of reform. Thus, the Communique of the Third Plenary Session of the 11th Central Committee of the Communist Party of China, issued on December 22, 1978, set the goals of the PRC's legal reform as follows:

> In order to safeguard people's democracy, it is imperative to strengthen the socialist legal system so that democracy is systematized and written into law in such a way as to ensure the stability, continuity and full authority of this democratic system and these laws; there must be laws for people to

follow, these laws must be observed, their enforcement must be strict and law breakers must be dealt with.[4]

Recently, the Constitution adopted on December 4, 1982, also stated in its preamble that "the Chinese people of all nationalities will continue . . . to improve the socialist legal system. . . ." [5] This Constitution has thirteen articles on the judiciary, while the 1978 Constitution had three[6] and the 1975[7] Constitution had only one. This arrangement also appears to indicate that the PRC is paying more attention to the role of law in its government structure and society.

In practice, the PRC has taken a series of steps, including legislative, judicial, educational and other measures, to strengthen its legal system. Moreover, legal research, which was virtually suspended between 1966 and 1976, has been revived and significantly expanded. The exchanging of visits of lawyers between the PRC and foreign countries has steadily increased since 1979. Legal publications have also flourished in the PRC and most of them are available to students of Chinese law outside China. While no one can predict how long the current trend of the PRC's legal development will continue, not since the founding of the PRC have prospects been brighter for Chinese efforts to establish a more stable legal system. In view of this reemphasis on the role of law in the Chinese government structure and society, it is clear that law can no longer be ignored in Chinese studies by the West.

Despite the excellent opportunity to study the PRC law now, with the exception of a few articles,[8] there has not been a book-length study of the most important aspect of Chinese law—the criminal justice system in the post-Mao period. The purpose of this book is to provide an introductory survey of the development, organization, and functioning of the criminal justice system in the present day PRC. It discusses not only the formal aspects of the criminal justice system, such as the court, the procuratorate, lawyers and criminal procedure, but also extrajudicial sanctions which play an important role in the Chinese system. No attempt is made here to describe all offenses under Chinese criminal legislation. Laws dealing with specific offenses are treated only within the administration of criminal justice.

The book's analysis and survey of the Chinese criminal justice system are primarily based on published Chinese materials and supplemented by published Western sources and interviews with Chinese lawyers in China or visiting in the United States. But the interpretation of the information provided by the interviewers is entirely that of the authors and should not be attributed to any person who was kind enough to help in this research.

To understand the post-Mao criminal justice reform and its limits, one must appreciate how the criminal justice system operated under Mao's rule. Therefore, Chapter two will deal with legal experience under Mao, including ideological background, Soviet influence and Chinese tradition.

Chapter three deals with law reform under the post-Mao Chinese leadership and its limits under the concept of socialist legality. The institutional aspects of criminal justice—the Courts, the procuracy, the Ministry of Justice, the lawyer system, the public security (police) and other extrajudicial apparatus—are analyzed in Chapter four.

Chapter five discusses the criminal process under the newly enacted Criminal Procedure Law and the Chinese approach to certain basic principles of criminal justice, such as presumption of innocence, equality before the law, right to defense, and judicial independence. Crime and punishment are the subjects of Chapter six. This chapter makes a concise survey of general principles and substances of the PRC Criminal Law, information on crime, problems of political offenses, and the postsentencing treatment of prisoners under the unique Chinese Reform Through Labor system. Also examined are extrajudicial sanctions in the PRC administered by the police under the Security Administration Punishment Act and the unique Reeducation Through Labor system.

The conclusion of the book provides the authors' assessment of the PRC's criminal justice system, including its unique aspects, problems and future prospects.

Since most of the important Chinese criminal and its related legislation is not readily available in the West, this book includes fourteen laws in its documentary section. However, in order to keep this book at a reasonable size, only excerpts of some legislation are provided. All translations not credited are those of the authors or revised by the authors from translations available in the *Foreign Broadcasting and Information Service*.

NOTES

Chapter One

1. Lawyers existed between 1954–57, but since then the number of lawyers was significantly reduced until 1966 when the Cultural Revolution broke out. At that time, being a lawyer was no longer a recognized profession. The authors were told by a Chinese lawyer that between 1959–66, there were only four lawyers in China, primarily handling cases involving foreigners.

2. The procuratorate system was in fact abolished in 1969 and the 1975 Constitution formally confirmed this by providing in Article 25, paragraph 2, that "the functions and powers of procuratorial organs are exercised by the organs of public security at

various levels." Chen Hefu, ed., *Zhongguo Xianfa Leibian* (Classified Collection of Chinese Constitutions), (Beijing: Chinese Social Sciences Publisher, 1980), p. 342.

3. See Gerd Ruge, "An Interview with Chinese Legal Officials," *The China Quarterly*, No. 61, March 1975, pp. 118–126.

4. "Quarterly Chronicle and Documentation (October-December 1978)," *The China Quarterly*, No. 77, March 1979, p. 172.

5. *Zhongguo Fazhi Bao* (Chinese Legal System Paper), December 5, 1982, p. 1.

6. See Chen Hefu, "Collection of Constitutions," see above note 2, pp. 15–16.

7. See Chen Hefu, "Collection of Constitutions," see above note 2, p. 342.

8. See the list of those articles in the bibliography.

China's Legal Experience Under Mao

Two forms of law have coexisted and competed with each other in the People's Republic of China. One may be called the jural (formal) model and the other the societal (informal) model. The former stands for formal, elaborate, and codified rules enforced by a regular judicial hierarchy; the latter focuses on socially approved norms and values, inculcated by political socialization and enforced by extrajudicial apparatuses consisting of administrative agencies and social organizations. It appears quite clear that Mao Zedong's bias against bureaucratization, preference for the mass line, and commitment to the continuous revolution constituted major reasons for the PRC's past emphasis on the societal model of law over the jural model and on the politicization of the entire legal process.[1]

As a background for understanding the current Chinese leadership's effort to promote the jural model of law, this chapter will examine the PRC's legal experience under Mao. The discussion will be divided into three parts: the influence of Chinese heritage and Communist ideology; the development of the Chinese legal order during 1949–1976; and the characteristic of the Maoist system of justice.

Chinese Heritage and Communist Ideology

Dong Biwu, late President of the PRC Supreme People's Court, described the "People's Democratic Legal System" as a product of many years of experiment through selective assimilation of Chinese and foreign experiences and particularly creative application of Communist doctrine and the Soviet model to the concrete conditions of China.[2] As a point of departure, we shall begin with a brief analysis of the traditional attitude toward law in Chinese society.

Fa (positive law) played only a supplementary role to Li (moral code, rite, or customary law) in Confucian China as a regulator of human behavior and social order. Although Confucius and his disciples recognized the utility of law, they insisted that the rule of Li through moral example and persuasion was superior to the rule of Fa through rigid codes and severe punishment. This view is well illustrated by one of Confucius' statements: "If the people are guided by laws and regulated by punishment, they will try to avoid the punishment but have no sense of shame; if they are guided by virtue and regulated by Li, they will have the sense of shame and also become good." [3]

To be sure, a number of impressive and detailed codes were promulgated by the imperial dynasties of China, the most notable ones being the Tang and Qing codes. They were, however, the embodiment of the ethical norms of Confucianism and were invoked only when moral persuasion and social pressure failed. Primarily penal and administrative in nature, the codified law of traditional China was less concerned with the defense of individual interests than with the protection of the social and political order. [4]

In the judicial system of old China, there was a rather well-prescribed procedure and a hierarchical structure of institutions for administering justice. An elaborate system of appeals also existed to allow the review of sentences by higher authorities, including the emperor himself. On the other hand, adjudication and common administration were vested in the same hands on the lower administrative levels. The county magistrate, for instance, had to perform the duties of judge, prosecutor, and police chief in addition to his other functions as the head of the local government. Since the chief objective of Chinese justice was to assert the power of the state and to punish those who violated the rules of order and good conduct, the imperial judicial practice contained certain features that put the individual at a definite disadvantage. These included the practice of presumption of the guilt of the accused, the nonexistence of defense attorneys, the use of torture for extracting confession, the analogous application of penal provisions, and the enforcement of group responsibility and group punishment. [5]

With good reasons, the Chinese traditionally preferred to stay away from the courts of law and considered litigation as strictly a last resort. It was customary for large areas of offenses and disputes to be handled by extrajudicial organs and procedures. [6] The clan, the guild, the village council, and other local groups usually did much to maintain peace and order by settling conflicts and imposing disciplinary sanctions. In line with the spirit of social harmony and compromise, the informal means of mediation and conciliation rather than the regular legal process became the prevailing forms of dispute resolution in old China. The following words of Confucius typify the time-honored Chinese attitude: "In presiding lawsuits, I am as good as any man. But the important thing is to cause lawsuits to cease in the future." [7]

There is little doubt that Mao and his supporters must have assimilated, intentionally or not, certain traditional Chinese attitudes toward law, such as subordination of law to a dominant political philosophy and preference for informality in settling disputes and imposing sanctions. However, it is from Marxist-Leninist ideology and the Soviet system that they drew the basic concepts and formulations of law and justice.

Communist jurisprudence stresses the class nature of law and its subordination to political dictates. As viewed by Marx and Engels, legal institutions are parts of the superstructure on an economic base; they are tools of class rule, designed to promote the interest of the ruling class.[8] Lenin also said: "Law is a political instrument. It is politics." [9]

Under this theory, the dictatorship of the proletariat is considered a transitional stage to a Communist society where the state will "wither away and law then is no longer needed." During the transitional period, the Proletariat uses state and law to ruthlessly suppress class enemies and to effect the transition to Communism free of any legal and ethical constraints.[10] Lenin said:

> The dictatorship of the proletariat produces a series of
> restrictions of liberty in the case of the oppressors, the
> exploiters, the capitalists. We must crush them in order to free
> humanity from wage slavery; their resistence must be broken
> by force; it is clear that where there is suppression there is
> also violence, there is no liberty, no democracy.[11]

In his official interpretation of Soviet legality, Andrei Y. Vishinsky defined law as the totality of the rule of conduct, reflecting the will of the dominant class and enforced by the coercive power of the state to secure and develop social relations and social orders desirable and advantageous to the dominant class. Socialist law, he asserted, "is entirely and completely directed against exploitation and exploiters . . . . It is invoked to meet the problems of the struggle with foes of socialism and the cause of building a socialist society." [12]

Fully in accord with the Marxist-Leninist concepts of revolutionary legality and class justice, Mao Zedong said, "Such state apparatus as the army, the police and the courts are instruments with which one class oppresses another. As far as the hostile classes are concerned these are instruments of oppression. They are violent and certainly not 'benevolent things.' " [13] He was echoed by a Chinese jurist, who described the socialist law in China as "a sharp weapon for carrying out class struggle in the hands of the broad masses of laboring people led by the proletariat," to be used primarily to suppress the enemy, protect the revolutionary order, and ensure the success of socialism.[14] From the perspective of his concept of continuous revolution, Mao regarded law as merely a useful tool to political ends and would not let formal rules hinder the interest of the revolution.[15] "Proper limits have to be exceeded," he contended, "in order to right a wrong, or else the wrong cannot be righted." [16]

Using the class line approach, Mao also provided a theoretical framework for differentiating and resolving social conflicts with his famous 1957 speech, "On the Correct Handling of Contradictions Among the People." In the speech, he drew a basic distinction between two types of contradictions: "Contradictions between ourselves and the enemy" (antagonistic contradictions) and "contradictions among the people" (nonantagonistic contradictions). Mao defined in broad terms "the people" as the "classes, strata, and social groups which approve, support and work for the cause of socialist construction" and "the enemy" as "the social forces and groups that resist the socialist revolution, and are hostile and try to wreck socialist construction." [17]

As the two contradictions are fundamentally different, the methods for solving them also differ. According to Mao, conflicts among the people are to be dealt with by the "method of democracy" and conflicts with the enemy by the "method of dictatorship." In settling "questions between right and wrong among the people," reliance should be placed on education and persuasion." In dealing with "reactionaries, exploiters, counterrevolutionaries, landlords, bureaucrat-capitalists, robbers, swindlers, murderers, arsonists, hooligans, and other scoundrels who seriously disrupt social order, measures of dictatorship and severe sanctions must be employed." Although "law-breaking elements among the people" should also be subjected to the discipline of law, stated Mao, "this is different in principle from using the dictatorship to suppress enemies of the people." [18]

DEVELOPMENT OF THE PRC'S LEGAL SYSTEM, 1949–1976

Prior to the founding of the People's Republic in 1949, the Chinese Communists had been engaged in revolutionary struggle for more than twenty years. During these years they drew upon the Soviet experience and, to a lesser degree, the tradition of China to develop legal institutions and procedures in response to the "objective" conditions of the revolution. The pre-1949 legal experience and experimentation of the Chinese Communist Party (CCP) later provided a valuable basis upon which for the PRC to build its system of "people's justice."

What should be noted here is the emergence of the two models of law, jural and societal, in the Communist-controlled areas before 1949. On the one hand, there were a number of basic laws enacted, and a regular judiciary system consisting of courts, procuracy, and people's assessors instituted along with elaborate judicial procedures providing for public trial, appeal, right of defense, etc. On the other hand, special encouragement was given to the development of mass line devices in judicial work, the use of mediation for handling civil cases, and the employment of extrajudicial organs and procedures in imposing sanctions and settling disputes. At times, "people's justice" was dispensed through the regular process by the judiciary. At others, it was done through the summary proceedings of revolutionary tribunals and public security organs. The alteration of procedures was determined not only by the nature of cases but more often by the relative intensity of the revolutionary struggle in a given time.[19]

While recognizing the utility of law, Mao nevertheless preferred informality and flexibility in approaching legal matters. He and his followers regarded those in favor of legal formality as "mechanistic," losing sight of the priority of the revolution.[20] Mao's position made its imprint in the years before 1949 and had an even more far-reaching impact in the post-1949 period upon the legal development of the PRC.

For the convenience of discussion, we shall divide the development of the PRC legal system under Mao into four major stages: (1) 1949–1953, (2) 1954–1957, (3) 1957–1965, and (4) 1966–1976.[21]

(1) 1949–1953

From 1949–1953 the Common Program adopted by the Chinese People's Political Consultative Conference (CPPCC) served as a provisional constitution for the new People's Republic of China. This period was one of internal consolidation and reorganization. In many respects it resembled the early years of the Soviet regime in Russia, when the notorious Cheka and revolutionary tribunals enforced the Red Terror to smash the hostile class and establish the new order.

In the early years of the People's Republic, the dual models of law continued to operate in a complimentary yet competitive manner. The Communist government abolished all Kuomintang (KMT, Nationalist) laws and judicial organs at the outset. It proceeded gradually to establish a three-level, two-trial (one appeal) judiciary system along with the procuracy.[22] According to Lan Chuanbu, a Chinese author, 148 important laws and regulations were also adopted from 1949 through 1953, the majority of which appeared in either experimental or provisional form.[23] Among the more important enactments were the Marriage Law (1950), the Land Reform Law (1950), the Trade Union Law (1950), the Act for the Punishment of Counterrevolutionaries (1951), and the Act for Punishment of Corruption (1952).[24]

In judicial practice, however, the people's courts as a rule would not indicate under which law and under what particular provisions the judgment was rendered.[25] Moreover, justice was often dispensed by administrative agencies, especially the police. Not infrequently, the public security organs disposed cases of ordinary offenders or of serious criminals without resort to the courts. Indiscriminate arrest, arbitrary detention, fatigue interrogation, corporal punishment, and wanton trial were those common police abuses reported by both Communist and other sources.[26]

During the nationwide mass campaigns, such as the Land Reform, Three-Anti, Five-Anti, and Suppression of Counterrevolutionaries Movements in 1950–1952, ad hoc people's tribunals conducted mass trials and dispensed revolutionary justice against "reactionaries" and "bad elements."[27] Even by Mao's own admission, some 800,000 "class enemies" were sentenced to death in such trials; many more were apparently sent to long terms of reform through labor.[28] These mass campaigns were, however, defended by a 1979 article in *Beijing Review* as necessary:

> In the early years of the People's Republic, the Communist Party initiated several mass movements on a nationwide scale. Direct mass action rather than the force of law fuelled these tempestuous revolutionary movements. The aim then was to break down the old, reactionary social order. Examples are the land reform movement of 1949–51 to overthrow the landlord class, the 1950 movement to suppress counterrevolutionaries and the 1952 *san fan* (three anti, i.e., anti-corruption, waste and bureaucratism) and *wu fan* (five anti, i.e., anti-bribery, tax evasion, stealing state property, cheating in workmanship and materials and stealing state economic intelligence) movements against the bourgeoisie. These mass movements were absolutely necessary because the reactionary forces riding on the backs of the people were still very powerful when the old society was being superseded by the new.[29]

Between 1952 and 1953, the Communist authorities carried out a judicial reform movement to purge holdovers from the Nationalist government and to "rectify and purify the people's judicial organs at the various levels politically, organizationally, and ideologically."[30] Undoubtedly, the movement marked an important step of the PRC toward the development of socialist legality. It laid a solid foundation, as observed by Shi Liang, "for the consolidation of the People's Democratic Dictatorship and the strengthening of the people's judicial work in New China."[31] Nevertheless, a prominent Chinese jurist acknowledged in a 1980 article that the 1952–53 Judicial Reform Movement overreacted in denouncing the viewpoints of "judicial independence" or "inheritability" of old or bourgeois law and therefore facilitated the subsequent abnormal development in which there was no differentiation between the Party and the government and between the Party and the law.[32]

(2) 1954–1957

There was a clear ascendency of the jural model in what may be called the era of the PRC's constitutional experiment, 1954–1957. During this period, Beijing closely modeled its programs of industrialization on the Soviet system through concentration on heavy industry. On the legal front, a serious move was made to lead the country in the direction of stability and codification.

The Constitution that the PPC promulgated in September 1954 underscored the regime's genuine attempt at institutionalization.[33] In the whole document, the Chinese Communist Party was mentioned just twice in the Preamble and only with reference to the CCP's leadership of the revolution and the democratic united front. In the Preamble, the PRC was characterized as "a people's democratic dictatorship" and in Article 1, as "a people's democratic state led by the working class and based on the alliance of workers and peasants".

According to the Constitution, the "highest organ of state authority" was the National People's Congress (NPC). Along with its Standing Committee, the NPC exercised broad powers of legislation, amendment, and appointment (Chapter Two, Section I). No deputy to the National People's Congress "may be arrested or placed on trial without the consent of the National People's Congress or, where the National People's Congress is not in session, of its Standing Committee" (Article 37).

The Chairman of the People's Republic of China, elected by the NPC for a four-year term, was the head of state with a number of executive, procedural, and ceremonial powers, including the authority to command the armed forces of the country (Chapter Two, Section II). The chief administrative organ was designated by the constitution as the State Council, which, together with the Supreme People's Court and Supreme People's Procuratorate, completed the central governmental structure. As stipulated by the Constitution, each of the three organs was accountable to the NPC, with its officials appointed or removed by the NPC or its Standing Committee (Chapter II, Sections III and VI).

In the local state hierarchy, all units of the three governmental levels (provincial, county, and basic) were required by the Constitution to have their own people's congresses (legislative) and people's councils (executive). The relationship between these bodies should be comparable to that between the NPC and the State Council (Chapter Two, Section IV). Article 56 prescribed an elaborate electoral procedure for direct election by the population of people's congresses at the lowest (basic) level and for indirect election by the people's congresses at the next lower level thereafter.

Bearing a striking resemblance to the 1936 Constitution of the USSR, the Chinese Constitution also contained in Chapter Three a comprehensive enumeration of people's rights and duties (Article 85 to 103). Among other things, this chapter guaranteed equality before the law, freedom of speech, of the press, of association, of demonstration, and of religion, as well as the right to work, to leisure, to education, and to social assistance. Article 89 specifically provided protection against arbitrary arrest by saying, "Freedom of the person of citizens of the People's Republic of China is inviolable. No citizen may be arrested except by decision of a people's court or with the sanction of a people's procuratorate." To implement this article, an Arrest and Detention Act was promulgated in December 1954 with provisions for concrete and detailed procedures.[34]

On September 28, 1954 the PRC promulgated organic laws of the People's Courts and the People's Procuratorates. These two laws, along with the relevant stipulations of the Constitution, gave the PRC judicial system a permanent structure. Under the National People's Congress and its Standing Committee, two separate but interlocking hierarchies were established. The people's courts, headed by the Supreme People's Court, were given the sole authority to administer justice; the people's procuratorates, culminating in the Supreme People's Procuratorate, were to exercise the supervisory power over the execution of the law. Below the Supreme People's Court, local courts were divided into higher people's courts, intermediate people's courts, and basic people's courts. A similar structure was also provided for local procuratorates.[35]

Both the Constitution and the Organic Law of the Courts introduced a number of democratic features to the new judicial system such as the right of legal defense and the principles of public (open) trial and withdrawal of judges. Probably more significantly, the PRC for the first time seemed to accept in a limited form the concept of judicial independence. With identical tones, Article 78 of the Constitution and Article 4 of the Organic Law stipulated: "In administering justice, the people's courts are independent, subject only to the law." Article 8 of the Constitution stated that the courts should be responsible to the people's congresses at corresponding levels and should report to them. This was in clear contrast with the earlier laws which required the subordination of the courts to the leadership of the people's governments.[36]

However, people's rights and judicial independence under the system remained qualified. For instance, a PRC scholar pointed out that "reactionaries" or "class enemies" had no rights whatsoever under the Constitution.[37] Nor did the Constitution's guarantee of equality before the law mean that "when the state enacts law, it would treat individuals from different classes equally in legislation." [38] Moreover, even in this period there was a continued informalization and politicization of the legal work in China.[39]

On the other hand, there is little question that an important trend toward more regularity and institutionalization was started. Besides the courts and the procuracy, a lawyer's system was established. It was reported in mid-1957 that there were 817 legal advisory offices and 2,528 full-time and 350 part-time lawyers in the country.[40] In addition to Constitutional and Organic enactments, the PRC adopted a large number of substantive and procedural laws and regulations during this period. As shown in the official statutory collections, over 600 laws, decrees, regulations, and decisions were passed between January 1954 and June 1957.[41] Efforts were also made to draft civil, criminal, and procedural codes. By 1957, for instance, more than twenty drafts of a criminal law had already been made.[42]

At the Eighth National Congress of the Chinese Communist Party in September 1956, Liu Shaoqi, then Vice Chairman of the CCP Central Committee, spoke of the reasons for regularizing the legal system:

> Now . . . the period of revolutionary storm and stress is past, new relations of production have been set up, and the aim of our struggle is changed into one of safeguarding the success for development of the productive forces of society; a corresponding change in the methods of struggle will consequently have to follow and a complete legal system becomes an absolute necessity. It is necessary, in order to maintain a normal social life and to foster production, that everyone in the country should understand and be convinced that as long as he does not violate the laws, his civil rights are guaranteed and will suffer no encroachment by any organization or any individual. Should his civil rights be

unlawfully encroached upon, the state will certainly intervene. All state organs must strictly observe the law, and our security departments, procurators' offices and courts must conscientiously carry out the system of division of function and mutual supervision in legal affairs.[43]

Similarly, the speech given by Dong Biwu, then President of the Supreme People's Court, and the resolution adopted by the CCP Central Committee at the Eighth Party Congress emphasized the need for codification and observance of law.[44] Mao Zedong, however, appeared to be less enthusiastic. In his speech before the same Congress he warned his party of the evil of bureaucratism and the danger of becoming isolated from the masses.[45]

3. 1957–1965

China's progress toward a stable legal order came to an abrupt end in the autumn of 1957 when the Communist elites launched an Anti-Rightist Campaign as a counterattack against strong criticisms of the Party evoked by the Hundred Flowers Blooming and Contending Movement of 1956–1957.[46] During the Movement, many jurists and scholars used the opportunity to criticize the government for the lack of basic laws and the defective administration of justice. Suggestions were made to restore certain legal concepts such as the "presumption of innocence" and the "benefit of the doubt for the accused." [47] In the ensuing Anti-Rightist Campaign, however, many leading jurists and even four judges of the Supreme People's Court were purged as "rightists." [48] Emphasis was placed on the class nature of the law. The independence of the judiciary was interpreted as subject to Party control and the concept of "presumption of innocence" and other liberal principles were dismissed as "theories of bourgeois jurisprudence," incompatible with the socialist judicial system.[49]

Equally important was the PRC's decision to abandon the Soviet model in favor of the Maoist developmental strategy (the Great Leap Forward) that stressed mass mobilization and "politics in command." [50] The impact on the legal field was a decisive shift from the jural model to the societal model. During the retrenchment years of the early 1960s, when Liu Shaoqi was the head of state, there was an occasional reappearance of legal discussion in judicial circles. Codification work on several basic laws was also resumed. In fact, the thirty-third draft of a criminal law was presented in 1963 to the Standing Committee of the CCP Political Bureau and Mao Zedong for examination.[51] On the whole, nonetheless, China's formal legal system continued to experience a steady decline in importance.[52] As pointed out by a recent Chinese publication, the malicious development during 1957–1965 of a phenomenon of looking down upon the legal system and substituting Party for government and officials' words for state laws really caused a complete standstill in the country's legislative work.[53]

In judicial practice, the criminal process became totally controlled by Party committees and was administered by public security organs. The pursuit of the mass line in judicial work, too, received a renewed emphasis. It called for integrating court trial with mass debate, bringing the courts directly to the people, simplifying and innovating rules and procedures, and carrying out justice on the spot.[54]

Under the circumstances, procedural guarantees and the citizens' fundamental rights provided by the Constitution and other legal documents appeared to have little relevancy in the administration of justice during this period. The case of Bao Ruo-wang is a good illustration. A dual national of France and China, Bao was arrested in December 1957 for engaging "in counterrevolutionary activities" and "violating the laws of the People's Republic of China." [55] Confined in the Interrogation Center where he was frequently interrogated and expected to write confessions constantly, Bao did not have his first trial until late December 1958. He was sentenced to twelve years' imprisonment on April 13, 1959 essentially based on his well-orchestrated "self-accusation" statement.[56] Nowhere in Bao's case did he even try to invoke the Constitutional protection afforded to the people and none of the officials involved in his case seemed to be concerned with any legal niceties.[57]

(4) 1966–1976

The Cultural Revolution, initiated in 1966 by Mao with the support of Lin Biao, Jiang Qing and others, was intended largely to revolutionalize and rectify the bureaucratic establishment and to impose Maoist values and norms upon the population and society. According to a resolution adopted by the CCP Central Committee on June 27, 1981, this turbulent campaign was "responsible for the most severe setback and the heaviest losses suffered by the Party, the state and the people since the founding of the People's Republic." [58]

Certainly, the formal legal structure received a most serious blow during the Cultural Revolution, as the Red Guards denounced Liu Shaoqi and his fellow "capitalist roaders," among others, for supporting the "bourgeois" concepts of "equal justice" and "defense counsel" and for resisting "leadership of the Party over legal work" in a document entitled "Completely Smash the Federal, Capitalist, and Revisionist Legal System." [59] The document also quoted Mao as saying, "Depend on the rule of man, not the rule of law." [60]

Following Mao's instruction to "smash Gongjianfa (police, procuracy, and courts)," the Red Guards singled out the Public Security Organs for special denouncement. They were attacked for abuse of power and for taking a reactionary stand. Moreover, its cadres were accused of failing to carry out the mass line according to the teachings of the Chairman Mao.[61] In an editorial titled, "In Praise of Lawlessness," the *People's Daily* called for the complete destruction of the "bourgeois" law so that the proletarian legal order could be established.[62]

To achieve the transformation of political-legal organs, Mao proceeded to have a large number of cadres purged without resort to any formal process. Among many law enforcement personnel removed from office were the President of the Supreme People's Court, the Chief Procurator, and the First Deputy Minister of Public Security. Liu Shaoqi, the primary target of the Cultural Revolution, was deprived of his post as the Chairman of the People's Republic of China by the decision of the Central Committee of the Chinese Communist Party in disregard of constitutional procedure.[63]

The dismantling of the "bourgeois" law enforcement apparatus during the Cultural Revolution was also accomplished through the wider use of mass line devices and the imposition of military control over Gongjianfa by the People's Liberation Army (PLA). The courts still existed but functioned only sparingly. There were occasional reports of participation of people's courts in the judicial process. More often there were reports of public judgment meetings or mass trials against counterrevolutionaries, class enemies, or common criminals, where judgments were rendered and sanctions imposed by "political and legal organs," "organs of dictatorship," "revolutionary committees," or "military control committees." [64]

Although 1969 marked the end of the Cultural Revolution, the PLA's supervision of the administration of justice continued beyond that year. It was only between 1970 and 1973 that military control over law enforcement gradually receded though the pace varied from region to region and from agency to agency. By 1973, "normalcy" appears to have been restored in the legal field. The courts did survive the Cultural Revolution, but the procuracy was abolished with its functions and powers transferred to the public security agency. This action was taken, according to a Chinese spokesman, "in order to simplify, improve and transform the structure which was not suitable to a socialist economic basis, and to simplify the procedure in the jurisdictional sphere for the convenience of the masses." [65]

What emerged from the Cultural Revolution was the clear ascendency of the societal model of law over the jural model and the complete dominance of the Party and the police in the administration of justice. In the early 1970's, for instance, the public notices announcing sentences were done "in accordance with the Party policy," particularly that of "dealing leniently with those who confess and severely with those who resist." [66]

More significantly, in January 1975, the Fourth National People's Congress (NPC) adopted a new Constitution for the PRC, which showed a strong Maoist influence with its stress on mass politics and Party supremacy.[67] Compared to the 1954 Constitution, the new one was much shorter; it had only thirty-six articles and contained about 4,500 words, while the 1954 one had 106 articles and contained about 14,000 words.

In contrast with the 1954 Constitution, the 1975 document proclaimed China as a "socialist state of the dictatorship of the proletariat" rather than "a people's democratic state" (Article 1). The new Constitution eliminated the chairman of the People's Republic of China from the state structure. It institutionalized the Party's direct control of the state. Article 2 declared: "The Communist Party of China is the core of the leadership of the whole Chinese people." Article 16 stated that "the National People's Congress is the highest organ of state power under the leadership of the Communist Party of China." Article 15 stipulated that the People's Liberation Army and the people's militia "are led by the Communist Party of China" and that the "Chairman of the Central Committee of the Communist Party of China commands the country's armed forces."

So far as the law is concerned, the 1975 Constitution confirmed the political reality of the consistent decline of the jural model in China since 1957. It abolished the procuracy and deleted the 1954 Constitution's protection of NPC deputies against arrest or trial without the consent of the NPC or its Standing Committee. There was a drastic reduction in the number of provisions regarding citizens' fundamental rights, from nineteen articles (Articles 85–105) in the 1954 Constitution to four articles (Articles 26–29) in the 1975 Constitution.[68] Omitted in the new document were the provisions on the freedom of residence, freedom to change residence, and freedom of scientific research, literary and artistic creation, and other cultural pursuits. While retaining the freedom to believe in religion, the 1975 constitution added the freedom not to believe religion and propagate atheism (Article 28). Reflecting the Maoist outlook, it also included certain new forms of freedoms, such as "freedom to strike" (Article 28) and "speaking out freely, airing views fully, holding debates, and writing big character posters" (Article 13).

The downgrading of legality was clearly demonstrated by the dramatic reduction in the coverage of the judicial system, from twelve articles (Articles 73–84) in the old Constitution to one article (Article 25) in the new Constitution. Provisions containing such "bourgeois" concepts of due process as equality before the law, public trials, right to defense, and protection against arbitrary arrest were eliminated.[69] The controversial provision providing for judicial independence was also dropped.[70] Underscoring the trend toward politicization and informalization of the legal order, Article 25 of the 1975 Constitution called for the subjection of the people's courts to the control of local political leadership (the revolutionary committees) at corresponding levels and the application of the mass line as the operational principle for procuratorial and trial work. It reintroduced mass trials to judicial proceedings in "major counterrevolutionary criminal cases." The Article further legitimized the dominant position of the police in law enforcement by stipulating that "the functions and powers of procuratorial organs are exercised by the organs of public security at various levels."

All in all, at the time of Mao's death in September 1976, the position of the societal model of law reached such a point that most offenses and disputes were handled by extrajudicial institutions led by Party committees and the police. The courts often played a subsidiary or ceremonial role in judicial proceedings. Under the circumstances, excesses and abuses in the administration of justice occurred easily and frequently. China's current leaders and spokesmen, in fact, have attacked Lin Biao and the Gang of Four for creating a state of lawlessness and "feudal-fascist" rule during of 1966–76.[71] The disgraced radicals have been accused of subjecting political opponents to arbitrary arrest, extended detention, and endless struggle meetings. Tens of thousand of innocent people are said to have been cruelly tortured and persecuted by the Gang of Four and their followers.[72] Regardless of one's view on the 1980–81 trial of the Gang of Four, there is little question that the decade immediately preceding the arrest of Jiang Qing and her associates was the most regressive period of China's legal life, a fact often emphasized by all types of Chinese the authors interviewed in recent years both inside and outside China.

CHARACTERISTICS OF PEOPLE'S JUSTICE[73]

Following the survey of the PRC's legal development under Mao, we can proceed to examine the features of the Maoist system of criminal justice. It should be noted that no code of substantive or procedural criminal law was ever enacted in Mao's China, even though there were 1,488 laws, regulations, and decrees of various kinds promulgated by the PRC's legislative and administrative bodies during the fourteen years of 1949–1963.[74] Among the issues of criminal justice under Mao, special attention should be given to class justice, mass mobilization campaigns, the Party's dominant role, and criminal as well as administrative sanctions.

Class Justice

One most notable characteristic of people's justice in Mao's China was to make an individual's class origin or political background a determining factor in the criminal process. As discussed before, the concept of class justice was expounded by Mao in his famous 1957 speech "On the Correct Handling of Contradictions Among the People." The theoretical formulation in this speech became the most frequently cited guideline for law enforcement in China and was incorporated with the Preamble of the 1975 Constitution. In order to correctly distinguish antagonistic from nonantagonistic contradiction, it was imperative for judicial and public security personnel to use a class standpoint to determine the nature of a problem. From a class viewpoint, the so-called "five black elements" (landlords, rich peasants, counterrevolutionaries, rightists and other bad elements) were considered "the enemy."[75] Persons with a bad class status or having a family background that included "five black elements" were treated as political outcasts and potential criminals. "They are held up," says one observer, "as 'negative examples' and living symbols of what happens to enemies of the regime."[76] When crimes were committed, such persons usually received harsher sanctions for the same offense than those among "the people."[77] This was particularly true during a political campaign when members of the "black elements" often provided convenient targets for class hostility and abuse.[78]

The strong class character of Chinese criminal law was clearly stated in an official textbook: "The criminal law of our country primarily deals blows to the counterrevolutionaries, to the criminals of homicide, arson, burglary, fraud, rape, and other offenses seriously obstructing social order and socialist construction. It must be understood that the point of our criminal law is chiefly directed toward the enemies of socialism."[79] Political considerations and the class line were not only applied to the sanctioning process but even to dispute resolution in Mao's China.[80] The concept of equality before the law for all persons certainly had no place in people's justice. Those Chinese leaders in favor of such a concept were severely attacked by the Maoists:

Class and class struggle is a great revolutionary magic weapon of Marxist-Leninism and the thought of Mao Zedong. . . . However, the handful of top capitalist roaders within the Party vainly attempted to wipe out fundamentally the dictatorship of the proletariat by means of law. . . .

Counterrevolutionary revisionist Peng Zhen even openly jumped forth to set the tune saying: "All citizens of ours can become equal and must be equal before the law." He advocated "equal treatment" and stated that "there is no need to adopt a class viewpoint in addition to law." He rejected the class character of law, thus overthrowing the proletarian dictatorship. In this way, the public security organs, procuratoriates, law courts and armed forces became ordinary organs instead of instruments of the dictatorship. The question of who should be defended or suppressed was obliterated at one stroke, and with no dividing line drawn between the enemy and ourselves, how could revolution be carried out? If such peaceful evolution were permitted to go on, our proletarian regime would not take long to end in capitalist restoration.[81]

The Party's Dominant Role

Throughout Mao's reign the Communist Party always played a dominant role in the administration of people's justice. It is, however, during the post-Mao period that details of the Party's control over judicial work have been made known.

During the years under review, 1949–1976, there were three nominal divisions in the PRC's formal structure of criminal justice: the public security (police), the procuracy (a victim of the Cultural Revolution), and the courts; in practice, all were under the direction of the Party committee at the same level, which made decisions as to arrest, prosecution, and sentencing in criminal cases. Dating back to the war years and the early period of the People's Republic, this practice was continued in spite of the adoption in 1954 by the Constitution of the principle that "the people's courts administer justice independently according to the law." [82] In fact, as a result of the 1957–58 Anti-Rightist campaign which attacked "judicial independence" and other bourgeois precepts, the system of having cases examined and approved by the Party committee became a permanent fixture of people's justice, to be known as "shuji pian" (approving cases by the secretary) since the Party committee often delegated the decision-making authority to its secretary in charge of political-legal affairs, lacking time to review the cases itself. Liao Junchang, a writer, describes the system as follows:

> Whether or not the facts of a case are clear, whether or not the evidence is convincing, whether or not the defendant should be subject to criminal sanction, and what criminal punishment should be imposed on the defendant—all must be sent to the secretary in charge of political-legal affairs of the local Party committee at the same level for review and approval. This is called the system of approving cases by the secretary.[83]

Liao criticizes this system for a number of reasons. First, he points out the harm done to the division of labor and mutually restrictive relationship among the three law enforcement organs (police, procuracy, and courts), by this type of interference from the Party committee. Second, "approving cases by the secretary" negated the trial system and legal process prescribed by law and made trial by the court only a formality. Third, this practice amounted to the substitution of the Party for the government and damaged the activism and creativity of judicial cadres. Finally, the political-legal secretary, concurrently in charge of many other administrative duties, just could not have time or energy to handle cases with care and competency.[84]

A study on judicial work by a group of teachers and cadres of the Southwest Political-Legal Institute also cites the following problems concerning the system of "approving cases by the secretary":

(1) Given the voluminous tasks to perform, the secretary found it not possible to review and approve cases for several months, thus causing delay in the administration of justice.

(2) The secretary's decision on cases often took the form of "surprise attack," handling several or even several dozen cases at one time. It was not possible for him to carefully study the facts, evidence, and the nature of each individual case.

(3) If a court should disagree with the handling of a case by the Party committee (i.e., the political-legal secretary), it could not secure the Party committee's reconsideration through any legal procedure, the only rule being "Whatever is approved (by the Party committee) should be executed."

(4) Since arrest and sentencing were all decided by the secretary on behalf of the Party committee, the court had to sentence the arrested in accordance with the decision of the Party committee, even if sometimes contrary to law.

(5) It was rather hard for the secretary to admit and correct his own mistakes. The prevailing attitude was one of "upholding the decisions of the Party committee" and of "not changing what has been approved by a leading cadre."[85]

Under the circumstances, it would appear entirely futile for a convicted person to challenge the judgment. What is more, under the PRC's principle of "leniency to those who confess and severity to those who confess," a refusal to confess or an appeal against conviction might be considered an aggravating factor leading to an increased sentence.[86] According to author Bao Ruo-wang, a fellow inmate named Bartek appealed a sentence of five-year imprisonment only to have it changed to life. Evidently, Bao observes, Bartek failed to accept the elementary truth in Mao China:

> An appeal against a sentence means the prisoner is not repentent for his crimes and has not accepted the government's lenience *ipso facto*, it is proof that he has not learned his lesson. An appeal, therefore, is a demand for further punishment.[87]

The Mass Line and Mobilization Campaigns

The application of Mao's mass line strategy to legal work was an inherent part of people's justice and took several forms. First of all, large numbers of minor contradictions and offenses were handled by a host of administrative agencies and mass organizations. Individual citizens got involved in the extrajudicial process through mediation committees, security defense committees, and other activist networks formed in residential, production, and occupational units.[88] Another way of implementing the mass line approach was to bring the courts to the people by holding trials in a factory, store, or commune. Still another was to disseminate materials on cases of political or educational value among the public for consideration in small group discussions. Opinions and suggestions resulting from such discussions were supposed to be consulted by the courts in reaching final judgments.[89] In practice, for important cases of a political nature, the public was usually given brief, conclusive materials referring to the offenses as "viciously attacking socialism" or "arousing the great anger of the masses." As a rule, the people followed the guidance of these documents and Party leaders in proposing punishment at small group discussions. In less important cases, however, there appears to have been more leeway for the people to express their views.[90]

Finally, political campaigns and mass trials were periodically employed to mobilize the masses and to heighten their vigilance against class enemies. The 1975 Constitution specifically provided in Article 25: "The mass lines must be applied in procuratorial work and in trying cases. In major counterrevolutionary criminal cases, the masses should be mobilized for discussion and criticism." [91] During political campaigns or mass movements, legal procedures were often totally disregarded and ad hoc organs were set up to arrest, investigate, and detain alleged offenders for almost unlimited periods.[92] Mass trials and public judgment meetings were held to dispense people's justices, which performed not only a deterrent function but a propaganda-education function of raising the people's political awareness.[93] For instance, in two mass trials held in Shanxi Province in 1970 involving 50,000 people, it was reported that the broad masses of the revolutionary people had learned a valuable lesson and vowed to follow Chairman Mao's instruction to protect the great achievement of the Cultural Revolution, to strike against a handful of counterrevolutionary and other criminal elements, and to consolidate the dictatorship of the proletariat.[94] On such occasions, public executions or harsh sanctions against the accused were usually used to achieve the purpose of "killing chicken to scare monkeys." [95]

Indeed, the political wind of a particular time in the PRC, especially the presence or absence of a mass movement, constituted a crucial factor in deciding the severity of punishment, if any, in criminal cases. During an "epidemic" of theft cases, for example, the authorities, with wide publicity, executed a thief.[96] On other occasions and in a different climate, a person committing theft might simply be subject to educational lectures and then set free. In the turbulent years of the Cultural Revolution, people were severely punished or imprisoned for shouting a wrong slogan or making uncomplimentary remarks on Lin Biao or Jiang Qing.[97] Many unintentional or accidental acts were also punished as in the so-called "damaging precious [Mao's] picture" cases.[98] In one case, a cadre who used a newspaper to wrap an article and accidentally broke the paper which contained Mao's picture was sentenced to eight years' imprisonment on a charge of engaging in counterrevolutionary activity.[99] In another case, a nineteen year old youth was sentenced to eighteen years' imprisonment on a charge of "malicious attack" on the "Great Leader" because he placed three crickets on a table of one of his fellow workers for fun, but behind that table there happened to be a picture of Mao.[100]

Criminal and Administrative Sanctions

There were three categories of sanctions in Mao's China: informal, administrative, and criminal. The informal sanctions for petty offenses imposed by work and residential units ranged from criticism to struggle meetings. The administrative sanctions imposed by the police included formal warning, fines and short detentions, supervised labor without segregation from society, and reeducation through labor in camps. The major criminal sanctions imposed by the courts were: control, similar to supervised labor; imprisonment for a fixed term; imprisonment for life; death sentence suspended for two years; and death sentence followed by immediate execution.[101]

In the absence of a criminal code, the PRC, for almost thirty years, had only a few statutes governing specific crimes such as the Act for Punishment of Counterrevolutionaries (1951) and the Act for Punishment of Corruption (1952).[102] The Act for Punishment of Counterrevolutionaries contained two catchall articles to cover almost every conceivable unforeseen situation. First, Article 18 made the Act retroactive to cover offenses committed before the establishment of the PRC in 1949. Second, Article 16 set forth the principle of crime by analogy: "Those who, with a counterrevolutionary purpose, commit crimes not covered by this Act may be given punishments prescribed for crimes [enumerated] in this Act which are comparable to the crimes committed." Moreover, the 1951 State Secret Act further expanded the scope of counterrevolutionary offenses by defining as state secrets almost anything not publicly released.[103]

The existence of many loopholes in the PRC's criminal legislation gave the Party dominated judicial system too much arbitrary power in applying criminal sanctions. As alluded to before, the severity of punishment was strongly affected by the offender's class status, his postcrime attitude, and the political situation of a given time. The most frequently used criminal sanction was imprisonment carried out in a reform through labor institution (camp, farm, or prison). In a report on "the ten major relationships," Mao Zedong emphasized the reform through labor rather than execution of counterrevolutionaries so as to convert "worthless things into useful ones" and to avoid making "irretrievable mistakes." [104] According to Article 1 of the 1954 Act for Reform Through Labor, this program was adopted "in order to punish all counterrevolutionary and other criminal offenders and to compel them to reform themselves through labor and become new persons." [105]

There is little doubt that the system of reform through labor performed useful functions for Mao's government by converting the dangerous elements of society into a source of economic and political strength. Through compulsory physical work, the inmates learned productive skills and contributed to the construction of China's public works and development projects. Moreover, the incessant process of political education and ideological indoctrination also served to break the resistence of hostile individuals and remold their values and attitudes to suit the needs of the socialist revolution.[106] As to the treatment of the individuals in Chinese corrective institutions, there have been conflicting claims. On the one hand, Chinese spokesmen described the government's humanitarian concern for the successful transformation of the offenders.[107] On the other, reports from ex-prisoners and other sources charged that the Chinese system of "forced labor" subjected millions of prisoners to cruelty and exploitation.[108] Many offenders, even at the end of their sentences, were retained in the same area where they undertook reform.[109] Those who were detained in prisons waiting for trials or after trials also suffered harsh treatment; this was especially true for political prisoners.[110]

In a 1982 interview with *The Washington Post*, a former school-teacher who spent twenty-one years in a labor camp in Southwest China before her release in 1979 provided a glimpse of the daily routine, living conditions, and inmates of one of Mao's prisons. According to her, tens of thousands of political undesirables and innocent intellectuals languished for years at the camp and were forced to work seven days a week with up to twenty hours a day of hard labor hauling coal or collecting manure. During her twenty-one years at the camp, thousands were said to have died of maltreatment, and in years of food shortages and extreme weather conditions, "as many as 40 percent of the camp population perished." [111]

As mentioned earlier, public security organs had the power to impose a series of administrative sanctions without judicial review. Under the Security Administration Punishment Act (SAPA) of 1957, the police could issue warnings, impose a fine, and detain a person up to fifteen days.[112] Furthermore, they were empowered to impose sanctions on acts not specifically prohibited in the SAPA by analogy.[113] The most serious administrative sanction was reeducation through labor governed by the State Council's Decision Relating to Problems of Reeducation Through Labor in 1957.[114] It was designed to control vagrants, minor offenders, and troublemakers who did not work properly or who refused to comply with work assignments or transfer, and people who were unemployed because they had been expelled from their place of work for a breach of discipline or for being antisocialist reactionaries. Since there was no time limit for placing a person under reeducation, those intellectuals who were labelled rightists in the late 1950s were detained for reeducation through labor for almost twenty years before their release in the post-Mao period. The harsh treatment of these people was similar to that meted out to those who were subject to the criminal sanction of reform through labor, although reeducation through labor carried less stigma and at times involved slightly better detention conditions.[115]

NOTES

Chapter Two

1. For a detailed discussion, see Shao-chuan Leng, "The Role of Law in the People's Republic of China as Reflecting Mao Tse-tung's Influence," *Journal of Criminal Law and Criminology*, Vol. 68, No. 3, 1977, pp. 356–73.

2. Dong Biwu, *Lun Shehui Zhuyi Minzhu Yu Fazhi* (On Socialist Democracy and the Legal System) (Beijing: People's Press, 1979), pp. 130–131.

3. *The Analects*, Book 1, Chapter 2.

4. For a comprehensive treatment of law in traditional China, see Derk Bodde and Clarence Morris, *Law in Imperial China* (Cambridge, Mass.: Harvard University Press, 1967); Chu Tung-tsu, *Law and Society in Traditional China* (Paris: Monton, 1961); Jean Escarra, *Le Droit Chinois* (Peking: Editions H. Vetch, 1936).

5. For traditional Chinese judicial practice, consult Sybille van der Sprenkel, *Legal Institutions in Manchu China* (London: The Athlone Press, 1962), Chapters 5–6; Robert van Gulik, *T'ang-yin-pi-shih, Parallel Cases From Under the Pear-tree* (Leiden: E. J. Brill, 1956), pp. 52–63.

6. The extrajudicial organs and procedures are examined in van der Sprenkel, Chapters 7–9; Hsiao Kung-chuan, *Rural China: Imperial Control in the Nineteenth Century* (Seattle: University of Washington Press, 1960).

7. *The Analects*, Book 12, Chapter 12.

8. Karl Marx and Frederick Engels, *Selected Works* (Moscow: Foreign Languages Publishing House, 1958), Vol. 1, pp. 49, 362, 623–625; Vol. II, pp. 493–495.

9. John N. Hazard, *Communists and Their Law* (Chicago: University of Chicago Press, 1969), p. 69.

10. Hans Kelsen, *The Communist Theory of Law* (London: Stevens & Sons, 1955), pp. 31, 51; Bernard P. Ramundo, *The Soviet Legal System: A Primer* (Chicago: American Bar Association, 1971), pp. 5–6.

11. V. I. Lenin, *Collected Works*, Vol. XXI–2 (New York: International Publishers, 1932), p. 219.

12. Andrei Y. Vyshinsky, *The Law of the Soviet State*, trans. Hugh W. Babb, (New York: Macmillan, 1948), p. 50.

13. Mao Tse-tung, *On People's Democratic Dictatorship* (Peking: Foreign Languages Press, 1951), pp. 16–17.

14. Zhou Xinmin, "Law Is a Sharp Weapon of Class Struggle," *Renmin Ribao* (People's Daily), October 28, 1964, p. 2.

15. For a discussion of Mao's concept of continuous revolution, see Stuart R. Schram, "Mao Tse-tung and the Theory of Permanent Revolution, 1958–69," *The China Quarterly*, No. 46, April-June 1971, pp. 221–244; John Bryan Starr, *Continuing the Revolution: the Political Thought of Mao* (Princeton: Princeton University Press, 1979).

16. "Report on the Investigation of the Peasant Movement," *Selected Works of Mao Tse-tung* (Peking, Foreign Languages Press, 1967), Vol. I, p. 27.

17. Mao, "On the Correct Handling of Contradictions Among the People," *Supplement to People's China*, No. 13, 1957, p. 4.

18. Ibid., pp. 4–6.

19. For the CCP's legal experience before 1949, see Shao-chuan Leng, *Justice in Communist China* (Dobbs Ferry, New York: Oceana, 1967), pp. 1–26; Patricia E. Griffin, *The Chinese Communist Treatment of Counterrevolutionaries: 1924–1949* (Princeton: Princeton University Press, 1976).

20. *The Chinese Communist Treatment of Counterrevolutionaries*, pp. 138–139; Leng, "The Role of Law in the PRC," see above note 1, p. 357.

21. In an article, three Chinese authors also have the same periodicalization of the PRC's legal development with the following descriptive titles: the creation period of the legal system (1949–1953); the development period (1954–1956); the period of stagnation when the work for building the legal system was subject to interference (1957–1965); the period of great destruction (1966–1976). Chen Shouyi, Liu Shengping, and Zhao Shenjiang, "Thirty Years of the Building Up of Our Legal System," *Faxue Yanjiu* (Studies in Law), No. 4, 1979, p. 1. See also Hungdah Chiu, *Chinese Law and Justice: Trends Over Three Decades* (Baltimore: University of Maryland School of Law Occasional Papers/Reprints in Contemporary Asian Studies, No. 7-1982(52), pp. 4–17.

22. Leng, *Justice in Communist China*, pp. 27–28; Hungdah Chiu, "The Judicial System Under the New PRC Constitution," *The New Constitution of Communist China*, ed. by Michael Lindsay, (Taipei: Institute of International Relations, 1976), pp. 70–72.

23. Lan Chuanbu, *Sanshi Nianlai Woguo Fagui Yange Gaikuang* (Survey of the Development of the Laws and Regulations of Our Country In the Last Thirty Years) (Beijing: Mass Press, 1980), pp. 3, 4.

24. Leng, *Justice in Communist China*, p. 32.

25. Chiu, "The Judicial System," see above note 22, p. 73.

26. Leng, *Justice in Communist China*, p. 34.

27. *Justice in Communist China*, pp. 35–39; Lung-sheng Tao, "Politics and Law Enforcement in China: 1949–1970," *American Journal of Comparative Law*, Vol. 22, 1974, pp. 715–720.

28. The number of people liquidated was contained in the unofficial version of Mao's major speech of February 27, 1957, "Problems Relating to the Correct Handling of Contradictions Among the People." *New York Times*, June 13, 1957, p. 8. See Jerome A. Cohen, *The Criminal Process in the People's Republic of China, 1949–1963* (Cambridge, Mass.: Harvard University Press, 1968), p. 10.

29. "Prospect and Retrospect: China's Socialist Legal System," *Beijing Review*, Vol. 22, No. 2, Jan. 12, 1979, p. 25.

30. Chen Shouyi, et al., "Thirty Years", see above note 21, p. 1.

31. Leng, *Justice in Communist China*, p. 44. Miss Shi (Shih in Wade-Giles) was then China's Minister of Justice.

32. Chen Shouyi, "A Review of New China's Research in Law During the Past Thirty Years", *Faxue Yanjiu*, No. 1, 1980, p. 2.

33. Text of the Constitution is in *Zhonghua Renmin Gongheguo Fagui Huibian* (Collection of Laws and Regulations of the People's Republic of China) *(FGHB)* (Beijing: Legal Press), Vol. I (1956), pp. 4–31. English translation is in *Constitution of the People's Republic of China* (Peking: Foreign Languages Press, 1954).

34. Text of the Regulations is in *FGHB*, Vol. I, pp. 239–242.

35. Text of the Organic Laws of the Courts and the Procuratorates are in *FGHB*, pp. 123–132 and 132–138, respectively. English texts of the two laws are in *Documents of the First Session of the First National People's Congress of the People's Republic of China* (Peking: Foreign Languages Press, 1955), pp. 185–199 and 201–211, respectively.

36. Leng, *Justice in Communist China*, p. 48.

37. Li Guangcan, *Woguo Gongmin Di Jiben Quanli He Yiwu* (The Fundamental Rights and Duties of the Citizens of Our Country) (Beijing: People's Press, 1956), pp. 7–8.

38. Ibid., p. 13.

39. See Jerome A. Cohen, "The Chinese Communist Party and 'Judicial Independence': 1949–1959," *Harvard Law Review*, Vol. 82, March 1969, pp. 967–1006; Victor Li, "The Role of Law in Communist China," *The China Quarterly*, No. 4, October-December 1970, pp. 80–88; Stanley Lubman, "Form and Function in the Chinese Criminal Process," *Columbia Law Review*, Vol. 69, April 1969, pp. 546–551.

40. *Zhengfa Yanjiu* (Political-Legal Studies), No. 4, 1957, p. 30.

41. See *Zhongyang Renmin Zhengfu Faling Huibian* (Collection of Laws and Decrees of the Central People's Government) *(FLHB)* (Beijing: People's Press, 1955), Vol. 1, and *FGHB*, Vols. I–V.

42. Peng Zhen, "Explanation on the Seven Draft Laws," *Main Documents of the Second Session of the Fifth National People's Congress of the People's Republic of China* (Beijing: Foreign Languages Press, 1979), p. 192.

43. *Eighth National Congress of the Communist Party of China*, Vol. 1, *Documents* (Peking: Foreign Languages Press, 1956), p. 82.

44. See above note 43, Vol. 2, *Speeches*, p. 87 and Vol. 1, *Documents*, pp. 128–129.

45. See above note 43, p. 9.

46. For a general discussion of the Hundred Flowers Movement, see Merle Goldman, *Literary Dissent in Communist China* (Cambridge, Mass.: Harvard University Press, 1967); Roderick MacFarguhar, *The Hundred Flowers Campaign and the Chinese Intellectuals* (New York: Praeger, 1960).

47. For a summary of these criticisms, see Leng, *Justice in Communist China*, pp. 57–63.

48. *Justice in Communist China*, p. 55.

49. *Justice in Communist China*, p. 63.

50. For a succinct analysis of the Great Leap, see Alexander Eckstein, *Communist China's Economic Growth and Foreign Trade* (New York: McGraw-Hill, 1966), pp. 29–37; Franz Schurmann, *Ideology and Organization in Communist China* (Berkeley: University of California Press, 1968), pp. 464–500.

51. Leng, "The Role of Law in the PRC," see above note 1, p. 358; "China's Socialist Legal System," *Beijing Review*, Vol. 22, No. 2, January 12, 1979, p. 26.

52. Peng Zhen, "Seven Draft Laws," see above note 42, p. 192.

53. Several PRC jurists had this to say: "In 1957, it was necessary to counterattack the attack launched by an extremely small number of bourgeois rightist elements; however, this class struggle was artificially expanded. Two years later, the struggle against the so-called rightist opportunism within the Party was improperly started, which caused unfavorable results as it undermined the democracy within the Party and people's democracy. In political-legal circles, the impact of this left thought was extremely obvious. The principles of democracy and the legal system provided in the Constitution were subject to criticism; the position was erroneously taken that the independent exercise of trial and procuratorial authority by the judicial organs were opposing Party leadership. Moreover, the leadership over subordinate organs and legal supervision over other state organs exercised by the procuratorial organs were accused of invoking law to resist the Party or opposing Party leadership; the principle of all citizens are equal before the law was considered as disregarding the class character of law and talking equality with counterrevolutionaries; the principle of relying on facts as basis and law as criterion (in trials) was described as abandoning party policy or favoring legal isolationism; the emphasis of doing business according to law was described as a bourgeois viewpoint of supremacy of law; the socialist defense system and lawyer system were described as defending bad elements and making no differentiation between us and the enemy. Thus, many laws and systems, which were in force and had proved their usefulness, were disturbed and undermined and many comrades who defended the principles of the Constitution were declared as rightists

and anti-Party elements under various false accusations which upset right from wrong. The result of such development greatly undermined the enthusiasm of the broad political-legal cadres and encouraged the tendency of left rather than right ideas and the doctrine of abolishing the law. As a result, an adverse development emerged which despised legal system, relying on the party to substitute for the government and using ('officials') words to replace law. The legislative work of the state was totally suspended. . . . Our country's legal work has (since then) continued to go downward and thus opened the gate for Lin Biao and the Gang of Four to take this opportunity to usurp power and occupy government positions to engage in counter-revolutionary restoration activities." Chen Shaoyi et al., "Thirty Years," see above note 21, p. 2.

54. For an examination of the judicial practice during this period, see Cohen, *The Criminal Process*, pp. 14–18; Leng, *Justice in Communist China*, pp. 63–74.

55. Bao Ruo-wang (Jean Pasqualini) and Rudolph Chelminski, *Prisoner of Mao* (New York: McCann and Geoghegan, 1973), pp. 27–28.

56. *Prisoner of Mao*, pp. 98–99.

57. For a similarly illustrative case of Yang Guoqing, see Chiu, "The Judicial System," see above note 22, pp. 83–85.

58. "On Questions of Party History," *Beijing Review*, Vol. 24, No. 27, July 6, 1981, p. 20.

59. Canton, *Fan Peng-Lo Heixian* (Anti-Peng and Lo's Black Line), No. 2, July 1968; English translation in *Selections from China Mainland Magazine* (Hong Kong: U.S. Consulate-General), No. 625, September 3, 1968, pp. 23–28.

60. *Selections from China Mainland Magazine*, No. 625, p. 23.

61. Leng, "The Role of Law in the PRC," see above note 1, p. 359.

62. *Survey of China Mainland Press (SCMP)* (Hong Kong: U.S. Consulate-General), No. 3879, February 14, 1967, p. 13.

63. Liu was expelled from the CCP "for all time" and stripped of all his state posts by the decision of the Central Committee of the Chinese Communist Party on October 31, 1968. *Renmin Ribao*, November 2, 1968, p. 1. However, the right to remove the head of state was reserved for the National People's Congress by Article 28 of the 1954 Constitution of the PRC. For a specific study of Liu, see Lowell Dittmer, *Liu Shao-ch'i and the Cultural Revolution* (Berkeley: University of California Press, 1974).

64. Leng, "The Role of Law in the PRC," see above note 1, pp. 359–360; Chiu, "The Judicial System," see above note 22, pp. 88–89. For a summary of the impact of the Cultural Revolution on the judiciary see Tao-tai Hsia, "The Tenth Party Congress and the Future Development of Law in China," *Oil and Asian Rivals* (Washington, D.C.: U.S. Government Printing Office, 1974), pp. 390–405.

65. Gerd Ruge, "An Interview with Chinese Legal Officials," *The China Quarterly*, No. 61, March 1975, p. 120.

66. For English translations of some of those notices, see Chiu, "The Judicial System," see above note 22, pp. 108–114.

67. The text of the 1975 Constitution can be found in *Documents of the First Session of the Fourth National People's Congress of the People's Republic of China* (Peking: Foreign Languages Press, 1975), pp. 5–29. For a detailed analysis of the Constitution, see Lindsay, *The New Constitution of Communist China;* Tao-tai Hsia and K. Haun, *The 1975 Revised Constitution of the People's Republic of China* (Washington, D.C.: Library of Congress—Law Library, 1975).

68. For the text of the 1954 Constitution, see above note 33.

69. E.g., Articles 76 and 85 of the 1954 Constitution. Article 89 of the 1954 Constitution stipulated that "no citizen may be arrested except by a decision of a people's court or with the sanction of a people's procuratorate" was replaced by

Article 28 of the 1975 Constitution that provided "no citizen may be arrested except by decision of a people's court or with the sanction of a public security organ." This actually meant no restriction on the arrest power of the police.

70. Article 78 of the 1954 Constitution.

71. "China's Socialist Legal System," see above note 51, pp. 26–27.

72. Chen Shouyi et al, "Thirty Years," see above note 21, p. 2. According to the Indictment of the Trial of the Gang of Four during November 1980–January 1981, a total of 729,511 people were allegedly framed and persecuted in the years of 1966–1976, of whom 34,800 were persecuted to death. *A Great Trial in Chinese History* (Beijing: New World Press, 1981), pp. 20–21; 173–184.

73. For a concise analysis of Chinese criminal justice and its problems before 1977, see generally Hungdah Chiu, "Socialist Legalism: Reform and Continuity in Post-Mao Communist China," *Issues & Studies*, Vol. 17, No. 11, November 1981, pp. 47–57.

74. See the chart on these laws and decrees in *Law Annual Report of China 1982–3* (Hong Kong: Kingsway International Publications, 1982), p. 9.

75. For a discussion of the PRC's class classification, see *Political Imprisonment in the People's Republic of China* (London: Amnesty International Publications, 1978), pp. 9–11.

76. A Doak Barnett, *Cadres, Bureaucracy and Political Power in Communist China* (New York: Columbia University Press, 1967), p. 404.

77. Cohen, *The Criminal Process*, pp. 511–512; Lubman, "Form and Function," see above note 39, pp. 560–561. See also Leng, "The Role of Law in the PRC," see above note 1, p. 364.

78. See above note 1, pp. 364–365; Randle Edwards, "Reflections on Crime and Punishment in China, with Appended Sentencing Documents," *Columbia Journal of Transnational Law*, Vol. 18, No. 1, 1977, p. 62; *Political Imprisonment in the PRC*, pp. 11–12.

79. Central Political-Judicial Cadres' School, *Lectures on the General Principles of Criminal Law in the People's Republic of China* (Peking, 1957), translated by Joint Publication Research Service (JPRS), No. 13331, 1962, p. 18.

80. Leng, *Justice in Communist China*, p. 174; Stanley Lubman, "Mao and Mediation: Politics and Dispute Resolution in Communist China," *California Law Review*, Vol. 55, No. 5, 1967, pp. 1339–1346.

81. "Completely Smash the Federal, Capitalist and Revision Legal System," see above note 59, pp. 23–24. Until his ouster during the Cultural Revolution, Peng Zhen was the mayor of Beijing and a close associate of Liu Shaoqi. Currently vice-chairman of the NPC Standing Committee, Peng has been a major architect in restoring the legal system in post-Mao China.

82. See the statement by President Jiang Hua of the Supreme People's Court in *Renmin Ribao*, August 25, 1980, p. 1.

83. Liao Junchang, "Independent Adjudication and Approving Cases by the Secretary," *Xinan Zhengfa Xueyuan Xuebao* (Journal of the Southwest Political-Legal Institute), No. 1, May 1979, p. 7.

84. See above note 83, pp. 7–9.

85. Special Group Assisting the Handling of Cases from the Southwest Political-Legal Institute, "Looking at Some Existing Problems in Judicial Work from the Practice of Handling Cases," *Xinan Zhengfa Xueyuan Xuebao*, No. 1, May 1979, pp. 26–27.

86. *Political Imprisonment in the PRC*, pp. 54–59. See also Leng, *Justice in Communist China*, pp. 151–153; Cohen, *The Criminal Process*, pp. 556–563.

87. *Prisoner of Mao*, p. 80.

88. For charts on these organizations and their relationships with Party and state apparatus, see Cohen, *The Criminal Process*, pp. 140–141 and Lubman, "Mao and Mediation," see above note 80, pp. 1313, 1331.

89. Gerd Ruge, "An Interview with Chinese Officials," *The China Quarterly*, No. 61, March 1975, pp. 121–122.

90. This is based on interviews with former Chinese cadres and residents in the early 1970's and confirmed by talks with Chinese nationals both inside and outside China in recent years.

91. For the text of the Constitution, see above note 67.

92. *Political Imprisonment in the PRC*, pp. 50–52.

93. For political purposes the authorities would execute even a minor offender to warn the public. Wang Rouwang, "Jokes Should not Be Considered as 'Law'," *Minzhu Yu Fazhi* (Democracy and Legal System), No. 1, 1980, pp. 25–26.

94. Leng, *Justice in Communist China*, pp. 35–39; Tao, "Politics and Law Enforcement," see above note 27, pp. 715–720.

95. Shanxi People's Broadcasting Station, February 17, 1970.

96. See the death sentence of a habitual thief reported in Cohen, *The Criminal Process*, pp. 540–541.

97. Remarks such as that Lin Biao was not well-built and that Jiang Qing was not the first wife of Mao. Yu Haocheng, "The 'Offense of Malicious Attack' and 'Six Articles of Public Security'," *Minzhu Yu Fazhi*, No. 1, 1979, p. 36. A Nanjing worker got five years' imprisonment merely because he inadvertently commented in public on Lin Biao's build. "China's Socialist Legal System," see above note 51, p. 61.

98. Wei Kemin, "Be Cautious!" *Minzhu Yu Fazhi*, No. 11, 1980, p. 27.

99. Tao Xijin, "Problems in the Study of Criminal Law," *Faxue Yanjiu*, No. 5, 1979, p. 4.

100. Ma Jian, "Three Crickets and Eighteen Years' Imprisonment," *Minzhu Yu Fazhi*, No. 10, 1980, p. 38.

101. Cohen, *The Criminal Process*, pp. 20–21; *Political Imprisonment in the PRC*, pp. 57–59.

102. Texts of the two Acts are in *FLHP*, see above note 41, Vol. II, pp. 3–5 and Vol. III, pp. 25–26. English translations are available in Cohen, *The Criminal Process*, pp. 299–302 and 308–311.

103. Article 2. Text of the Act is in *FLHP*, Vol. II, pp. 19–22, republished in *Renmin Ribao*, April 11, 1980, pp. 1, 3. English translation is in Foreign Broadcast Information Service (FBIS), *Daily Report: PRC*, April 14, 1980, pp. L7–L11.

104. Leng, "The Role of Law in the PRC," see above note 1, p. 368.

105. Text of the Act is in *FGHB*, see above note 33, Vol. V, pp. 33–43. English translation is in Cohen, *The Criminal Process*, pp. 589–594.

106. Consult Robert J. Lifton, *Thought Reform and the Psychology of Totalism* (New York: Norton, 1961); W. Allyn Rickett and Adele Rickett, *Prisoners of Liberation* (New York: Cameron Associates, 1957); Martin K. Whyte, *Small Groups and Political Rituals in China* (Berkeley: University of California Press, 1974).

107. See Gu Fangping, "The Great Victory of the Policy of Reforming Criminals," *Zhengfa Yanjiu*, No. 6, 1959, pp. 36–37; Zhou Keyong, "The Great Achievement in Work of Reforming Criminals Through Labor," *Jiangxi Ribao (Jiangxi Daily)*, December 17, 1959, cited in Cohen, *The Criminal Process*, p. 587; Edgar Snow, *The Other Side of the River* (New York: Random House, 1962), pp. 47–48.

108. See Bao Rue-wang, *Prisoner of Mao; Political Imprisonment in the PRC*, pp. 73–150; *White Book on Forced Labour and Concentration Camp in the People's Republic of China* (Paris: Commission Internationale Contre Le Regime Concentrationnaise, 1957), 2 vols.

109. *Political Imprisonment in the PRC*, pp. 142–146.

110. See Fox Butterfield, "Peking Dissident, in Rare Account, Tells of Political Prisoners' Torture," *New York Times*, May 7, 1979, pp. A1, A10, and "Excerpts From the Wall Poster Describing How Detainees Are Treated," *New York Times*, May 7, 1979, pp. A1, A10.

111. Michael Weisskopf, "Ex-Inmate Recalls Life in China's Gulag," *The Washington Post*, February 12, 1982, pp. A1, A44–45.

112. Text of the SAPA is in *FGHB*, Vol. VI, pp. 245–261. English translation and comments are in Cohen, *The Criminal Process*, pp. 200–237.

113. Article 31 of the Act.

114. Text of the Decision is in *FGHB*, Vol. VI, pp. 243–244, English translation is in Cohen, *The Criminal Process*, pp. 248–250.

115. *Political Imprisonment in the PRC*, pp. 81–83; also interviews with five individuals who have undergone reeducation through labor.

Law Reform Under the Post-Mao Leadership

The death of Mao Zedong in September 1976 and the subsequent ouster of the Gang of Four ushered in a new era of reforms and limited liberalization in China. One of the most noticeable developments of the new era is the commitment of the post-Mao leadership headed by Deng Xiaoping to a stable legal order and a regular criminal justice system.

In a series of measures undertaken from early 1978 to the present (1983), the PRC has twice revised the Constitution, codified a number of important laws, restructured the judicial system, and restored and expanded legal education and research. The jural model of law has more than regained the respectability it once enjoyed in the mid-1950s. Law and the legal system, in fact, have become the most popular topic of discussion today, second only to the four modernizations. In contrast with the scarcity of information on Chinese law just a few years ago, barely a single day passes now without the appearance of new legal materials in the PRC news media and other publications.

The ensuing chapters will analyse in detail the structure and operation of the PRC's evolving criminal justice system. In this chapter, we shall examine the reasons for the post-Mao leadership to strengthen socialist legality and the various steps taken to such an end.

REASONS FOR SEEKING LEGAL STABILITY

In a sharp departure from the Maoist emphasis on continuous revolution and class struggle, the present leadership in China has instead made economic development and socialist modernization the focal point of its attention. As we may recall, Liu Shaoqi observed in 1956 that "the period of revolutionary storm and stress is past, new relations of production have been set up, and the aim of our struggle is changed into one of safeguarding the success for development of the productive forces of society; a corresponding change in the methods of struggle will consequently have to follow and a complete legal system becomes an absolute necessity." [1] Disgraced in the Cultural Revolution, Liu has been rehabilitated posthumously by Deng and his statement quoted above has also been echoed by some Chinese pronouncements in the post-Mao period. One recent instance was the CCP Central Committee's resolution on Party history, dated June 27, 1981. According to this significant document, the principal contradiction in China today is no longer class struggle but between the growing material and cultural needs of the people and the backwardness of social production. Thus, the overriding objective of "the Party's struggle in the new historical period is to turn China step by step into a powerful socialist country with modern agriculture, industry, national defense, and science and technology and with a high level of democracy and culture." [2]

Undoubtedly, the resurgence of the PRC's interest in law is closely linked to the commitment of its new leaders to the four modernizations. After the "lost decade" of chaos and struggle, China badly needs a regular legal order to ensure stability, unity, and an orderly environment essential to the successful development of its economy. In an article on the new legal system, *Beijing Review* quoted a noted Chinese jurist as saying:

> Having had enough of a decade of turmoil caused by Lin Biao and the Gang of Four, the people want law and order more than anything else. Democratization and legalization which the Chinese people have long been yearning for are now gradually becoming a reality. [3]

Other Chinese writings have described the socialist legal system as a "sharp weapon" for safeguarding the four modernizations because it maintains and strengthens the stability and unity of the socialist order. [4]

The post-Mao leadership also realizes that in order to get the population in general and intellectuals in particular enthusiastically involved in the program of modernization, it is necessary to have a system of law to help create an atmosphere of security and to overcome the "disease of lingering fear" referred to by former President Jiang Hua of the Supreme People's Court. [5] After all, not only the common people but many top officials, including Deng Xiaoping himself, were victims of arbitrary treatment and lawless cruelties during the Cultural Revolution. In his report to the second session of the Fifth National People's Congress on June 18, 1979, Hua

Guofeng articulated the regime's position with the following statement:

> Strengthening of our socialist democracy and socialist legal
> system is urgently needed for the sake of consolidating the
> socialist state system which is led by the working class and
> has its masters the entire working people, for the sake of
> solidifying the political foundation on which the country can
> carry out socialist modernization in stability and unity, for the
> sake of bringing into full play the enthusiasm and initiative of
> our whole people in modernization and for the sake of
> ensuring that there are no further serious loopholes in our
> political system which can be taken advantage of by
> conspirators like Lin Biao and the gang of four in their
> attempts at counterrevolutionary restoration.[6]

Furthermore, the PRC has reason to expect a growing demand for
economic legislation with the progress of its modernization program.
Chinese spokesmen have acknowledged the need for a variety of
economic statutes, decrees, and rules to regulate production processes
and the relationships among production units in the interest of the
overall economic development.[7]

Last but not least, China obviously needs to have a formal legal
system as a prerequisite to secure international cooperation and
support for its four modernizations. In order to expand external trade
and to attract foreign investment, the PRC must project itself as a
stable and orderly society and enact relevant laws to protect the
interests and rights of foreigners in areas of patents, trademarks, joint
ventures, etc.[8] Chinese effort in this regard was clearly underscored
by Mr. Ren Jianxin, Director of the Legal Affairs Department of the
China Council for the Promotion of International Trade (CCPIT), in
the opening remarks of his speech presented to a delegation of the
American Bar Association in Beijing during May 1981:

> China's long-term strategic policy for accelerating the
> realization of four modernizations is to exert our efforts with
> the prerequisite of self-reliance in taking in all merits of
> foreign countries, developing foreign trade, importing advanced
> technology, utilizing foreign capital and expanding economic
> cooperation and technological exchange with foreign countries.
> In order to insure the implementation of the policy, it has, at
> present, become a task of prime importance to continuously
> ameliorate and strengthen our foreign economic and trade law-
> work.[9]

THE EVOLVING CONSTITUTIONAL ORDER

In the course of examining the various steps taken by the post-Mao leadership to strengthen China's legal system, we shall begin with a brief discussion of the revised Constitution adopted in March 1978. As generally conceived, this new fundamental charter of the PRC was a sort of compromise between the "liberal" document of 1954 and the Maoist document of 1975.[10] Resembling the 1975 version, it described the PRC as "a socialist state of the dictatorship of the proletariat" (Article 1) and proclaimed that "the Communist Party of China is the core of leadership of the whole Chinese people" (Article 2). Similarly, it did not restore the post of Chairman of the PRC abolished in 1975 and declared that "the Chairman of the Central Committee of the Communist Party of China commands the armed forces of the People's Republic of China" (Article 19). While restoring some powers granted to the National People's Congress (NPC) by the 1954 document but omitted by the 1975 session, the 1978 Constitution, at the same time, failed to reinstate other relevant provisions of 1954, such as protection of NPC deputies against arrest.[11]

There were, however, many important similarities between the 1978 and 1954 Constitutions. The new document restored many 1954 provisions on legality and individual rights omitted by its immediate predecessor. Of the sixteen articles on the fundamental rights and duties of citizens (Articles 44–59) in the 1978 Constitution, fourteen essentially revived the stipulations in the 1954 document. Conspicuously missing was the "freedom of residence and freedom to change residence," apparently in the interest of keeping millions of urban youth in the countryside.[12] The new leaders also found it politically wise to incorporate a few novel items from the 1975 document in the 1978 one: namely, the freedom to strike, the right to speak out freely, air their views fully, hold great debates and write big-character posters (Article 45), the freedom not to believe in religion and propagate atheism (Article 46), and the duty to support the leadership of the Communist Party of China (Article 56).[13]

In the judicial field, the 1978 Constitution revived the rights of the accused to defense and to an open trial and the participation of people's assessors in the administration of justice (Article 41). While failing to restore the 1954 provisions on equality before the law and the independence of the courts, the 1978 Constitution did deemphasize the mass line in trying cases and made the local courts again accountable to the local people's congresses (Article 42) instead of to both the local people's congresses and their executive organs as required by the 1975 document. It also reinstituted the procuracy and established the requirement for the police to have the approval of the judiciary or the procuracy before making an arrest (Articles 43 and 47). It did not revive the 1954 system of "vertical leadership" under which the local procuratorates were only responsible to higher-level organs within the procuratorial hierarchy. Instead, the new Constitution made the local procuracies accountable to the people's congresses at corresponding levels (Article 43).[14]

When the Eleventh Central Committee of the Chinese Communist Party held its Third Plenary Session in December 1978, the party elites apparently decided to go a step further than the new Constitution in strengthening the legal system. The Communique of the Third Plenum made, among other things, qualified commitment to "judicial independence" and "equality before the law," the two controversial concepts contained in the 1954 Constitution but unrestored in the 1978 document:

> In order to safeguard people's democracy, it is imperative to strengthen the socialist legal system so that democracy is systemized and written into law in such a way as to insure the stability, continuity and full authority of this democratic system and these laws. There must be laws for people to follow, these laws must be observed, their enforcement must be strict and lawbreakers must be dealt with. From now on, legislative work should have an important place on the agenda of the National People's Congress and its Standing Committee. Procuratorial and judicial organizations must maintain their independence as is appropriate; they must faithfully abide by the laws, rules and regulations, serve the people's interests, keep to the facts; guarantee the equality of all people before the people's laws and deny anyone the privilege of being above the law.[15]

As part of the overall plans to improve the status of law, the current leadership in China has adopted other liberalization measures to win back popular confidence and to right the wrongs of its predecessor. One important move has been the removal of bad class labels from certain groups of people in China. For instance, some 110,000 persons who had been detained as rightists since 1957 were released in June 1978 and the labels of still other rightists were lifted later that year.[16] The Chinese leaders also decided in early 1979 to restore political and civil rights to the social groups labeled "enemies of the people" for thirty years: "landlords and rich peasants." Discrimination would no longer be practiced against members of former class enemies and their descendants with respect to school enrollment, job allocation, and political activity "as long as they support socialism." [17]

Steps have also been taken by the present regime to rectify the injustice and repressions allegedly committed by the Gang of Four and their followers. There have been numerous reports of reversals of unjust and wrong verdicts. Among the most celebrated was the reversal of the verdict of 1976 Tiananmen Square incident; rioters are now labelled "revolutionary heroes" instead of "counterrevolutionaries." [18] In another equally well-known case, the three authors of the 1974 Li Yi Zhe poster "On Socialist Democracy and the Legal System" were released from prison and exonerated in early 1979.[19] Even more important politically was the posthumous rehabilitation of Liu Shaoqi in 1980.[20] Between 1977 and mid-1980 more than 2,800,000 people reportedly had their unjust verdicts reversed and were rehabilitated, some posthumously like Liu Shaoqi.[21]

Moreover, the post-Mao leadership has shown greater willingness to permit some degree of political relaxation and limited forms of free expression. In fact, there were times during 1978–1979 when the regime tolerated open advocacy of democracy and public airing of complaints in wall posters, street demonstrations, and underground publications. However, alarmed at the danger of the Democracy Movement and pressed by the Party's hard-liners, Deng Xiaoping and his supporters had to reverse their policy by closing down the Democracy Wall in Beijing, arresting political dissidents, and deleting from Article 45 of the Constitution the Four Big Rights (Sida): "to speak out freely, air views freely, hold great debates, and write big character posters." [22]

Despite this retreat from the liberalization experiment, the present Chinese leadership continues to proclaim its determination to expand democracy, strengthen socialist legality, and protect the people's rights. Cited as proof of such commitment was the adoption of a new Constitution at the end of 1982. It should be noted that the 1978 Constitution had been amended twice before 1982. In July 1979, the National People's Congress adopted the following amendments: that a standing committee be established for local people's congresses at and above county level, that local revolutionary committees at various levels be changed into local people's governments, that deputies to the people's congresses of counties be elected directly by the voters, and that the relationship between higher and lower people's procuratorate's be changed from that of supervision to one of leadership.[23] Again in September 1980 the NPC amended Article 45 of the Constitution by deleting the controversial provision for the Four Big Rights (Sida).[24]

More importantly, the Chinese authorities decided to prepare a new constitution to replace the 1978 one which they considered as containing a number of "outmoded and erroneous" ideas and provisions that "do not conform to the conditions and needs of the current new period of historical development." [25] To this end, the Committee for the Revision of the Constitution was established in September 1980. After more than a year of soliciting opinions from various quarters and of serious and detailed deliberations, the Committee formulated the Draft of the Revised Constitution of the PRC, which was published and circulated for discussion in April 1982 by the NPC standing committee. After a period of nationwide discussion and further changes, the document was finally adopted by the National People's Congress on December 4, 1982.[26]

The new Constitution of 138 articles appears to be more liberal than the 1978 document with emphasis on the united front and the legal system. To be sure, the present document takes as the guiding ideology for China's modernization the upholding of the four basic principles, namely, socialism, the People's Democratic Dictatorship, Marxism-Leninism and Mao Zedong thought, and the leadership of the Chinese Communist Party (Preamble). Nonetheless, it gives a special attention to the united front and the People's Political Consultative Conference (Preamble) and describes China as a socialist state under "the people's democratic dictatorship" (Article 1) instead of "the dictatorship of the proletariat" as used in the 1975 and 1978 documents.

While the leadership of the CCP is never questioned, the new Constitution does attempt to make a clear distinction between the functions of the state and those of the Party, thus curbing the Party's interference in state affairs. For one thing, it provides for restoring the post of the Chairman of the State (Articles 79–84). The new head of state will fulfill many ceremonial functions but will no longer command China's armed forces or chair the Council of National Defense, as provided by the 1954 Constitution.[27] For another, the Constitution establishes a Central Military Commission to lead the armed forces of the country (Articles 93–94) and removes, at least formally, the direct command of the PLA by the Central Committee of the Party.[28] Moreover, the Party is also expected to carry out activities within the extent of the Constitution and the law, as required of every individual and organization by Article 5 of the Constitution.[29]

The new Constitution strengthens the system of people's congresses and enlarges the powers of the Standing Committee of the National People's Congress. The NPC will continue to adopt criminal, civil, and other basic laws but its Standing Committee will have the authority to adopt all other laws as well as to make partial amendments to the basic laws formulated by the NPC (Articles 62 and 67). Moreover, the Constitution restores the provision in the 1954 Constitution that no deputy to the National People's Congress may be arrested or placed on trial without the consent of the presidium of the NPC or its Standing Committee (Article 74) and retains the stipulation in the 1978 Constitution that NPC deputies have the right to address inquiries to the state organs, which are under obligation to answer (Article 73). It also adds a new stipulation that deputies to the NPC shall not be called to legal account for speeches or votes at its meetings (Article 75).[30] Another important feature of the Constitution regarding the state structure is the provision for reinstating organs of township state power in rural areas (Article 95) according to the principle of separating government administration from commune management.[31]

Of particular interest to our study is the serious attempts of the new Constitution to institutionalize the rule of law. Article 5 says that all organs of state and people's armed forces, all political parties and public organizations and all enterprises and institutions must abide by the Constitution and the law. In the judicial field, the new Constitution goes one step further than the 1978 Constitution by restoring the 1954 provisions that people's courts and people's procuratorates exercise their respective authority independently according to the law and are not subject to interference by administrative organs, public organizations* or individuals (Articles 126 and 131). As in the case of other top state officials, the term of office of the President of the Supreme People's Court and the Chief Procurator of the Supreme People's Procuratorate is stipulated for five years. They may be reelected, but shall not serve more than two consecutive terms (Articles 124 and 130).[32]

The new document also puts more emphasis on individual rights than the 1978 Constitution. It has twenty-four articles on the fundamental rights and duties of citizens as against sixteen articles in the 1978 document. Except for the missing stipulation on freedom of residence, the Constitution restores or expands the provisions on individual rights and freedoms in the 1954 Constitution. The most notable one is equality before the law for all citizens of the People's Republic of China (Article 33).[33] In religious freedom, the Constitution drops the right to propagate atheism as contained in the 1978 Constitution. It says that "the state protects normal religious activities" but adds that no religious affairs may be "subject to any foreign domination" (Article 36). The Constitution guarantees the "freedom

---

* It is not clear whether the term "public or social organizations" would include the Chinese Communist Party.

and privacy of correspondence" and at the same time, permits public security or procuratorial organs to censor correspondence in accordance with procedures prescribed by law to "meet the needs of state security or of investigation into criminal offenses" (Article 40).[34]

Among the major new additions of the Constitution is the provision that the "personal dignity of citizens of the People's Republic of China is inviolable. Insult, libel, false charge of frame-up directed, or slander against citizens by any means is prohibited" (Article 38). There is also an added statement on the freedom of person: "Unlawful deprivation or restriction of citizens' freedom of person by detention or other means is prohibited; and unlawful search of the person of citizens is prohibited" (Article 37). The Constitution specifically stresses that the rights of citizens are inseparable from their duties (Article 33). Chinese people not only have the right but also obligation to work (Article 42) and to receive education (Article 46). Added to the list of citizens' duties are to safeguard state secrets (Article 54) and to refrain from infringing "upon the interests of the state, of society and of the collective or upon the lawful freedoms and rights of other citizens" when exercising their freedoms and rights (Article 51). These vaguely phrased provisions can be invoked by the PRC authorities to restrict citizen freedoms provided in the Constitution. However, the new Constitution does not make the support of the leadership of the CCP a specific duty for Chinese citizens as done in Article 56 of the 1978 Constitution. This may only indicate a subtle shift of emphasis in the drafting skill of the Constitution as the Preamble of this Constitution affirms the adherence of the Four Basic Principles, including the leadership of the CCP. The Constitution also eliminates the provision for the freedom to strike, which, along with the Four Big Rights, was incorporated into Article 45 of the 1978 Constitution, as a result of the Maoist influence.[35] Despite the fact that in the past several PRC Constitutions were almost totally disregarded by the leaders in power, there is no seemingly effective mechanism in this Constitution to interpret and to supervise the enforcement of the Constitution. Article 62 provides that the National People's Congress shall, among other functions, "supervise the enforcement of the Constitution" and Article 67 provides that NPC Standing Committee shall, among others, "interpret the Constitution and supervise its enforcement, . . . enact and amend statutes . . . interpret statutes." How these arrangements could guarantee the enforcement of the Constitution is rather difficult to perceive. It seems unlikely that the NPC Standing Committee would interpret any statute or amendments to statutes as inconsistent with the Constitution or with the basic principles of those basic statutes (such as Criminal Law) adopted by the NPC itself. Since most members of the Standing Committee are of military and political backgrounds, there is a natural tendency to play their role from a political point of view and underemphasize or even disregard legal provisions in the Constitution or statutes.

Whatever its flaws and problems, the new Constitution appears to signify a triumph of the policy of moderation and pragmatism and an attempt of the Chinese elites to promote the jural model of law and to separate the functions of the Party from those of the state. The degree of its implementation will undoubtedly affect the extent of success in China's quest for a modernized economy and a stable and rationalized political-legal system.[36]

LEGISLATIVE ACTIVITY

Closely related to the evolving constitutional order in post-Mao China is Beijing's effort to renew and expand legislative activity. After the adoption of the Constitution in early 1978, Chinese leaders and the media began to call for codification and enactment of statutes and regulations. In a speech on strengthening China's legal system delivered on October 13, 1978, Zhao Cangbi, then Minister of Public Security, spoke of the need for expanding the body of legislation and for the adoption of some specific laws, such as a criminal code, a civil code, an environmental protection law, etc.[37] Party leadership in the legislative process was also clearly indicated in Zhao's speech. According to him, all proposed enactments must be examined and approved by the Central authorities (the Central Committee of the CCP). For major codes, the Party Central Committee's Political-Legal Group should first organize a special team to prepare a draft and seek opinions around the country. After several revisions, the draft would be presented to the Party Central Committee for approval and then to the NPC Standing Committee for adoption and promulgation.

Since Zhao's talk, however, there have been some noticeable changes in the legislative process. The Party Central Committee's approval is still essential to the adoption of all legislation in the PRC, but the major responsibility for legislative work now appears to rest with the NPC.[38] The Communique of the Third Plenum of the 11th Central Committee of the CCP declared in December 1978 that in the future "legislative work shall have an important place on the agenda of the National People's Congress and its Standing Committee."[39] This was followed by the establishment in early 1979 of a Legal Affairs Commission by the NPC Standing Committee and the appointment as the Commission's chairman Peng Zhen, former mayor of Beijing.[40] It may be recalled that Peng Zhen was purged during the Cultural

Revolution because of his association with Liu Shaoqi and identification with the PRC's past attempts at codification.

From all the information that is available, a picture of the current legislative process in the PRC may be drawn. In the case of codifying a substantive or procedural law, the Legal Affairs Commission of the NPC Standing Committee, together with the Legal Research Institute of the Chinese Academy of Social Sciences and the concerned departments and agencies, organizes a special group to prepare a draft. This group often designates a smaller group of prominent experts and jurists as the key member of the tasks, and also gathers pertinent data through investigation, study, and suggestions from various quarters. Once the first draft is complete, it is printed and sent to the concerned units all over the country for comments. After several rounds of revisions and comments, a final draft is submitted to the National People's Congress for approval and promulgation.[41]

In regard to its legislative output, post-Mao China has proceeded with surprising speed to enact new codes and revised old laws or affirm their validity. Among the 1979 enactments were a Forestry Law (February), a revised Act on Arrest and Detention (February), and an Environmental Protection Law (September). More importantly, in July 1979, the Fifth National People's Congress adopted the two long-awaited Criminal Law and Criminal Procedure Law along with five other laws: one Organic Law of the Local People's Congresses and Local People's Governments, an Electoral Law for the NPC and the Local People's Congresses, an Organic Law of the People's Courts, an Organic Law of the People's Procuratorates, and a Law on Joint Ventures Using Chinese and Foreign Investment.[42] In September 1980, the NPC also enacted a Nationality Law, a revised Marriage Law, a Joint Venture Income Tax Law, and an Individual Income Tax Law. Other new laws adopted in 1980 included the Act on Academic Degrees (February) and the Provisional Act on Lawyers (August).[43] The Fifth Session of the Fifth National People's Congress adopted in December 1982 the following four new or revised laws: the Organic Law of the National People's Congress, the Organic Law of the State Council, the Organic Law of the Local People's Congresses and Governments, and the Electoral Law for the National People's Congress and the Local People's Congresses.[44] On September 2, 1983, the Second Session of the Sixth NPC Standing Committee adopted the Law on the Safety of Maritime Traffic and also revised both the Organic Law of the People's Courts and the Organic Law of the People's Procuratorates.[45]

The PRC's other legislative activities have been centered recently on two areas. One is the codification of two basic laws: a civil law and a law of civil procedure. The draft of a Civil Law has been circulated throughout the country for examination while the Civil Procedure Law was adopted in March 1982 for trial implementation.[46] The other area is economic legislation. Important enactments in the field include the Economic Contract Law (December 1981), Act on Land Requisition for National Construction (May 1982), Trademark Law (Aug. 1982), Law on Marine Environmental Protection (Aug. 1982), and Law on Statistics (December 1983).[47] According to *Xinhua News Agency*, of the 300 laws issued in recent years, nearly 250 concern themselves with economic matters. There were around 150 more economic laws and regulations being drafted in 1982,[48] among them a factory law, labor law, patent law, company law and planning law.[49] Currently, in keeping with Beijing's policy of restructuring government departments, there are also increasing calls for developing administrative legislation. The argument is that administrative laws and regulations are essential to the improvement of administrative efficiency and to the strengthening of socialist democracy and the legal system.[50] Altogether, it was reported that between 1979 and 1983, the National People's Congress and its Standing Committee, along with the State Council and its ministries and commissions, have enacted or issued some 700 laws, decrees, and regulations.[51]

Aside from making good progress in new legislation, Beijing has also taken steps to settle the status of the laws and regulations adopted after the founding of the People's Republic. On November 29, 1979, the NPC Standing Committee declared in a resolution that all laws and decrees promulgated since 1949 would remain in full force if not in conflict with the Constitution or laws and decrees enacted by the Fifth National People's Congress and its Standing Committee.[52] Besides this rather broadly stated resolution, Beijing has republished specific pieces of past legislation with or without minor changes. Among them are the 1954 Organic Regulations of the Urban Street Offices, 1954 Organic Regulations of the Urban Residents' Committees, 1952 Provisional Regulations Governing the Organization of the Security Defense Committees, and 1954 Provisional General Rules Governing the Organization of the People's Mediation Committees (all republished in January 1980).[53] Others include the 1957 Security Administration Punishment Act (SAPA) republished in February 1980, the 1957 Decision of the State Council on Reeducation Through Labor, republished along with supplementary provisions approved by the NPC Standing Committee in November 1979, and the 1951 Provisional Act on Guarding State Secrets, republished in April 1980.[54]

LEGAL EDUCATION AND RESEARCH

One significant aspect of China's legal development in the post-Mao era is the restoration and expansion of legal education.[55] Prior to the Cultural Revolution, there were six comprehensive universities with law departments (Beijing University being one of them) and four political-legal institutes in China to offer legal training at the college level. In 1961, the enrollment figure was estimated to be three thousand.[56] By 1966, when all law departments and political-legal institutes were forced to close, they reportedly had graduated some 19,000 students since 1949.[57]

Since 1977, law departments that had existed before the Cultural Revolution have begun to reopen with Beijing University, Kirin University, and the Chinese People's University leading the way. In addition, new law departments have been formed in eighteen other comprehensive universities. Today, there are twenty-nine universities in China with law departments.[58] Similarly, in 1979 the Beijing Political-Legal Institute, the East China Political-Legal Institute in Shanghai, and the Southwest Political-Legal Institute in Chungqing were reopened and a new Northwest Political-Legal Institute was established. Plans have also been under way to reopen the Central-South Political-Legal Institute and a new South China Political-Legal Institute.[59] In May 1983, the Beijing Political-Legal Institute was incorporated into the new China Political-Legal University, which consists of an undergraduate school, a graduate school, and a school for training cadres.[60] The current enrollment of all the law departments and institutes is said to be around 13,000.[61] More than 5,000 law students are expected to be graduated in 1985.[62]

Both the university law departments and the political-legal institutes are under the joint leadership of the Ministries of Education and Justice. Students are selected through the nationwide examination system. Some graduates of the university law departments may pursue academic careers but the majority of them are bound for the courts, procuratories, public security bureaus and other practical fields. Graduates of the political-legal institutes tend to be even more oriented toward the practical types of work. There are now both graduate and undergraduate programs available in the university law departments as well as in the political-legal institutes. While the graduate program, (usually three years) permits students to choose areas of specialization, the curricula of the four-year undergraduate program generally include the following subjects: Marxism and Leninism, history of the Communist Party, political theory, political philosophy, political economy, China's legal history, logic, foreign language, theories of law and the state, foreign legal history, constitutional law, administrative law, economic law, criminal law and procedure, civil law and procedure, marriage law, public and private international law, and criminal investigation. Compared to the university law departments, however, the political-legal institutes do give more attention in instruction to practical subjects such as evidence, investigation, and forensic medicine. In accord with the PRC's policy of combining theory with practice, law students are required to do "clinical" work in judicial or public security organs as a part of their program of study. Again, this receives a greater emphasis in the political-legal institutes than in the university law faculties.[63]

In addition, the Ministry of Justice is reported to have requested that the Ministry of Public Health create a department of legal medicine in a number of medical schools and that the Ministries of Railways Communications, Forestry, Foreign Affairs, and Foreign Trade set up departments of law or offer law courses in their affiliated institutions of higher learning.[64] Recently, a five-year evening law college has been established in Beijing by the Municipal Department of Justice and the Beijing branch of the Nine-Three Society in collaboration with the Law Department of Beijing University.[65]

Below the institutions of higher learning, the PRC has various junior college level and senior high school level programs as well as ad hoc, short-term training classes to offer legal education. The Ministry of Justice has under its jurisdiction two Central Political-Legal Cadre Schools and a number of local political-legal cadre schools in the provinces and municipalities. The Public Security Organs also have their own cadre schools offering law courses.[66] Spare-time law schools, two-year judicial schools, and middle-level law schools have also been set up in China.[67] Moreover, the PRC frequently provides basic legal training to its current judicial cadres and others through a variety of ad hoc, flexible programs. Between January 1980 and December 1981, Beijing's Judicial Bureau organized seven training classes for more than 600 judicial cadres.[68] From October to December 30, 1981, the Water Transport Political-Legal Class organized by the Ministry of Communication trained fifty-two cadres.[69] During a four-and-a-half-month period (September 1981–January 15, 1982), several tens of thousands of former PLA cadres received intensive training in politics and law at various collective training centers throughout the country in preparation for new jobs on the political and legal front.[70] The PRC is reported to have at present eleven schools that provide on-the-job training for judicial cadres. In the past few years, 7,000 judicial cadres have received professional training, 11,000 are currently being trained, and more are enrolled in correspondence and television training programs.[71]

In addition to formal legal education, the PRC has used a mass propaganda campaign to educate the public about socialist legality. When the seven major laws were promulgated in 1979, Beijing mobilized its mass media to publicize them, especially the Criminal Law and the Criminal Procedure Law.[72] This has been repeated regarding other new laws and the Draft of the Revised Constitution. In 1983 the PRC launched a "Legal System Publicity Month" to focus on the safeguarding of the legitimate rights and interests of women and children.[73]

To familiarize the people with the laws and cultivate their faith in legality, the present government has employed some novel and innovative means. Among them are legal exhibits in city neighborhoods and formal legal education exhibitions in major urban centers.[74] Traditional operas on the legendary Judge Bao and contemporary plays such as *"The Accused"* and *"Save Her"* are staged to stress the concepts of law and justice.[75] There is even a children's song titled "We Should Observe the Law From Childhood." [76] Legal education is further propagated through popular publications, group discussion meetings, and the inclusion of a basic legal knowledge course in the curricula of colleges, middle schools, and primary schools.[77]

Along with the vigorous development of legal education in recent years, legal research and publication have also been revived and expanded under the present Chinese leadership. Leading the way is the Legal Research Institute of the Chinese Academy of Social Sciences in Beijing, which has worked closely with the Legal Affairs Commission of the NPC Standing Committee in drafting laws. This institute and other national or regional law related research institutes and societies have been carrying on research and publication work and sponsoring scholarly conferences on legal affairs. Their research activities cover a wide variety of issues, including topics considered taboo in the past such as the inheritability of law, rule by man and rule by law, and equal justice before the law.[78]

In terms of both quality and quantity, legal publication in China today is already exceeding the level of the mid-1950s. There are six major legal journals being published, i.e.: *Faxue Yanjiu* (Studies in Laws), bi-monthly, published by the Legal Research Institute of the Chinese Academy of Social Sciences; *Minzhu Yu Fazhi* (Democracy and Legal System), monthly, published by the Shanghai Law Society and the East China Political-Legal Institute; *Faxue Zazhi* (Law Magazine), bi-monthly, published by the Beijing Law Society; *Faxue* (Jurisprudence), monthly, published by the East China Political-Legal Institute; *Faxue Yicong* (Law Translation Series), bi-monthly, published by the Legal Research Institute of the Chinese Academy of Social Sciences; *Guowai Faxue* (Foreign Law), bi-monthly, published by

Beijing University Department of Law and the Commercial Press.[79]
Three other journals are now published in China but not available
to the public: *Renmin Sifa* (People's Judiciary), published by the
Supreme People's Court; *Renmin Jiancha* (People's Procuracy), published by the Supreme People's Procuratorate; and *Renmin Gongan*
(People's Public Security), published by the Ministry of Public Security. A weekly publication by the Ministry of Justice is *Zhongguo
Fazhi Bao* (China's Legal System Paper), which began in 1980 and
has now a circulation of more than one million. Academic journals
on the humanities and social sciences also frequently carry scholarly
articles on law. Moreover, special columns and articles on legal issues
make a regular appearance in the *People's Daily* and the *Enlightenment
Daily*.[80]

Scholarly monographs and popular books in the legal field have
also been published in increasing numbers. Practically all important
subjects from criminal procedure to international law are treated. A
comprehensive law dictionary, *Faxue Cidian*, was published in 1980.[81]
And in the same year the PRC resumed publication of its two official
Gazettes: the *Quanquo Renmin Daibiao Dahui Changwu Weiyuan Hui
Gongbao* (Gazette of the Standing Committee of the National People's
Congress) and *Zhonghua Renmin Gongheguo Guowuyuan Gongbao* (Gazette of the State Council). Both Gazettes are now available to
foreigners.[82]

To facilitate legal development, scholarly conferences have been
organized, legal societies and associations formed, and contacts with
foreign jurists and legal organizations promoted in recent years. In
March 1979, the Legal Research Institute of the Chinese Academy
of Social Sciences sponsored a Conference on Legal Research Planning
which adopted a national-legal research development outline for
1979–1985.[83] Other conferences convened since then include the
Conference on Chinese Legal History and the History of Legal
Thought, September 1979, which resulted in the formation of the
Chinese Association for Legal History,[84] the Inaugural Conference of
the Chinese Society of International Law, February 1980, the Beijing
Conference on the Role of Law in the United States and China, June
1982, and the Shanghai Conference on the Theory of Law, April
1983.[85] Of the professional legal associations established in the PRC,
the China Law Society is probably the most prominent. There are
fifteen municipal and provincial Law Societies in operation, and the
National Law Society was inaugurated in July, 1982 to help strengthen
China's legal studies and development and promote exchanges between Chinese and foreign legal circles.[86]

Since 1979 there has been a marked increase in the flow of visiting
jurists between China and foreign countries. Apart from individual

Chinese scholars visiting abroad, the PRC has been sending delegations to foreign countries in its efforts to learn more about certain branches of law and different legal systems and experiences. The following are just a few examples. In 1979, Deputy Head Han Youtong of the Legal Research Institute of the Chinese Academy of Social Sciences led a delegation to visit Austrian judicial institutions.[87] During the same year the Chinese Academy of Social Sciences also sent a delegation to visit the Institute of Comparative Jurisprudence in France,[88] and another group went to Yugoslavia to study its legal system.[89] In the year of 1980, a legal delegation of the Chinese Academy of Social Sciences went to West Germany to study its legal institutions, a delegation of Chinese lawyers visited the United States to study its lawyers' system, and a delegation of Chinese scholars from the Sino-Japanese Friendship Association went to Japan for the observation of its environment protection legislation.[90] In 1981, the Chinese Academy of Social Sciences sent a legal delegation to Japan to survey its studies on the history of the legal system.[91] Also a Chinese legal group visited Austria to study its criminal legislation.[92] During 1982, a Chinese Judicial Delegation, led by Justice Minister Liu Fuzhi, visited the courts, youth reformatories, prisons, and mediation committees of Rumania and Yugoslavia, and another group of Chinese jurists went to West Germany, France, and United Kingdom to study economic law.[93] Among Chinese delegations going abroad in 1983 were a judicial delegation to Australia and New Zealand and a legal delegation to the United States.[94]

SOCIALIST LEGALITY AND THE FOUR BASIC PRINCIPLES

The discussion in the preceding pages clearly shows the serious efforts of present Chinese leaders to institute a stable legal system in the name of socialist legality. While considerable progress has been made in Beijing's legal reform, there exist many problems to overcome in China's path to a sound legal order. Throughout the book these problems will be examined in one form or another; here we cite a few problems as illustrations. One difficulty generally recognized is the dire shortage of well-qualified personnel resulting from the disruption of legal education in the past. The recent revival and expansion of legal education constitutes "only a small first step towards meeting the country's vast need for legal expertise." [95] Another problem is the attitude toward law commonly held by both the populace and the bureaucracy. Not only is there a general ignorance about the law in the PRC, but the people also tend to be skeptical over the current regime's determination to enforce the law after experiencing many years of political upheavals and frequent shifts of Party lines. It appears that much time and effort will be needed to repair the damage and effect an attitudal change in this respect.

More basically, in our analysis of the prospect for the rule of law in China, we must address ourselves to the issue of socialist legality which is officially identified with the PRC's legal order. To help understand where the Chinese legal system stands in terms of stability and predictability and protection of the individual against arbitrary state action, it is pertinent and necessary to examine how socialist legality is interpreted by Chinese spokesmen.

First of all, socialist legality is viewed by the Chinese as legality compatible with the needs of socialism and with the will and interests of the proletariat and the entire people.[96] Second, the Communist Party plays a leading role in formulating socialist laws, but Party policies and state laws should be differentiated in spite of their close linkage. This point is stressed by the following comments of a Chinese writer:

> Socialist laws are enacted under the leadership of the Party; they are the finalization, standardization, and codification of the Party's line, principles, and policies. By getting through the state's leading legislative, judicial, and executive organs to enact and carry out the laws, the Party raises the will of the class to that of the state and uses the compulsive power of the state to insure the enforcement of these laws . . . the Party must arm the people of whole country with Marxism-Leninism-Mao Zedong thought and use it to guide work on all fronts. However, Marxism-Leninism-Mao Zedong thought is not law and cannot replace law . . . Marxism is a scientific truth and belongs to the ideological sphere. We can only make people accept Marxism through propaganda and education but cannot use compulsory means to make them believe in Marxism. Laws are quite different. They are codes of conduct for everyone to observe and reflect the will of the ruling class raised to that of the state. Their enforcement is insured by the compulsive power of the state. Anyone who violates the law and commits a crime shall be punished. Hence, Marxism and the socialist legal system are things of different categories. They should not be lumped together nor should Marxism be used to replace socialist laws.[97]

Third, Chinese spokesmen also take pains to point out the stable and equitable elements of their new socialist laws. Marshall Ye Jianying, for instance, has stated: "Laws, rules and regulations, once they are framed and adopted, must be stable, have continuity, and enjoy full authority. They must not be subject to the will of any leader and can be revised only through proper legal procedure . . . Everyone, without exception, must abide by the laws of the state. All citizens are equal before the law, whether or not they are Party members and whatever their rank, social position and social origin." [98]

On the other hand, the legal system, like China's other institutions, is expected to operate within the so-called Four Basic Principles, namely, the socialist road, the People's Democratic Dictatorship (i.e., the dictatorship of the proletariat), the leadership of the Communist Party, and Marxism-Leninism-Mao Zedong thought. The upholding of these principles was advocated by Deng Xiaoping in March 1979 on behalf of the CCP Central Committee.[99] Deng is believed to have done so in an attempt to placate the leftist opposition which challenged his liberalization program at that time.[100] Regardless of the motive behind Deng's action, upholding the Four Basic Principles has since become the most important norm of behavior in the PRC, reiterated by the CCP Central Committee's Resolution on Questions of Party History on June 27, 1981 and by the 1982 new Constitution of the People's Republic of China.[101]

Despite the restrictive nature of the Four Basic Principles, Chinese spokesmen insist that upholding them is entirely consistent with the emancipation of the mind and the strengthening of the legal system.[102] A prominent jurist has this to say: "The socialist legal system is the Party's policy transformed and solidified into legal provisions. It will therefore have to uphold socialism, the People's Democratic Dictatorship, the leadership of the Party, and Marxism-Leninism-Mao Zedong thought." [103] Another legal author, however, goes into some length to discuss the limits of freedom and permissible behavior set by socialist legality and the Four Basic Principles:

> Under the socialist system, civil rights enjoyed by citizens not only must be guaranteed by law to ensure their realization, but the scope and limits of the citizens' exercising their liberties must also be regulated by law. Socialist liberties are liberties that do not violate the basic interest of the broad masses of people; they are liberties that observe the social order and the necessary discipline; they are the liberties of the vast majority of the people. They must obey the socialist laws which reflect the will and interest of the broad masses of people. The socialist laws must impose sanctions on every act which violates the people's democratic rights and at the same time, restrict extreme democracy and anarchism as well as people who abuse freedom and other civil rights. Without these restrictions, there will be no socialist liberties . . . In

conjunction with the development of the four modernizations, we should further summarize experiences, continue to strengthen pertinent legislation and constantly use legal means to ensure that the people really enjoy their freedoms and rights. Taking freedom of the press for example, we should enact publication law to guarantee that the people have the right to publish their works but should also prohibit some people from using the "freedom of the press" to carry out illegal activities to publish works which violate the Four Basic Principles and harm the four modernizations, to sell illegally reactionary publications, etc. As for freedom of assembly, in enacting the assembly law, we should guarantee the citizens' rights to hold meetings but should also guarantee the order and discipline necessary for the country's normal political life; no one would be allowed to gather a crowd for inciting riots or to confuse and poison people's minds with reactionary propaganda, harmful to the political stability and unity and to the smooth progress of the four modernizations. In regard to freedom of association, again in our legislation we should guarantee that the people have the right to form all types of learned societies and research associations for cooperative endeavor and mutual consultation in order to promote the development of science and culture and advance the Socialist cause; at the same time, we must absolutely ban all the illegally formed reactionary groups and organizations.[104]

The above quotation is interesting in that it articulates and justifies official restrictions on citizens' freedoms and rights under China's socialist laws and that the same argument has been used by the authorities to explain actions taken toward the Democracy Wall and against Wei Jingsheng, Fu Yuehua, and other political activists and dissidents.[105]

Post-Mao China has undoubtedly made long strides in its efforts to restore the respectability of the jural model of law, to stress rule by law over rule by man, and to provide some measure of stability and predictability to its newly renovated legal system.[106] Nevertheless, unless the policy of upholding the Four Basic Principles is modified or diluted, the PRC's legal system is likely to function the same way as its counterpart in the Soviet Union—no principle, however normatively stated in the Constitution or law, is permitted to conflict with the policy needs of the Communist Party, though in normal situations, the legal system still operates generally in a reasonable and predictable manner.[107] More light will be shed on the Chinese concept of socialist legality through our examination of China's current criminal justice system in the ensuing chapters.

NOTES

Chapter Three

1. *Eighth National Congress of the Communist Party of China*, Vol. 1. *Documents* (Peking: Foreign Languages Press, 1956), p. 82.

2. "On Questions of Party History," (Adopted by the Sixth Plenary Session of the 11th Central Committee of the Chinese Communist Party), *Beijing Review*, Vol. 24, No. 27, July 6, 1981, pp. 35–37. See also Xie Wen, "Class Struggle and the Principal Contradiction in Socialist Society," *Hongqi* (Red Flag), No. 20 1981, pp. 26–31, 6.

3. "Publicizing the New Laws," *Beijing Review*, Vol. 22, No. 29, July 20, 1979, p. 4.

4. Liu Guangming, "The Socialist Legal System Is a Sharp Weapon for Building a Modern and Strong State," *Liaoning Daxue Xuebao* (Journal of Liaoning University), No. 3, 1978, p. 37; Wu Lei, "A Sharp Weapon for Defending the Four Modernizations," *Guangming Ribao* (Enlightenment Daily), July 14, 1979, p. 3. Chen Weidian and Zhou Xinming, "Strengthen the Legal System, Ensure Stability and Unity," *Faxue Yanjiu* (Studies in Law), No. 1, 1980, pp. 35–36.

5. *Renmin Ribao* (People's Daily), October 21, 1978, p. 1.

6. Hua Guofeng, "Report on the Work of the Government," *Main Documents of the Second Session of the Fifth National People's Congress of the People's Republic of China* (Beijing: Foreign Languages Press, 1979), pp. 62–63.

7. See, for example, Peng Zhen, "Report on the Work of the Standing Committee of the NPC," *Main Documents of the Third Session of the Fifth NPC of the PRC* (1980), pp. 96–100; Zhang Youyu, "The Year of Strengthening the Socialist Legal System," *Zhongguo Baike Nianjian, 1980*, (Chinese Encyclopedia Yearbook, 1980) (Beijing: Chinese Encyclopedia Press, 1980), pp. 442–443; Huang Yifeng, "Drafting Economic Laws and Regulations Is An Urgent Task in the Current Drive to Realize the Four Modernizations," *Minzhu Yu Fazhi* (Democracy and Legal Systems), No. 8, 1980, pp. 8–9.

8. Fox Butterfield, "Peking Issues Rules to Lure Investment," *New York Times*, July 9, 1979, p. A1; Masao Sakuru, "Investing In China: The Legal Framework," *JETRO China Newsletter*, No. 37, 1982, pp. 7–12, 32.

9. Copies of Mr. Ren Jianxin's 12-page speech entitled "China's Foreign Economic And Trade Law Work is Progressing" were distributed to the members of the ABA delegation at the CCPIT briefing session on May 30, 1981.

10. One legal expert, for instance, calls the 1978 Constitution "a halfway house between the 1975 document on the left and the 1954 document on the right." Jerome A. Cohen, "China's Changing Constitution," *The China Quarterly*, No. 76, December 1978, p. 836. The English text of the 1978 constitution is in *Documents of the First Session of the Fifth National People's Congress of the People's Republic of China* (Beijing: Foreign Languages Press, 1978), pp. 125–172. For the English text of the 1954 and 1975 constitutions, see Michael Lindsay, ed., *The New Constitution of Communist China* (Taipei: Institute of International Relations, 1976), pp. 291–311 and 328–336 respectively.

11. For a thorough discussion of the 1978 Constitution regarding institutional restraints on the executive, see Cohen, "China's Changing Constitution," pp. 809–827.

12. For the PRC's policy of transferring educated youth to rural China, see Thomas P. Bernstein, *Up to the Mountains and Down to the Villages* (New Haven: Yale University Press, 1977).

13. It should be noted that the 1978 constitution balanced the freedom to strike with the revival of the citizens' duty to maintain labor discipline (Article 57). Article 100 of the 1954 Constitution required citizens to uphold labor discipline.

14. For a discussion of the restoration of the procuracy, see Cohen, "China's Changing Constitution," see above note 10, pp. 812–817; Tao-tai Hsia and Kathryn A. Haun, *The Re-Emergence of the Procuratorial System in the People's Republic of China* (Washington, D.C.: Library of Congress, 1978).

15. "Communique of the Third Plenary Session of the 11th Central Committee of the Communist Party of China," *Peking Review*, Vol. 21, No. 52, December 29, 1978, p. 14.

16. *New York Times*, June 6, 1978, p. 1; *Xinhua New Agency*, November 16, 1978.

17. *Beijing Review*, Vol. 22, No. 4, January 26, 1979, p. 8.

18. "Heroes of Tien An Men Square," *Peking Review*, Vol. 21, No. 46, November 17, 1978, pp. 13–15.

19. "Big-Character-Poster Authors. 'Li Yi Zhe' Exonerated," *Beijing Review*, Vol. 22, No. 12, March 23, 1979, pp. 15–16. For the analysis and translation of the poster, see Anita Chan and Jonathan Unger, eds., "The Case of Li I-che," *Chinese Law and Government*, Vol. 10, No. 3, 1977, pp. 3–112.

20. See the "Communique of the Fifth Plenary Session of the 11th Central Committee of the CCP, February 29, 1980," *Beijing Review*, Vol. 23, No. 10, March 10, 1980, p. 9; Editorial: "Restore the True Future of Mao Zedong Thought on Liu Shaoqi's Rehabilitation," *Renmin Ribao*, May 16, 1980, p. 1.

21. Jin Zitong, "Reverse Unjust and Wrong Verdicts," *Chinese Encyclopedia Yearbook, 1981*, p. 189.

22. The treatment of political dissent in post-Mao China will be examined in Chapter Six, Section on Political Offenses, of this book.

23. For the detailed changes in the relevant Constitutional provision, see the NPC's resolution on July 1, 1979 in *Renmin Shouce. 1979* (People's Handbook. 1979) (Beijing: People's Daily Press, 1980), pp. 263–264.

24. *Chinese Encyclopedia Yearbook, 1981*, p. 182.

25. Hu Sheng, "On the Revision of the Constitution," *Beijing Review*, Vol. 25, No. 18, May 3, 1982, p. 15; Editorial: "A Major Event in the Country's Political Life," *Hongqi*, No. 9, 1982, p. 7.

26. See Peng Zhen, "Report on the Draft of the Revised Constitution of the People's Republic of China," *Beijing Review*, Vol. 25, No. 50, December 13, 1982, pp. 9–10. Text of the new Constitution is in *Renmin Ribao*, Dec. 5, 1982, pp. 1–4. Its English translation is in FBIS (Foreign Broadcast Information Service), *Daily Report: China*, Dec. 7, 1982, pp. K1–K28.

27. Xu Chongde, "On Head of State," *Faxue Yanjiu*, No. 3, 1982, p. 20.

28. Both Article 15 of the 1975 Constitution and Article 19 of the 1978 Constitution provide for the Chairman of the CCP Central Committee to command the Chinese armed forces.

29. Hu Sheng, see above note 25, pp. 16–17.

30. See Zhang Shangzhou, "New Development of Socialist Democracy and the Legal System," *Renmin Ribao*, May 11, 1982, p. 5.

31. According to the Vice-Chairman of the Committee for Revision of the Constitution this measure only takes out the communes' functions and powers as state power organs whereas the ownership of enterprises of the communes, production brigades and production teams as well as of their other property remains unchanged. Peng Zhen, "Explanations on the Draft of the Revised Constitution of the PRC," *Beijing Review*, Vol. 25, May 10, 1982, p. 26. For different views, see David Bonavia, "Communes Plunged Under," *Far Eastern Economic Review*, April 30, 1982, p. 24.

32. This reflects the current leaders' policy of abolishing the practice of "life tenure" for Party or State officials. See Yan Jiaqi, "Enforce the Limited Tenure System for the Highest Leading Offices," *Minzhu Yu Fazhi*, No. 6, 1982, p. 6.

33. Article 90, paragraph 2 of the 1954 Constitution provides that the PRC citizens shall have "freedom of residence and freedom to change their residence", but this was omitted in the 1975 and 1978 constitutions. The present constitution is the same. This indicates that the present policy of rigid control over movement of the people will continue.

34. This makes one Western observer wonder whether people's mail will be really protected since no one is sure about either the existence of these legal procedures or the definition of "state secrets." Frank Ching, "Chinese Nationwide Mull Their New Constitution," *Asian Wall Street Journal*, June 24, 1982, p. 6. For reports about the PRC's practice of opening people's mail, see Fox Butterfield, *China: Alive in the Bitter Sea* (New York Times Books, 1982), pp. 323–324.

35. According to a Chinese jurist, the freedom to strike (first adopted in the 1975 Constitution) was a product of ultraleftist ideas, unsuitable to the interest of socialist development or to China's concrete conditions. Zhang Youyu, "On the Revision of the Constitution of China," *Faxue Yanjiu*, No. 3, 1982, p. 3–4.

36. For a study of the 1982 PRC Constitution, see Byron S. J. Weng, ed., *Studies on the Constitutional Law of the People's Republic of China*, in *Chinese Law and Government*, Vol. 16, Nos. 2–3 (Summer-Fall 1983), pp. 3–195.

37. Text of Zhao's speech is in *Renmin Ribao*, October 29, 1978, p. 2. The speech was given at a forum held before the Central Political-Legal Group.

38. Just at what points the Party Central Committee, probably through its Political-Legal Committee, now examines and approves the drafts of laws is not entirely clear. We failed to clarify this point when our American Bar Association Delegation held a meeting in Beijing with Mr. Gao Xijiang and six others from the Legal Affairs Commission of the NPC Standing Committee on June 1, 1981.

39. *Peking Review*, Vol. 21, No. 52, December 29, 1978, p. 2.

40. *Beijing Review*, Vol. 22, No. 9, March 2, 1979, pp. 3–4.

41. This is based on the following sources: Interviews with Chinese jurists; discussion sessions with the PRC legal groups, including the one with the Legal Affairs Commission of the NPC Standing Committee on June 1, 1981, see above note 38; Huang Shuangzhuan, "Drafting Groups for Civil Law and Civil Procedure Law Were Established to Strengthen Civil Legislation," *Chinese Encyclopedia Yearbook, 1981*, pp. 187–188.

42. Texts of all these laws are in *Renmin Shouce, 1979* (People's Handbook), pp. 397–431, 432–435.

43. Texts of the Six laws cited here are in *Chinese Encyclopedia Yearbook, 1981*, pp. 184–187, 188–189, 190–191.

44. Texts of these laws are in *Renmin Ribao*, Dec. 15, 1982, pp. 1–2 and Dec. 16, 1982, pp. 1–3.

45. Texts of the new law and revisions are in *Zhongguo Fazhi Bao* (China's Legal System Paper), Sept. 9, 1983, pp. 2–3.

46. Text of the Civil Procedure Law is in *Zhongguo Fazhi Bao*, March 12, 1982, pp. 2–3.

47. Texts of the three laws are in *Zhongguo Fazhi Bao*, Dec. 12, 1982, pp. 2–3; December 25, 1981, p. 2; May 28, 1982, p. 2; Aug. 27, 1982, p. 2; Dec. 16, 1983, p. 2.

48. *Zhongguo Fazhi Bao*, Aug. 27, 1982, p. 1.

49. Tao Xijin, "On the Current Legislative Work," *Zhongguo Fazhi Bao*, Jan. 29, 1982, p. 1. Chen Sui, "On Economic Legislation," *Chinese Encyclopedia Yearbook, 1981*, pp. 396–397; Wang Changshuo and others, "Strengthening the Legislation of Labor

Protection," *Faxue Yanjiu,* No. 2, 1982, pp. 39–42; Ren Jianxin, see above note 9, pp. 1–2; Sun Yaming, "Some Proposals Concerning the Acceleration of Economic Legislation," *Renmin Ribao,* August 5, 1980, p. 5. The Research Center on Economic Laws Under the State Council is reported to have discussed and examined some forty economic laws and regulations in the first nine months of 1983. *Zhongguo Fazhi Bao,* Oct. 14, 1983, p. 1.

50. Wu Biao, "Building Up Administrative Laws and Regulations Is the Current Urgent Task," *Minzhu Yu Fazhi,* No. 6, 1982, pp. 17–19; Xia Shusheng, "Restructuring of Government Departments and Administrative Laws," *Renmin Ribao,* March 15, 1982, p. 5; Xia Shuzhang, "From the Standpoint of the Draft of the Revised Constitution View the Role of Administrative Legislature," *Renmin Ribao,* June 29, 1982, p. 5.

51. Zhang Zhiye, "Legislative and Judicial Work in China," *Beijing Review,* Vol. 26, No. 33, Aug. 15, 1983, p. 19.

52. *Renmin Ribao,* November 30, 1979, p. 1. For an official explanation of the PRC's policy, see Peng Zeng's Report, see above note 7, pp. 86–88.

53. Texts of these regulations are in *Renmin Shouce, 1979,* pp. 436–438.

54. For the text of the SAPA, see *Renmin Shouce,* pp. 472–474. For the texts of the Decision and Supplementary Provisions on Reeducation, see *Gongan Faguei Huibian, 1950–1979* (Collection of Laws and Regulation on Public Security), (Beijing: Mass Press, 1980), pp. 113–122. The text of the Provisional Act on Guarding State Secrets is in *Gongan Faguei Huibian,* pp. 472–476, republished in *Renmin Ribao,* April 11, 1980, pp. 1, 3.

55. For a detailed discussion, see Timothy A. Gelatt and Frederick E. Snyder, "Legal Education in China: Training for a New Era," *China Law Reporter* Vol. 1, No. 2, 1980, pp. 44–60. See also R.S.J. MacDonald, "Legal Education in China Today," *Dalhousie Law Journal,* Vol. 6, 1980, pp. 313–337.

56. Shao-chuan Leng, *Justice in Communist China* (Dobbs Ferry, New York: Oceana, 1967), p. 97.

57. *Xinhua News Agency,* August 26, 1980.

58. *FBIS, Daily Report: China,* Sept. 21, 1983, p. K15.

59. Zhao Yusi, "Legal Education Should Be Greatly Expanded," *Renmin Ribao,* October 10, 1980, p. 5; *Chinese Encyclopedia Yearbook, 1981,* p. 475 (Table on Classified Institutions of Higher Learning, 1980); interviews with Chinese jurists.

60. *Remin Ribao,* May 8, 1983, p. 4; FBIS, *Daily Report: China,* Sept. 21, 1983, p. K15; "Legal Studies of America in China," *China Exchange News,* Vol. 11, No. 3, Sept. 1983, p. 9.

61. Jerome A. Cohen, "Rebuilding China's Shattered Legal System," *Asia,* November/December 1983, p. 48.

62. As estimated by Li Yunchang, First Vice-Minister of Justice, *FBIS, Daily Report: China,* September 22, 1982, p. K-11.

63. This section is based on the following sources: Gellatt and Snyder, see above note 55, pp. 43–50; information gathered through visits to Beijing University, the Peoples University, Nanjing University, Zhongshan University, the Beijing Political-Legal Institute, and the Southwest Political-Legal Institute. See also "Legal Studies of America in China," see above, note 60, pp. 7–12.

64. Information provided by Dr. Tao-tai Hsia of the Far Eastern Law Division of the Library of Congress. Illustrative is the exchange of letters concerning legal medicine in Zhongshan Medical School published in *Zhongguo Fazhi Bao,* February 26, 1982, p. 2.

65. *Zhongguo Fazhi Bao,* February 5, 1982, p. 1.

66. Pan Nienzhi, "The Construction of the Legal System in 1980," *Chinese Encyclopedia Yearbook, 1981,* p. 185.

67. See, for instance, "Tainjin Opens Spare-Time Law School," *Renmin Ribao,* July 10, 1979, p. 7; "Wuhan Establishes a Judicial School," *Zhongguo Fazhi Bao,* March 26, 1982, p. 1; "Training Personnel in Political Science and Law," *Beijing Review,* Vol. 22, No. 23, June 8, 1979, p. 7.

68. *Zhongguo Fazhi Bao,* February 5, 1982, p. 1.

69. *Zhongguo Fazhi Bao,* January 22, 1982, p. 1.

70. *Zhongguo Fazhi Bao,* January 22, 1982, p. 1.

71. Zhang Zhiye, see above, note 51, pp. 21–22.

72. See Gelatt and Snyder, see above, note 55, p. 57.

73. *FBIS, Daily Report: China,* Nov. 21, 1983, pp. K14–K16.

74. *FBIS, Daily Report: China,* pp. 57–58; Ellen R. Eliasoph and Susan Grueneberg, "Law on Display in China," *The China Quarterly,* No. 88, December 1981, pp. 669–685; "Shanghai Publicizes the Legal System," *Beijing Review,* Vol. 26, No. 33, Aug. 15, 1983, pp. 22–24.

75. Both plays are said to attract popular attention. *Zhongguo Fazhi Bao,* June 18, 1982, p. 1.

76. See *Zhongguo Fazhi Bao,* June 4, 1982, p. 4; July 9, 1982, p. 4.

77. See *Zhongguo Fazhi Bao,* August 7, 1981, p. 1 and "How We Have Educated our Middle-School Students on the Legal System," *Zhongguo Fazhi Bao,* July 16, 1982, p. 2. For current Chinese fictions on crime and justice, see Cen Ying, ed., *Zhongguo Dalu Zuian Xiaoshuo Xuan* (A Selection of Chinese Mainland Crime Stories), (Hong Kong: Tongjin Publishers, n.d., preface October 1980) and Jeffery C. Kinkley, *Law in Chinese Crime Fiction,* (A paper presented to the Modern Language Association Convention, New York, December 29, 1981).

78. Qi Naikuan, "Legal Research," *Chinese Encyclopedia Yearbook, 1980,* p. 444.

79. *Chinese Encyclopedia Yearbook, 1980,* p. 447; "Principal Legal Journals in China," *China Exchange News,* Vol. 11, No. 3, Sept. 1983, p. 12.

80. The latter, for instance, has in each week a "legal system" section on page 3.

81. Shanghai: Dictionary Press, 1980. A more concise law dictionary was published in 1982. *Jianmin falu cidian* (Concise law dictionary), (Hubei Province: Hubei People's Press, 1982).

82. The Library of Congress and major U.S. University Libraries, including that of the University of Virginia and University of Maryland Law School, now receive both Gazettes regularly.

83. Qi Naikuan, "National Conference on the Planning of Legal Research," *Chinese Encyclopedia Yearbook, 1980,* pp. 444–445.

84. Xiao Yongqing and others, "Subjects and Methods of Research on the History of the Legal System," *Faxue Yanjiu,* No. 5, 1979, pp. 17–20.

85. *FBIS, Daily Report: PRC,* February 6, 1980, pp. L2–L3; Hung Xiang, "On Expanding Research Into International Law," *Faxue Yanjiu,* No. 2, 1980, pp. 9–11; "A Conference on the Theory of Law Held in Shanghai," *Faxue Yanjiu,* No. 3, 1983, p. 3. The Beijing Conference of 1982 was sponsored by the Ford Foundation and the Chinese Academy of Social Sciences, with participants from both U.S. and Chinese legal circles. *China Exchange News,* Vol. 11, No. 3, Sept. 1983, pp. 11–12. For a report on increasing activities of Chinese experts in international law, see Gerd Kaminski, "International Law: A Robust Plant Among the Hundred Flowers of China's Law Reform," *Asian Thought and Society,* Vol. VII, March 1982, p. 3–17.

86. *Zhongguo Fazhi Bao,* July 23, 1982, p. 1.

87. "Brief Introduction to the Judicial System of Austria," *Zhongguo Fazhi Bao,* No. 1, 1980, pp. 45–57.

88. See Wang Zhongfang "A Visit to the Institute of Comparative Jurisprudence of France," *Faxue Yanjiu,* No. 5, 1980, pp. 55–60.

89. "Yugoslavia Is a Socialist State Ruled by Law," *Faxue Yanjiu*, No. 3, 1980, pp. 55–61.

90. Wang Baoshu, "Observation of Foreign Legal Systems," *Chinese Encyclopedia Yearbook, 1981*, p. 397.

91. "A Survey Concerning the Researches in the History of Legal Systems in Japan," *Faxue Yanjiu*, No. 6, 1981, pp. 51–85.

92. Zeng Qingmin, "The Theory and Practice of Criminal Legislation in Austria," *Faxue Yanjiu*, No. 3, 1982, pp. 61–64.

93. *Zhongguo Fazhi Bao*, Oct. 29, 1982, p. 1; Wang Jiafu and Others, "An Investigation on Economic Law in West Germany, France and Britain," *Faxue Yanjiu*, No. 4, 1983, pp. 61–72.

94. *Zhongguo Fazhi Bao*, Nov. 11, 1983, p. 1. The Chinese legal delegation from Beijing, which toured mainly U.S. Law Schools, came to the University of Virginia Law School for a two-day visit in September 1983.

95. Gellett and Snyder, see above note 55, p. 57. Deng Xiaoping is reported to have stated in January 1980 that China would need one to two million trained legal cadres. *FBIS, Daily Report: PRC*, March 11, 1980 (Supplement), p. 20.

96. Chen Chunlong, *et al.*, *Falu Zhishi Wenda* (Questions and Answers in Legal Knowledge) (Beijing: Beijing Publishing House, 1979), p. 18; Zhao Canbi, "Strenthen the Concept of the Legal System and Act Strictly According to the Law," *Hongqi*, No. 8, 1979, p. 41.

97. Li Buyun, "On the Scientific Character of the Concept of Rule by Law," *Faxue Yanjiu*, No. 1, 1982, p. 9.

98. "Closing Address," *Main Documents of the Second Session of the 5th NPC of the PRC* (1979), pp. 224–225.

99. Dai Zhou, "Foundation of Unity: Guarantee of Victory On Upholding the Four Basic Principles," *Banyue Tan* (Semi-monthly Talks), No. 14, July 25, 1981, p. 5.

100. Parris H. Chang, "Chinese Politics: Deng's Turbulent Quest," *Problems of Communism*, Jan–Feb. 1981, pp. 11–12.

101. For the new Constitution, see the earlier discussion in this chapter. English text of the Central Committee's 1981 "Resolution on Certain Questions in the History of Our Party Since the Founding of the People's Republic of China" is in *Beijing Review*, Vol. 24, No. 27, July 6, 1981, pp. 10–39. See earlier reference to the Four Basic Principles.

102. Wang Guiwu, "Upholding Four Basic Principles: Continuously Emancipating Our Minds," *Faxue Yanjui*, No. 2, 1979, pp. 21–23; Song Hua, "Adhere to the Four Basic Principles and Continue to Emancipate the Mind," *Guangzhou Ribao*, May 3, 1981, p. 1.

103. Zhang Youyu, "Revolution and the Legal System," *Minzhu Yu Fazhi*, No. 7, 1981, p. 9.

104. Li Maoguan, "Citizens' Freedom and the Law," *Faxue Yanjiu*, No. 2, 1981, pp. 7–8. English translation of this article is available in JPRS (Joint Publication Research Service) 79550, No. 30, 1981, pp. 49–52. However we only used JPRS for reference in translating the quotation in question.

105. For a discussion of the PRC's treatment of political dissent, see Chapter VI of this book.

106. There is, for instance, a recent book with collected essays on the question of rule by law or rule by man. Although containing no conclusions, the book is unmistakenly in favor of rule by law. See *Fazhi Yu Renzhi Wenti Taolun Ji* (Collection of Discussions on the Question of Rule by Law and Rule by Man) (Beijing: Mass Press, 1981).

107. A good discussion of Soviet concepts of socialist legality and socialist democracy is in Bernard Rasmundo, *The Soviet Legal System, A Primer* (Chicago: American Bar Association, 1971), pp. 27–28. Even a publication in Hong Kong sympathetic to the PRC maintains that the draft of the new Chinese Constitution has a serious flaw in that in upholding the Four Basic Principles in the Preamble, it emphasizes the Party's leadership of the state. Editorial: "The Big Leaky Hole of the Draft of the New Constitution," *Cheng Ming*, No. 56, June 1982, p. 3. The editorial urges the CCP to make a breakthrough on the question of "Party leadership" in order to "resolve the crisis of trust and realize the genuine rule of law."

Restructuring of the Judicial System

One major aspect of the present Chinese leaders' policy of building a stable legal order and a regular criminal justice system is the various steps that have been taken in recent years to restructure China's judicial institutions seriously damaged by the Cultural Revolution. They include the reorganization and expansion of the court structure, restoration of the procuracy, revival of the Ministry of Justice, and resurrection of the lawyer system.

This chapter will examine the structure and functions of these formal legal organs in post-Mao China. Reference will also be made to public security organs (police) and other extrajudicial apparatus that continue to play important roles in the administration of justice and exercise of social control.

COURTS

As in the mid-1950s, the courts, together with the procuracy and police, are the principal political-legal organs that divide and share responsibilities and complement and restrict one another in the formal administration of justice in China today.[1] The new Organic Law of the People's Courts was adopted in July 1979 and came into effect on January 1, 1980. Compared to the 1954 Organic Law, the new Court Law has made only a few but relevant changes.[2] The court system is still composed of the Supreme People's Court, local people's courts, and special people's courts. The local courts are divided into three levels:

(1) the higher people's courts of provinces, autonomous regions, and municipalities directly under the central government (Article 26);

(2) the intermediate people's courts of prefectures, autonomous prefectures, municipalities directly under the central government, and municipalities directly under the provinces (Article 23); and

(3) the basic people's courts of counties, autonomous counties, cities, and municipal districts (Article 18).

The special courts include military courts, railway transport courts, water transport courts, and new forestry courts (Article 2).

With minor modifications, the new Organic Law of the Courts reiterates the 1954 provisions concerning judicial independence, equality before the law, public (open) trials, the right to defense, people's assessors, the collegiate system, adjudication (judicial) committees, and the two-trial (one appeal) system.[3] One significant change in the revised Court Law is to make the court accountable only to the people's congress and free the court from direct supervision by local governments. According to Articles 35 and 36, the presidents of the people's courts at all levels are elected and recalled by the corresponding people's congresses, and their vice-presidents, chief judges, and other judges are appointed and removed by the standing committees of the corresponding people's congresses. Under the 1954 Law, however, the vice-presidents and other officials of the local courts were appointed and removed by the people's councils (administrative organ) at the corresponding levels.[4]

As prescribed by the law, the term of office for the presidents and other judges of the Supreme People's Court is five years; the term for the president and other judges of the higher court or the intermediate court is also five years; the term for the president and other judges of the basic court is three years.[5] They can be reelected but shall not serve more than two consecutive terms in the future, so stipulated by the PRC new Constitution adopted on December 4, 1982.[6]

Another important feature of the 1979 Court Law is to provide the Supreme People's Court with additional power. While the authority to interpret the Constitution and laws in the PRC is reserved for the Standing Committee of the NPC[7], the Supreme People's Court is bestowed with the power to give "explanations on questions concerning specific applications of laws and decrees in judicial procedure" in addition to its adjudication functions.[8] The requirement adopted by the NPC in 1957 that all death sentences must have the approval of the Supreme People's Court, is also incorporated into the new Organic Law of the Courts as Article 13.[9] As will be further examined in later chapters, however, the NPC Standing Committee adopted a resolution on June 10, 1981 to temporarily delegate the Supreme People's Court's right to approve death sentences, except those for counter-revolutionaries and embezzlers, to the provincial-level higher people's courts for the years of 1981–1983.[10] This change became further formalized on Setpember 2, 1983 when the NPC

Standing Committee in its revision of the Court Law modified Article 13 to read: "Except for those cases handed down by the Supreme People's Court, cases involving the death penalty should be reported to the Supreme People's Court for approval. Whenever necessary, the Supreme People's Court may authorize the higher people's courts in provinces, autonomous regions and municipalities directly under central authority to exercise the power of approval in cases of murder, rape, robbery, use of explosives and other cases seriously endangering public security and social order which involve the death penalty." [11]

Under the Organic Law, the people's courts of all levels are essentially organized the same; each court is composed of a president and a number of vice-presidents, chief judges, associate chief judges, and judges (Articles 19, 23, 27 and 31). In May 1982, the NPC Standing Committee cut down the number of the Supreme People's Court's vice-presidents from seven to four and also lowered, as a result, the average age of the vice-presidents of the Court from 69.5 to 62.5. Two of those relieved of their posts as vice-presidents were simultaneously appointed as advisers to the Supreme People's Court.[12]

The people's courts at all levels have a criminal division and a civil division. Each division is headed by a chief judge and associate chief judges. In addition, the lower courts have recently followed the example of the Supreme People's Court and set up economic divisions to deal specifically with civil economic disputes and criminal acts against the socialist economic order. By the end of 1980, economic divisions had been established in 1,002 people's courts of all levels, of which twenty-eight were higher people's courts, 277 were intermediate people's courts, and 697 were basic people's courts. More than 600 other people's courts were also prepared to establish economic divisions.[13] In his report to the National People's Congress on December 7, 1981, President Jiang Hua of the Supreme People's Court listed the Supreme People's Court, all the higher people's courts, 297 intermediate people's courts, and an unspecified number of basic people's courts as having set up economic divisions.[14] According to his report to the NPC on June 7, 1983, the people's courts at various levels tried more than 33,000 cases of economic offense and handled 49,000 cases of economic disputes during the year of 1982.[15]

There are in China more than 3,000 regular courts at all levels: the Supreme People's Court, 29 higher people's courts, about 300 intermediate courts, and approximately 3,000 basic courts.[16] Restoration of special courts have also been underway. It should be noted that the PRC had in the mid–1950s three types of special courts: military courts, railway transport courts, and water transport courts. The latter two were abolished in 1957.[17] The military courts continued to operate until the Cultural Revolution when they ceased to function. They were, however, revived in October 1978 and open military trials resumed two months later.[18] Since then, the other special courts, along with the new forestry courts, have been established in accordance with the specific listing by Article 2 of the Organic Law of the People's Courts. To provide more flexibility, however, the Article has recently been revised to read just "military courts and other special people's courts." [19]

To staff the courts is still a serious problem for the PRC as the disruptions of the Cultural Revolution contributed heavily to the present shortage of well-qualified judicial personnel. However, the Chinese have been making determined efforts, as shown in the preceding chapter, to alleviate the situation by restoring and expanding university law departments, political-legal institutes, political-legal cadre schools, ad hoc training classes, etc. Progress has been reported not only in the training of new cadres but also with the return of veteran workers to their original posts. In September 1981, Li Yunchang, Chinese First Vice-Minister of Justice, reported that China had 200,000 judicial workers.[20] In August 1982, Liu Fuzhi, Minister of Justice, gave a figure of one million people engaged in political-legal work.[21] Of course, the qualifications of China's current judicial personnel are understandably uneven and their backgrounds are quite diverse. For instance, many military officers have been tansferred to political-legal work.[22] Increasing numbers of women have also joined the ranks of judicial cadres. According to one report, there are more than 4,800 female judges, more than 3,100 female procurators, and some 50,000 policewomen in China today.[23]

Recently, the people's courts at various levels have been also carrying out organizational reforms. The emphasis appear to be on expertise and youth. Article 34 of the recently revised Court Law, for instance, adds the following statement: "The judges of people's courts must possess professional judicial knowledge." [24] According to Jiang Hua, members of the readjusted leading judicial bodies are in some measure more revolutionary, younger in age, more competent professionally, and better educated.[25] It may be noted that his successor as President of the Supreme People's Court in June 1983 is 70-year-old Zheng Tianxiang, five years younger than Jiang.

In order to have a fuller understanding of how the people's courts operate, we now turn our attention to the following features and related organs of the Chinese judiciary.

Collegiate System

Both the Organic Law of the People's Courts and the Criminal Procedure Law provide that the people's courts use the collegiate system in adjudicating cases. Except for minor cases, justice is administered in cases of original jurisdiction by a collegiate bench composed of one to three judges and two to four people's assessors. In cases of appeal or protest, the collegiate bench consists of three to five judges.[26] The president of the court or the chief judge appoints one judge as the presiding jduge of the collegiate bench; when the court president or the chief judge participates in adjudication, he serves as the presiding judge.

The members of a collegiate bench are supposed to enjoy equal rights. In adjudicating a case, the entire process of investigation, trial, and sentencing should be jointly and fully discussed by all the members of the collegiate bench. If there is no unanimous agreement, the majority rules, but the minority opinion must be entered into the official record.[27]

Adjudication (Judicial) Committees

The people's courts at all levels are required by law to set up adjudication committees to insure "collective leadership" over judicial work. Members of adjudication committees of the people's courts are appointed and removed by the Standing Committees of the People's Congress at corresponding levels upon the recommendation of the presidents of the people's courts.[28] As a rule, the adjudication committee include the president, vice-presidents, chief judges, and associate chief judges of the court. In 1979, eleven members were listed on the Adjudication Committee of the Supreme People's Court.[29]

Among the major functions of the adjudication committee are to "sum up judicial experience and to discuss major or difficult cases as well as other issues regarding judicial work." [30] Another important task of the adjudication committee is to review a legally effective court decision if some actual error is found in the determination of facts or application of law.[31] The adjudication committee shall also decide whether the chief judge of the court should withdraw from handling a case.[32] In addition, once a case is submitted by the chief judge to the adjudication committee for discussion, its decision shall be carried out by the collegiate bench of the court.[33]

Meetings of adjudication committees are presided over by the presidents of the people's courts. The chief procurators of the people's procuratorates of the corresponding levels have the right to participate in the discussions at such meetings as nonvoting representatives.[34] In the view of a Chinese writer, this is the way to place judicial work under the supervision of the procuracy and help the procuratorates and courts complement, coordinate, and restrict each other.[35]

People's Assessors

Article 9 of the Organic Law of the People's Courts stipulates that the people's courts apply the system of people's assessors in adjudicating all cases of the first instance, except in minor civil and criminal matters. According to the Organic Law, citizens over twenty-three years of age who have the right to elect or be elected and have not been deprived of political rights may be elected people's assessors (Article 38). The method of selecting people's assessors is twofold: (1) Election: people's assessors are elected by local residents directly or by the basic-level people's congresses, (2) Invitation: specific invitations are used by the courts when cases that come up demand people's assessors with special and technical knowledge.[36]

Under the Organic Law of the Courts, people's assessors enjoy equal rights with the judges in performing their duties (Article 38). They can examine the files of a case, verify all facts and evidence, and question the parties and witnesses at the trial. Along with the judges, they also have the right to decide on a judgment and sign the court decision.[37] PRC writers have listed three major advantages of the system of people's assessors. First, it manifests the people's right to control the state and thus gives the masses a sense of responsibility in national affairs. Second, the system helps increase the efficiency of trial work, prevent the miscarriage of justice, and minimize the occurrence of biased and subjective judgements. Third, as a bridge between the people and the courts, the assessors are in a position to facilitate education and propaganda on the legal system.[38]

On the other hand, since few assessors have professional knowledge of law, their presence in court proceedings has caused certain practical problems. In an effort to alleviate this situation, the NPC Standing Committee revised, on September 2, 1983, Article 10 of the Court Law by replacing the requirement of a collegiate bench of judges and assessors at initial trials with a more flexible provision: "In handling initial trials, the people's courts form a collegiate bench of judges or a collegiate bench of judges and assessors who are representatives of the masses." [39]

People's Reception Offices

As in the past, people's reception offices of the courts at all levels receive letters and visits from people, hear their complaints, and resolve uncomplicated problems. They are a useful channel through which the authorities maintain close contacts with the masses to facilitate the promotion of social order and correct handling of cases. Procuracy, public security, and other organs have also taken active steps to encourage letters and personal visits from the people.[40]

Mediation Committees

Below the basic people's courts are mediation committees which, along with other extrajudicial organs, perform the functions of settling civil disputes and disposing minor criminal cases at the grassroots level. We may recall that the informal process of dispute resolution enjoyed its heyday under Mao when the societal model of law overshadowed the jural model.[41] Even today the mediation committees continue to play a useful role in complementing the PRC's formal judiciary structure and relieving the courts of responsibility for processing cases which would otherwise be too time-consuming.

There are now in China more than 800,000 mediation committees. Composed of five to eleven members each, the mediation committees operate in urban neighborhoods, industrial and mining units, and rural production brigades. The near six million mediators are elected by popular vote for a two-year term and can be reelected. They serve without pay and may be removed at any time by the electors for dereliction of duty.[42]

According to the 1954 Provisional General Rules Governing the Organization of People's Mediation Committees, reissued by the PRC in 1980, all committee work must be carried out in accordance with state laws and policies and under the direction of the courts and political authorities at basic levels.[43] In addition to handling civil disputes and minor criminal cases, mediation committees are also responsible for conducting legal and moral education as well as propaganda. Legally, mediation is not a required procedure for persons involved in disputes and cannot be used to impede an attempt to get cases tried in formal courts.[44] Nevertheless, up to 90 percent of the civil cases in China have been resolved through mediation in the past few years, as stated by Zhang Youyu, Vice-President of the Chinese Academy of Social Sciences. He further pointed that mediation committees handled 12.8 times as many civil and minor criminal cases as basic people's courts in 1981.[45] Other reports also stressed the success of China's mediation work and the raving comments on the people's mediation committees made by foreign visitors, including U.S. Chief Justice Warren Burger.[46]

PROCURACY

Article 43 of the PRC's 1978 Constitution reinstituted the procuracy. The new Organic Law of the People's Procuratorates, promulgated in 1979, retains the same structure of the procuracy established by the 1954 Organic Law, namely, the Supreme People's Procuratorate, local people's procuratorates, and special people's procuratorates.

Parallel to that of the local people's courts, the hierarchy of the local procuratorates consists of three levels: people's procuratorates of provinces, autonomous regions, and municipalities directly under the central authority; branches of the above and people's procuratorates of prefectures and counties directly under the provincial governments; and people's procuratorates of counties, cities, autonomous counties, and districts directly under the city governments.[47]

The new Law on the procuracy introduces some important innovations on the basis of Chinese conditions, thus departing from the Soviet model on which the 1954 Statute was closely patterned.[48] First, it drops the controversial principle of "vertical leadership" adopted in 1954 under which local procuratorates were free of control by local state organs and were responsible only to higher level organs of the procuracy.[49] Instead, the new Law applies the principle of dual leadership, making the procuratorates at all levels accountable to the people's congresses and their Standing Committees at corresponding levels and at the same time placing local procuratorates under the leadership of the procuratorate at the next higher level (Article 10). As in the case of court officials, the power to elect or recall chief procurators and to appoint or remove deputy chief procurators and other procurators at various levels is vested in the corresponding people's congresses and their Standing Committees, respectively (Articles 21–24).[50]

Second, the new Law defines the procuratorates as "state organs of legal supervision" (Article 1) but omits the 1954 provisions detailing the procuracy's power of general supervision over the legality of the actions of all state organs.[51] The procuratorates are now to deal with state functionaries only when they violate the Criminal Law (Articles 5–6). "Ordinary cases concerning breaches of Party or government discipline but no violation of the Criminal Law," in the words of Peng Zhen, "shall all be handled by the discipline inspection departments of the Party or the organs of government."[52] In its specifically designated role of supervising the administration of criminal justice, the procuracy is empowered by the new Law to carry out investigation of criminal cases, oversee the activities of the police in the criminal process, institute prosecution, scrutinize the trial activities of the courts, and supervise the execution of judgements and the activities of correctional activities (Article 5). Reflecting the current political need in China, the procuracy also has the power to "exercise procuratorial authority with regard to cases of treason, of attempts to split the country, and other major criminal cases of serious disruption of unified implementation of state policies, laws, decrees, and administrative orders" (Article 5).[53] The independence of the procuracy reinstated conditionally by the 1978 Third Plenum of the

Eleventh Central Committee of the Chinese Communist Party appears to be fully restored in Article 9 of the 1979 Procuratorial Law, which reads: "People's Procuratorates shall exercise their procuratorial authority independently in accordance with the law and shall not be subject to interference by other administrative organs, organizations, or individuals." [54] The same wording is contained in Article 131 of the PRC's new Constitution, except adding "public (social)" before "organizations."

An important organizational feature of China's procuratorates that has been passed on from the 1954 Law to the present is procuratorial committees. Under Article 3 of the new Organic Law, people's procuratorates at various levels are required to set up procuratorial committees, which, under the direction of chief procurators, will discuss and decide on major legal cases and other important questions relating to their work. If the chief procurator disagrees with the decision of the majority on important questions, he can submit his objections to the Standing Committee of the people's congress at the corresponding level for a decision.[55] In the words of Huang Huoqing, China's Chief Procurator until June 1983 when replaced by Yang Yichen, this provision "ensures full practice of democracy" and also "helps give full play to collective wisdom and avoids one-sideness in making decisions by one person so that they may be more accurate." [56]

There are in China over 3,000 procuratorates with some 110,000 cadres.[57] In addition to the regular procuracies at the various levels, special procuratorates which include military procuratorates, railway transport procuratorates, and water transport procuratorates have been set up.[58] Recently, the procuratorates of all levels have expanded their procuratorial work in the economic area and increased their activities in combating corruption, bribery, and other economic crimes. In accordance with Article 2 of the Organic Law, the procuratorates at provincial and county levels have been establishing people's procuratorates in industry and mining, land reclamation, and forestry areas with the approval of the Standing Committees of the people's congresses at the corresponding levels.[59]

According to official statistics, during the first nine months of 1981, 99.7 percent of the persons prosecuted by the people's procuratorates at all levels were found guilty by the people's courts; in the same period the procuratorates handled more than 16,000 malfeasance cases and more than 31,000 criminal cases in the economic field.[60] In 1982, the procurators of all levels also investigated more than 33,000 economic cases, of which some involved embezzlement, bribery, smuggling and fraud and more than 17,000 cases were prosecuted before the people's courts.[61]

Chinese press and journals have publicized from time to time model procurators in the PRC. Some have carried out their duties courageously in struggle against evil practices of higher-ups. Others have handled cases impartially regardless of personal relationships. All appear to be incorruptible and upright procurators, who are devoted to the upholding of justice and administration of law without deviation.[62]

Still, it is officially conceded that the procuratorial organs are confronted with a number of problems and difficulties. As described by former Chief Procurator Huang Huoqing, there are a shortage of backbone personnel and a lack of work experience among procuratorial cadres. To build up the procuratorial ranks both quantitatively and qualitatively, he said, China would have to train the existing cadres, cultivate and promote young and middle-aged cadres, and strengthen the leadership at various levels so that more younger, knowledgeable and professional people would become leading members in procuratorial organs.[63]

Another issue of major concern is the degree of independence the procuratorates may enjoy in performing their duties. Article 9 of the Organic Law of the People's Procuratorates stipulates: "People's procuratorates exercise their procuratorial authority independently in accordance with the law, and are not subject to interference by administrative organs, organization or individuals." Nevertheless, there have been reports about continuing interference in procuratorial work. One procurator lost his job because of conflicts with a Party secretary; another needed the support of the Party committee to overcome all kinds of obstacles to the exercise of his legal authority.[64] Thus, Chinese leaders like Ye Jianying and Peng Zhen have found it necessary to urge procurators and judges to be fearless and ready to die in upholding the dignity of the legal system.[65]

There have been considerable number of legal publications discussing the issue of procuratorial independence. The consensus is that the procuratorates can faithfully perform their sacred duty of legal supervision only if they can exercise their procuratorial authority independently according to the law, not to be influenced and interfered with by others. This, however, does mean the negation of Party leadership over the procuratorial organs. It is said by one official that while Party committees should refrain from direct involvement in concrete procuratorial activities, they also must strengthen their leadership over the procuratorates so as to ensure the latter's independent exercise of functions and powers according to the law and correct implementation of the Party's principles and policy lines.[66] One legal article even suggests that "when they encounter different opinions over cases from the concerned departments and leading comrades, the procuratorates should rely on the Party committees for proper solutions." [67]

MINISTRY OF JUSTICE

A Ministry of Justice existed in the early years of the PRC but was abolished in 1959 with its judicial administrative functions transferred to the Supreme People's Court.[68] In September 1979, however, the Ministry of Justice, along with its nationwide bureaucracy, was reestablished as a means to strengthen the legal system.[69]

Under the guidance of the State Council, the Ministry of Justice carries on its judicial administrative work with the support of provincial level judicial departments, county level judicial bureaus, and grassroots level judicial assistants. Its main tasks are as follows: handle the judicial administrative work of the people's courts at all levels; manage and train judicial cadres; supervise and expand political-legal institutes; publicize the law and educate the people in the legal systems; supervise the work of the organizations of lawyers and notaries; exercise leadership over the organization and work of people's mediation committees; compile collections of laws and decrees; conduct researches on jurisprudence in cooperation with scholarly institutions and organize the publication of books and periodicals on law; and manage external affairs in connection with judicial work.[70]

Since its restoration, the Ministry of Justice is reported to have accomplished many things. It has, for instance, consolidated and expanded the Beijing, East China, Southwest, and Northwest Political-Legal Institutes and helped educational departments set up law departments at twenty-nine universities. It has also guided the establishment of more than 2,000 legal advisory offices and more than 800,000 mediation committees with nearly six million mediators.[71] To further strengthen judicial administration, Justice Minister Liu Fuzhi in 1982 suggested that, among other things, China establish judicial bureaus, legal advisory offices, notarial offices and judicial assistants in perfectures, cities, and counties where these organs are still nonexistent and strengthen the consolidation and rotational training of judicial cadres on the job.[72]

LAWYERS

A system of people's lawyers was established by the PRC in the mid-1950s. By June 1957, there were more than 800 legal advisory offices and nearly 3,000 lawyers all over the country.[73] The organization and activity of the Chinese bar were governed by the Provisional Rules for Lawyers of 1957.[74] However, China's overall legal development was abruptly disrupted by the Anti-Rightist Campaign of 1957–1958, and as a result, practicing lawyers all but ceased to exist.[75]

One aspect of the new legal policy of the post-Mao leadership is the resurrection of the Chinese bar. In August 1980, the Standing Committee of the National People's Congress adopted the twenty-one Article Provisional Act on Lawyers, which closely resembled the 1957 Provisional Rules and came into force on January 1, 1982. According to the new statute, China's lawyers are "state's legal workers" and have the duty to "safeguard the interests of the state, the collectives and the legitimate rights and interests of citizens" (Article 1). There are a number of major functions for them to perform:

(1) To act as legal advisers to state organs, enterprises and institutions, social groups, and people's communes;

(2) To serve as agents for litigants in civil suits;

(3) To defend the accused involved in criminal cases on request of the defendant or upon the assignment of the people's court; take part in litigation on request of the party which initiates a private prosecution or of the injured party or their close relatives involved in a public prosecution;

(4) To furnish legal advice to parties in a nonlitigious matter or act on their behalf in mediation or arbitration;

(5) To answer questions on law and to draft documents for litigation and other documents related to legal matters. Moreover, lawyers are expected to "propagate the socialist legal system" through their entire professional activities.[76]

To ensure the proper performance of their services, the Provisional Act also confers the following rights to Chinese lawyers. First, they are protected by the law of the state and are free from interference by any unit or individual in the course of their work (Article 3). Second, they have the right to refuse to serve as defense counsel for dubious clients (Article 6). Third, lawyers participating in litigious activities have the right "to examine and to read the materials relevant to their cases and to make inquiry to relevant units and individuals" (Article 7). However, this right does not include access to adjudication committees' records, judges deliberations in certain cases, and other materials which might provide leads to other cases.[77] Fourth, as defense counsels, lawyers have the right to visit and correspond with the accused persons in custody. They are also obligated to keep confidential "state secrets" and their clients' "personal secrets" (Article 7).[78]

One prerequisite for law practice in China is Chinese citizenship. Article 8 of the Provisional Act specifies that all lawyers must be Chinese citizens who support the socialist system and have the right to elect and be elected. This requirement, as stated by a Chinese official, rules out the possibility of foreign lawyers appearing in Chinese courts, handling legal cases, or acting as legal advisers to any Chinese organization or enterprise.[79] Chinese citizens who qualify as lawyers include:

(1) graduates with a law major from institutions of higher learning with two or more years in judicial work, teaching of law, or legal research;

(2) those who have received training in a law major and worked as judges and procurators;

(3) those who have received higher education, have done three or more years of economic, scientific, technological, or other work, are proficient in their fields and in the laws and decrees related to their field, have gone through training in a law major and are suitable to engage in lawyers' work; and

(4) those who possess the same level of legal knowledge as listed in items (1) and (2) above, have the cultural level of graduates of institutions of higher learning, and are suitable to be lawyers (Article 8).[80]

Finally, it is necessary for the judicial departments at the provincial level to evaluate, approve, and issue the lawyers' certificate to those candidates who have met the requirements and register such certificates with the Ministry of Justice (Article 9). Under certain circumstances, written examinations may also be required.[81]

There are two types of organizations for lawyers in China. The first is legal advisers offices, which exist at the county, municipality, and municipal district levels. When necessary, specialized legal advisers offices can be established in enterprises or institutions with the approval of the Ministry of Justice. These offices are led and supervised by the state judicial administrative organs which train, examine, assign and transfer lawyers. They are the work organs through which lawyers operate in China, where no private practice is permitted.[82] Each legal advisers office elects its director and deputy directors with the approval of the provincial judicial administrative department. It oversees the professional activities of lawyers, collects fees from clients, and distribute work to its members.[83] The other type of organization is lawyers' associations. Labelled as social groups, lawyers' associations are organized by lawyers themselves at the provincial, municipal and autonomous regional levels.[84] Their functions are "to protect the legitimate rights and interests of lawyers, to exchange work experience, and to promote lawyers' work and contacts between legal workers both at home and abroad." [85]

As in the past, lawyers are paid by the state, but it is not clear whether the 1956 Provisional Rules for Lawyers' Fees, which established a close relation between a lawyer's salary and his performance, will be followed.[86] Fees are paid by clients to the legal advisers office in accordance with the cost of living and the type of work done. The amount is quite moderate as set by the Tentative Methods for Charges for Legal Counsel. For example, the charges range from 0.5 yuan to 10 yuan for legal inquiries or drafting legal papers; 5–30 yuan for drafting contracts and agreements; 10–30 yuan for handling criminal or civil cases; 10–30 yuan for estates amounting to over 10,000 yuan. Fees may be reduced or exempted if the client proves too poor to pay, or is involved in pension or alimony claims, or has other justifiable claims.[87]

Since the resumption of legal counseling in 1979, considerable progress has been made by the PRC in recruiting lawyers and expanding their organizations and operations. Beijing, for instance, had only two legal advisers offices and seventy-three lawyers in early 1981.[88] By mid-1982, however, there were legal advisers offices in the capital's nineteen different districts and counties with a total staff of 303 lawyers serving the city's nine million people.[89] In September 1981, there were 1,300 legal advisers offices and 4,800 lawyers in China.[90] As of mid-1983, 2,350 legal advisers offices and more than 12,000 professional and part-time lawyers were reportedly operating throughout the country.[91]

Chinese lawyers' work appears to be heavily weighted on criminal defense. In the session the American Bar Association Delegation had with members of the Shanghai Lawyers' Association in June 1981, the delegations were told by Chinese colleagues that 78 percent of the Shanghai lawyer's average daily workload was devoted to criminal defense matters and approximately 22 percent devoted to civil and family law matters.[92] By the same token, incomplete data on a nationwide basis indicates that lawyers in China handled more than 90,000 criminal cases during 1982.[93] At the same time, there is a trend toward increasing participation of lawyers in economic disputes and civil litigation in line with the PRC's focus on the four modernizations. In 1982, lawyers in various places handled more than 23,000 civil suits and more than 12,000 out-of-court settlements.[94]

Undoubtedly, the number of Chinese lawyers is still too small for a country of over one billion population. The level of their professional competence also leaves much to be desired. Furthermore, there are a number of problems for lawyers to overcome, such as the Chinese negative attitude toward lawyers, ever present political interference in legal work, and other related issues that will be examined in connection with legal defense in Chapter Five of this book. Nevertheless, a foundation for legal counseling has already been built and the post-Mao leadership is showing every indication it is determined to develop the lawyers system as an integral part of China's growing socialist legality.

PUBLIC SECURITY APPARATUS

The public security apparatus (the police) has retained an important role in the maintenance of law and order in post-Mao China. Article 135 of the new Constitution, for instance, states: "The People's courts, people's procuratorates and public security organs shall, in handling criminal cases, divide their functions, each taking responsibility for its own work, and shall coordinate their efforts and check each other to ensure correct and effective enforcement of law."

At the top of the apparatus is the Ministry of Public Security in the State Council. Under this Ministry are four levels of public security organs in the following descending order: public security departments at the provincial and special municipal level; public security bureaus at the county and municipal level; public security subbureaus at the rural or urban district level; and public security stations at the commune and city district level.[95] The two governing enactments of the 1950s that still remain in force are the Regulations for the Organization of Public Security Stations (December 1954) and the Regulations on the People's Police (June 1957).[96]

Below the official structure and supplementing the work of the public security organs are wide-ranging networks of grassroots mass organizations that maintain social order and public security and settle disputes among local residents. Those extrajudicial institutions, which have formed important parts of the PRC's highly effective system of control over the lives of the people, were established in the 1950s and have been reaffirmed by the post-Mao leadership.[97] At the basic level of the Chinese control structure are street offices, residents' committees (supervising 100 to 600 households with a staff of seven to seventeen members), and residents' groups (supervising fifteen to forty households) in the cities; communes, production brigades (200 to 300 households), and production teams (twenty to fifty households) in the countryside. In addition, mediation committees, security defense committee, and other popular organizations are formed in residential, production, and occupational units. We have already discussed the organization and functions of the mediation committees earlier, so our attention here should be given to the security defense (protection) committees. Originally organized in 1952 and revitalized since the Cultural Revolution, the security defense committees operate within street committees, production brigades or teams, factories, mines, enterprises and schools. Composed of three to eleven members each, these committees are subject to the direction of the basic-level governmental and public security organs and may establish small security teams of three to five activists with the approval of appropriate public security authorities. The duties of these committees are to assist the police in maintaining public order, combating criminal activities, and teaching the masses in the observance of state laws and policies. Since the committee members are all local residents who know their neighbors fairly well, they have proven to be a valuable aid in the extension of the public security system.[98]

As an important instrument of the People's Democratic Dictatorship, the public security organs continue to perform, as they did in the past, a wide variety of tasks in the PRC. They are competent to arrest, detain, and investigate suspected criminals in accordance with the law. They have the authority to impose as well as administer punishment. They monitor internal travel and manage labor reform institutions. They are also in charge of traffic control, fire prevention, public health, census registration, border patrol, and protection of economic and military installations.[99]

In June 1983, the PRC established a new Ministry of State Security to "ensure the security of the state and strengthen counterespionage work." According to Minister Ling Yun, former Vice-Minister of Public Security, the new Ministry and the Ministry of Public Security work in close coordination for different tasks under the State Council. The State Security Ministry will "ensure the security of the state through effective measures against enemy agents, spies and counterrevolutionary activities designed to sabotage or overthrow China's socialist system." [100] While the regular police work remains a part of the public security structure, the new Ministry of State Security is to control the People's Armed Police Force, which was established in early 1983 to include China's border guards and special units that guard government buildings, embassies, and residence compounds set aside for foreigners.[101]

Measures have been taken by the post-Mao leadership to prevent the abuse of power by the public security apparatus. The new Criminal Procedure Law and the revised Act on Arrest and Detention, promulged in 1979, have placed restrictions on police powers regarding arrest, investigation, and search.[102] As will be examined in Chapter Five, these laws set proper procedure and time limits to prevent illegal arrests and prolonged detentions; they also prohibit the use of torture, threat, deceit, or any other illegal means to collect evidence. The Regulations Governing the Use of Weapons and Arms by the People's Police, adopted in 1980, allow the police to fire the pistol only in self-defense or some other emergencies. Use of batons, sirens, police lights, and whistles are also governed by the Regulations.[103] At the same time, two old laws have been revived by the NPC Standing Committee to enable the public security organs to impose administrative sanctions. The first one is the Security Administrative Punishment Act (SAPA) of 1957, under which the police can issue warnings, impose a modest fine, and detain a person up to fifteen days.[104] The second one is the Decision on Reeducation Through Labor of the same year, under which the police and civil administrative organs can send a wide range of offenders to reeducation through labor camps without trial for a period of one to four years.[105]

One difficulty with China's public security cadres is that many of them are still not accustomed to do things according to law. Some even regard the law as a hindrance, tying their hands and feet in the fight against criminals.[106] Consequently, legal restraints notwithstanding, arbitrary arrest and detention as well as other abuses by the police have continued to occur. Some have been reported by foreign reporters,[107] others by Chinese press and journals.[108] More details will be examined in Chapters Five and Six of this book.

To overcome the lingering problems and to improve police image, public security personnel have been instructed to set an example for the masses in the observances of law. "Love the people month" is revived as an annual affair. The title of "Lei Feng type People's Police" is awarded periodically to cadres who selflessly perform their duties and do their best to serve the masses.[109] In a recent article, the Public Security Minister stressed the need to raise the overall level of public security cadres with special attention to youthfulness, knowledge, specialization, and revolutionary spirit. He also called for the police to be brave and incorruptible, to enforce strictly the law and to devote themselves to the promotion of the people's interest and the realization of four modernizations. To those who misuse power for personal gain in violation of law and discipline, he promised severe punishment.[110]

As mentioned before, the PRC public security system goes beyond the bureaucratic structure to include such mass organizations and social groups as resident committees and security defense committees. The existence and operation of those groups make the Chinese control networks unusually tight, pervasive, and even terrifying. According to one Chinese informant, for instance, the police are supposed to have a warrant to search one's house, but the street committee members can come in whenever they want to inspect the household registration certificate and to check for any illegal residents from the countryside, relatives of the family, or rusticated youth who have snuck back into the cities.[111]

NOTES

Chapter Four

1. Zhang Youyu and Wang Shuwei, *Faxue Jiben Zhishi Jianghua* (Lectures on Basic Knowledge of Jurisprudence) (Beijing: China Youth Press, 1979), p. 154.

2. Text of the new Organic Law of the People's Courts is in *Renmin Shouce, 1979 (People's Handbook, 1979)* (Beijing: People's Daily Press, 1980), pp. 403–406. English translation is in *FBIS, Daily Report: PRC*, July 27, 1979 (Supplement), pp. 20–27.

3. Articles 4–12 of the new Law. For a discussion of the Courts under the 1954 Organic Law, see Shao-chuan Leng, *Justice in Communist China* (Dobbs Ferry, New York: Oceana, 1967), pp. 77–101. Text of the 1954 Organic Law is in *Zhonghua Renmin Gongheguo Fagui Huibian* (Collection of Laws and Regulations of the People's Republic of China) (FGHB) (Beijing: Legal Press, 1956), Vol. 1, pp. 123–132.

4. See Article 32 of the 1954 Law.

5. Article 36 of the 1979 Organic Law states that term of office for the presidents of People's Courts at various levels shall be the same as that for People's Congresses at the corresponding levels. For the prescribed terms of the various People's Congresses, see Articles 21 and 35 of the 1978 PRC Constitution in *Documents of the First Session of the Fifth National People's Congresses of the People's Republic of China* (Peking: Foreign Languages Press, 1978), pp. 146–147, 157.

6. For instance, see Article 124 of the new Constitution. Text of the Constitution is in *Renmin Ribao* (People's Daily), Dec. 5, 1982, pp. 1–4 while its English version is in *FBIS, Daily Report: China*, Dec. 7, 1982, pp. K1–K28.

7. Article 25 of the 1978 Constitution; also Article 67 of the new Constitution.

8. Articles 32 and 33 of the 1979 Organic Law of the People's Courts. In response to a number of questions put forth by various localities and departments, the NPC Standing Committee adopted on June 10, 1981 a resolution on strengthening the interpretation of law. Among other provisions, it reiterated that all questions arising from court trials concerning the specific application of laws and decrees shall be interpreted by the Supreme People's Court. *Renmin Ribao*, June 11, 1981, p. 1; FBIS, *Daily Report: China*, June 11, 1981, p. K4.

9. "Resolution of the Fourth Session of the First National People's Congress of the People's Republic of China to the effect that death penalty cases should be decided or approved by the Supreme People's Court" (adopted July 15, 1957), *FGHB*, Vol. 6 (1958), p. 296.

10. *Renmin Ribao*, June 11, 1981, p. 1.

11. *Zhongguo Fazhi Bao* (China's Legal System Paper), Sept. 9, 1983, p. 2.

12. *Zhongguo Fazhi Bao*, May 7, 1982, p. 1; *Xinhua News Agency*, May 4, 1982.

13. Huang Laiji, "Setting up the Economic Divisions and Strengthening Economic Procuratorial and Trial Work," *Zhongguo Baike Nianjian, 1981* (Chinese Encyclopedia Yearbook, 1981) (Beijing: Chinese Encyclopedia Press, 1981), p. 190.

14. "Report on the Work of the Supreme People's Court," *Renmin Ribao*, December 16, 1981, p. 2. It should be noted that Articles 19 and 24 were revised on September 2, 1983 to formally provide for the lower courts to set up economic divisions. *Zhongguo Fazhi Bao*, September 9, 1983, p. 2.

15. "Report on the Work of the NPC," *Renmin Ribao*, June 26, 1983, p. 2.

16. *Renmin Ribao*, August 1, 1980, p. 1; *Zhongguo Fazhi Bao*, March 27, 1981, p. 1.

17. Leng, *Justice in Communist China*, pp. 80–81.

18. David Barlow and Daniel Wagner, "Public Order and Internal Security," *China: A Country Study* (Washington, DC: U.S. Government Printing Office, 1981), p. 439.

19. According to Wang Hanbin, Secretary General of the NPC Standing Committee, to delete references to "railway transport courts, water transport courts, and forestry courts" is necessary because "there is no concensus on what special courts, except for military courts, should be established or on the structural system, functions, and areas of jurisdiction of special courts." *FBIS, Daily Report: China*, September 6, 1983, p. K14.

20. *FBIS, Daily Report: China*, Sept. 22, 1981, p. K11.

21. *FBIS, Daily Report: China*, Aug. 25, 1982, p. K14; *Zhongguo Fazhi Bao*, Aug. 27, 1982, p. 1.

22. See the report of the political-legal training of several tens of thousands of former PLA cadres during Sept. 1981—Jan. 1982 for new jobs on the political and legal front. *Zhongguo Fazhi Bao*, Jan. 22, 1982, p. 1; also articles on "From Military Officers to Judges" in *Minzhu Yu Fazhi* (Democracy and Legal System), No. 7, 1981, pp. 12–14.

23. *Zhongguo Fazhi Bao*, March 5, 1982, p. 1.

24. *Zhongguo Fazhi Bao*, September 9, 1983, p. 2.

25. *Renmin Ribao*, June 26, 1983, p. 2.

26. Article 10 of the Organic Law of the People's Courts and Article 105 of the Criminal Procedure Law. Text of the latter is in *Gongan Fagui Huibian, 1950–1979* (Collection of Laws and Regulations on Public Security) (GAPGHB) (Beijing: Mass Press, 1980), pp. 35–65.

27. Chen Chunlong *et al*, *Falu Zhishi Wenda* (Questions and Answers on Law) (Beijing: Beijing Press, 1980), pp. 176–177.

28. Article 11 of the Organic Law of the People's Courts.

29. *Renmin Shouce*, 1979, p. 296.

30. Article 11 of the Organic Law. The judicial experiences summed up by adjudication committees have been used in the past to guide and improve judicial cadres' work and to provide the legislative body with relevant material for drafting laws. Leng, *Justice in Communist China*, pp. 85–87. In his "Explanation on the Seven Draft Laws" made on June 26, 1979, Peng Zhen said that the various laws were drafted and revised "after much investigation and study and the summing up of past experience." *Main Documents of the Second Session of the Fifth National People's Congress of the PRC* (Beijing: Foreign Languages Press, 1979), p. 192.

31. Article 14 of the Organic Law; Article 149 of the Criminal Procedure Law.

32. Article 24 of the Criminal Procedure Law.

33. Article 107 of the Criminal Procedure Law.

34. Article 11 of the Organic Law.

35. Xu Lisheng, "The Role of the Adjudication Committee," *Renmin Ribao*, Feb. 5, 1980, p. 2.

36. Chen Chunlong, *et al*, see above note 27, p. 171.

37. Chen Chunlong, *et al*, pp. 171–172.

38. Chen Chunlong, *et al*, pp. 170–171; Chang Cong, "A Fine Status on the People's Judicature," *Faxue Yanjiu* (Studies in Law), No. 4, 1979, p. 37. For the PRC's past experience with the assessor system, see Leng, *Justice in Communist China*, pp. 87–91 and Jerome A. Cohen, *The Criminal Process in the People's Republic of China, 1949–1963* (Cambridge, Mass.: Harvard University Press, 1968), pp. 430–435.

39. *Zhongguo Fazhi Bao*, September 9, 1983, p. 2; *FBIS, Daily Report: China*, September 6, 1983, p. K14.

40. See, for example, "People's Letters and Visits—Bridge Between the Party and Masses," *Minzhu Yu Fazhi*, No. 6, 1982, pp. 13–16.

41. See Shao-chuan Leng, "The Role of Law in the People's Republic of China as Reflecting Mao Tse-tung's Influence," *Journal of Criminal Law and Criminology*, Vol. 68, No. 3, 1977, pp. 361–363. For the role of mediation committees in the past, see Stanley Lubman, "Mao and Mediation," *California Law Review*, Vol. 55, No. 5, 1967, pp. 1339–1346.

42. *Xinhua News Agency*, March 8, 1982; Zhou Zheng, "China's System of Community Mediation," *Beijing Review*, Vol. 24, No. 23, 1981, p. 23; "Opening of the First National Conference on Mediation Work," *Zhongguo Fazhi Bao*, Aug. 21, 1981, p. 1.

43. Articles 2 & 6 of the Provisional General Rules in *Renmin Shouce*, 1979, p. 438.

44. Article 6 of the Provisional General Rules.

45. *Xinhua News Agency*, March 8, 1982.

46. Editorial: "Fully Develop the Work of People's Mediation Committees," *Zhongguo Fazhi Bao*, Aug. 28, 1981, p. 1; "Burger Praised Our People's Mediation Committees," *Zhongguo Fazhi Bao*, Sept. 18, 1981, p. 1; "One of China's Creations: People's Mediation Committees," *Zhongguo Fazhi Bao*, Feb. 5, 1982, p. 2; Wang Jian, "Actively Participate in the Comprehensive Management of Social Order; Lift People's Mediation Work to a New Level," *Minzhu Yu Fazhi*, No. 12, 1981, pp. 2–3.

47. Article 2 of the Organic Law of the People's Procuratorates. English translation of the law is in *FBIS, Daily Report: PRC*, July 27, 1979 (Supplement), pp. 27–33. Text of the 1954 Organic Law is in *FGHB*, Vol. 1, pp. 133–38.

48. For a discussion of the Soviet Procuracy, see Harold J. Berman, *Justice in the U.S.S.R.* (New York: Vintage Books, 1963), pp. 238–47. In an interview with one of the authors in Beijing in November, 1979, Mr. Sun, deputy chief of the Legal Research Bureau of the Supreme People's Procuratorate, said that rather than follow the Soviet model, China had to make some changes regarding the procuracy in order to meet its specific conditions and needs.

49. For past attacks against the tendency to free the procuracy from local party cadres' interference, see Leng, *Justice in Communist China*, pp. 114–19.

50. On September 2, 1983 the NPC Standing Committee revised Articles 22 and 23 of the Law of Procuratorates by deleting references to the "appointment and removal of deputy chief procurators and other procurators." *Zhongguo Fazhi Bao*, September 9, 1983, p. 2.

51. See Articles 3, 4, 8, and 19 of the 1954 Organic Law. For a discussion of the procuratorial power, see Jin Mosheng, "People's Procuratorial Work," *Renmin Ribao*, July 13, 1981, p. 5; The Legal System Propaganda Group of the Supreme People's Procuratorate, "Earnestly Implement the Organic Law of the People's Procuratorates," *Faxue Yanjiu*, No. 3, 1979, pp. 13–16.

52. *Main Documents of the Second Session of the Fifth NPC*, p. 210.

53. See also Zeng Longyue, "Legal Role and Functions of Procuratorial Organs in Criminal Proceedings," *Faxue Yanjiu*, No. 3, 1980, pp. 26–29.

54. For comparison, Article 6 of the 1954 Law reads, "The Local people's procuratorates are independent in the exercise of their authority and are not subject to interference by local state organs." The CCP Central Committee's Third Plenum of 1978 is discussed in the section on "The Evolving Constitutional Order" in the preceding chapter.

55. This is different from the provision of Article 2 of the 1954 Law, which gave the chief procurator a decisive voice in case of disagreements.

56. "China's Procuratorates—An Interview with Chief Procurator Huang Huoqing," *Beijing Review*, Vol. 22, No. 52, Dec. 28, 1979, pp. 16–19.

57. "Procuratorates at All Levels in the Country have Achieved Notable Results," *Zhongguo Fazhi Bao*, Oct. 1, 1982, p. 1.

58. "National Conference of Chief Procurators," *Zhongguo Fazhi Bao,* Dec. 4, 1981, p. 1.

59. "Move Further to Expand Economic Procuratorial Work and Insure the Smooth Process of Economic Adjustment," *Zhongguo Fazhi Bao,* Dec. 4, 1981, p. 3; Liu Zhongya, "The Role of the Economic Judicature," *Faxue Yanjiu,* No. 2, 1981, p. 35.

60. "Work Report of the Supreme People's Procuratorate, Dec. 7, 1981," *Renmin Ribao,* Dec. 16, 1981, p. 2.

61. "Work Report of the Supreme People's Procuratorate," *Renmin Ribao,* June 26, 1983, p. 3.

62. See e.g., "Break Up the 'Net of Relationship' And Arrest 'Underground Tiger'," *Minzhu Yu Fazhi,* No. 8, 1982, p. 22; "A Battle Between Law and Power," *Minzhu Yu Fazhi,* No. 12, 1981, pp. 32–33; "An Upright and Incorrupt Procurator Chen," *Zhongguo Fazhi Bao,* Nov. 5, 1982, p. 4; Commentator, "Let Us Hope There Will Be More People Like Wang Chengbao," *Renmin Ribao,* March 14, 1982, p. 2.

63. "Huang Huoqing's Work Report on Sept. 2, 1980," *FBIS, Daily Report: PRC,* Sept. 23, 1980 (Supplement), p. 48; "Huang's Report on Dec. 7, 1981," *Renmin Ribao,* Dec. 16, 1981, p. 2.

64. *Cheng Ming* (Contending), No. 35, September 1980, p. 87; *Guangming Ribao* (Enlightenment Daily), Aug. 11, 1981, p. 32.

65. *Beijing Review,* Vol. 22, No. 9, March 2, 1979, p. 3; "Strengthening the Building of the Legal System and Work for the Four Modernizations," *Renmin Ribao,* July 29, 1979, p. 1.

66. See Jin Mosheng, "On the Exercising Procuratorial Authority Independently," *Faxue Yanjiu,* No. 3, 1981, pp. 33–35; Wang Guiwu, "Independent Exercise of Procuratorial Authority is the Fundamental Principle of Legal Supervision," *Minzhu Yu Fazhi,* No. 2, 1979, pp. 9–10.

67. Gao Xun, "Insist on the Independent Exercise of Procuratorial Authority According to the Law Under the Party's Leadership," *Zhongguo Fazhi Bao,* Nov. 5, 1982, p. 3.

68. Leng, *Justice in Communist China,* p. 80.

69. Wang Gangxiang, "Establishment of the Central Ministry of Justice," *Zhongguo Baike Nianjian, 1980* (Chinese Encyclopedia Yearbook) (Beijing: Chinese Encyclopedia Press, 1980), p. 276.

70. *Zhongguo Baike Nianjian,* p. 276; "New Minister of Justice Interviewed, "Beijing Review Vol. 22, October 19, 1979, pp. 3–4; "Justice Minister Liu Fuzhi Answered Questions of A Xinhua Reporter," *Zhongguo Fazhi Bao,* July 30, 1982, p. 1; Wang Yuetang, "Several Problems in the Present Judicial Administrative Work," *Minzhu Yu Fazhi,* No. 2, 1981, pp. 11–12.

71. *Zhongguo Fazhi Bao,* July 30, 1982, p. 1; *Xinhua News Agency,* March 8, 1982; *FBIS, Daily Report: China,* September 21, 1983, p. K15.

72. "Justice Minister Interviewed on New Laws," *FBIS, Daily Report: China,* Aug. 25, 1982, p. K14.

73. He Bian, "China's Lawyer," *Beijing Review,* Vol. 25, June 7, No. 23, 1982, pp. 14–15; Leng, *Justice in Communist China,* pp. 135–136; Sun Yinji & Feng Caijin, *Lushi Jiben Zhishi* (Basic Knowledge about Lawyers) (Beijing: Mass Press, 1980), pp. 13–14.

74. Leng, *Justice in Communist China,* p. 137.

75. In a talk given at the University of Virginia in the fall of 1982, Ma Rongjie, editor of *Faxue Yanjiu,* said that after the Anti-Rightist Campaign, only 4 lawyers were allowed to function in China, he being one of the four.

76. Article 2 of the Provisional Act. Text of the Act originally appeared in *Zhonghua Renmin Gongheguo Guowuyuan Gongbao* (Gazette of the State Council of the PRC), No. 10, Oct. 8, 1980, pp. 283–286. English translations are available in Tao-tai Hsia

and Charlotte Hambley, "Provisional Regulations on Lawyers," *China Law Reporter*, Vol. 1, No. 4, Fall 1981, pp. 217–221; "Text of Provisional Regulations on Lawyers," *FBIS, Daily Report: PRC*, Aug. 28, 1980, pp. L6–L9. A revised translation of the Act appears in Document 14 of this book.

77. See the joint statement made on April 27, 1981 by the Supreme People's Court, Supreme People's Procuratorate, Ministry of Public Security and Ministry of Justice, reported in *Zhongguo Fazhi Bao*, May 15, 1981, p. 1.

78. For a discussion of defense counsel's preparatory work, see Sun Yinji & Feng Caijin, see above note 73, pp. 53–64.

79. Frank Ching, "Foreign Law Firms Barred from Practicing in China," *Asian Wall Street Journal*, Jan. 8, 1982, p. 1.

80. In answering questions on how to acquire qualifications for lawyers, a legal journal encourages those interested to take the road of independent study. It cites an example that the East China Political-Legal Institute's correspondent department has adopted an independent study and examination system to prepare people to qualify for lawyers. *Minzhu Yu Fazhi*, No. 12, 1981, p. 43.

81. First Vice-Minister of Justice Li Yunchang, "Several Points of Explanations Concerning the Provisional Act on Lawyers of the PRC," *Renmin Ribao*, Aug. 29, 1980, p. 4. The 1957 Rules made no reference to any examination and had even more flexible standards for lawyers than the current Act. See Leng, *Justice in Communist China*, pp. 137–139.

82. As stated by Vice-Justice Minister Li Yunchang in *Renmin Ribao*, Aug. 29, 1980, p. 4.

83. Articles 13–18 of the Provisional Act.

84. He Bian, "China's Lawyers," *Beijing Review*, p. 16.

85. Article 19 of the Provisional Act.

86. Text of the 1957 Rules is in *FGHB*, Vol. 4, pp. 235–238.

87. He Bian, "China's Lawyers," *Beijing Review*, p. 17; Zhang Zhiye, "How do China's Lawyers Work?" *Beijing Review*, Vol. 26, No. 23, June 6, 1983, p. 27.

88. "More Legal Advisory Offices in Beijing," *Beijing Review*, Vol. 24, Feb. 16, 1981, p. 4; "Lawyer Meeting Ends in Beijing 21 May," *FBIS, Daily Report: China*, May 22, 1981, pp. R3–R4.

89. "Lawyers in Beijing," *Beijing Review*, Vol. 25, No. 23, June 7, 1982, p. 15.

90. *FBIS, Daily Report: China*, Sept. 22, 1981, p. K11.

91. *Zhongguo Fazhi Bao*, Aug. 27, 1982, p. 1.

92. James C. Tuttle, "Development in China's Legal System: Introduction and Delegation Overview," *China Law Reporter*, Vol. II, No. 1, Spring, 1982, p. 46.

93. "Lawyer Work in Our Country Has Achieved Notable Results," *Zhongguo Fazhi Bao*, Oct. 1, 1982, p. 2; Zhang Zhiye, "How Do China's Lawyers Work?" p. 20.

94. Zhang Zhiye, "How Do China's Lawyers Work," p. 20.

95. See Leng, *Justice in Communist China*, p. 121; Barlow & Wagner, "Public Order and Internal Security," see above note 18, p. 443; Chu Pufu, *Zhonggong Renmin Jingcha Toshi* (Perspective on the People's Police in Communist China) (Hong Kong: Freedom Press, 1955), pp. 23–40. Victor Li, "The Public Security Bureau and Political-Legal Work," in John W. Lewis, ed., *The City in Communist China* (Stanford: Stanford University Press, 1971); Liu Nianci, *Renmin Jingcha* (People's Police) (Hong Kong: Commercial Press, 1950).

96. Texts of the laws are in *GAFGHB* (see above note 26), pp. 436–437 and 441–444 respectively.

97. For instance, the PRC republished in January 1980 the following regulations: Organic Regulations on Street Offices in Cities (Dec. 21, 1950); Organic Regulations on Urban Resident Committees (Dec. 31, 1954); Provisional Regulations Governing

the Organization of Security Defense (Protection) Committees (Aug. 10, 1952); and Provisional General Rules Governing the Organization of People's Mediation Committees (March 22, 1954). See *Renmin Shouce, 1979*, pp. 436–438 and FBIS, *Daily Report: PRC*, Jan. 24, 1980, pp. L2–L9.

98. Luo Fu, "City Dwellers and the Neighborhood Committee," *Beijing Review*, Vol. 23, No. 44, Nov. 3, 1980, p. 20.

99. For a discussion of powers and functions of the police before the Cultural Revolution, see Leng, *Justice in Communist China*, pp. 122–124. The table of contents in *GAFGHB*, (see above note 26) illustrate the various tasks and functions of the public security apparatus. See also Tian Yun, "The Police and the People," *Beijing Review*, Vol. 26, No. 21, May 23, 1983, pp. 22–27.

100. "Ministry of State Security Established," *Beijing Review*, Vol. 26, No. 27, July 4, 1983, p. 6.

101 Christopher S. Wren, "Peking to Create New Security Unit," *New York Times*, June 7, 1983, p. A11.

102. Texts of the two laws are in GAFGHB, pp. 35–65 and 87–90, respectively.

103. Text of the Regulations is in *Renmin Ribao*, July 15, 1980, p. 1.

104. Text of the SAPA is in *GAFGHB*, pp. 113–122, republished in *Renmin Ribao*, Feb. 23, 1980, p. 4.

105. Text of the Decision in *GAFGHB*, pp. 391–392, republished in *Renmin Ribao*, Feb. 24, 1980, p. 4. There will be more discussion on this Decision in Chapter Six.

106. Zhao Cangbi, "Strengthen the Concept of the Legal System and Act Strictly According to the Law," *Hongqi* (Red Flag), No. 8, 1979, p. 43; also interviews with Chinese legal circles during one of the authors 1979 and 1981 visits.

107. Fox Butterfield, *China: Alive in the Bitter Sea* (New York: Times Books, 1982), pp. 9–10, 414–415; "Correspondence," *SPEAHRhead*, No. 12/13, 1982, p. 26.

108. *Xinhua News Agency*, Oct. 1, 1980; *Minzhu Yu Fazhi*, No. 7, 1980, p. 34 and No. 3, 1981, p. 10.

109. See, for instance, "Public Security Ministry Awards Shao Yuqiao the Title of 'Lei Feng Type People's Police," *Zhongguo Fazhi Bao*, March 3, 1982, p. 1.

110. Zhao Cangbi, "For the Realization of the Party's General Task, Build a More Stable Social Order," *Zhongguo Fazhi Bao*, Nov. 19, 1982, p. 1.

111 Butterfield, *China: Alive in the Bitter Sea*, p. 325.

Criminal Process

China's trial of the Gang of Four and six other members of the "Lin-Jiang cliques" in November 1980 to January 1981 was a subject of world-wide attention. Chinese spokesmen have pictured the trial as a landmark: the end of a lawless era, a successful test of the new legal system, and a demonstration that all are equal before the law.[1] Contrary to Chinese leaders' expectations, however, many foreign observers considered the trial as essentially a political rather than legal exercise.[2] On the other hand, the holding of this trial appeared to reflect, among other things, Beijing's desire to publicize its commitment to legality, and the controlled and selected reporting of the court sessions gave the outside world glimpses of the judicial process under China's new and emerging legal order.

This chapter attempts to provide a preliminary and general survey of the procedure through which criminal justice is administered, in law and in practice, in post-Mao China. Special attention will be given to the applicability of certain universal principles of the rule of law in relation to criminal cases, including public trials, presumption of innocence, equality before the law, right to defense and appeal, judicial independence, etc.

ENACTMENT OF CRIMINAL LEGISLATION

Until mid-1979 the People's Republic of China did not have a code of substantive or procedural criminal law, although there were a few statutes governing criminal justice such as the Act for the Punishment of Corruption of 1952, the Act on Arrest and Detention of 1954, and the Security Administration Punishment Act (SAPA) of 1957.[3] In July 1979, the National People's Congress enacted for the first time in the PRC's history the Criminal Law and the Criminal Procedure Law.[4] By comparison, the PRC's new Criminal Law of 192 articles and Criminal Procedure Law of 164 articles are rather short, as either the Soviet codes or Nationalist Chinese codes are several times longer.[5] Still, the adoption of these two laws was a landmark development in the Chinese system of justice, for these measures define punishable acts and penalties and regularize the sanctioning process in the PRC.

According to Peng Zhen, before their enactment, both laws went through many drafts, dating back as early as the 1950s. The Criminal Law finally adopted is, in fact, a revised version of the thirty-third draft.[6] China's Criminal Law and Criminal Procedure Law, said former Public Security Minister Zhao Cangbi, were not copied from any foreign country but were formulated with Marxism-Leninism-Mao Zedong thought as the guide on the basis of the Constitution and in the light of China's concrete experience in exercising the People's Democratic Dictatorship.[7] There is, however, little doubt that Soviet codes served as models for the Chinese draftsmen. On the basis of the texts alone, as pointed out by specialists on Soviet law, one can see a strong Soviet influence on the language and style as well as on the policy of the Chinese laws.[8] There are also striking differences between the Chinese and Soviet laws. For one thing, the Chinese laws are "much more simple, much more general, much more pro-grammatic, and much more moralistic in their syntax and style." For another, the Chinese use of the principle of analogy and of the terms "counterrevolution" and "counterrevolutionary" distinguish the cur-rent Chinese Criminal Law from the 1960 Russian Criminal Code although linking it with the Russian Criminal Code of 1926.[9]

It is precisely over such problems as the retention of analogy and the vague definition of counterrevolution that the Chinese Criminal legislation is vulnerable to criticism.[10] Despite that, the presence of the Criminal Law and the Criminal Procedure Law clearly constitutes a welcome and significant advancement in post-Mao China's move toward legality.[11] Together they prescribe appropriate legal standards to guide judicial work and the framework for "due process" to protect the individual. Their enforcement, on the other hand, is certainly no easy task. One authority on Chinese law states that "the relatively small number of well-trained and disciplined police, prosecutors, judges, and Party officials concerned with law, the limited availability of legal education, the inadequacy of communications in a vast, largely rural nation, and the lack of legal awareness among the masses would all impose objective restraints on implementation of the codes." [12]

The two laws officially came into force in January 1980. Never-theless, the NPC Standing Committee decided in February 1980 that: "If there are too many cases, and personnel handling cases is in-sufficient and thus unable to handle cases according to the time limits prescribed by the Criminal Procedure Law . . . within the year 1980, the standing committee of (provincial-level) people's congresses may approve extensions of the times for handling cases." [13] In September 1981, the NPC Standing Committee passed another decision concerning extension of the time limit. According to the decision, criminal cases received on or after January 1, 1981 should, in general, be handled in accordance with the time limits in the Criminal Procedure Law. However, if, in a small number of criminal cases "where the circumstances of the case are complex or which take place in outlying districts to which transportation is inconvenient", the time limits set in Articles 92, 97, 125 and 142 of the Criminal Procedure Law cannot be observed, the standing committees of the provincial-level people's congress are authorized, from 1981 to 1983, to decide or approve appropriate extensions of the time periods for handling cases.[14]

In the following pages we shall examine the process through which criminal justice is administered in China and the major issues pertinent to the judicial procedure.

PRETRIAL PROCEEDINGS

According to the Criminal Procedure Law, "the public security organ is in charge of investigation, detention and preliminary review of criminal cases. The people's procuratorate approves arrest, conducts procuratorial proceedings (including investigation) and institutes public prosecution. The people's court is responsible for adjudicating cases. No other organ, institution or individual has the right to exercise such powers" (Article 3).[15] "In handling litigation, the people's court, the people's procuratorate and the public security organ must rely on the masses, base themselves on facts and take the law as the yardstick" (Article 4) and should "perform their respective functions while coordinating with and checking each other to guarantee that the law is accurately and effectively enforced" (Article 5).

The pretrial proceedings of the Chinese criminal process are composed of two principal parts:

(1) arrest and detention and

(2) investigation.

To prevent illegal arrests and prolonged detentions, proper procedure and strict time limits are set by the Criminal Procedure Law as well as by the revised Arrest and Detention Act promulgated in February 1979 to replace the old enactment in 1954.[16] In carrying out an apprehension or in making an arrest, the police must produce a warrant. The family of the detainee or the arrested should be notified of the reasons for the action and the place of confinement within twenty-four hours, "unless in the situation where investigation may be hampered or notification is impossible" (Article 5). Interrogation must start within twenty-four hours after any apprehension or arrest, and the detainee or the arrested must be released immediately if no legitimate grounds are found. When the public security organ deems it necessary to declare a detainee arrested, the matter should be submitted to the procuratorate for approval within three days or, in special circumstances, seven days. The procuracy must either sanction the arrest or order the release of the detainee within three days.[17] However, Article 47 of the Criminal Procedure Law provides the procuracy with the right to have supplementary investigation if needed for decisions. It is not clear whether the suspect should be released by the police under such circumstances.

During the stage of investigation, the tasks include interrogation of the accused and witnesses, search and seizure, examination of evidence, and preparation of the indictment. Mindful of past abuses, the Criminal Procedure Law stipulates that in collecting various kinds of evidence throughout the entire judicial process, the police, judges, procurators are strictly forbidden to extort confessions by torture and use of threat, enticement, deceit or any other illegal means (Article 32). At the time of search, except in emergency situations, investigators shall show the searched a search warrant (Article 81). The Criminal Procedure Law further provides that detention of an accused pending investigation should not exceed two months. If necessary, a one month extension may be granted by the procuratorate at the next higher level (Article 92).[18] A procuratorate is required to decide whether or not to prosecute a case sent to it by police within one month to one and a half months (Article 97).

In practice, the shortage of trained personnel and persistence of negative and erroneous views about the law have hampered the full implementation of the provisions of the Criminal Procedure Law. As noted earlier, the NPC Standing Committee has twice extended the time limits beyond those provided in the Criminal Procedure Law. Some police and judicial cadres regard the law as a hindrance tying their hands and feet in the fight against crimes.[19] Others cling to the old prejudice that the suspect in a criminal case is guilty and should be dealt with as such.[20] Consequently, it is not too surprising to find the frequent occurrence of illegal arrests and detentions and unlawful search and seizure in Chinese society.[21] What has happened to some political dissidents is only a part of this phenomenon.[22]

Educational and other efforts have been made by the PRC to combat the negative attitude toward the law. A 1979 textbook on the Criminal Procedure Law, for example, warned against the unlawful practice of prolonged detentions and the use of "continuous interrogation" and other forms of "disguised torture" to extract a confession from the accused.[23] A 1980 article in the *Enlightenment Daily* also took pains to explain the reasons for banning torture in extracting confessions.[24] Still, violations have been taking place. In one case, an African student in Beijing was allegedly arrested by the police, held in prison six days and tortured because of his supposed relations with several Chinese women.[25] In another case, a policeman in Shanghai was reported to have illegally detained and cruelly beat a stranger over a minor dispute.[26] Still another case involved a widow who complained about her unlawful detention of fifty-two days by the public security organ for her property dispute with her parents-in-law.[27] A most celebrated case was the one concerning Liu Qing, a political activist, whose arrest and imprisonment along with other dissidents will be examined later in Chapter Six. According to Liu's personal account, he was detained by the police for several months without a formal trial; he was brusquely interrogated and received and witnessed physical abuse while in detention. During an inter-rogation session, Liu protested his detention as illegal, and the reply from the police was, "This is the place of dictatorship." [28]

Chinese spokesmen have shown their full awareness of these abuses by candidly admitting that even after the promulgation of the Criminal Procedure Law, many basic-level cadres have continued to illegally detain people, arbitrarily interrogate them, extort confes-sions by torture, and unlawfully search people's homes. Attributing the leftist influence as a major cause, they call for the combined use of sanctions and legal education to prevent future recurrences.[29] According to a 1980 report of the Supreme People's Procuratorate, the organs of the procuracy at various levels prosecuted in 1979 and 1980 more than 10,000 cases in infringement upon citizens' personal and democratic rights, such as illegal detention, illegal search, and extorting confessions by torture.[30] Citing an incident where public security personnel in Tianchung County, Anhui Province illegally detained an eight-year-old child and his mother, a *People's Daily* commentator wrote a special article on April 18, 1983 urging the education of police and judicial officials in observing the law and severe punishment for those lawbreakers.[31]

While some of these abuses of infringement upon citizens' personal rights, such as illegal arrest or detention, may be due to what the PRC described as "leftist influence", in certain political sensitive cases, a violation of a citizen's personal right appears to be the deliberate policy of the PRC government.

In several recent cases, the PRC authorities appeared to apply the escape clause of Article 5 of the 1979 Arrest and Detention Act to hold a person incommunicado indefinitely, from several days to more than a year, apparently on the ground that any information on his detention, if released even to his family member, would "hamper" the investigation. The case of Hansen Huang is a recent example. Mr. Huang is a Hong Kong Chinese and graduated from Harvard Law School in 1976. He at first worked for an American law firm and later went to China to teach law at the Beijing Institute of Foreign Trade and Beijing University. Later, he became a legal consultant to China International Trust & Investment Co. (CITIC), set up by China to lure foreign capital into China. In January 1982, he called his mother in Hong Kong to tell her that he had a change of hotel in Beijing. His mother, however, did not hear from him until almost two years later.[32] On February 1, 1984, a spokesman of the PRC Ministry of Justice said, "He (Huang) was arrested, tried and convicted of espionage and sentenced to 15 years' imprisonment." [33] The PRC, however, has not yet released the text of the judgement against him, nor provided any information on his arrest and trial situation.[34]

As part of Beijing's effort to publicize its legal system, prominent Chinese jurists in a radio broadcast answered questions concerning the 1980–81 trial of the Gang of Four and six others. One of the procedural issues raised was why Jiang Qing and other defendants were just brought to trial after having been under detention for several years. In his explanations, Zhang Youyu, Vice-President of the Chinese Academy of Social Sciences, said that more time was needed to conduct investigation for this important case and to reconstruct China's badly damaged judicial system and put it back into operation:

> The reason for the delay of the trial until now is that the case was of such extraordinary and grave nature and required us to do tremendous work in thoroughly and meticulously checking and verifying the evidence. Moreover, during the ten turbulent years, legal organs at all levels in our country had been destroyed and all the laws were abrogated. It was in 1978—two years after the downfall of the Gang of Four—that the new Constitution was formulated. Also, it took quite some time to set up the organization, train cadres and make other legal preparations.[35]

TRIAL PROCEEDINGS

According to Article 100 of the Criminal Procedure Law, when the procuratorate finds conclusive and sufficient evidence for prosecution of the accused, it will initiate a public prosecution by the filing of an indictment with a court. The indictment shall include basic information about the accused, facts and evidence of the offense, and article or articles of the law violated.[36]

The procedure of adjudication, as stipulated by the Criminal Procedure Law, is divided into four stages:

(1) investigation,

(2) debate,

(3) appraisal by the collegiate bench, and

(4) judgment (Part III, Chapter II).

Except for minor cases, trials are conducted in cases of original jurisdiction by a collegiate bench of a judge and two assessors. In cases of appeal or protest, a collegiate bench of three to five judges is required (Article 105).

All cases are heard in public except those involving minors, state secrets, or personal intimacies (Article 111).[37] However, at panel discussions held by NPC Deputies in September 1980, a delegate from Tianjin pointed out that the overwhelming majority of the courts in China lacked the necessary facilities and funds for conducting public trials.[38] Western observers criticized the trial of the Gang of Four as not an open (public) one because of the exclusion of foreigners and severe restrictions on Chinese attendance.[39] Jurist Zhang Youyu, on the other hand, argued that the limitation of the trial attendance to representatives of selected Chinese groups was fully in accord with the general practice of all states to restrict the number of people attending a court session. As for the exclusion of foreigners, he contended, it was necessitated by the grave nature of the case and the involvement of many important state secrets.[40] In practice, public trials in China are generally open only to people with admission tickets which are obtained from oganizations selected by the authorities. For instance, the trial of Wei Jingsheng, a leading political dissident, on October 16, 1979 was announced to be open to the public, but Wei's relatives and friends as well as foreign journalists were all denied entrance by officials who said all tickets had been given out. About 400 spectators were taken in, but a woman who attended said afterward that she had received her ticket the day before the trial at her workplace and had been instructed to attend.[41]

The Criminal Procedure Law also provides that at the beginning of the court session the presiding judge shall inform the parties of their right to require the withdrawal of judges and other participants who may be parties to the case or close relatives of the parties or who may have an interest in the case or whose close relatives may have an interest in the case.[42] Critics of the trial of the Gang of Four cite its complete disregard for this provision, as both Jiang Hua, President of the Special Court, and Huang Huoqing, Chief of the Special Procuratorate, were among the alleged victims listed in the indictment.[43] Moreover, among the thirty-five judges, at least twenty had allegedly been persecuted during the Cultural Revolution, and most of the others were directly related to people who had suffered similarly.[44] Jiang Hua, however, defended the Special Court's decision to deny the defendants the right to request the withdrawal of the adjudication personnel on the grounds that since the Gang of Four had persecuted so many people in the past, especially judicial and procuratorial cadres, it was necessary to impose a restriction on their right to demand withdrawal otherwise there would have been no one left in China to prosecute and try them.[45]

Right of Defense

Article 125 of the Constitution states that "the accused has the right of defense." To elaborate on this point, the Criminal Procedure Law provides that besides exercising the right to defend himself, an accused may have for his defense a lawyer, a relative, a guardian, a citizen recommended by a people's organization or designated by the court for him (Articles 26 and 27). The responsibility of a defender is, on the basis of the facts and the law, to present "materials and opinions to prove that the defendant is innocent or committed a less severe offense or should receive a mitigated sentence or be exempted from criminal responsibility in order to safeguard the legitimate rights and interests of the defendant" (Article 28).

While the law permits laymen to act as counsel, lawyers are considered better equipped with legal knowledge, experience, and rights than others to act as defenders.[46] It should be noted here that the right to counsel before trial is not provided in the Chinese legislation. As stipulated by Article 110 of the Criminal Procedure Law, defense counsel apparently becomes involved in a case only after the court has decided to "open the court session and adjudicate the case." In contrast, the Soviet defense counsel may become involved at some point in the preliminary investigation.[47]

To prepare for the defense, the Chinese lawyer is empowered by law to study the materials relevant to the case, acquaint himself with the circumstances of the case, and interview and correspond with the defendant in custody.[48] He may take notes on the case file but may not have access to the records of the adjudicating committee or the collegiate bench or materials "on clues" to other cases.[49] At the trial, the defense lawyer has the right to question witnesses, experts, and the defendant, summon and question new witnesses, introduce new evidence, and participate in courtroom debates. If necessary, he can also, with the consent of the defendant, lodge an appeal from the judgment and present his version of the case to the court of the second instance.[50]

In performing his functions, the Chinese lawyer is expected to "act on the basis of facts, take the law as the criterion, and be loyal to the interest of the socialist cause and the people." At the same time, he is protected by the law from any unit or individual.[51] According to Chinese writers, the defense counsel is not an agent of the defendant in a criminal proceeding. He is an independent party in the litigation and is not bound by the will of the accused. He must carry out his activities within the legal framework and under no circumstances should he fabricate evidence, distort facts, or use deceptions to help his clients. If the evidence presented by the prosecution is incorrect in whole or in part, the lawyer should try to prove the innocence of the defendant or mitigate his guilt. If, on the other hand, the crime has been established beyond any doubt, then the counsel should defend the accused from the standpoint of certain extenuating circumstances, such as motives and means of the crime, the age of the defendant, the degree of his repentence, or the objective reasons for the crime. The lawyer should not say anything detrimental to the defendant at the trial but must persuade the defendant to reveal to the court concealed facts to seek its leniency. All told, the purpose of the defense counsel is considered well-served if he can help the court to render a just verdict and protect the legitimate rights and interests of the defendant.[52]

From time to time there have been reports of some Chinese lawyers' success in defending their clients. In one case, for instance, a lawyer was able to secure an acquittal from the Hubei Provincial Higher People's Court in appeal for his client, who was sentenced to six years' imprisonment by the court of first instance for the alleged offense of harboring a murderer.[53] In another case where the defendant was charged with the offenses of arson and theft, his lawyer succeeded in persuading the court to exempt him from punishment for the alleged theft.[54] The third case involved a "model" lawyer, who turned down gift after gift from the relatives of those individuals he had successfully defended at trial.[55] Notwithstanding such nice stories, a number of problems do exist for the defense counsel in the PRC.

One major problem facing the Chinese lawyer in defending a criminal suspect is the traditional prejudice against legal defense. During the years when the PRC was experimenting with the lawyer system, many people regarded the presence of a lawyer at a criminal trial as troublemaking and even traitorous.[56] This hostile attitude appears to be persisting in China today. For instance, one reader complained to a legal journal that "the negative views on lawyers that some judicial cadres have continued to harbor are the main reason for the difficulty of finding defense attorneys." [57] A defense lawyer also wrote to the same journal about the improper treatment by a court, which first "summoned" him for appearance at the hearing and then questioned him about his political background and personal history.[58] In an article entitled "Correctly Understand and Support the Defense Lawyer System," a Beijing radio commentator stated: "In some places some comrades still do not quite understand the meaning and role of lawyers. Therefore, they take a rather strong dislike to defense lawyers, and, in some places, even openly prevent lawyers from performing their duties. All this is very wrong." [59] In a forum on "restoring and strengthening the lawyer system" spon- sored by the journal *Democracy and the Legal System* and the Shanghai Law Society, several speakers emphasized the importance of removing mistaken ideas and lingering fears about defense counsel.[60] An article writer went to considerable lengths to show that it would be erroneous to "view a lawyer being on the side of the enemy" or to "assume defendants being necessarily the same as criminals." [61] In a more recent forum on the implementation of the Provisional Act on Law- yers, a Shanghai attorney cited certain prevalent misconceptions in China about defense lawyers in criminal proceedings. Some think that their presence at trials is just to put on a show and go through the motions, while others consider lawyers as opposite to judges and procurators and suggest "Let the lawyer talk but the court will decide the case just the same regardless of his argument." [62]

Another touchy issue is whether PRC lawyers can function in- dependently and how far they may go to defend their clients. One Chinese lawyer is quoted by *Beijing Review* as saying, "There is no such thing as absolute independence. We are government function- aries and as such, must handle affairs strictly in accordance with state laws . . . . I think we practice law more independently than those hired by big firms or wealthy people." [63] China's First Vice- Minister of Justice also spoke of the difference between Chinese and Western lawyers. According to him, lawyers in capitalist countries act only in terms of their clients' interest while lawyers in China must proceed from a "proletarian stand" in their work.[64] Commen- taries from other Chinese legal sources further suggest that in doing their job as defense counsel, "proletarian lawyers" should not act like "bouregois lawyers" who are willing to manipulate facts and bend the law to win a case and help an accused escape criminal responsibility.[65]

Given the various constraints, it is little surprising that defense lawyers in China generally play a passive role in court proceedings. They tend to confine their defense to pleading for leniency and are reluctant to challenge the prosecution or to exercise such rights as cross-examining government witnesses and calling witnesses of their own as provided by the Criminal Procedure Law (Articles 115 and 117). At a robbery trial in Beijing open to foreign observers, the defense lawyer was reported to have spoken only once during the three-hour session, when he asked for a lighter penalty because of the defendant's confession and past contribution. No attempt, however, was made either to examine the two witnesses or to ask questions of the police and the prosecutor.[66] This pattern has been repeated in other reported trials, and in the two trials witnessed by one of the authors, including the one attended with fellow members of the American Bar Association delegation in the Shanghai Intermediate Court on June 9, 1981.

In the 1980–81 trial of the Gang of Four and other radical leaders, five defendants did appoint or accept the Court's appointment of two defense lawyers each, while Jiang Qing and four others did not accept or request the appointment of defense counsel.[67] Officials listed the following functions for defense lawyers in this case:

(1) to protect the legitimate rights and interests of the defendants,

(2) to contribute to the correct handling of the trial in the Special Court,

(3) to publicize socialist democracy and socialist legality, and

(4) to help persuade the defendants to acknowledge guilt, obey the law, and accept reform.[68]

Judging from the limited official news release, however, the lawyers appeared to be not too active during trial proceedings and made statements for their clients only at the time when the court was concluding the debates on each defendant. There were no reports of objection to the prosecution's questions, cross-examination of witnesses, or evidence presented by the defense.[69]

In this trial, a uniform line of defense was essentially used by the attorneys for Chen Boda, Li Zuopeng, Jiang Tengjiao, Wu Faxian, and Yao Wenyuan. The lawyers basically agreed with the government that the defendants had committed serious crimes but argued that they were not "principal culprits" and should be given lenient punishment because of their guilty pleas and repentent attitudes.[70] Minor exceptions were taken to some specific charges made by the prosecution against the accused. Li Zuopeng's lawyers, for instance, pointed out that as shown in the court investigation, he did not participate in drawing up the project for the armed coup, nor was any evidence showing that he had taken a direct part in the counterrevolutionary activities of engineering the coup.[71] Lawyers for Chen Boda said that the defendant should bear "an unshirkable responsibility" for making a speech to "trump up" a case against the party organization of eastern Hebei Province. Nevertheless, they argued that there was no evidence to show that his speech alone caused the death of thousands of people and the persecution of tens of thousands.[72] Yao Wenyuan's lawyers also said that it "could not be established" that Yao was involved in a plot by two other members of the Gang of Four, Zhang Chunqiao and Wang Hongwen, to stage an armed rebellion in Shanghai in October 1976, as charged in item forty-six of the indictment.[73]

Presumption of Innocence

The real importance of the presumption of innocence, as observed by a group of international jurists, lies not in the abstract principle but in the extent to which in actual practice an accused person is in a position to "assert the principle against an over-eager prosecutor or police official who may find it easier to build up a case of intimidation of the accused, based on assumption of guilt, than by laborious collection of independent evidence."[74] In the past, the assumption of guilt and emphasis on confessions have been the prevailing mode of the PRC's criminal justice.[75] One noticeable change found in the current Criminal Procedure Law is the premium now placed on facts and hard evidence. Article 31 of the Law stipulates that evidence can be used as the basis of judgment only after it has been verified. In collecting various kinds of evidence to prove the innocence or guilt of the accused, use of illegal means including extortion of confessions by torture is strictly forbidden (Article 32).[76] The Law also provides that in all cases, "stress shall be laid on the weight of evidence and on investigation and research, and one should not readily believe confessions. When there is only a confession by the defendant and no other evidence available, the defendant should not be considered guilty or sentenced; when there is no confession by the defendant but there is abundant, reliable evidence against him, the defendant may be considered guilty and so sentenced" (Article 35).

However, there still appears to be considerable resistence to the adoption of the presumption of innocence in China's criminal proceedings. Certainly, the present Criminal Procedure Law is ambiguous enough to be used to support arguments for or against the presumption of innocence.[77] During 1956–57, some liberal Chinese jurists did urge the acceptance of this principle, but it was rejected as a "reactionary bourgeois doctrine" in the ensuing Anti-Rightist Campaign. The official line was that to assume the accused innocent in penal prosecution would only mean "the protection of guilty persons from punishment" and "the restriction of the freedom of the judicial organs and the masses in their fight against counterrevolutionary and other criminal elements." [78] Since 1979, the debate on this principle has been again revived among Chinese legal circles. This time, nevertheless, it has been conducted on a broader scale and in a more open atmosphere.

Among the proponents of the presumption of innocence, some advocate its critical assimilation into the Chinese criminal process. Despite certain contradictions within this principle, they argue, China should selectively absorb its spirit and essence and reject its "dregs" and unreasonable elements so as to ensure the protection of the innocent and keep wrong or unjust judgments to a minimum.[79] Others even go a step further to urge the adoption without qualifications of the presumption of innocence as one of the basic principles of China's criminal procedure. They justify their stand not only in terms of the importance of this principle in guiding the correct handling of cases but also in terms of its compatibility with the socialist legal system. First of all, according to them, the principle of presumption of innocence is a true expression of materialism, because it insists that a judgment can only be made by reliable, objective evidence rather than by subjective views inherent in the feudalistic tradition of "presumption of guilt." Moreover, what the presumption of innocence stands for is in complete accord with a number of principles in the Chinese Criminal Procedure Law, such as "base . . . on facts and take the law as the yardstick" (Article 4), "stress be laid on the weight of evidence and on investigation and research, and one should not readily believe confession" (Article 35). Therefore, the incorporation of the presumption of innocence into Chinese law, in the eyes of its advocates, would have the benefits of reinforcing the aforementioned democratic principles and facilitating the full realization of the PRC's socialist legality.[80]

Those who hold an opposite view on this issue may be divided into two groups. The hard-liners brand the presumption of innocence as a legacy of the capitalist countries, used by the bourgeois class as a means to oppress the people. Unscientific and reactionary, it violates the fundamental spirit of China's Criminal Procedure Law. To adopt this principle would create much confusion, tie the hands of law enforcement personnel, and leave many criminals unpunished.[81] Some even raise the following question: If the defendant is "innocent," why has he been arrested and preferred a public charge against? [82] Others tend to take a more moderate position by saying that there is no need for socialist China to adopt either the feudal principle of presumption of guilt or the bourgeois principle of presumption of innocence although an analysis of both may be useful. The primary responsibility for Chinese judges in a criminal trial, as suggested by the argument, is to investigate the facts and evaluate the evidence with an open mind and from all sides so that the accused's guilt or innocence can be rightfully proven and a correct verdict can be rendered.[83] This position seems to reflect somewhat the current official line, even though the debate on the presumption issue is continuing. In a *Xinhua News Agency* reported interview on the trial of the Gang of Four, jurist Zhang Youyu explained the Chinese attitude toward the principle of presumption of innocence. According to him, China's criminal procedure operates neither on the presumption of guilt nor of innocence but adheres to the principle of "basing ourselves on facts and taking law as the criterion." In so doing, "we can insure the correctness of the judgment and avoid an erroneous judgment arising from preconceived ideas. The exercise of this principle can avoid wronging the innocent and allowing the guilty go unpunished. This complies to the social system and concrete conditions of China." [84]

Question of Judicial Independence

The 1954 Organic Law of People's Courts had, as does the current Law, the provision that "the People's Courts administer justice independently and are subject only to the law." [85] Unfortunately, those legal scholars and practioners who took this provision seriously were branded in the late 1950s as "rightists" challenging Party leadership.[86] As a result, in the ensuing years, Party control over judicial work continued to be so dominant that the Party committee reviewed and approved cases tried by the court at the same level. This system has come to be known as "Shuji pian" (approving cases by the secretary) since the Party committee frequently delegated the decision-making authority to its secretary in charge of political-legal affairs.[87]

Several problems arising from this past practice have been pointed out by critics in the post-Mao era. First, it is impossible for the Party committee (i.e., its political-legal secretary) to have time to investigate all the cases, which may result in either unreasonable delays of administering justice or making careless and erroneous decisions. Second, the Party committee's direct involvement in concrete court cases has tended to weaken the spirit and enthusiasm of judicial personnel in their work. Third, this has had the effect of rendering court trials a mere formality and causing the people to lose confidence in the PRC's legal system.[88]

In view of all this, the Central Committee of the Chinese Communist Party explicitly abolished the practice of reviewing and approving cases by Party committees in an instruction issued in September 1979 on the full implementation of the Criminal Law and the Criminal Procedure Law.[89] At a criminal trials conference in August 1980, then President Jiang Hua of the Supreme Court also urged the Party Central Committee's instruction be resolutely carried out. According to him, it was necessary for Party committees to review and approve cases during the war and in the early years of the People's Republic. After the principle that "the People's Court administer justice independently according to the law" was established in 1954, the practice of reviewing and approving cases by Party committees should have been gradually changed. However, for various reasons, it was not done. Now the Party Central Committee's decision to revoke the system of reviewing and approving cases by Party Committees is a major step of reform to ensure "independent adjudication according to the law" and "proper Party leadership over judicial organs in principles and policy lines and not in concrete and routine matters." [90]

Along the same line other official statements and legal writings have tried to reconcile the principle of judicial independence with the principle of Party leadership by allowing some functional freedom for judicial organs without relinquishing the leadership of the Party. To begin with, the Chinese point out that insofar as their judicial system operates within the framework of Party leadership, it would be wrong to equate the socialist principle of "administering justice independently" with "the separation of the three powers" and "the independent judiciary" proclaimed by the bourgeoisie.[91] Equally mistaken, from their perspective, is to interpret Party leadership to mean substituting the Party for the courts and interfering by Party committees in the details of judicial operation.[92] Moreover, they stress the fact that insistence on the principle of "administering justice independently according to the law" is entirely consistent with the strengthening of Party leadership in legal work:

> Our country's law is made by the National People's
> Congress under the guidance of the Party. It embodies the
> will of the people and the policy of the Party. Determination
> to carry out the law is determination to carry out the people's
> will and the Party's policy. Therefore, independent

adjudication by the courts according to the law really stands for accepting Party leadership and not seeking independence from the Party. . . . With the strengthening of the socialist legal system, Party leadership over the people's courts must be strengthened, not weakened. This leadership, however, is exercised primarily to strengthen the Party's political-ideological guidance so as to make the people's courts see the right direction in the complicated class struggle and resolutely implement the Party's political line, principles, and policies. . . . In the meantime, Party committees must also be required to select and train a large group of proletarian judges, who are loyal to the law, to the system, to the people's interests, as well as to true facts.[93]

By following the above prescriptions and refraining from handling concrete cases, Party committees are said to be in a position to assert more effective leadership in the legal field, as they can concentrate on what is essential without getting bogged down by trivial matters.[94]

In spite of all this, there is evidence that Party officials have continued to interfere in the performance of adjudication functions by the judicial organs. At a panel discussion held by NPC deputies in September 1980, Yang Xiuteng from Tianjin suggested, among other things, that the PRC must guarantee the independence of the People's court in administering justice. "Some cadres," he said, "do not grasp the principle of independent trial according to the law and adopt an attitude of passive resistance. Others even interfere with the court's judicial authority and seek to replace the law with words. In some cases, judicial cadres who have held firmly to principles and handled cases according to the law have been transferred or replaced. Such a situation must resolutely be rectified." [95] In an informal discussion session sponsored by the *Enlightenment Daily* in October 1980, Ma Rongjie, Editor of *Studies in Law*, also called attention to the continuing practice of substituting the Party for the government in judicial work. This usurpation, as he observed, manifests itself principally in two areas: (1) in some localities, the election, appointment, and removal of presidents and judges of the people's courts and chief procurators and other procurators of the people's procuratorates are actually decided by Party committees, contrary to the provisions of the Organic Laws of the Courts and the Procuracy. Ma cited a case in which the president and vice-president of a municipal intermediate court were removed by the first secretary of the municipal Party committee because of their refusal to bend the law to change a judgment; (2) the supposedly abolished practice whereby cases are reviewed and approved by Party committees is still in effect in certain localities.[96] The same newspaper also carried an article on July 17, 1981 which said that some responsible cadres not only proclaimed court decisions as "inconsequential" but even tore up written judgments in public.[97]

The problem referred to by Ma Rongjie regarding the practice of some Party secretaries to remove judicial officials and to change court sentences was confirmed and deplored by a Chinese jurist in a 1981 legal journal article.[98] Similarly, this issue was raised by an article in the *Beijing Daily* on January 23, 1981 which pointed out that the revocation of the practice of reviewing cases by Party committees "has been passively resisted by some comrades and overtly challenged by others." Two instances were cited. One responsible person of a certain county Party committee interfered in a trial and unjustifiably dismissed the chief procurator from his post. Another county Party committee seriously infringed upon the right of a court to conduct adjudication independently and refused to carry out the verdict so as to prevent the close of case.[99] According to a judicial worker's letter to a legal journal, the people's court at Yu County, Henan Province, under the pressure of the county Party's political-legal committee, sentenced on January 7, 1983 a commune member named Dong to six months of detention, even though during the trial the defendant's advocate, the procurator, and adjudication personnel all regarded Dong's act in question as not a criminal offense.[100]

To combat unlawful interference in judicial work and to overcome the passive attitude of some judicial personnel, Chinese leaders like Ye Jianying and Jiang Hua have called for fearless judges and procurators ready to sacrifice their lives for the dignity of the legal system.[101] There are reports about courageous, professional and incorruptible workers in the fashion of the legendary Judge Bao.[102] One is said to have taken a great risk to save a innocent man from the death penalty and have his verdict reversed after twenty-three years.[103] Several others have resisted bribery and various types of pressure in an effort to enforce the law and uphold justice.[104] At the same time, there are also reports concerning those judicial cadres who have been slow, reluctant, or unable to carry out their duties. In Pingding county of Shanxi province, a demobilized soldier was reported to have been unjustly arrested, tortured, and sentenced to prison during 1976–78 because of his criticism of Dazhai (a production brigade in Xiyang County, Shanxi Province, the pacesetter of China's agricultural front) and its leaders. Even after his release he failed in his attempts to have the verdict reversed by the courts. Finally, the intermediate court of Jingzhong did so in August 1980 after a rehabilitation meeting called by the Pingding County Party committee had completely exonerated him.[105] In a letter to a law journal, one reader reported another victim of unjust imprisonment in Qingpu County near Shanghai. Even after the true facts became known, the county court continued to delay any action to "rehabilitate" him for fear of the opposition of certain Party committee members. Only after the repeated urging of the municipal higher court did the county court eventually reverse the verdict.[106] Writing to the same journal, two members of the people's court in Jingan district of Shanghai complained that a legally effective judgment of their court could not be executed due to the resistance from some cadres in the branch office of the China Shipping Fuel Supply Company.[107] The *People's Daily* on October 12, 1983 contained two articles which deplored the fact that a "notorious despot" named Zhang Jinjun, son of a veteran Red Army man, had managed to be in and out of the house of detention and prison several times and urged that legal and public security organs never allow "human relations to break the net of justice." [108]

Development in recent years seems to indicate that while the practice of reviewing and approving cases by Party Committees is officially abolished, the Chinese authorities are engaged in a restrictive interpretation of the concept of judicial independence. According to Jiang Hua's speeches made in early 1981, the provision that "the people's court adjudicate independently according to the law" only governs the courts' relations with outside organs, groups, and individuals. Internally, decisions of judges and collegiate benches must still be approved by court presidents and chief judges.[109] In his address given in November 1981, Jiang Hua said that the courts should take the initiative to report to and seek instructions from the Party committee over significant polity questions and the handling of important and complicated cases. The courts should also regularly keep the Party committees informed of the conditions of judicial work.[110] As a matter of fact, judicial cadres in China today still find it prudent, as in the past, to secure advice and consent from Party committees in dealing with many criminal cases. Sometimes it takes direct intervention from Party committees to settle cases of controversial or political nature.[111]

Concerned with the rising crime wave in China, the Political-Legal Committee of the CCP Central Committee convened a forum on public order in May 1981, which led to the adoption in June by the National People's Congress of strong measures against criminals.[112] In an editorial on August 17, 1981 regarding social order, the *People's Daily* stressed the importance of strengthening Party committees' leadership over political and legal organs and urged the Party secretaries to be directly involved in the drive against criminal offenders.[113] In July 1982, a large-scale conference on China's political and legal work was held in Beijing, again under the sponsorship of the Political-Legal Committee of the CCP Central Committee. After the conference, the *People's Daily* wrote an editorial on political and legal work and made special comments on relations between the Party and judicial organs:

> Strengthening Party leadership is a fundamental guarantee for the proper handling of political and legal work. Various political and legal departments must consciously place themselves under the leadership of the Party. Leadership by Party committees over political and legal departments has to do chiefly with attention to general and specific policies, control over the handling of things according to the law, the supervision of cadres, and the control of political and ideological work. Party committees must protect courts and procuratorates to exercise independently their respective adjudication and procuratorial rights according to the law. They must also support political and legal departments in taking the initiative to carry out professional activities independently.[114]

On July 4, 1983 the Political-Legal Committee of the CCP Central Committee held a telephone conference calling for all judicial procuratorial and public security organs to follow the leadership of Party committees and people's governments at various levels to strengthen their work and improve public order. Chen Pixian, member of the CCP Central Committee Secretariat, and Liu Fuzhi, Secretary General of the Political-Legal Committee and new Minister of Public Security, spoke at the Conference. They both stressed that to ensure social stability, swift and severe blows must be dealt to serious criminal activities.[115] As will be examined more fully in the next chapter, following the conference a vigorous nationwide anticrime campaign was soon started in Tangshan and Beijing in the form of mass arrests and public executions. These measures were legitimized later by the NPC Standing Committee on September 2, 1983 when it amended a number of provisions in the Criminal Law and the Criminal Procedure Law.

What has emerged from the PRC's campaign against violent and economic crimes is a renewed emphasis on Party leadership over judicial work. How it may further develop is, of course, a matter of concern. Nevertheless, indications are that the Chinese leadership is likely to continue to give its blessings to a limited form of judicial independence: the courts can decide their cases on a day-to-day basis, without Party interference, but must always accept the Party's political-ideological guidance, a departure from which will invoke direct Party intervention.

Equality Before the Law

Article 5 of the Organic Law of the People's Courts as well as Article 4 of the Criminal Procedure Law provides that in judicial proceedings all citizens are equal before the application of law, irrespective of their nationality, race, sex, occupation, social origins, religious belief, education, property status, or duration of residence. The same principle of equality was stipulated in the 1954 Constitution (Article 85) and in the 1954 Organic Law of the People's Courts (Article 5). However, it never took roots in Mao's China and was repudiated as a bourgeois concept in the 1957–58 Anti-Rightist Campaign. During the Cultural Revolution, the radicals attacked Peng Zhen, among other things, for advocating this anti-Party principle.[116] In fact, Chinese justice under Mao put so much stress on an individual's class background that persons from the "enemy" class usually received harsher sanctions for the same offense than those among the people.[117]

The post-Mao leadership, on the other hand, has attempted to change the past policy both in law and in practice. As mentioned before, Beijing declared in early 1979 that former landlords, rich peasants, and their descendants would no longer be discriminated against "as long as they support socialism."[118] According to the author of a legal article, conditions in China are now ready for the application of the principle of "equality before the law." "The broad masses of the working class have already become the masters of China; the political dominance of the exploiting class has been overthrown; private ownership of the means of production has been eliminated; public ownership under socialism has been established; the toiling masses have achieved economic equality. All this has wiped out the social roots for inequality before the law."[119] In administration of criminal justice, another author writes in the *Red Flag*, "The criterion for measuring the penalty for a criminal is determined by the extent of harm to society caused by the nature of the crime and the criminal offense itself as well as by the extent of the offense. It is not determined by whether his class element is good or bad, whether his years of revolutionary experience are long or short, or whether his work position is high or low."[120] Since the law in China reflects the will of the Party and the people of the whole country, Peng Zhen asks, "Before this law, how can there be any inequality? . . . How can a landlord be found guilty and a worker or a poor peasant not guilty after committing the same crime or murder? How can an ordinary person found guilty and a cadre not guilty after committing the same crime of murder?" [121]

Indeed, "no special privilege is allowed before the law" is specifically incorporated into the respective equality provisions of the current Organic Law of the Courts (Article 5) and the Criminal Procedure Law (Article 4), in contrast to the 1954 relevant legal provisions that contained no such statement. This reflects the present leadership's concern about the abuse of power by Party and state officials without regard for the law. In an address delivered at the 1979 fifth NPC, Ye Jianying said:

> All citizens are equal before the law, whether or not they
> are Party members and whatever their rank, social position
> and social origin. . . . All leading cadres, no matter how
> highly placed, are public servants of the people. They are
> under obligation to serve the people diligently and
> conscientiously and have no right whatsoever to place
> themselves above the law. . . . While most of our leading
> cadres at all levels are good or fairly good, it is also true that
> there are a few who, by flaunting the laws and institutions of
> the state or by taking advantage of certain imperfections in
> our legal system, have abused the power entrusted them by
> the people to seek personal gain. With regard to such bad
> practices as bureaucracy, the pursuit of privilege, "back-door
> dealings" and suppression of democratic rights, the Party and
> government must take resolute and effective measure to rectify
> them. [122]

Ye's view has been echoed by journal and press articles. "Equality before the law" is described as a sharp weapon against special privileges. [123] To think that one is above the law and cannot be restrained by law "reflects actually the mentality of the ruling feudal landlords in China thousands of years ago." [124] The socialist legal system, on the other hand, is said to be ". . . applicable to all men. Whoever breaks the law and commits a crime, no matter how high his seniority, how important his office and how great his contributions, shall not be shieded but shall be punished according to the law. Otherwise, the principle of the socialist legal system will be undermined, the Party's prestige impaired, and the authority of judicial organs defied." [125]

Actual cases have been used by the press to show the application of the "equality" principle in China today. Three rapists of a gang of seven, for instance, were sentenced to death in June 1980 by an intermediate people's court in Changchun, Jilin, with the chief culprit being the son of a leading cadre at the municipal level. In a commentary, the *China Youth News* said, "Gone are the days when Lin Biao and the Gang of Four lorded it over the people. In the eighties of socialist China, no one who breaks the law can escape the arms of justice." [126] A Beijing intermediate people's court also sentenced on August 9, 1980 four young men to imprisonment for illegal detention and extortion; three were the sons of high-ranking officials. This case was the talk of the town and cited as yet another example of upholding the principle of "equality before the law." [127] A dramatic demonstration that no one is above the law was the punishment of top officials responsible for the offshore drilling rig disaster in Bohai Bay that claimed seventy-two lives on November 25, 1979. Not only was the Minister of Petroleum Industry removed from office by the State Council, but four oil industry supervisors were also given prison sentences for criminal negligence by an intermediate people's court of Tianjin on September 2, 1980.[128] Radio Beijing praised the verdicts as giving expression to the sanctity of the socialist legal system and upholding the principle of "equality before the law." [129] On January 25, 1981, China's Special Court concluded the well-publicized trial of ten leaders of the Cultural Revolution with guilty judgments against the defendants. Jiang Qing and Zhang Chunqiao, former Vice-Premier, received death sentences suspended for two years, while eight others got sentences ranging from sixteen years to life in prison. In an editorial entitled, "The Just Court Verdicts," the *People's Daily* called the trial a great victory for the socialist legal system and for the principle that all are equal before the law.[130] Also in an editorial, the *Red Flag* said that the trial "swept away the long standing pernicious influence of feudalism and shattered the decadent idea that the 'penalties are not imposed upon officials.' All ten principal defendants occupied top leadership positions in the Party, government, or Army. Throughout the trial they were not give special consideration or protection because of their former high positions or previous merits. The court stood firm in protecting the people's interests and pronouncing the appropriate judgments according to the law." [131]

Official statements notwithstanding, the trial of the Gang of Four and others appears to be a poor case to show off Chinese legality. Most foreign observers have regarded the trial as primarily political.[132] Even a Chinese writer in a Hong Kong-based, pro-PRC journal criticized the political interference in the trial. He wondered how is it possible for the Chinese authorities to reconcile their commitment to the principle of "equality before the law" with the fact that they have routinely executed embezzlers and rapists while sparing the life of Jiang Qing[133] who persecuted thousands of people and caused the death of many during the Cultural Revolution.[134] Concerning the handling of the oil rig disasters, two NPC deputies, speaking at a panel discussion in September 1980, stated that they and many of their colleagues were not fully satisfied. In their view, "we have attacked just flies but not tigers" and only by discontinuing the "feudal" practice favoring the privileged "can we truly succeed in having everyone equal before the law." [135]

In the recent Chinese drive against crimes, there have been complaints about failure of the law to reach people of power and influence or those related to them.[136] One reader's letter to a law journal raised the question "Are All Citizens Equal Before the Law?" when one soldier charged with attempted rape was sentenced to five years imprisonment while an army cadre's son charged with robbery and attempted rape only received a two-year prison term.[137] There is little doubt that the present Chinese leadership has been making a genuine effort to rectify the situation. Nevertheless, even some of the reported cases where the culprits have been brought to justice demonstrate certain deep-rooted problems and obstacles for the PRC to overcome in the enforcement of law. For instance, among the convicted corrupt officials was Wang Weijing, Director of the Guangzhou Telecommunications Bureau and Secretary of the provincial CCP Committee. For years he had been known for his smuggling and profiteering activities, but it was not until the spring of 1982 that he was arrested, tried, and then sentenced to two years imprisonment.[138] A young offender named Mao Xiaohong was able to make rapid advances in his career despite his early criminal record and continuation of unlawful activities, including speculation and rape. Mao's "success" in escaping legal sanctions until recently was attributed to the help of his protective father, once the Secretary of the Beijing Municipal CCP Committee.[139] In contrast, in a more publicized case involving the rape of a young woman by three cadres' sons, the ring leader's father, a senior army commander, wrote a letter to the Party leadership, dated March 16, 1982, to support the imposition of severe punishment on his son according to the law.[140] On April 12, 1982, the Chengdu Intermediate People's Court sentenced He Deming, the ring leader, to life imprisonment and his two accomplices to fifteen and ten years imprisonment, respectively.[141] The Chinese press again used the occasion to emphasize the principle of equality before the law. Commenting on the court's decision, reporters of the *People's Daily* had this to say: "During the court hearing of this case, there were no such phenomena which were common years ago when some senior cadres took advantage of their power or sought help from their friends to cover their children's crimes or absolve them from punishment. Nor did people see the old practice where some courts applied the law differently on different people or imposed lenient punishment for serious crimes." [142] In the 1983 crime suppression campaign, a grandson of the late Marshall Zhu De was reported to have been executed for rape and other offenses, and many children of senior officials were also arrested.[143] Still, as pointed out by one observer, the PRC's drive against corruption and other economic crimes has so far only punished some midrank cadres, and no high officials (12-grade up) have ever been criminally prosecuted and sentenced for their wrongdoings.[144] Thus, much remains to be done for the PRC to establish the credibility of the equality principle and to attack tigers and flies alike in applying criminal sanctions.

APPEAL AND REVIEW

Under the two-trial system as stipulated in Article 12 of the Organic Law of the People's Courts, a judgment or ruling of the court of first instance may be appealed to the court of the next higher level. An appeal may be initiated by the defendant or the procuracy. In the past, the fear of incurring heavier punishment seriously deterred the Chinese from exercising their right of appeal.[145] To remedy the situation, Article 137 of the Criminal Procedure Law specifically provides that in adjudicating a case appealed by a defendant or his advocate, the court of second instance may not increase the penalty, although this limitation is inapplicable in a case appealed by the procuracy.[146] With this protection, more people have now sought redress through appellate proceedings. In his report to the NPC on December 7, 1981, Jiang Hua said that from October 1980 to September 1981, the courts at all levels handled more than 240,000 appeals of criminal cases.[147] As pointed out by Harold Berman and his colleagues, however, since Article 137 of the Chinese Criminal Procedure Law does not have the Soviet provision (Article 347 of the Russian Code) that if the procurator protests on the ground of the mildness of the punishment, the case may be remanded for a new trial, it apparently allows the appellate court to increase the punishment itself when both the accused and the procurator appeal.[148] A Shanghai intermediate court did just that on June 9, 1981 at an appellate trial witnessed by Professor Berman as well as one of the authors.

A legally effective judgment in the PRC is also subject to a form of review called adjudication supervision if a definite error in the determination of facts or application of the law is found. Article 149 of the Criminal Procedure Law provides the following procedure of judicial supervision for such a situation:

(1) The president of the court which gave the judgment in question may refer it to the adjudication committee for disposal.

(2) The Supreme People's Court or an upper court may review the case themselves or direct the lower court to conduct a retrial.

(3) The Supreme People's Procuracy or an upper procuracy may lodge a protest against the given judgment in accordance with the procedure of adjudication supervision.

This system of review, says one authoritative publication, ensures that erroneous or unjust judgments are to be corrected and that criminal offenders are to be duly punished.[149]

In fact, the post-Mao leadership has taken vigorous steps to reverse unjust and wrong verdicts of the past. As reported by Jiang Hua, by the end of June 1980, the people's courts had reviewed over one million criminal conviction cases handled during the Cultural Revolution and had rectified more than 251,000 cases of injustice involving over 267,000 persons.[150] The guiding principle has been to "seek truth from facts and correct mistakes whenever discovered."[151]

It should be noted here that besides the appeal procedure, there are special review procedures for death penalty cases. Article 43 of the Criminal Law stipulates that except for those imposed by the Supreme People's Court, all other death sentences should be submitted to the Supreme People's Court for examination and approval. According to Articles 15–17 of the Criminal Procedure Law, the court of the first instance for capital crime cases is the intermediate people's court or above. Part three, Chapter Four of the same law provides detailed review procedures for death sentences. Whether appealed or not and whether imposed by an intermediate people's court or by a higher people's court, a death sentence has to be ratified by the Supreme People's Court (Articles 144–145). As to death sentences with a two-year suspension of execution handed down by the intermediate people's court, only the approval of the higher people's court is required (Article 146).[152]

Chinese officials and jurists generally agree that it is necessary to retain capital punishment in China because of its deterrent value in dealing with major counterrevolutionary crimes and other most heinous offenses that seriously endanger society or incur great popular indignation.[153] Nevertheless, they contend that the underlying principle of China's criminal legislation is to reduce and restrict the use of the death penalty and to combine punishment with leniency in the spirit of revolutionary humanism. As evidence, they cite the special review procedures provided for death penalty cases, the two-year suspension of death sentences for the convicted to reform, and the exemption from capital punishment of young people committing crimes while under eighteen years of age and of women found to be pregnant during trial.[154]

Undoubtedly, the legal provisions mentioned above reflect the current Chinese leadership's policy to employ capital punishment with care and to avoid the past abuses of mass trials and "exemplary" public executions. There is, however, still a tendency on the part of the PRC to use harsh measures and to depart from legal requirements on occasions of political and social tensions. During 1979–1980, for example, there were a number of mass sentencing and public execution meetings, some of which even had their proceedings televised.[155] More important was the 1981 decision of the NPC Standing Committee for a temporary modification of Articles 144 and 145 requiring the approval of death sentences by the Supreme People's Court. In a move to mete out swift and severe punishment to criminals seriously endangering social order, the Committee adopted a resolution on June 10, 1981 granting for 1981–83 the right to approve death sentences to the provincial-level higher people's courts in cases of murder, robbery, rape, bombing, arson, poison, breaching of dikes, or sabotage of communications and power facilities. The approval of the Supreme People's Court shall continue to be required for death sentences passed on counterrevolutionaries and embezzlers.[156]

More far reaching was the harsh crime crackdown campaign launched in the second part of 1983, during which there were mass arrests, "summary executions," and public denunciation and humiliation of those convicted of serious crimes, particularly capital offenses. To put a legal stamp to the Beijing regime's policy of swift and stern punishment of criminals seriously endangering social order, the NPC Standing Committee adopted on September 2, 1983 resolutions to amend several exiting laws. It revised Article 13 of the Organic Law of People's Courts to allow the Supreme People's Court to delegate the authority to approve death sentences to the provincial-level higher people's courts in cases of murder, rape, robbery, use of explosives, and other serious offenses.[157] It also revised the Criminal Law to sharply increase the number of capital offenses to cover virtually any serious crime and ordered the courts to impose stiffer penalties, including execution, on people convicted of violent crimes.[158]

For persons accused of murder, rape, armed robbery and other violent crimes, the NPC Standing Committee suspended practically all guarantees of due process. In its decision on the procedure to try those persons, it removed Article 110 of the Criminal Procedure Law that requires the defendants to receive a copy of the indictment at least seven days before the trial to prepare their defense. It also changed the time limit for appeals to three days from the ten days stipulated in Article 131 of the Criminal Procedure Law.[159] This decision was defended by Wang Hanbin, Secretary General of the NPC Standing Committee, who said: "If criminals who are involved in homicide, rape, robbery, use of explosives, and other activities that seriously threaten public safety and should be sentenced to death are handled in accordance with those stipulations, we will not be able to try swiftly some cases that need to be tried right away, thus hindering our efforts to frighten the criminals, frustrate their arrogance, maintain public order, and protect the life and property of the people." In most of these cases, according to Wang, the facts are clear and the evidence is conclusive so legal procedure should not be permitted to hinder the exercise of the Dictatorship of People's Democracy.[160]

The zeal and determination of the PRC to strike a "swift and resolute blow" at violent offenders has resulted not only in the removal of some procedural guarantees in the criminal process but also the revival of the public humiliation of condemned criminals practiced in the past. What is described below has caused concerns among human rights advocates:

> Persons convicted during the anticrime campaign were often taken before "mass sentencing meetings" attended by thousands of people. . . . After those who had been convicted confessed or publicly denounced at such meetings, in many cases they were sentenced to death. They were then paraded through the city with placards around their necks specifying their crimes, before they were executed by firing squads.[161]

PRELIMINARY OBSERVATIONS

It would be unrealistic to expect too much from the PRC's emerging criminal justice system. After all, the two major criminal laws only became effective on January 1, 1980, and the full implementation of the Criminal Procedure Law has been particularly hampered by technical and practical difficulties. Nonetheless, even at this stage of its development, the criminal process in the PRC today is a substantial improvement over the Maoist system of justice in the protection of the individual against the arbitrary power of the state. Certainly, the presence of legal rules, the stress on evidence rather than confessions, and the de-emphasis of class justice all appear to give the accused in a criminal case—now more than before in the history of the People's Republic—a more meaningful opportunity to defend himself.

On the other hand, thirty years of political uncertainty and policy shifts have instilled a sense of cynicism in the people of the PRC about the durability of the current regime's commitment to the rule of law. Their confidence has not been increased by the trials of Wei Jingsheng and other dissidents and the administrative sanctions applied against other political dissidents. Chinese leaders appear to be aware of the problem and have stressed the importance to observe the law. In a report to the NPC Standing Committee in April 1980, Jiang Hua said, "The Criminal Law and the Criminal Procedure Law promulgated by our country have attracted the attention of the world. Whether they can be implemented to the letter is a matter of great importance concerning whether we can win the trust of the people." [162]

Another troubling question is the relationship between the Party and the judicial organs. Despite the prescription of official spokesmen that Party leadership over the judiciary should be exercised in areas of guidelines and policies and not in the handling of individual cases, some Party cadres have continued to intervene in the administration of justice. Furthermore, there are cases where Party discipline has replaced state law in applying sanctions against criminal offenders. A serious incident at a construction site in Shanghai resulted in loss of lives; however, the two persons in charge were only given disciplinary demerits and were not prosecuted according to Article 114 of the Criminal Law.[163] A Party official in Xiyang County, Shanxi, allegedly committed many crimes, including rape and extortion. Again, he was reported to have been subjected to Party disciplinary sanctions and not legal punishment.[164] These and other similar occurrences have promoted critical comments in the press and legal journals.

The fact that these criticisms and others cited elsewhere in this chapter can be voiced freely in China is itself an encouraging sign. At the same time, rather disconcerting are the measures used by the PRC in its latest anticrime campaign. While Beijing may indeed have good reasons and even some popular support for its drive against violent crimes, the removal of procedural guarantees in the interest of swift justice and the revival of public humiliation of the condemned to frighten the criminals, however, do not, in the long run, promote people's confidence in the rule of law nor the stability of the PRC's legal system. Hopefully, Chinese leaders are aware of this problem. This and other related issues will be further examined in the next chapter on crime and punishment to help us to construct a complete picture of China's criminal justice at work.

NOTES

Chapter Five

1. See, for example, "The Just Court Verdicts," *Renmin Ribao* (People's Daily), January 26, 1981, pp. 1, 4; *A Great Trial in Chinese History* (Beijing: New World Press, 1981), pp. 135–148.

2. See, for instance, Frank Ching, "Robes Of Justice Sit Uneasily on Gang of Four Judges," *The Asian Wall Street Journal*, November 28, 1980, p. 4; Fox Butterfield, "Revenge Seems to Outweigh Justice at Chinese Trial," *New York Times*, December 6, 1980, p. 2; David Bonavia, "Give Them Rice and Circuses," *Far Eastern Economic Review*, Vol. 110, No. 50, December 5–11, 1980, p. 12; Editorial: "Peking's Trial and Error," *New York Times*, January 5, 1981, p. A-14; James C. Hsiung, ed., *Symposium: The Trial of the "Gang of Four" and Its Implications in China* (Baltimore: University of Maryland School of Law Occasional Papers/Reprints Series in Contemporary Asian Studies, No. 3, 1981); Hungdah Chiu, "Certain Legal Aspects of the Recent Peking Trials of the 'Gang of Four' and Others," *Asia Thought & Society*, Vol. 6, No. 16, April 1981, pp. 54–62. Professor Jerome A. Cohen, however, considers the trial as China's effort to bring a political case under the legal process. He also would compare the trial to the Nuremburg war crimes trials following World War II. *The Associate Press*, Beijing, December 6, 1980.

3. Texts of the Counterrevolutionaries Act and the Corruption Act are in *Zhongyang Renmin Zhengfu Faling Huibian* (FLHB) (Collection of Laws and Decree of the Central People's Government) (Beijing: People's Press) Vol. II (1953), pp. 3–5 and Vol. III (1954), pp. 25–28, respectively and texts of the SAPA and the Arrest Act are in *Zhonghua Renmin Gongheguo Fagui Huibian* (FGHB) (Collection of Laws and Regulations of the People's Republic of China) (Beijing: Law Press), Vol. I (1956), pp. 239–242 and Vol. VI (1957), pp. 245–261, respectively.

4. Texts of the Criminal Law and the Criminal Procedure Law are in *Gongan Fagui Huibian, 1950–79* (Collection of Laws and Regulations on Public Security) (Beijing: Mass Press, 1980), pp. 4–34 and 35–65 (hereinafter GAFGHB). English translations appear in *FBIS, Daily Report: PRC*, July 27 (Supplement), pp. 33–62 and July 30, 1979 (Supplement) pp. 1–31, respectively. More recent translations done by J.A. Cohen, T.A. Gelatt, and F.M. Li are in *Journal of Criminal Law and Criminology*, Vol. 73, No. 1, 1982, pp. 138–237.

5. See translations of the Soviet codes in Harold Berman and J. Spindler, *Soviet Criminal Law and Procedure: The RSFSR Codes* (Cambridge, Mass.: Harvard University Press, 1972); and translations of Nationalist Chinese codes in *A Compilation of the Laws of the Republic of China* (Taipei; David C. C. Kang, 1971), Vol. 2, pp. 181–281 and 333–460.

6. Peng Zhen, "Explanation on the Seven Draft Laws," *Main Documents of the Second Session of the Fifth National People's Congress of the People's Republic of China* (Beijing: Foreign Languages Press, 1979), pp. 192–193.

7. Zhao Canbi, "Strengthen the Concept of the Legal System and Act Strictly According to the Law," *Hongqi* (Red Flag), No. 8, 1979, p. 41.

8. Harold Berman, Susan Cohen, and Malcolm Russell, "A Comparison of the Chinese and Soviet Codes of Criminal Law and Procedure," *Journal of Criminal Law and Criminology*, Vol. 73, No. 1, 1982, p. 256.

9. Berman, et al, "A Comparison of the Chinese and Soviet Codes of Criminal Law and Procedure," pp. 256–257.

10. See, for example, Hungdah Chiu, "China's New Legal System," *Current History*, Vol. 79, No. 458, September 1980, p. 31; Fox Butterfield, "Definition of Crime Clarified

by Peking," *New York Times*, July 10, 1979, p. A-11; "The Criminal Law," *China News Analysis*, No. 1160, August 3, 1979, p. 6–8.

11. As one Western jurist comments, the mere promulgation of the Criminal Law is already an act of courage on the part of the present government. M.J. Meijar, "The New Criminal Law of the People's Republic of China," *Review of Socialist Law*, Vol. 6, No. 2, 1980, p. 138.

12. Jerome A. Cohen, "Foreward—China's Criminal Codes," *Journal of Criminal Law and Criminology*, Vol. 73, No. 1, 1982, p. 136.

13. Text of the Standing Committee's Decision Regarding the Questions of Implementation of the Criminal Procedure Law (Feb. 12, 1980) in *Renmin Ribao*, Feb. 13, 1981, p. 1; English translation in FBIS, *Daily Report: PRC*, February 13, 1980, p. L6. In Beijing, for instance, the Municipal People's Congress was reported to have extended the maximum pretrial detention time to seven months. *Beijing Ribao* (Beijing Daily), April 2, 1980.

14. Text of the decision (September 10, 1981) in *Renmin Ribao*, Sept. 1, 1981, p. 1; English translation in *FBIS, Daily Report, China*, Sept. 15, 1981, p. K5. The People's Congress of Zhejiang Province decided on Nov. 1, 1981 a one-month extension beyond the time limits in Articles 92, 97, 125 and 142 of the Criminal Procedure Law. *Zhejiang Ribao*, Nov. 4, 1981, p. 3; JPRS (Joint Publication Research Service), 79808, Jan. 6, 1982, pp. 4–5.

15. For the text of the Criminal Procedure Law and its English translations, see above note 4. A revised translation appears in Document 6.

16. Text of the revised Act is in *Renmin Ribao*, Feb. 25, 1979, p. 1. Translation of the Act appears in Document 3. Text of the 1954 Act, ignored in the past, is in *FGHB*, Vol. 1, pp. 239–242.

17. See Articles 38–52 of the Criminal Procedure Law & Articles 2–8 of the Act on Arrest and Detention. The difference between "detention" and "arrest" is clearly described in a 1968 study as follows: detention is the emergency apprehension and confinement of a suspect for the purpose of investigating whether there is sufficient evidence to justify his arrest; arrest is the apprehension and confinement, or the continuing confinement, of a suspect for the purpose of investigating whether there is sufficient evidence to justify prosecution. Jerome A. Cohen, *The Criminal Process in the People's Republic of China* (Cambridge, Mass: Harvard University Press, 1968), p. 28.

18. As explained by a Chinese jurist, the three month period before the trial is needed because China is so vast in size and transportation is difficult. Ronald C. Keith, "Transcript of Discussions With Wu Daying and Zhang Zhonglin Concerning Legal Change and Civil Rights," *The China Quarterly*, No. 81, March, 1980, pp. 44–45.

19. Zeng Longyao, "Upholding the Principle of Mutual Coordination and Restriction by the Public Security Organs, Procuratorial Organs and People's Courts," *Faxue Yanjiu*, No. 1, 1979, pp. 44–45.

20. Luo Ping, "The Principle of Measuring Penalty in China's Criminal Law," *Hongqi* (Red Flag), No. 9, 1979, pp. 71–72; Teaching and Research Office of the Beijing Political-Legal Institute, *Zhonghua Remin Gongheguo Xingshi Susong Fa Jianghua* (Lectures on the Criminal Procedure Law of the People's Republic of China) (Beijing: Mass Press, 1979), p. 74.

21. Qin Huaihe, "Need to Ensure People's Power to Direct State Affairs," *Cheng Ming* (Contending), No. 37, Nov. 1, 1980, p. 82.

22. See, for example, Fox Butterfield, "Four Arrested in China at Democracy Wall," *New York Times*, Nov. 13, 1979, p. A5; Arlette Laduguie, "The Human Rights Movement," *Index on Censorship*, Vol. 9, No. 1 (February 1980), pp. 18–26. According to the report of the underground publication *Dadi* (Great Earth) on Nov. 4, 1979, when

Wei Jingsheng was arrested on March 27, 1979, he demanded that the public security personnel show him their arrest warrant, but was told, "We want to arrest you, why do we need an arrest warrant! " A week later, the arrest warrant was issued by a people's court. Chiu, "China's New Legal System," p. 32.

23. *Lectures on the Criminal Procedure Law*, pp. 52, 63–64.

24. Wang Shunhua, "Why Is It Necessary to Strictly Ban Torture in Extracting Confession?" *Guangming Ribao* (Enlightenment Daily) March 19, 1980, p. 3.

25. Fox Butterfield, "Chinese Said to Torture African Student in Sex Inquiry," *New York Times*, June 1, 1980, p. 3.

26. *Minzhu Yu Fazhi* (Democracy and Legal System), No. 8, 1980, p. 31.

27. *Minzhu Yu Fazhi*, No. 2, 1981, pp. 47–48.

28. Michael Weisskopf, "A Glimpse of Life in China's Prisons," *The Washington Post*, Sept. 15, 1981, pp. A1, A14. For translation of a shorter version of the alleged manuscript written by Liu, see "Prison Writings of Dissident Liu Qing Published," JPRS 80461, March 31, 1982, pp. 110–159.

29. Han Xiaobai and Liu Chunda, "A Brief Discussion of the Offense of Illegal Detention," *Minzhu Yu Fazhi*, No. 11, 1981, pp. 35–36; "Legal and Disciplinary Cases Must be Resolutely Investigated and Dealt With," *Minzhu Yu Fazhi*, p. 36; Guangdong Provincial Broadcast in FBIS, *Daily Report: PRC*, October 27, 1980, p. P2.

30. *Xinhua News Agency*, October 1, 1980.

31. Commentator, "Their Mistake Was in Knowingly Violating the Law," *Renmin Ribao*, April 18, 1983, p. 4.

32. "Hong Kong 'Compatriots' Missing in China," *Asian Wall Street Journal Weekly*, October 11, 1982, pp. 4, 17. According to this report:

> "(Hong Kong Chinese, While Visiting China,) can be—and are—held for prolonged periods without any formal charges being lodged against them; they haven't any right to see friends or relatives, and, if there is a hearing it is held without publicity." They simply disappear.
>
> No one knows how many Hong Kong Chinese travellers have vanished in China. One magazine editor here (Hong Kong) estimates that 100 people have been arrested so far this year (1982), for one reason or another." Ibid., p. 4.

33. "China Confirms Jailing of an Ex-U.S. Lawyer," *New York Times*, February 2, 1984, p. A7. See also, Frank Ching, "Lawyer Who Worked at American Firms Imprisoned in China as Spy for the U.S.," *Asian Wall Street Journal Weekly*, January 23, 1984, p. 3.

34. See also the case of another Hong Kong Chinese. "PRC Upholds 10-Year Sentence for Hong Kong Man," FBIS, *China*, September 9, 1983, p. W1.

35. FBIS, *Daily Report, PRC*, November 21, 1980, p. L3.

36. *Lectures on the Criminal Procedure Law*, p. 87.

37. One Chinese writer maintains that "public trial" not only serves educational purposes but also puts adjudication under the people's supervision. Zhuang Huichen, "On Public Trial," *Faxue Yanjiu*, No. 5, 1980, pp. 35–38. Cases involving personal intimacies (Yinci) are said to mean those concerning sex offenses. *Zhongguo Fazhi Bao* (China's Legal System Paper), Nov. 13, 1981, p. 3.

38. *Xinhua News Agency*, Sept. 15, 1980.

39. Frank Ching, "Justice Must be Seen to be Done to Gang of Four," *Asian Wall Street Journal*, October 3, 1980, p. 6.

40. *Renmin Ribao*, Nov. 22, 1980, p. 4. A similar view was expressed by Wang Hanbin, Vice-Chairman of the Legal Affairs Commission of the NPC Standing Committee, when interviewed by a *Xinhua News Agency* reporter. *Renmin Ribao*, Dec., 17, 1980, p. 4.

41. Fox Butterfield, "Leading Chinese Dissident Gets 15-year Prison Term," *New York Times,* October 17, 1979, p. A3.

42. Article 113. See also Article 23.

43. See "Indictment of the Special Procuratorate," *A Great Trial of Chinese History,* p. 156.

44. See James P. Sterba, "Former Chinese Leaders Given Long Prison Terms," *New York Times,* January 26, 1981, p. A3.

45. "A Good Model for Public Adjudication," *Zhongguo Fazhi Bao,* February 13, 1981, p. 1.

46. Sun Yinji and Feng Caijin, *Lushi Jiben Zhishi* (Basic Knowledge about Lawyers) (Beijing: Mass Press, 1980), pp. 51–52.

47. The Soviet defense counsel may participate in the preliminary investigation after the investigator has issued an indictment and may also participate from the beginning of the preliminary investigation in certain types of cases. Berman *et al,* "A Comparison of the Chinese and Soviet Codes," see above note 8, p. 241. For comparing the PRC code with Soviet, ROC, and Western European laws on this issue, see Timothy A. Gelatt, "The People's Republic of China and the Presumption of Innocence," *Journal of Criminal Law and Criminology,* Vol. 73, No. 1., 1982, pp. 287–288.

48. Article 29 of the Criminal Procedure Law; also Article 7 of the Provisional Act on Lawyers, adopted on August 26, 1980 and becoming effective on January 1, 1982. The text is in *Renmin Ribao,* August 27, 1980, p. 4, translated by Tao-tai Hsia and Charlotte Hambley in *China Law Reporter,* Vol. 1, No. 4, 1981, pp. 217–221. A revised translation appears in Document 14 of this book.

49. "Joint Circular of the Supreme People's Court, Supreme People's Procuratorate, Ministry of Public Security, and Ministry of Justice on Certain Specific Regulations for Lawyers' Participation in Litigation," *Zhongguo Fazhi Bao,* May 25, 1981, p. 1; *FBIS, Daily Report: China,* May 15, 1981, p. K23.

50. Articles 114, 115, 117, 118, 129, 139 and 141 of the Criminal Procedure Law; Sun Yingjie and Feng Caijin, see above note 46, pp. 72–78; Lin Guoding, "The Criminal Advocacy of Lawyer," *Faxue Yanjiu,* No. 5, 1981, pp. 21–23. According to the editor of a law journal, as a "participant in the litigation," the lawyer may also study case materials in the second trial. *Minzhu Yu Fazhi,* No. 7, 1981, pp. 47–48.

51. Article 3 of the Provisional Act on Lawyers.

52. Sun Yingjie and Feng Caijin, *supra* note 46, pp. 63–66; Lin Guoding, "The Criminal Advocacy of Lawyer," p. 23; Ye Chuangu, "How Do the Lawyers Carry on Their Task of Defense Amidst the Drive to Mete Out Severe and Swift Punishment to Current Major Offenders?" *Minzhu Yu Fazhi,* No. 8, 1981, pp. 10–11.

53. Zhu Kaihua, "How Did I do to Defend the Man Named Xia?" *Minzhu Yu Fazhi,* No. 6, 1981, p. 37.

54. "Implement the Policy of Severe and Swift Punishment; Improve the Worth of Criminal Defense," *Zhongguo Fazhi Bao,* Oct. 9, 1981, p. 2.

55. "Lawyer He Qingyuan Refused Gifts," *Zhongguo Fazhi Bao,* Feb. 12, 1982, p. 1.

56. Shao-chuan Leng, *Justice in Communist China* (Dobbs Ferry, NY: Oceana, 1967), p. 144.

57. *Minzhu Yu Fazhi,* No. 2, 1979, p. 36.

58. *Minzhu Yu Fazhi,* No. 2, 1981, p. 47.

59. *FBIS, Daily Report: PRC,* Sept. 24, 1980, p. L14.

60. *Minzhu Yu Fazhi,* No. 4, 1980, pp. 10–11.

61. Xiao Yang, "Should Correctly Treat Lawyers' Work," *Minzhu Yu Fazhi,* No. 4, 1980, pp. 14–15. In October 1983, a lawyer, Wang Xiangguang, while filing an appeal for an accused who was wrongfully sentenced to death, was arrested by the Procur-

atorate Office in the Hainan Island. The reason for appeal was that the youth, at the time of committing the alleged offense, had not yet reached eighteen years old so, under Article 44 of the Criminal Law, should not be receiving death sentence. After Wang was detained for several months and his residence searched, he was released for lack of evidence in committing any offense. See Reuter Dispatch from Beijing, March 16, 1984, in *Zhong Bao* (Centre Daily News), March 17, 1984, p. 2.

62. See remarks made by Ye Chuangu in *Zhong Bao*, No. 1, 1982, p. 12.

63. *Beijing Review*, Vol. 23, No. 23, June 9, 1980, p. 26.

64. *Renmin Ribao*, August 29, 1980, p. 4.

65. Timothy A. Gelatt, "Resurrecting China's Legal Institutions," *Asian Wall Street Journal*, March 29, 1980, p. 4.

66. Fox Butterfield, "Peking Criminal Trial, in Bank Robbery Case, Opened to Foreigners," *New York Times*, June 18, 1980, p. A3.

67. *Zhongguo Fazhi Bao*, Feb. 6, 1981, p. 1.

68. Jiang Qing initially wanted lawyers to represent her but failed to reach an agreement with the three lawyers recommended by the court. *Guangming Ribao*, November 11, 1980, p. 1.

69. John Rodenick, "Gang of Four: Baffling Trial in China," *AP*, December 6, 1980; Fox Butterfield, "Revenge Seems to Outweigh Justice at Chinese Trial," *New York Times*, December 6, 1980, p. 2.

70. See *FBIS, Daily Report: PRC*, December 2, 1980, pp. L2–3; December 19, 1980, pp. L2, L4–5; December 22, 1980, p. L6; December 29, 1980, pp. L11–12. See also *A Great Trial in Chinese History*, pp. 113–127.

71. *FBIS, Daily Report: PRC*, December 29, 1980, p. L11; *A Great Trial in Chinese History*, pp. 123–124.

72. *FBIS, Daily Report: PRC,* December 19, 1980, p. L2; *A Great Trial in Chinese History*, pp. 116–117.

73. *FBIS, Daily Report: PRC*, December 22, 1980, p. L6; *A Great Trial in Chinese History*, pp. 113–114.

74. *The Rule of Law in a Free Society: A Report on the International Congress of Jurists, New Delhi, India, 1979* (Geneva: International Commission of Jurists, 1959), p. 249.

75. Leng, *Justice in Communist China*, pp. 164–165: Cohen, *The Criminal Process*, pp. 49–50; Luo Ping, "The Principle of Measuring Penalty," see above note 20, pp. 71–72.

76. Article 31 of the Criminal Procedure Law lists the following six categories of evidence: (1) Material evidence and documentary evidence; (2) Testimony of witnesses; (3) Statements of victims; (4) Statements and explanations of defendants; (5) Conclusions of expert evaluations; and (6) Records of inspection and examination.

77. For an excellent dicussion of the PRC's treatment of the presumption of innocence, see Gelatt, "The PRC and the Presumption of Innocence," see above note 47, pp. 259–316.

78. Leng, *Justice in Communist China*, pp. 63, 165.

79. Chen Guangzhong, "The Principle of Presumption of Innocence Should be Critically Assimilated," *Faxue Yanjiu*, No. 4, 1980, pp. 34–36; Liao Zengyun, "View on the Principle of Presumption of Innocence," *Faxue Yanjiu*, No. 5, 1980, pp. 32–34.

80. Wang Bingxin, "Exploration on the Principle of Presumption of Innocence," *Xinan Zhengfa Xueyuan Xuebao* (Journal of the Southwest Political-Legal Institute), No. 1, 1979, pp. 10–15; Zhao Hong and Dou Jixiang, "Comprehension on the Principle of Presumption of Innocence," *Faxue Yanjiu*, No. 3, 1979, pp. 47–48; Wang Xiaohua and Ma Qingguo, "Argue for the 'Presumption of Innocence'," *Faxue Yanjiu*, No. 1, 1980, pp. 63–64.

81. *Lectures on the Criminal Procedure Law*, p. 55; Wang Zhaosheng and Wei Ruoping, "A View on the Principle of Presumption of Innocence," *Faxue Yanjiu*, No. 2, 1979, pp. 47–48; Zhang Zipei, "Analysis of the Principle of 'Presumption of Innocence'," *Faxue Yanjiu*, No. 3, 1980, pp. 30–33; Yu Zhi, "Presumption of Innocence Cannot Serve as a Guiding Concept in Criminal Procedure," *Minghu Yu Fazhi*, No. 3, 1980, pp. 20–21.

82. Zhang Zipei, *Faxue Yanjiu*, No. 3, 1980, p. 32; Yi Xiaozhong, "Principle of 'Presumption of Innocence' Is Poles Apart From Our Country's Regulations on Arrest and Detention," *Faxue Yanjiu*, No. 1, 1980, p. 63.

83. See, for example, Yang Guanda, "A Concrete Analysis Should be Made of 'Presumption of Innocence'," *Faxue Yanjiu*, pp. 63, 28.

84. *A Great Trial in Chinese History*, pp. 141–142; *Renmin Ribao*, November 22, 1980, p. 4.

85. Article 4 of both the 1954 Law and the 1979 Law. English text of the new Organic Law of the People's Court is in *FBIS, Daily Report: PRC*, July 27, 1979 (Supplement), pp. 20–27. Text of the 1954 Organic Law in *FGHB*, Vol. 1, pp. 123–132.

86. Leng, *Justice in Communist China*, pp. 61–63, 98–101; Cohen, *The Criminal Process*, pp. 483–506.

87. Liao Junchang, "Independent Adjudication and Approval of Cases by the Secretary," *Xinan Zhengfa Xueyuan Xuebao* (see above note 80), No. 1, 1979, pp. 6–9.

88. Liao Junchang, pp. 7–9; Special Group Assisting the Handling of Cases from the Southwest Institute of Politics and Law, "Looking at Some Problems Existing in Judicial Work from the Practice of Handling Cases," *Xinan Zhengfa Xueyuan Xuebao*, No. 1, 1979, pp. 26–27; Cui Min and Wang Liming, "Strengthen Party Leadership; Adjudicate Independently According to the Law," *Minzhu Yu Fazhi*, No. 2, 1979, p. 13.

89. Yu Haocheng, "Party Committees Should Not Continue Reviewing and Approving Cases," *Beijing Ribao*, January 23, 1981, p. 3.

90. *Renmin Ribao*, August 25, 1980, p. 1.

91. Liu Guangming, "The People's Courts Administer Justice Independently," *Faxue Yanjiu*, No. 3, 1979, pp. 31–32.

92. Chen Shouyi, "A Review of New China's Research in Law During the Past Thirty Years," *Faxue Yanjiu*, No. 1, 1980, p. 6.

93. Chang Gong, "A Fine Statute on the People's Judicature," *Faxue Yanjiu*, No. 4, 1979, pp. 35–36.

94. Peng Zhen, "Several Questions on the Socialist Legal System," *Hongqi*, No. 11, 1979, p. 7.

95. *Xinhua News Agency*, Sept. 15, 1980. For similar complaints on the legal system by other deputies, see *Renmin Ribao*, Sept. 16, 1980, p. 3 and Sept. 18, 1980, p. 3.

96. "Strengthen Theoretical Study; Promote Institutional Reform: Excerpts of Comments from the Theoreticians Forum Held in the National Capital, I," *Guangming Ribao*, October 10, 1980, p. 2.

97. Yang Kedian, "Correctly Implement the Principle of Independent Adjudication," *Guangming Ribao*, July 17, 1981, p. 3.

98. According to Hua Xiao, a Chinese jurist, unless there is a change of this practice, the authority of China's legal system is being undermined. Hua Xiao, "On the Blindness towards Justice," *Faxue Zazi* (Law Journal), No. 3, 1981, p. 34.

99. Yu Haocheng, "Party Committees Should Not Continue Reviewing and Approving Cases," *Beijing Ribao*, January 23, 1981, p. 3. The first example Yu cited apparently refers to an episode that occurred in Fuding County of Fujian Province. Ji Zhili, secretary of the county Party committee, came into conflict with Zhou Zongshuang, Chief procurator of the county, over the disposal of a case. Ji questioned

Zhou, "Which is superior, the law or the Party committee secretary?" and had Zhou dismissed on the pretext of his "resistence to Party leadership." This was reported in Beijing's *Zhongguo Fazhi Bao* and also in Hong Kong's *Cheng Ming*, No. 35, Sept. 1980, p. 87. Because of the wide publicity of the incident, Zhou has since been reinstated to his post as chief procurator and Ji has been under investigation. For a comment on this episode, see Mao Rongjie, "Which is Superior, the 'Official' or the Law?" *Renmin Ribao* July 29, 1981, p. 5.

100. *Minzhu Yu Fazhi*, No. 8, 1983, p. 35.

101. *Beijing Review*, Vol. 22, No. 9, March 2, 1979, p. 3; FBIS, *Daily Report: PRC*, Sept. 23, 1980 (supplement), p. 4.

102. In a book on crime stories of contemporary China (see above Chapter Three, note 70), some fictitious Judge Bao figures are also included. See "Public Procurator from Beijing" and "After Cracking the Case," Cen Ying, ed., *Zhongguo Dalu Zuian Xiaoshuoxuan* (A Selection of Chinese Mainland Crime Stories) (Hong Kong: Tongjun Publishers, n.d., Preface October 1980), pp. 15–29, 218–225.

103. Luo Ting, "The Prisoner Condemned to Die is Still Alive," *Cheng Ming*, No. 57, July 1982, pp. 73–74.

104. See "A Model Court President," *Zhongguo Fazhi Bao*, Feb. 19, 1982, p. 1.; "A Respectable Chinese Procurator," *Zhongguo Fazhi Bao*, May 26, 1982, p. 4; "The Leader of the People's Court of Nanpiao," *Zhongguo Fazhi Bao*, July 2, 1982, p. 1; "The Youxi Intermediate Court Insists Upon the Principle of Seeking Truth from Facts," *Minzhu Yu Fazhi*, No. 2, 1981, p. 34.

105. "Strange Injustice of Taihang," *Guangming Ribao*, Sept. 20, 1980, p. 3; *Renmin Ribao*, Sept. 21, 1980, p. 3.

106. *Minzhu Yu Fazhi*, No. 6, 1980, pp. 24–25.

107. *Minzhu Yu Fazhi*, No. 3, 1980, p. 25.

108. " 'The Tiger Who Returned to the Mountain' Has Fallen into the Net of Justice Once Again—On the Arrest of Zhang Jinjun" and "We Must Never Allow Human Relationships to Break the Legal Net," *Renmin Ribao*, October 12, 1983, p. 4; FBIS, *Daily Report: China*, October 19, 1983, pp. K13–K19.

109. For Jiang Hua's speeches on the question of independent adjudication, see *Minzhu Yu Fazhi*, No. 6, 1981, pp. 4–5 and *Zhongguo Fazhi Bao*, May 29, 1981, p. 1. An eloquent argument for the abolition of approving court judgments by court president and chief judges is presented by Liu Chunmao's article in *Minzhu Yu Fazhi*, No. 1, 1981, pp. 30–31. Other articles on the issue are in pp. 34–36.

110. A speech made at the Third National Conference on Criminal Trial Work on November 18, 1981, reported in *Zhongguo Fazhi Bao*, Nov. 27, 1981, p. 1.

111. See Hsin Fei [Xin Fei in Pinyin], "Tests For the Chinese Communist Legal System," *Chung-pao Yueh-k'an* (Zhongbao Yuekan in Pinyin, Center News Monthly), No. 46, November 1983, pp. 54–56.

112. "Suppression of Criminality," *China News Analysis*, No. 1215, Sept. 11, 1981, pp. 2–3. Details will be examined in Chapter Six of this book.

113. Editorial: "Advance From Our Victory to Improve Social Order," *Renmin Ribao*, Aug. 17, 1981, p. 1.

114. Editorial: "Political and Legal Work Must Render More Conscious Services to the Four Modernizations" *Renmin Ribao*, Aug. 3, 1982, p. 1, translated in FBIS, *Daily Report: China*, Aug. 4, 1982, pp. K1–K2.

115. *Renmin Ribao*, July 15, 1983, p. 1.

116. Shao-chuan Leng, "The Role of Law in the People's Republic of China as Reflecting Mao Tse-tung's Influence," *Journal of Criminal Law and Criminology*, Vol. 68, No. 3, 1977, p. 365.

117. *Journal of Criminal Law and Criminology*, pp. 363–365; J. A. Cohen, "Reflections on the Criminal Process in China," *Journal of Criminal Law and Criminology*, pp. 335–337; *Political Imprisonment in the People's Republic of China* (London: Amnesty International Publications, 1978), pp. 7–13. See also Chapter Two of this book.

118. *Beijing Review*, Vol. 22, No. 4, January 26, 1979, p. 8.

119. Chang Gong, "A Fine Statute on the People's Judicature," *Faxue Yanjiu*, No. 4, 1979, p. 36.

120. Luo Ping, "The Principle of Measuring Penalty in China's Criminal Law," *Hongqi*, No. 9, 1979, p. 75. A similar stand is taken in He Bingsong, "On the Democratic Principle of our Country's Criminal Law," *Faxue Yanjiu*, No. 4, 1980, p. 26.

121. Peng Zhen, "Several Questions on the Socialist Legal System," *Hongqi*, No. 11, 1979, p. 5.

122. Ye Jianying, "Closing Address," *Main Documents of the Second Session of the Fifth National People's Congress of the People's Republic of China* (Beijing: Foreign Languages Press, 1979), pp. 225–226.

123. Yuan Xiaofan, "On the Equality of the Application of Law," *Faxue Yanjiu*, No. 2, 1980, p. 26.

124. Pan Nianzhi and Qi Naikuan, "On 'Everyone is Equal Before the Law'," *Guangming Ribao*, February 9, 1980, p. 3.

125. Cui Min, "How Should We Interpret 'Everyone is Equal Before the Law'," *Renmin Ribao*, July 24, 1979, p. 3.

126. *FBIS, Daily Report: PRC*, July 2, 1980, p. L6.

127. For this case, *Beijing Ribao* on August 9 carried a commentator's article entitled "Warn Those Cadres' Children and Younger Brothers Who Violate the Law and Commit Crimes," *Renmin Ribao*, August 9, 1980, p. 4. See also "High Officials' Sons Punished," *Beijing Review*, Vol. 23, No. 35, Sept. 1, 1980, pp. 7–8.

128. *Xinhua News Agency*, September 2, 1980; "Oil Rig Accident Sternly Dealt With," *Beijing Review*, Vol. 23, No. 36, Sept. 8, 1980, pp. 7–8.

129. *FBIS, Daily Report: PRC*, September 4, 1980, p. L23.

130. *Renmin Ribao*, January 26, 1981, pp. 1, 4.

131. "Advance in the Direction of Strengthening Socialist Democracy and the Legal System," *Hongqi*, No. 3, 1981, p. 15.

132. The delay in the Court's sentencing of the radicals, for instance, was reported to have been caused by the split of the Chinese leadership over the fate of Jiang Qing, and the final judgments were said to have been a compromise approved by the CCP Politburo. See "China's Leaders Said to be Split on the Sentencing of Jiang Qing," *New York Times*, January 11, 1981, p. 7 and James P. Sterba, "Former Chinese Leaders Given Long Prison Terms," *New York Times*, Jan. 26, 1981, p. A1.

133. On January 25, 1983, Jiang's suspended death sentence was reduced to life imprisonment, see *Renmin Ribao*, January 26, 1983, p. 1.

134. Li Ming-fa (Li Mingfa in Pinyin), "The Chinese Leadership's Dispute Over the Sentencing of Jiang Qing," *Cheng Ming*, No. 40, 1981, p. 23.

135. See remarks made by Deputy Yang from Jiangxi and Deputy Zhang from Sichuan in *Renmin Ribao*, Sept. 18, 1980, p. 3.

136. See Lu Ming, "Big Cases and Little People," *Minzhu Yu Fazhi*, No. 3, 1982, pp. 25–26; Chen Lang, "Flies and Tigers," *Minzhu Yu Fazhi*, No. 4, 1982, p. 5; *Tianjin Ribao* commentator's article, "Strengthen Leadership and Concentrate Efforts on Investigating and Handling Big, Serious Cases," FBIS, *Daily Report: China*, August 10, 1982, pp. R4–R5; Xu Xing, "Besides Flies, It Would be Good to Attack Tigers Too," *Cheng Ming*, No. 53, March 1982, pp. 42–45.

137. *Minzhu Yu Fazhi*, No. 7, 1982, p. 42.

138. Luo Ping, "Following Deng Xiaoping on a News Gathering Trip," *Cheng Ming*, No. 53, March 1982, p. 4 (also *FBIS, Daily Report: China*, March 4, 1982, p. W4); "Wang Weijing Jailed for Two Years," *Dagong Bao* (L'Impartial), April 4, 1982, p. 1.

139. Luo Ping, *Cheng Ming*; Shan Feng and Hu Di, "How Many People Have Turned on the 'Green Light' for Him?" *Minzhu Yu Fazhi*, No. 1, 1981, pp. 28–30.

140. *Renmin Ribao*, April 14, 1982, p. 2.

141. *Renmin Ribao*, April 13, 1982, p. 1.

142. Xi Ping and Luo Maocheng, "Uprightness Triumphs Over Evil," *Renmin Ribao*, April 19, 1982. According to them, the two other cadres expressed similar support for punishment of their sons. See also "Senior Cadres Support Sentences on Their Criminal Sons," *Beijing Review*, Vol. 25, May 17, 1982, p. 5.

143. David Bonavia, "A Comradely Crackdown," *Far Eastern Economic Review*, Vol. 122, No. 44, November 3, 1983, p. 43; *AP*, Beijing, October 12, 1983.

144. Hsin Fei, "Tests For the Chinese Communist Legal System," see above note 111, p. 56.

145. Leng, *Justice in Communist China*, pp. 151–153; Cohen, *The Criminal Process*, pp. 556–563.

146. This stipulation is interpreted as important to the removal of defendants' fear to appeal and to the protection of innocent people against unjust and wrong verdicts. Tao Mao and Li Baoyue, "The Principle of 'Not Increasing Sentences on Appeal' Should Not Be Negated," *Minzhu Yu Fazhi*, No. 2, 1980, pp. 25–26.

147. *Renmin Ribao*, Dec. 12, 1981, p. 3.

148. Berman, *et al*, "A Comparison of the Chinese and Soviet Codes," see above note 8, pp. 245–246.

149. *Lectures on the Criminal Procedure Law*, p. 118.

150. *FBIS, Daily Report: PRC*, Sept. 23, 1980 (supplement), p. 42.

151. "Continue to Reverse Unjust and Erroneous Verdicts Based on False Charges," *Guangming Ribao*, June 28, 1979, p. 1.

152. This provision is described as a design to simplify procedures and to reduce the workload of the Supreme People's Court. The decision on this arrangement was first made by the Supreme People's Court in 1958 and is now confirmed by this article. *Lectures on the Criminal Procedure Law*, p. 112.

153. See Zhao Canbi, "Strengthen the Concept of the Legal System and Act According to the Law," *Hongqi*, No. 8, 1979, pp. 42–43; Ge Ping and Wang Honggu, "On Capital Punishment," *Faxue Yanji*, No. 1, 1980, pp. 29–32, 44; Chen Yiyun and Kong Qingyun, "On Capital Punishment," *Renmin Ribao*, February 25, 1980, p. 3.

154. The provision concerning the underage youth and pregnant women is in Article 44 of the Criminal Law. Article 154 of the Law of Criminal Procedure also provides that execution will be stayed if the condemned is found to be pregnant and the case will be submitted to the Supreme People's Court for resentencing according to law.

155. "Beijing Rapist-Murderer Executed," *Xinhua News Agency*, August 18, 1979; "Beijing TV Shows Execution of Hangzhou Rapist," *FBIS, Daily Report: PRC*, Dec. 6, 1979, pp. L9–L10.

156. *Renmin Ribao*, June 11, 1981, p. 1; *FBIS, Daily Report: China*, June 11, 1981, p. K4.

157. *Renmin Ribao*, September 3, 1983, p. 3.

158. See Chapter Six for more details.

159. *Renmin Ribao*, Sept. 3, 1983, p. 3.

160. *Renmin Ribao*, p. 4; *FBIS, Daily Report: China*, September 6, 1983, pp. K12–K13.

161. Department of State, *Country Report on Human Rights Practices For 1983* (Washington, D.C.: U.S. Government Printing Office, 1984), "China," p. 743. For other

preports, see Colin Campbell, "To Shame Its Felons, China Puts Them on Parade," *New York Times,* September 16, 1983, p. A2.

162. "Briefing by People's Court President," *New York Times,* April 14, 1980, p. L2.

163. "Party Discipline Should Not Replace State Law," *Jiefang Ribao* (Liberation Daily), Oct. 7, 1980, p. 3.

164. *Renmin Ribao,* Oct. 4, 1980, p. 3.

Crime and Punishment

As noted before, China under Mao had no criminal codes to guide judicial work; statutes governing specific crimes such as counterrevolution and corruption as well as unpublished regulations on penalties for murder, rape, arson, and other offenses did exist.[1] Mao's emphasis on the societal model of law and on "politics in command" also resulted in the frequent application by the police of administrative sanctions against antisocial behavior and the habitual use by judicial cadres of the Chairman's speeches, Party directives or the *People's Daily's* editorials as guidance to their adjudication activity.[2]

Among the major changes in the post-Mao era was the enactment of China's substantive and procedural criminal laws in 1979. Composed of 192 articles, the new Criminal Law is the first comprehensive law of its kind to define punishable acts and appropriate sanctions for judicial work in the PRC. Like the Criminal Procedure Law, it bears a strong resemblance to its Soviet counterpart, the 1960 Russian Soviet Federated Socialist Republic (RSFSR) Criminal Code; however, it has many features distinctively Chinese.[3] Prominent examples are the Chinese Criminal Law's emphasis on punishment of wrongdoers rather than wrongful acts; its use of highly moralistic words such as "heinous" and "monstrous" to describe the elements of some offenses; and its inclusion of many types of crimes closely related to specifically Chinese circumstances, ranging from forging or reselling ration coupons to the "brutalitization" of family members.[4]

The purpose of this chapter is to discuss the aims and principles of China's criminal justice under the new Law and the measures used to handle adult crimes, juvenile delinquencies, and political offenses; the role of noncriminal, administrative sanctions will also be examined.

Principles and Criteria for Determining Criminality and Sanctions

The main objective of the Chinese criminal justice system is to protect, first of all, the socialist order and next, the people's personal rights. According to Article 2 of the Criminal Law, the task of the new Law is to "use punishment to struggle against all counterrevolutionary and other criminal acts" in order to

(1) protect the system of proletarian dictatorship;

(2) safeguard socialist property of the whole people, property collectively owned by the laboring masses, and legitimate private property of citizens;

(3) protect citizens' personal, democratic and other rights:

(4) maintain public order and order in production, order in work, order in education and research, and order in people's lives; and

(5) ensure the smooth progress of the socialist revolution and socialist construction.[5]

Article 10 of the Law defines crime as any act which endangers society and is punishable by law.[6] As seen from legal provisions and Chinese jurists' commentaries, there are three basic criteria for differentiating criminal from noncriminal conduct. First, an offense is an act that endangers society. The emphasis is on a "socially dangerous act." The mere possession of an "erroneous thought" should not be considered a crime. Second, criminal conduct is an act that violates China's Criminal Law. Those socially dangerous acts which violate civil law or administrative regulations are not crimes. Only an act that endangers society seriously enough in violation of the Criminal Law is an offense. Third, a crime is an act that is punishable by law. To constitute an offense, the act in question must be a socially dangerous one committed intentionally or through negligence and subject to criminal punishment as prescribed by the Criminal Law.[7]

The Criminal Law stipulates eight types of crimes and their penalties in the Special Part. These offenses are:

(1) counterrevolutionary offenses;

(2) offenses of endangering public security;

(3) offenses of undermining the socialist economic order;

(4) offenses of infringing the personal rights or democratic rights of the citizens;

(5) offenses of encroachment upon property;

(6) offenses of disrupting the governing of social order;

(7) offenses against marriage or family; and

(8) malfeasance.[8]

Counterrevolutionary Crimes (Articles 90–104)

The Special Part of the Criminal Law begins with major crimes against the state, so-called "counterrevolutionary offenses," the equivalent of what the Soviet Criminal Code now calls "especially dangerous crimes against the state." [9] In the view of Harold Berman and his colleagues, the Chinese Criminal Law contains some vague and sweeping provisions on "counterrevolution," reminiscent of the 1926 Russian Criminal Code. [10]

Article 90 of China's Criminal Law defines counterrevolutionary crime as "acts done for the purpose of overthrowing the political power of the dictatorship of the proletariat and the socialist system and endangering the People's Republic of China." Among the specific acts of counterrevolution listed by the Criminal Law are conspiring with a foreign state to jeopardize the sovereignty and security of China, plotting to overthrow the government or split the country, instigating an armed rebellion, committing espionage or supporting the enemy, and carrying out sabotage with a counterrevolutionary motive. Also labeled as a counterrevolutionary offense is "using counterrevolutionary slogans, leaflets or other means to spread propaganda inciting the overthrow of the regime of the dictatorship of the proletariat and the socialist system" (Article 102). Although the new Law is definitely an improvement over the old statute on counterrevolution,[11] its inclusion of the above provision, nevertheless, cannot but cause some concern in view of the past and potential abuses. In 1958, for instance, a twelve-year-old youth was sentenced to a five-year prison term for allegedly shouting wrong slogans in a parade: "Oppose World Peace" and "Oppose U.S. Withdrawal from Lebanon." [12] In 1974, the authors of the famous Li Yi Zhe poster "On Socialist Democracy and the Legal System" were also imprisoned for "counterrevolutionary activity" and were not released and exonerated until early 1979.[13] Aware of this problem, Chinese commentators blame Lin Biao and the Gang of Four for past injustices and urge that special care be taken to differentiate counterrevolutionary conduct from unintentional and careless errors, especially those made by innocent junveniles.[14]

Offenses of Endangering Public Security (Articles 105–115)

Any acts that harm public safety or harm the security of person or property of the public belong to this category. They range from destruction of enterprises, communications, and transport facilities by arson, possession of arms and ammunition, and violation of regulations on the control of dangerous substances, thus causing serious accidents.

Offenses of Undermining the Socialist Economic Order (Articles 116–130)

They include, among others, smuggling, speculation, tax evasion, and counterfeiting of national currency. Article 119 provides that a state functionary who takes advantage of his position to engage in smuggling, speculation, and profiteering shall be severely punished.[15]

Offenses of Infringing the Personal Rights or Democratic Rights of the Citizens (Articles 131–149)

Among the offenses enumerated by the Law are homicide, inflicting injury, rape, kidnapping, forcing women into prostitution, interfering with the elections, and tampering with someone else's mail. To prevent the recurrence of flagrant abuses of the past, the Law prohibits extortion of confessions through torture or gathering a crowd for "beating, smashing and looting" (Articles 135–7). Penalties are also stipulated against false charges, perjury, illegal detention, illegal searches or entries, and slander and libel, including the use of wall posters (Articles 138, 143–5). State functionaries who abuse their power, indulge in jobbery, or retaliate against complainants, petitioners or critics shall be subject to criminal sanction (Article 146).

Offenses of Encroachment Upon Properties (Articles 150–156)

They include the offenses of robbery, theft, swindling, plundering, extortion, destruction of property, and embezzlement of public funds by state officials.

Offenses of Disrupting the Governing of Social Order (Articles 157–178)

Included in the long list of offenses under this category are obstruction of official business, mob disturbances, hoodlum activities, harboring of criminals, manufacturing or selling narcotics or pornography, engaging in business for gambling or prostitution, damaging or illegally transporting valuable cultural relics, and violation of border control regulations.

Offenses Against Marriage or Family (Articles 179–184)

The Law imposes criminal sanctions on six offenses which violate the Marriage Law and disrupt marriage and the family.[16] They are:

interference with the freedom of marriage; bigamy; breaking up a military marriage; maltreatment of a family member; abandonment of the old, the young or the invalid; and abducting minors under the age of fourteen.

Malfeasance (Articles 185–192)

In addition to some relevant provisions on state personnel mentioned earlier, these articles here are specifically stipulated against malfeasance in office. Among the offenses listed are: bribery, divulging of "state secrets" (see pages 26, 130, 182–187); dereliction of duty; fraudulent practices in judicial work; and maltreatment of persons under detention and surveillance.

The offenses outlined above are stipulated with their respective penalties. As done in the past, the Criminal Law categorizes punishment into principal and supplementary ones. The principal punishments are:

(1) control, a special Chinese practice, which ranges from three months to two years of work with pay;

(2) detention of fifteen days to six months during which time appropriate pay is given for work done and one or two days leave is granted each month;

(3) fixed-term imprisonment from six months to fifteen years;

(4) life imprisonment; and

(5) the death sentence, including the one with a two-year reprieve.

The supplementary punishment consists of fines, deprivation of political rights, and confiscation of property.[17]

China's criminal sanctions are intended not only to punish offenders but to reform criminal elements through education and corrective labor. They also serve to educate the general public with the use of open trials or sentence-pronouncing mass rallies.[18] Imprisonment is actually synonymous with reform through labor and can be served in a prison or in a labor camp where inmates are expected to be transformed into new men under the policy of uniting productive labor with political education.[19] Capital punishment, according to the Criminal Law, is imposed only for those counterrevolutionary offenses that "are seriously endangering the state and the people or the situation of a particularly heinous nature" (Article 103) and for other most heinous crimes such as homicide, robbery, arson, rape, dike-breaching, planting explosives, and embezzling public property (Articles 106, 110, 132, 139, 150 and 155).[20] The Chinese regard capital punishment as a necessary deterrent to protect the socialist order and the people's interest. Sensitive about the image of the PRC's past record, they stress the limitations placed on the employment of the death penalty by the present Criminal Law.[21] Article 44 of the Law, for instance, exempts from capital punishment young people committing crimes while under eighteen years of age and women pregnant during trial. Article 43 provides that "except for a death sentence rendered by the Supreme People's Court, all others shall be submitted to the Supreme People's Court for examination and approval." [22] The Law also retains a unique PRC innovation to suspend (in most cases) the death penalty for a two-year period during which reform through labor will be carried out to see if the offender shows evidence of repentance to warrant commutation (Articles 43 and 46).[23]

While the principle of combining punishment with reform constitutes basic guidelines for the PRC's criminal justice, the phrase "taking the facts as the basis and law as the criterion" appears to govern the application of Chinese criminal penalties.[24] Article 57 of the Criminal Law states: "Punishment for the offender should be determined by the facts, nature and circumstances of the offense and the degree of its harm to society. Sentence shall be based on the provisions of the Criminal Law." In the words of Chinese writers, full facts of a crime and its consequences rather than subjective assumptions should be the basis for conviction and measuring penalties. Thorough investigation and hard evidence should be stressed. No longer is the employment of torture or other illegal means to secure confessions tolerated. Nor is it permissible to use the offender's social origin and class background as a premise to mete out punishment; continuing to do so would be in violation of the principle that in judicial proceedings all citizens are equal before the application of law, provided by Article 4 of the Criminal Procedure Law.[25]

The requirement of "taking law as the criterion" is truly a significant feature of criminal justice in post-Mao China. Having laws instead of words to rely on, judicial officials now can name offenses and determine appropriate penalties more precisely and confidently in accordance with the provisions of the Criminal Law. Although continuing to pay lip service to the importance of Mao's famous 1957 speech on "Correct Handling of Contradictions," some Chinese jurists nevertheless openly argue that the Criminal Law rather than Mao's theory of contradictions should serve as the standards for the assessment of offenses and measurement of punishments.[26]

In circumstances where a heavier or lighter penalty is imposed on an offender, the sentence shall fall within the scope of maximum and minimum punishments prescribed by the Criminal Law (Article 58). With the approval of the Adjudication Committee of the People's Court, a penalty below the minimum may also be legally imposed (Article 59). However, the Criminal Law does not provide a list of aggravating and mitigating circumstances to guide the court in determining the penalty in a given case. The existence of such latitude, some Chinese authors contend, is necesary so that law enforcement may be adapted to the needs of the political situation. According to them, the basis for measuring penalties is the degree of harm to society, and degree of harm to society is not only determined by the sum total of all the components of the crime in question but also influenced by current, extraneous conditions. It was for this reason that the NPC Standing Committee adopted in June 1981 and again in September 1983 strong measures to deal with the pressing problems of crime.[27]

Obviously, the offender's attitude toward his crime and the degree of his repentance are among the pertinent factors considered in sentence determination. Although the principle of "leniency to those who confess and severity to those who resist" is not formally incorporated into the Criminal Law, its spirit appears to run through the entire Law.[28] There are provisions for heavy punishment for recidivists (Article 61) and reduced penalties for offenders who voluntarily surrender or perform meritorious service (Article 63). In a resolution adopted in March 1982 by the NPC Standing Committee to punish economic criminals, there was a specific stipulation for "lenient treatment of those who acknowledge their crimes and severe punishment of those who stubbornly refuse to do so." [29]

A major problem in China's past criminal legislation has been the application of analogy and retroactivity.[30] The present Law eliminates the use of retroactivity by stipulating that offenses committed before the date of its promulgation shall be dealt with in accordance with the laws, decrees and policies at the time when the infractions occurred (Article 9). However, it does retain the principle of analogy with certain restrictions, as Article 79 provides: "A person who commits crimes not explicitly defined in the specific parts of the Criminal Law may be convicted and sentenced, after obtaining the approval of the Supreme People's Court, according to the most similar article in this Law." Most Chinese jurists defend the "restrictive" use of analogy as necessary and realistic but suggest that in the future China may work to adopt the principle of nullum crimen, nulla poena sine lege.[31]

Another issue of concern about China's past penal regulations has been the presence of many vague and sweeping provisions, open to a wide range of interpretations. The present Criminal Law is clearly an improvement but some problems remain. Take, for example, the term "state secrets" referred to in Article 186 of the Criminal Law.[32] The Chinese definition of this term is so broad as to give rise to considerable international attention and criticism. In 1980, the PRC republished the Provisional Act on Guarding State Secrets, first issued in 1951. The Act enumerates fifteen categories of state secrets to include those concerning national defense, the armed forces, foreign affairs, the police, state economic planning, transportation and communication systems, natural resources, culture, education, public health, and legislative and judicial affairs. In addition, the Act has two all-embracing categories: the sixteenth covers "all state affairs which have not yet been decided upon or which have been decided upon but have not been made public" and the seventeenth goes on to add "all other state affairs which should be kept secret." [33]

State secrets as defined above would indeed mean almost anything not publicly released.[34] In 1979, a teacher used his position as a member of the admission committee of his county high school to help his son and younger brother with examination questions; he was later tried, convicted, and sentenced to one year in prison (with the punishment suspended for two years) for disclosing state secrets as prescribed in Article 182 of the Criminal Law.[35] The same Article was invoked by a People's Court in early 1982 to sentence a Chinese editor to a five-year imprisonment for leaking details of the agenda of a Communist Party meeting to a Japanese reporter. As this incident caused an uproar among foreign journalists, *Beijing Review* found it necessary to defend the sentence and offered the following interpretation: "Before they are made public, all of the Party's private activities are state secrets." [36] Another international incident, which occurred in late May–early June 1982, involved the detention and expulsion of an American graduate student, Lisa Wichser, on charges of participating in the theft of "state secrets". The American girl was reported to have obtained the CCP Central Committee materials on economic subjects for preparing her dissertation.[37] In May 1983, China disclosed that Lo Chengxun, editor in chief of a pro-Communist daily in Hong Kong, *Xin Wanbao* (New Evening Post) had been sentenced in Beijing to ten years in prison on charges of supplying "important secret information" on China's political, diplomatic, and military affairs to an unidentified U.S. intelligence agency.[38] More recently, it was officially confirmed that Hanson Huang, a Hong Kong-born and Harvard-trained lawyer, who disappeared in China in 1982, had been arrested, tried, and convicted for espionage and sentenced to a fifteen-year imprisonment. According to Hong Kong news report, Mr. Huang was accused of passing classified information about China's energy resources to the United States.[39]

CRIME SITUATION

The preceding pages have examined the basic legal framework for determining criminal offenses and appropriate penalties in post-Mao China. In the following section our attention will be focused on the way certain types of crimes have been handled by the Chinese authorities.

Reluctance on the part of the PRC to report crimes in the past has helped create a myth that Mao's China was practically a crime-free society.[40] In recent years, however, the Chinese have been more open in admitting existing social problems and have occasionally given out crime figures. At a speech to a U.N. crime conference in August, 1980, Vice-Justice Minister Xie Bangzhi disclosed that China's present crime rate averaged about 570,000 a year. From 1950 to 1965, he said, the average number of cases annually was only 290,000.[41] In a report to the National People's Congress in August, 1980, Chief Procurator Huang Huoqing also talked about the increase of crime in the country. According to him, during the first half of 1980, more than 84,000 criminal offenders were prosecuted and more than 50 percent of them were suspects of serious crimes.[42] Both Xie and Huang cited the disrupting impact of the Cultural Revolution on China's social order and ethics and the growth of the young population as chief reasons for the rise of crime rate.

Aside from the above official explanation, China's increasing lawlessness and social disturbances may also be attributed to the problem of unemployment and the frustration and resentment of disaffected groups and individuals. In October 1980, for example, a man who had not been allowed to return to his home in Beijing after being forcibly resettled in the countryside ten years ago, set off an explosion in the Beijing Railroad Station killing nine people, including himself, and injuring eighty-one others.[43] In early 1981, the army was called to maintain order in Shanghai where some 1,000 unemployed people demonstrated for jobs.[44] In January 1982, a disgruntled taxi driver in Beijing docked of her bonus after a dispute with her superior over wages, drove her car at a high speed into a crowd at Tienanmen Square, killing five persons and injuring nineteen.[45]

Another factor causing the rising crime rate appears to be the tendency of people to abuse the new economic freedoms offered by the present leadership and by trade and other contacts developed with foreign countries. In 1980, procuratorial organs at various levels reportedly handled 14,532 criminal cases of an economic nature, including corruption, bribery, tax evasion, speculation, and smuggling.[46] The State Council issued a special directive, calling on the various localities to strengthen market control and punish those engaged in smuggling and speculation.[47] The South in general, and Guangzhou (Canton), in particular, took stiff measures against smuggling, black-marketing and other economic offenses.[48] An official of an Overseas Chinese Association in Fujian Province was sentenced to death with a two-year reprieve by an intermediate court for embezzlement of huge sums of overseas Chinese remittances and bank savings.[49] Applauding strong sanctions against economic criminals, *Nanfang Ribao* of Guangzhou (Canton) stated that their illegal activities were not merely economically harmful but would also "affect the activism of the masses in building the four modernizations, corrupt our social atmosphere, corrode and poison the ideology of the people, and undermine the consolidation of the proletarian rule."[50]

As a move to restore public order and curb the wave of serious crimes, Chinese authorities were reported to have increased the use of capital punishment in 1979–80. A check of official press and courthouse notices revealed that at least 198 persons had been executed and another 214 sentenced to death with a two-year reprieve in the year ending June 30, 1980.[51] Most of those executed were convicted of murder and rape; some for crimes of armed robbery, drug peddling and gold speculation. An infamous embezzler named Wang Shouxin was executed in February 1980 for taking about $350,000 from the fuel company where she was manager.[52] An even more publicized case was the Hangzhou rape trial and the execution of Xiong Ziping, leader of the gang. On November 14, 1979, the intermediate court of Hangzhou held a mass sentencing meeting, attended by some 6,000 people, to announce the sentencing of Xiong Ziping to death. The condemned was immediately executed and later the whole proceedings were shown in a four minute report on China's television news.[53]

Despite these measures, violent and other major crimes continued to cause concern in the first half of 1981. *Hebei Ribao* reported rampant criminal activities in some areas where criminals "have stolen firearms and killed people, have committed arson and set off explosions, have waylaid people, and have raped or gang-raped women."[54] An article in *Sichuan Ribao* also stated that "major cases seriously endangering social order are still occurring." If we should fail to deal resolute blows at the criminal activities, it said, "economic readjustment and political stability will be sabotoged, and people's democratic rights and even their rights of existence will be endangered."[55] Amidst the reported official concerns and public dissatisfaction with the situation, the Political-Legal Committee of the Chinese Communist Party Central Committee convened a forum at Beijing in mid-May, 1981, on public security in the five large cities of Beijing, Tianjin, Shanghai, Guangzhou (Canton) and Wuhan. The forum participants agreed, among other things, that "it is imperative to continue meting out heavy and swift punishment according to law to a small number of murderers, robbers, rapists, bomb throwers, arsonists and other criminals who seriously endanger society and especially to the abettors, prime culprits, and recidivists." The emphasis was on heavy and swift punishment. As pointed out by the forum, "Severity means to impose the maximum penalty within the scope of the law, not outside it. Swiftness means being prompt not dilatory in handling cases according to the time limit set by law." [56]

In response to this and other views expressed throughout the country, the NPC Standing Committee adopted on June 10, 1981 three resolutions concerning legal matters to cope with the pressing problems of crime.[57] Two of these resolutions served to modify or supplement the Criminal Law; one on approval of the death penalty and the other on escapees and recidivists.[58] The first one granted for the period of 1981–83 the right to approve death sentences on murderers, robbers, rapists, bomb throwers, arsonists, and saboteurs to the higher people's courts of the provinces, autonomous regions, and municipalities directly under the central authorities.[59] Approval of the Supreme People's Court, however, shall continue to be required for death sentences passed on counterrevolutionaries and embezzlers.[60] The second resolution provided heavy penalties for escapees who are under reform through labor or reeducation through labor. Heavier or additional punishments will be imposed on recidivists who refuse to mend their ways after release from reeducation through labor or reform through labor. After the escapees or recidivists serve their new terms, they are required to get jobs on farms and not to return to their home cities.[61]

These resolutions were hailed by the Chinese press as important and necessary decisions for dealing timely and telling blows at active perpetrators of serious crimes.[62] In an editorial, the *People's Daily* put blame on the pernicious influence of Lin Biao—Jiang Qing cliques and the failure of political and judicial departments to take effective measures against criminals for poor public security in some places. It urged all localities and all judicial and public security personnel to conscientiously study, publicize, and enforce the NPC Standing Committee's resolutions.[63] To improve public security, an editorial in the *Liberation Daily* also called for resolute, severe and swift punishment of criminals according to these resolutions and the Criminal Law. "By severe punishment," it said, "we mean we must base ourselves on facts, follow the legal procedure and impose severe penalties within the range of punishments as stated in the law." "By swift punishment, we mean that measures must be taken to investigate the basic facts of major crimes in order to crack down criminal cases, prosecute and try them and impose penalties as quickly as possible." [64] This editorial and the other press commentaries all suggested that mass rallies be held to pronounce judgment on important cases so as to give wide publicity to the legal system, display the might of the people's democratic dictatorship, enhance the morale of the general public, and strike terror into criminal hearts.[65]

What followed was a vigorous nationwide drive against crime. Conferences were held from Beijing to Guizhou province to discuss ways to implement the NPC Standing Committee's resolutions, to publicize the socialist legal system, and to strike timely and heavy blows at offenders who commit crimes of murder, robbery, rape, arson, and bombings.[66] Reports of mass meetings to pronounce death sentences became frequent. For instance, on June 16, 1981, the Nanning Municipal Intermediate People's Court held a judgment-pronouncing mass meeting of 40,000 people at the Nanning Municipal Stadium. A murderer, robber, and escapee was sentenced to death, and executed immediately after the meeting.[67] On June 23, 1981, the Nanjing Municipal Intermediate People's Court convened a 10,000 people mass rally, where a "cruel" murderer named Luo received the death penalty and was immediately executed. The interesting point of this case is that it took only eight days for the whole legal process from the arrest of Luo to his execution, including the trial, sentencing, and his appeal to the Guangxi Provincial Higher Court.[68] On June 27, 1981, the Harbin Municipal Intermediate People's Court held a rally at the Harbin Workers Gymnasium, attended by 5,000 people, to pronounce sentences on eleven criminals, involved in four criminal cases of robbery, murder and gang rape. Four were sentenced to death, one received the death penalty with a two-year reprieve, and the other six were given various terms of imprisonment. After the rally, six other offenders who had been sentenced to death in May on charges of robbery and murder were executed.[69] On June 27, 1981, the Guangzhou Municipal Intermediate People's Court also held a 6,000 people mass meeting on four cases involving a total of fourteen rapists, robbers and spies. Sentenced to death and executed immediately was Gua Lianhong, leader of a clique of rapists and robbers and two-time escapee from reform through labor and reeducation through labor camps.[70] On July 18, 1981, the Beijing Municipal Intermediate People's Court convened a mass meeting of 18,000 people at the Beijing Gymnasium to pronounce verdicts on six persons for crimes of murder, rape, and armed robbery. Five were sentenced to death and were escorted to the execution ground to be shot, while the sixth, having "established merits" by exposing the others, was given a death sentence with two-year reprieve.[71] Reports of all the cases cited here indicated that the death sentences had been reviewed and approved by the higher people's courts in advance. Only Gua Lianhong's sentence is said to have been reported to the Supreme People's Court for ratification.[72]

There were other examples of implementing the policy of severe and swift punishment of criminals according to the law. The people's courts at various levels in Wuhan reportedly disposed of 204 criminal cases in just twenty days. In the 122 serious cases, eighty-three offenders were sentenced to imprisonment for terms of over six years, three to life imprisonment, and eight to death.[73] As a result of the anticrime campaign in 1981–1982, official sources reported a decrease in crime and an improvement in social order both nationally and in some large cities. According to the statistics of eighteen cities, within the month after the adoption of the anticrime resolutions by the NPC Standing Committee in June 1981, over 4,000 law offenders surrendered themselves, over 820 escapees returned to reformatories, and more than 1,600 escapees from labor camps were caught. Incomplete statistics from sixteen provinces, municipalities, and autonomous regions also indicate that during 1981 the masses reported more than 168,000 criminal cases and turned over some 68,000 offenders to the authorities.[74] In the first six months of 1982, there were 57,000 criminal cases in the eighteen major cities with populations exceeding one million, which was 25.1 percent fewer than during the same period of 1981, and 10.4 percent fewer than the latter half of 1981.[75] Throughout the country some 750,000 crimes were reported for the year of 1982.[76] Although low by the Western standards, the figures were still considered too high by the Chinese authorities, who were particularly concerned that the rates of serious crimes, including murder and rape, had not dropped appreciably in recent years. In his report to the National People's Congress on June 6, 1983, for instance, Premier Zhao Ziyang had this to say:

> There has been improvement in recent years thanks to the efforts by various quarters, but public order is still not as good as in the best years after the founding of the People's Republic. Such criminal offences as murder, robbery, rape and larceny pose quite a problem in some places. The recent plane hijacking indicates that there are serious loopholes and defects in our system of management, that public security, procuratorial and judicial departments have failed to perform

some of their functions effectively as organs of dictatorship . . .[77]

According to a pro-PRC Hong Kong publication in 1983, over 40,000 Chinese cadres and civilians had been slain in the past three and a half years and only some 8,000 killers had been apprehended.[78] The most notorious criminals were two Wang brothers who were wanted for murdering scores of people from Manchuria to the south, and were finally killed by the police in September 1983.[79] Social order became so bad that even Deng Xiaoping's motorcade was reported to have been attacked by a gang of hooligans in the summer of 1983 near the seaside resort of Beidaihe.[80] Though Deng was not harmed, the incident apparently prompted Beijing to inaugurate a new coordinated nationwide anticrime campaign in 1983.

As mentioned in Chapter Five, at a telephone conference called by the Political-Legal Committee of the CCP Central Committee in early July 1983, Party leaders all stressed the need for swift and severe blow against serious criminal activities. Around the end of July, the latest major crackdown on crime was launched in Tangshan, Hebei Province, where 105 persons accused of belonging to six gangs were arrested by police.[81] Following this, thirty condemned criminals were executed immediately after the sentence-pronouncing mass meeting of 100,000 people held at the Beijing Workers' Gymnasium in August.[82] Other cities and areas across the country also took similar measures in the drive against the so-called "dregs of society."

To facilitate the campaign and to legalize the measures already undertaken by the authorities, the NPC Standing Committee adopted on September 2, 1983 decisions to amend certain stipulations of China's criminal laws for the purpose of "swiftly and severely punishing criminals who seriously jeopardize public security." Besides revising the Criminal Procedure Law to deprive some felons of procedural guarantees as discussed in Chapter Five, the Committee amended Articles 160, 134, 141, 112, 99, 140, and 169 of the Criminal Law. In so doing, it increased the number of capital offenses to 29 by including the following new categories: leading a criminal gang; intentionally injuring or causing death to others or attacking government workers and citizens attempting to stop a crime; kidnapping and trafficking in women and children; illegal making and trading firearms; organizing reactionary and secret societies; enticing, housing, or forcing women to prostitution; corrupting, inciting, or forcing young people to commit offenses by unrepentant recidivists.[83]

Standing Committee Chairman Peng Zhen said that the new drive would enable China to return to the standard of social order it had enjoyed during the late 1950s and early 1960s (crime rate being 2.3

per 10,000 people).[84] Quotas for arrests and executions were reported to have been assigned to provinces and municipalities. Many of those arrested were sent to labor camps in Qinghai and other remote areas. Those condemned to death were often denounced at large public rallies before being executed. The crime suppression campaign was said to have resulted in 100,000 arrests and some 5,000–10,000 executions by January 1984.[85]

Amnesty International sent a letter to Chinese President Li Xiannian on October 21, 1983 urging that China halt the wave of executions. The PRC rejected this appeal and described the executions as "normal measure and routine work" in maintaining public order.[86] Sensitive to foreign criticisms, Chinese spokesmen, nevertheless, have made efforts to defend the anticrime campaign. An article in *Beijing Review*, for instance, argued that criminals had been coddled far too long and that they must be rounded up and severely punished to maintain social stability and safeguard the people's lives and property.[87] Another article in the same publication said that meting out stern punishment "will not only give these lawbreakers what they deserve, but will also serve a warning to other offenders and prevent future crimes." [88] An editorial of *People's Daily* also contended: "Only when we severely crackdown on criminal activities can our country effectively avoid the incurable diseases common in Western capitalist countries, such as unchecked criminal activities, social unrest, and moral degeneration, while our economy gradually becomes prosperous and our people steadily become rich." [89] According to a report of *China's Legal System Paper*, crime rates throughout China have dropped considerably since the inauguration of the law-and-order campaign in August 1983. Criminal cases recorded an overall drop of 46.7 percent nationwide from August to September, with a 38.7 percent decrease in major crimes. In October, there were 11.5 percent fewer criminal cases than in September, while major cases dropped a futher 28.5 percent.[90]

Besides violent crimes, criminal activities in the economic field has also been China's main concern. Reported cases of smuggling, speculation, profiteering, graft, and other economic crimes have been on the increase, particularly in the three coastal provinces of Guangdong, Fujian and Zhejiang where smuggling poses a special problem. Many of the cases have involved state and Party officials, who have abused their positions with corrupt and other illegal practices. Wang Weijing, former CCP secretary and director of the Guangzhou Municipal Telecommunications Bureau, was one such example. Along with his wife (a retired cadre), Wang was arrested, tried, and sentenced to two years in prison in early 1982 on charges of speculation, smuggling and illegal purchase of foreign currency.[91]

Thus far only officials of middle and lower levels have been exposed and punished, but the Chinese leadership seems determined to punish all economic offenders, including top-ranking cadres in order to restore official integrity and protect the program of modernization. The Party's Discipline Inspection Commission, together with the state's judicial organs, has led the drive against corruption and other economic crimes—a current preoccupation of the press and legal and political journals in China.[92]

Just as it did on June 10, 1981 to make changes in the Criminal Law to deal with violent crimes, the Standing Committee of the NPC amended certain provisions of the Criminal Law on March 8, 1982 in a resolution on "Severely Punishing Criminals Who Do Great Damage to the Economy." According to this resolution, whoever commits particularly serious crimes of smuggling, illegal purchase of foreign exchange, speculation for huge profit, selling narcotics, or stealing and exporting cultural relics will be sentenced to ten or more years of imprisonment, life imprisonment, or death (amendments to Articles 118, 152, 171 and 173 of the Criminal Law with heavier penalties for relevant offenses). State functionaries who exploit their office to commit such crimes will be severely punished. The resolution also stated that a state functionary who extorts or accepts bribes will be punished as commiting the crimes of embezzlement. It means that he may be sentenced to life imprisonment or death as provided by Article 155 of the Criminal Law on embezzlement instead of a fix-term imprisonment for bribery prescribed in Article 185. Reflecting the spirit of the principle of "leniency to those who confess and severity to those who resist," the resolution further stipulated that offenders who give themselves up before May 1, 1982 or who, already in custody, confess truthfully all their crimes and report the crimes committed by others will be handled according to the relevant legal provisions existing prior to the enforcement of this resolution on April 1, 1982. Otherwise, they will be considered as perpetuating their crimes and will be handled resolutely in accordance with this resolution.[93]

Unquestionably, the adoption of this resolution demonstrates that whenever the socialist system is perceived to be threatened, Beijing will not hesitate to use harsh measures and revise its laws to meet the challenge. In an editorial on March 10, 1982, the *People's Daily* explained the necessity for severe sanctions against economic offenders:

> The various criminal activities in the economic field,
> especially certain grave cases, are seriously interfering with the
> implementation of the Party's principles and policies,

disturbing social and economic order, endangering the
country's economic construction, undermining the socialist
legal system, harming our national sovereignty, corrupting the
cadres and masses, debasing the Party style and social
atmosphere, and constituting a most serious danger to our
country's socialist cause and the people's interest both
politically and economically. . . . Only by severely punishing
such criminal activities, can we uphold the four fundamental
principles and guarantee the smooth progress of the building
up of socialist material and spiritual civilization.[94]

Following the NPC Standing Committee's resolution of March 8,
1982, there was a rash of confessions to meet the deadline of May
1 for lenient treatment. By April 16, 1982 nearly three thousand
people were reported to have voluntarily surrendered for economic
offenses and have returned stolen money and other stolen property.[95]
Still, economic crimes are continuing to plague the PRC. As observed
by a Western journalist, "Bribery and speculation are now so prevalent
in China that they have become a live political issue, which the
Communist Party says will be a matter of life and death for the
socialist cause and even the party itself. It is not only individuals
who are involved, but whole production brigade, factories and administrative bureaus." [96]

In response to the troubling situation, the CCP Central Committees
and the State Council jointly adopted on April 13, 1982 a decision
on "dealing blows at serious criminal activities in the economic
field." [97] The following summarizes a few important points of the
decision:

(1) Over the past two or three years, serious criminal activities
of smuggling, corruption, bribery, speculation, swindling, and theft
of state and collective property have markedly increased. Sometimes
such activities are carried out under the signboard of state and
collective undertakings and some are even backed up by leading
cadres;

(2) The current struggle is a major mainfestation of class struggle
in the economic sphere of China's socialist society under new historical conditions. It is bound to be protracted;

(3) The law must be enforced strictly and impartially to punish
offenders who have seriously harmed the society, no matter who
they are, what units they belong to, or whatever official posts they
hold. There must be no exceptions. It is absolutely impermissable
for anyone to try to shield them or plead for lenient treatment.

Anyone who violates this principle will be held responsible and punished accordingly;

(4) The current struggle will not take the form of a mass movement, although the mass line should be followed in dealing with major and key cases. Serious investigation and study should be carried in all cases. Under no circumstances should confessions be extorted and credence given to them, and under no circumstances should innocent relatives and friends be implicated;

(5) In the present struggle, Party members must take a clear-cut and resolute stand. Those Party members and state cadres who have committed crimes and done harm to the socialist cause must be given due punishment according to Party, government and military discipline, and state law, respectively.[98]

It is interesting to note that the press reported in July 1982 the first case in the current campaign of a senior official receiving administrative, though not criminal, punishment for "serious mistakes" committed in the economic field. Yang Yibang, Vice-Minister of Chemical Industry, was placed on probation within the Party for two years and stripped of all his Party posts by the CCP Central Committee's Discipline Inspection Commission, which also recommended that he be dismissed from his government position. Among his "mistakes" were the acceptance of bribes in disguised form and mismanagement of international trade business that caused the state to lose hundreds of thousands of dollars.[99]

In a report on July 25, 1983, Han Guang, Secretary of the CCP Central Discipline Inspection Commission, spoke of notable results in the struggle against economic crimes. By the end of April 1983, he said, more than 192,000 cases of economic offenses had been investigated and over 131,000 cases, 71 percent of the total, had been resolved. His information also included the following figures: "More than 30,000 offenders have been sentenced; of the Party members involved, over 8,500 have been expelled from the Party; more than 24,000 people across the country have voluntarily surrendered and confessed their offenses." [100] Despite all this, according to a more recent official source, so far few economic criminal cases have been exposed in major factories, mines, enterprises, and state organizations at the central government and provincial levels. It shows that there are areas practically untouched by the current crackdown and that the fight against serious economic crimes is a prolonged and difficult task.[101] Against this background, a commentator of the People's Daily has taken pains to urge that Party and government leaders adhere to the principle of equality before law and bravely breakthrough obstacles in the struggle against serious economic criminality:

> When cadres commit crimes they must be punished according to law regardless of their level. Their sons and daughters are no exception. Anyone trying to place obstacles or to harbor evildoers must also be dealt with according to party discipline and state law. Under no circumstances must we tolerate him.[102]

JUVENILE DELINQUENCY

One serious social problem troubling the post-Mao leadership is the fact, as pointed out by a 1981 public security forum, that "the overwhelming majority of those disrupting public order are young people, children of workers, peasants, and intellectuals who have grown up in the new society." [103] Jiang Hua also told the National People's Congress in 1983 that "the overwhelming majority of criminals in China today are working people and their sons and daughters." [104] According to one report, China has had ten times more juvenile delinquency recently than in the early 1960s.[105] Other sources indicate that of the criminal offenders apprehended in recent years, some 80 percent have been young people under twenty-five.[106] Most of the cases involve fist-fighting, theft, and hooliganism, while assault and murder account for only 10 to 15 percent. Problems arising from drunkenness appear to be rare and there is no report of drug addiction among Chinese youths and teenagers.[107]

An article in a social science journal of Liaoning Province shows a current trend in continuous growth of juvenile delinquency, with the offenders becoming younger of age and the main offences being rape, robbery, and theft.[108] Another phenomenon, as reported from Jiangsu and Hubei Provinces, is that most of the inmates in the reform through labor and reeducation through labor camps are young people from proletarian families.[109] Moreover, there are children of high-ranking officials who have been reportedly engaged in illegal activities. According to foreign press accounts, fifty-one of them have been under investigation on suspicion of smuggling, black-marketeering, and taking bribes.[110] Some of them have already been arrested.[111] In connection with a gang rape case in which the son of a senior officer of the People's Liberation Army in Chengdu was sentenced to life imprisonment, the Discipline Inspection Commission of the CCP Central Committee issued a notice on April 10, 1982 to warn the whole Party against the danger of youngsters going astray. "Crimes committed by children of leading cadres," the notice said, "are rare but have strong repercussions and, if not duly handled, can directly undermine the Party's prestige and its relations with the masses." [112]

One of the most striking features of China's latest crime suppression drive has been the young age of those arrested or executed for rape, robbery, and other felonies. For instance, none of the thirty criminals executed in Beijing on August 23, 1983 were older than thirty-five.[113] Also, of the fifty-one criminals executed in Beijing in a week of October 1983, forty-three were under thirty and nineteen of these were between ages of eighteen and twenty.[114] As referred to previously, a grandson of the late Marshall Zhu De was reportedly executed in September 1983 for being a gang leader and rapist.[115]

In explaining the causes of juvenile delinquency in China today, official pronouncements attribute the problem, first of all, to the ten turbulent years of the Cultural Revolution, when impressionable young people were brought up in an environment in which "beatings, smashing and looting" were considered "revolutionary actions" and rebellion was actively encouraged. As a result, many of the present young people are unable to distinguish right from wrong and good from evil.[116] Other main reasons given are the inability of a large number of urban youths to find jobs and the failure of the families to give their children a strict upbringing.[117] There are also suggestions that corruptive influences of bourgeois ideology and the bourgeois way of life abroad have contributed to the PRC's current rate of juvenile offenses.[118] Lacking the discriminating ability, one official said, some Chinese youths "are simply fascinated by certain decadent things abroad and ape them avidly. For instance, a young teenager overwhelmed by some of the scenes in an imported film was led to commit rape." [119] Foreign observers, on the other hand, tend to view the problem as a manifestation of the prevailing cynicism, resentment, and alienation of the young people in China. Indeed, "no way out" is a phrase frequently used by Chinese youths to underscore their sense of helplessness and meaninglessness.[120]

Whatever official explanations may be given, the Chinese leadership is undoubtedly aware of the depth and complexity of the youth problem. Our interest here is to see how the PRC now deals with juvenile delinquents and young offenders. The guiding principle of China's Criminal Law is to use education as the primary means and punishment as the auxiliary in handling minors who commit crimes.[121] Article 14 provides: "An offender who is above 16 years of age should bear criminal responsibility. An offender who is between 14 and 16 years of age should bear criminal responsibility if he commits homicide, inflicts serious injury on a person, or commits robbery, arson, repeated theft or other offenses which seriously undermine social order. An offender who is between 14 and 18 years of age should receive a lighter or mitigated penalty. An offender who is exempted from punishment because of not reaching 16 years of age should be required to be disciplined and educated by his parents or guardians. If necessary, he may be taken into custody by the government for upbringing." [122] Article 44 exempts from capital punishment any person who has not reached the age of eighteen at the time of the commission of the crime and also provides the death penalty with a two-year reprieve for any person between sixteen and eighteen years of age who has committed a particulaly serious crime.

Except for serious cases where imprisonment of juvenile delinquents is required by law, the post-Mao leadership appears to have given special attention to the education and transformation of the young. Beijing's policy is aimed at restoring juvenile offenders' self-respect, showing love and concern for them, and educating and helping them to reform with the patience of parents treating their sick children or doctors taking care of their patients.[123] The devices employed by the PRC to discipline—educate the youngsters vary according to the nature of their offenses.

In minor cases of law infraction, teenage offenders are turned over to neighborhood organizations, parents, and teachers for help. Educational aid teams are organized by street committees, residential groups, schools, factories, enterprises, parents, and the police to reeducate the problem youth and make them improve their ways. Chongqing and Wuhan are cited for their excellent work in this field as over half of the delinquents "have turned over a new leaf." [124] In the Siming district of Amoy, sixty-eight educational aid teams have been set up, and one of its residential committees alone has reportedly found employment for over 200 reformed youngsters.[125]

As for cases too difficult for the neighborhood organizations to handle, work-study schools under the local education bureau or board have been especially established in Chinese urban centers to train, educate and correct the teenagers in question. As soon as they have improved, they are to be sent back to either their former factories or to their old schools.[126]

When juveniles commit more serious offenses which call for sterner sanctions, they are not sent to prisons or reform through labor camps but to the corrective centers for juvenile offenders (reformatories). These corrective centers are designed to conduct reform through education of juvenile offenders between the age of thirteen and eighteen.[127] There are in each large Chinese city several reformatories, run jointly by the bureau of education and the bureau of public security. Only the provincial and municipal governments are authroized by law to establish reformatories and reeducation farms (for

young offenders above eighteen).[128] Probably the best known reform
school is the Beijing Municipal Reformatory, which has about 1,000
students between thirteen to sixteen years of age, of whom 5 percent
are girls. They spend half a day on study and half on work. Most
of them work in the fields while some have jobs at the reformatory's
machinery plant. The goal of the institution is to rehabilitate those
children with the combination of painstaking education and strict
discipline. Many juveniles have been released before completing their
terms. The recidivism rate is estimated to be 8–10 percent and most
youngsters are said to have reformed themselves upon release and
have resumed their places in society.[129]

Because, at present, large numbers of offenses are committed by
young people in their late teens and mid-twenties, the Communist
elites have adopted a new policy of "education, reform, and salvation"
towards young offenders in the reform through labor camps as well
as in the reeduction through labor camps. Cadres in charge of these
camps are told to handle young offenders "as parents handle children
with contagious diseases, as doctors handle patients, and as teachers
handle students" to carry out the painstaking task of education and
rehabilitation.[130] Considerable publicity has been given to the work
of some of the camps. The reeducation through labor camp in
Qinhuangdao, for example, is described as a democratically administered institution, where top priority is given to the work of reeducating and helping the erring young people to change.[131] Another
showcase is the reeducation through labor farm in Tuanhe, south of
Beijing. For the first time in the summer of 1982, foreign journalists
were allowed to visit the camp and talked to its inmates.[132] Some
prisons and reform through labor camps in Zhejiang Province are
also reported to have properly treated the young offenders by combining cultural and technical education with the cultivation of spiritual
life.[133] In a series of articles in China's Legal System Paper, the Fourth
Squadron of the No. 2 Prison in Hebei Province has offered its
successful experience in educating and remolding young offenders.[134]
Occasionally, there are reports about certain young offenders who
have passed examinations to achieve the level of engineers and some
others have been permitted to take the entrance examination for
institutions of higher education after being released before the completion of their terms.[135]

Despite government expectations, however, placing reformed youths
after their release is in reality no easy task. Many factories and
schools have reportedly been reluctant to accept youngsters with a
criminal past.[136] On a tour of Beijing's reform institutions, the legal
affairs group of the National Committee of the Chinese People's
Political Consultative Conference discovered that the number of

youngsters who found employment after leaving work-study school and reformatories was small.[137] A public security forum held in 1981 specifically urged that the concerned departments and units not neglect or discriminate against released juveniles in arranging schools and jobs.[138] According to the Deputy Director of the Beijing Municipal Bureau of Public Security, two measures have been adopted to solve the problem. One is to persuade the leadership of the units concerned to accept the reformed youth and the other is for the state to set up a certain quota in labor recruitment for these people.[139]

The more basic solution, of course, lies in the prevention and reduction of juvenile delinquency. To this end, attention is given to the improvement of the social and family environment for the young people and to the cultivation of their law-abiding spirit and habit.[140] Lei Feng again is used as a model for the young to emulate for his hard work, selflessness, patriotism, and commitment to law and order. Not only political education but legal education is emphasized in schools. Since the fall of 1981, China's middle schools have been offering a special course on legal knowledge. The purpose of this course is to teach the young students how to understand and observe the law and how to distinguish what is legal or illegal so that their awareness of social democracy and the socialist legal system can be strengthened and their eagerness to wage struggles against criminal activities can be developed.[141] Family education, too, is being stressed. In a notice issued on April 10, 1982, the CCP Central Committee's Discipline Inspection Commission asked leading cadres at various levels to shoulder the responsibility of educating their children to be law-abiding citizens.[142] Legal journals have also published thoughtful articles on juvenile delinquency and youth crime.[143] A national symposium on juvenile delinquency problems was held in Nanning of Guangxi Province in June 1982. At the symposium, the Society of Juvenile Delinquency of China was established. The announced goal of the Society is to study ways for the protection of youths and juveniles and the prevention of their crimes and also to propose comprehensive measures to deal with juvenile delinquents and young offenders.[144] In the midst of the anticrime campaign in late 1983, a commentator of *China's Legal System Paper* made a special appeal to political-legal workers to use the opportunity to educate, transform, and save those youngsters involved with minor law infraction.[145]

POLITICAL OFFENSES

The term "political offenses" had a broad range of meanings during Mao's time. In fact, anyone who dissented from official policy could easily be labelled as a "counterrevolutionary" or a "rightist" and be punished accordingly.[146] The post-Mao leadership has taken measures to rectify the wrongs and arbitrariness of its predecessor. It released in June 1978 some 111,000 persons who had been detained as "rightists" since 1957.[147] It also decided in early 1979 to restore political and civil rights to members of former "class enemies": former landlords and rich peasants and their descendents.[148] At the end of June 1980, the people's courts at various levels were said to have reviewed over 1.13 million criminal conviction cases handled during the Cultural Revolution and had redressed more than 261,000 cases (over 175,000 counterrevolutionary cases) in which people were unjustly, falsely, and wrongly charged and sentenced.[149]

As mentioned earlier, the present Criminal Law defines in clearer terms than before a long list of acts of counterrevolutionary offenses and their appropriate punishments. To avoid the recurrence of past injustices, the NPC Standing Committee decided on its resolution of July 10, 1981 not to modify the requirement of the Supreme People's Court's approval of capital punishment in counterrevolutionary cases. The recent reports of increasing numbers of executions in the PRC have actually included only a few counterrevolutionaries. One offender named Wen Zhiquan, for instance, was sentenced to death and executed by shooting in Yichun, Heilongjiang Province, for the crime of working for the Soviet Union.[150] Another named Wang Xiwen met the same fate in Handan, Hebei Province, on charges of murder and counterrevolutionary activities in support of the Gang of Four.[151] Still another man named Liu Zhangguang was executed in Sichuan on conviction of stealing guns and explosives,, printing "counterrevolutionary" pamphlets and injuring a policeman.[152] Other executions involved five "counterrevolutionaries" who failed in their attempt to hijack a plane flying from Xian to Shanghai on July 25, 1982.[153] During the latest drive against crime, five alleged agents of Taiwan are also said to have been executed.[154] Other than these, hardly any political offenders have been reportedly put to death. In the most publicized trial of the Lin-Jiang countervoluntionary cliques during November 1980–January 1981, the heaviest punishment meted out to the ten defendants by the Special Court was the death penalty with a two-year reprieve for Jiang Qing and Zhang Chunqiao.[155]

All this must be considered a marked departure from the rule of the fanatical Maoists. Still a pertinent question here is just how the present leaders have otherwise treated Chinese political activists and dissidents. It should be noted that there were times during 1978–1979 when public airing of complaints and open advocacy of democracy were tolerated in China. Wall posters, underground publications, and street demonstrations sprung up in Beijing, Shanghai, Guangzhou (Canton) and other cities to usher a democracy movement with demands for human rights, legality, free elections, freedom of thought and expression, better living conditions, and greater educational opportunities.[156] However, confronted with the potential threat of this movement and the pressure from the conservative elements within the CCP, Deng Xiaoping and his associates soon had to retreat from their bold experiment of political liberalization.

In March 1979, the Chinese authorities began to put restrictions on wall posters and demonstrations. A couple of activists, including Wei Jingsheng, were arrested.[157] On December 6, 1979, in the name of safeguarding social order and protecting stability, Beijing closed down the Democracy Wall in Xidan and assigned another site for posters.[158] In September 1980, the National People's Congress adopted a resolution to amend Article 45 of the Constitution by deleting from it the provision about the Sida ("Four Big Rights"): "to speak out freely, air views freely, hold great debates, and write big-character posters." [159] This meant the banning of all wall posters and underground publications. According to the official explanation, Article 45 of the 1978 Constitution already provided for freedom of speech, correspondence, publication, assembly, association, procession, demonstration, and the freedom to strike; adding Sida to the Constitution was like adding feet to a picture of a snake—absurdly irrelevant.[160] It is further pointed out Sida had close ties with the Gang of Four who used it as a tool to wage unwarranted struggle and throw the country into chaos.[161] "To impose limitations on the irresponsible use of freedom of speech and delete Sida does not in any way limit people's freedom, but protects it," says a prominent Chinese jurist.[162]

Together with the abolition of wall posters and underground journals as an outlet for political expression, the Chinese authorities also arrested leading activists in the tiny democracy movement. Among them was Wei Jingsheng, editor of an underground journal, *Exploration*. Wei wrote a wall poster in March, 1979 demanding democracy and giving a sensational account of life inside the Communist party political prison called Qin Cheng. Subsequently, he and his deputy were arrested for "counterrevoluntionary activity." [163] On October 16, 1979, more than six months after his arrest, Wei was brought to trial by a Beijing Municipal Intermediate Court and sentenced to fifteen years' imprisonment for passing on military secrets regarding the Sino-Vietnamese War to a foreigner and for carrying out counterrevolutionary agitation.[164] The Court invoked as the legal basis for the judgment several articles of the 1951 Counterrevolutionary Act, including Article 16 providing punishment for crime by analogy.[165] Wei lodged an appeal to the Beijing Municipal Higher People's Court, which decided on November 6, 1979 to uphold the original judgment of the lower court. As reasoned by the official line, Wei wrote and distributed "reactionary" articles and launched direct attacks on the "Four Basic Principles" stipulated in the Constitution, namely, the socialist system, the proletarian dictatorship, the leadership of the CCP, and Marxism-Leninism-Mao Zedong thought. His behavior, therefore, went beyond the bounds of holding different views and constituted counterrevolutionary acts aiming at overthrowing the Chinese Socialist system.[166]

Another well-known activist, Fu Yuehua, was sentenced on December 24, 1979 to two years in prison on charges of violating public order and for having led demonstrations of a group of poor people in Beijing early in the year.[167] Among those arrested in 1979, several also received prison sentences in 1980. Two were Shanghai activists, Qiao Zonglin and Wang Fuchen, sentenced to three years' imprisonment for having branded Mao Zedong as a dictator.[168] Another was Liu Qing, a founder of the underground magazine, *April 5 Forum*, who was placed under three years of reeducation through labor for, among other things, having distributed the verbatim record of the trial of Wei Jingsheng.[169] According to his personal memoirs available to the outside world, Liu was detained by the police, brusquely interrogated, thrown into solitary confinement for five months, locked in a Beijing jail, and finally, nine months after his arrest, sent to a labor camp in Shanxi Province with a three-year reeducation. All this was done without a formal arrest, an indictment, or a trial.[170]

Despite Beijing's various measures of curtailment, the small number of Chinese political activists continued to voice their views, publish "newsletters," and maintain unofficial organizations. In an important speech given at the Central Work Conference on December 25, 1980, Deng Xiaoping attacked some "bourgeois" elements' antipathy and antisocialist activities and urged the strengthening of the state machinery to break up various influences disruptive to stability and unity.[171] This speech is said to have reflected both Deng's effort to appease the conservative faction in the Politburo and the deep concerns of the Party leadership about the spurt in the antigovernment protests, civil disobedience, and organization of independent unions in Chinese factories.[172] It was followed by articles in China's influential publications. The *Liberation Daily* said in an article on January 10, 1981, "Certain counterrevolutionary elements have brazenly caused explosions and distributed counterrevolutionary leaflets to oppose the people's democratic dictatorship; some people have formed illegal organizations, published illegal journals, spread antiparty and antisocialist sayings, and also secretly established ties with one another under the pretext of running the election in certain basic-level democratic election activities." The article warned, "If we fail to deal blows at this type of activity, the people's democratic rights and even their right to existence will be endangered." [173] In an article rejecting the "bourgeois" concept of absolute freedom of speech, the CCP's theoretic journal, Red Flag, stated on April 1, 1981 that while not making people "ideological criminals," China, however, would not let anyone spreading counterrevolutionary opinions go unopposed and unpunished. "To those who have deliberately carried out counterrevolutionary agitation, established secret ties, held clandestine meetings, printed illegal publications, and conspired to spread chaos, we must mete out punishment according to the relevant provisions of our Criminal Law." [174]

Pursuant to the call for striking at "disruptive elements," public security personnel started another drive to round up some key political dissidents. Xu Wenli, editor of the April 5 Forum, and his aide Yang Jing were reportedly arrested in Beijing in April 1981.[175] Also arrested about the same time were Wang Xizhe, a pioneer of Chinese dissent in Guangzhou, Su Feng of the Foam of Waves in Qingdao, and He Qin and Fu Shengqi, prime movers of the National Association of Unofficial Publications, in Beijing.[176] By the end of 1981, most of the leaders of China's democratic movement had been arrested. The total number of the dissident leaders arrested is estimated to be around fifty.[177]

However discouraging to China's fragile democracy and human rights movement, the latest crackdown appeared unlikely to lead to a major campaign against political and intellectual dissenters as ferocious and devastating as the Anti-Rightist Campaign of the 1950s or the Cultural Revolution of the 1960s. Time, decision makers and national priorities have changed significantly since the days of Mao Zedong. There have been indications of important debates going on among the Chinese leaders regarding the degree of political liberalization and the limits of free expression in the PRC. The controversial film, "Unrequited Love" (Ku Lian) which draws a gloomy picture of the Cultural Revolution, is an example. In a savage blast on the film, the Liberation Army Daily criticized the screenplay writer, Bai Hua, for besmirching China's image and the reputation of the Party and socialism.[178] But two top Party leaders, Hu Yaobang and Deng Yingchao (Zhou Enlai's widow) later urged an end to the attack and called for conciliation.[179] Finally, Bai Hua did engage in some form of self-criticism. Nevertheless, he has not been disciplined and has since been back at his writing.[180] Even the campaign against "spiritual pollution" and other unwanted bourgeois influences that began in October 1983 has come to a halt apparently as a result of one group of Party leaders prevailing over another in the split within the Chinese elites.[181]

One of the best known activists that fell victim to the government's clampdown in 1979, Fu Yuehua, is reported to have been released from the Beijing prison in early 1981 after serving a two-year sentence.[182] Our concern is about the fate of other dissidents whose arrest may have or may not have been reported. It is true that in the aforementioned speech by Deng Xiaoping in December 1980, the Chinese leader stressed that the struggle against various "disruptive activities" must be waged "within the bounds of Law." [183] However, loopholes do exist in China's legal system to make the protection of citizens against arbitrary arrest and confinement not always effective. As will be further examined in the next section, the NPC Standing Committee revived in a 1979 resolution a 1957 State Council decision on reeducation through labor, which permits the police and administrative organs to send without trial or court review a wide range of offenders to labor camps for a period of one to four years. Already this measure has reportedly been used by local authorities with increasing frequency against political dissidents.[184] One source estimates the number of persons imprisoned for their political beliefs to be in the thousands.[185]

PARTY DISCIPLINE AND STATE LAW; ADMINISTRATIVE AND CRIMINAL SANCTIONS

Confusion about Party discipline, administrative discipline, and state law is a persistent problem in the PRC, especially when dealing with economic offenses. Two main reasons for this confusion are given by a legal analysist. First, because of the complex nature of many economic issues, it is difficult to differentiate between transgression of Party or administrative discipline and violation of the Criminal Law. Secondly, some misguided cadres are reluctant to employ the legal weapon to strike at crimes committed by other cadres and tend to use Party or administrative discipline as a substitute for state law in applying sanctions.[186] Recently, the press reported a case in which the Yunan Provincial CCP Committee upheld Party discipline by expelling Cheng Zhanbiao, a veteran cadre, from the Party on the ground that he used his position to secure a divorce for his daughter and help her to go to Hong Kong to become the concubine of a merchant, who had showered Cheng's family with luxurious gifts.[187] However, a reader wrote to a legal journal, *Democracy and Legal System*, saying that Cheng's loss of Party membership could not offset his offense and that the authority of China's legal system would be undermined if he was not criminally punished.[188] In another issue of the same journal, an article writer also warned against the practice of applying only the disciplinary measure of criticism-education in handling cadres who violated the law.[189]

In an effort to clarify the confusion, a number of newspaper articles on this specific problem have been published. An article in the *Enlightenment Daily,* for instance, pointed out the differences between Party discipline, administrative discipline, and the legal code: Party discipline is applied to all members of the CCP who have committed errors; administrative discipline is applied to all workers of state administrative organs who have committed errors; the legal code is applied to all those who have broken the law, including Party members and state cadres who have violated Party or administrative discipline as well as the Criminal Law. According to the article, a transgressing Party member or government employee should be subject to criticism and education and, in a more serious case, to disciplinary measures. The disciplinary sanctions of the Party in order of the severity of the errors committed are warning, serious warning, removal from Party office, probation within the Party, and expulsion from the Party; the disciplinary sanctions of government organs are warning, demerit, serious demerit, demotion in grade, demotion in office, removal from office, probationary expulsion, and expulsion. If transgressing Party members or state cadres have also violated the law, they should be subject to, besides disciplinary measures, criminal sanctions that range from control to imprisonment and the death sentence.[190]

An article in the *People's Daily* listed two reasons why the Party's discipline inspection organs should intervene in the area of the judiciary's responsibility in leading the struggle against economic crimes. First of all, the adverse effect of economic crimes on China's modernization and the involvement of Party personnel, including some leading cadres, in such crimes are said to have made it imperative for the Party's Discipline Inspection Commissions to take a direct hand in the anticrime drive. Secondly, to resolve the confusion concerning the investigation and handling of complicated economic cases, it would be better to have coordinated actions by the Party's Discipline Inspection Commissions, the judicial organs, and other relevant units under the unified leadership of the Party committees. The article, on the other hand, was quick to stress the differences between Party discipline and state law. The former is enforced by the Party's Discipline Inspection Commissions on the basis of the Party Constitution; state law is enforced by the judicial organs according to the provisions of the Criminal Law.[191] In answering questions on Party membership after crimes, a special column of the *People's Daily* also made the following interesting statements: When a Communist Party member violates the Criminal Law, the judicial organs should proceed to arrest, prosecute, and try him according to legal procedures without waiting for the Party to take disciplinary action first. As a rule, a Party member who is punished by the Court for a criminal offense should be expelled from the Party. However, there are exceptions—when the offense is not serious and the penalty imposed is rather light, a Party member may not be expelled from the Party but must be subject to other disciplinary sanctions within the Party.[192]

Another issue of concern in the PRC is the practice of the public security organs to bypass the legal process for administrative sanctions in dealing with certain politically or socially deviant individuals. As noted in Chapter Two, one prominent feature of the Maoist system of justice was the far-reaching power of the police and the abuses associated with it in imposing administrative sanctions without judicial review. Since Mao's death, genuine efforts have been made by the present leadership to put legal constraints on the police and to prevent the recurrence of past abuses. Still, some problems remain. On November 29, 1979, the NPC Standing Committee declared that all laws and decrees promulgated since 1949 would remain effective if not in conflict with the present Constitution and new laws.[193] Among the old statutes thus revived are the Security Administrative Punishment Act (SAPA) of 1957 and the Decision on Reeducation through Labor of the same year. Under the SAPA, the police can issue warnings, impose a modest fine, and detain a person up to fifteen days.[194] Under the Decision on Reeducation through Labor, the police and civil administrative organs can send a wide range of offenders to special camps to labor and reeducate themselves. The offenders are to include people who have no decent occupation, who behave like hoodlums, and who engage in theft, swindling, and other antisocial conduct; counterrevolutionaries and antisocial reactionaries not subject to criminal prosecution; people who refuse to work or to comply with work assignments or transfer; and troublemakers who refuse to correct themselves despite repeated criticism. Although similar to reform through labor in many aspects, reeducation through labor is a noncriminal punishment not subject to court approval and those assigned to reeducation are paid a salary according to their work and output.[195] Since the original decision fixed no specific length of time for reeducation, the police could send "undesirable elements" to labor camps for an indefinite period.[196]

In republishing the 1957 decision on November 29, 1979, the NPC Standing Committee also passed "Supplementary Regulations Concerning Reeducation Through Labor" to make some improvements. First, special committees composed of public security, civil affairs, and labor officials will be established for provinces, autonomous regions, and large and medium cities to direct and administer the work of reeducation through labor. The range of "admittance" is confined to those people in large and medium cities who need reeducation through labor. Second, the duration of reeducation through labor is limited from one to three years and may be extended for another year. Third, after their release, those who have undergone reeducation through labor shall not be discriminated against in employment or schooling. Fourth, the People's Procuratorates shall exercise supervision over organs of reeducation through labor.[197] In addition, the State Council adopted a decision in February 1980 to curb the use of such administrative methods as "forced labor" and "taking in for investigation" by consolidating them with reeducation through labor.[198] Chinese writers have also taken pains to emphasize the distinction between reform through labor, a criminal sanction imposed by the Court, and reeducation through labor, a milder noncriminal sanction for those who have not been deprived of their political rights.[199]

Some reeducation through labor farms, like those in Qinhuangdao and Tuanhe (South of Beijing), have recently been selected by the government to show off the good conditions of these camps, the special care given to the inmates, and the positive results of transforming them.[200]

Despite all this, the continuation of police power to send undesirable elements, including political activists, to labor camps for up to four years is rather disconcerting. Reports indicate that Chinese authorities have used this administrative measure to detain thousands of people from vagrants to political dissidents in rural camps.[201] An editor of one unofficial magazine committed suicide by throwing himself under a train before he and other activists were about to be sent to a labor camp.[202] Liu Qing, a well-known dissident, was given, in July 1980, a three-year sentence of reeducation through labor at the Lotus Flower Temple, a penal farm, in Shanxi Province. According to Liu's account, there were different categories of inmates in the penal farm: those sent for reform through labor and others, like him, given reeducation through labor. In spite of these distinctions, in practice all inmates were treated the same.[203]

It may be useful at this juncture to say a few words about reform through labor that convicted offenders serve in prisons or labor camps and farms. Information available in recent years has provided chilling accounts of Chinese corrective institutions under Mao where the prisoners reportedly suffered from exploitation, hunger, harsh treatment, and long hours of hard labor (up to twenty hours a day in some cases).[204] The post-Mao leadership appears to have been making efforts to improve prison conditions and to project a better image of China's labor reform policy. Municipal prisons in Beijing and Shanghai have received special attention from the media. The guiding principle of these institutions is said to be "reform first, production second." Inmates work eight hours a day, spend two hours on study, and one hour on recreational activities in the evening. They have a day off every week and days off on national holidays. There is a hospital in each of the prisons. There are also films and TV programs available to the inmates.[205] In an interview with a reporter, Public Security Minister Zhao Cangbi at the time had this to say about China's labor reform policy: "We have implemented revolutionary humanitarianism and treated criminals as human beings . . . We have provided them with sufficient food and clothes and normally they do not work more than eight hours a day. We have actively improved their living and sanitation conditions and provided them timely treatment when they are sick. Local and foreign visitors who have visited our prisons and reform through labor units have all admitted that the prisons and farms for reforming criminals through labor are actually schools, plants, and farms." [206] Many reformed offenders, Zhao further stated, have becomed skilled workers and some even engineers, technicians, medical doctors and technologists.[207] An author in *Studies in Law* also reported that "one prison in Hebei Province has, in the course of reforming criminals through labor, trained 110 architectual engineering technicians, one fifth of whom have already passed the examination to achieve the level of engineers." [208]

Granting that there is some truth in the Chinese claims, the question remains whether the reported improvements and accomplishments are not just confined to certain showcase corrective institutions. Unlike model prisons or reformatories in Beijing and Shanghai now routinely shown to foreign visitors, including one of the authors, Chinese labor camps or farms in the countryside remain somewhat a mystery and often a controversial subject. Stories about camp life in China's northwestern regions are particularly depressing.[209] The present government can certainly strengthen its credibility by improving the conditions of these camps and by making information on, or limited access to, them available to outside observers. Another problem relating to reform through labor is the fact that former inmates have found, because of their criminal record, greater difficulties in getting employment than those who have undergone reeducation through labor. Two former political offenders, for instance, decided to get married and stay on at the farm in Xinjiang where they had served sentences. "The Party's policy was to give us work here," the man said. "If we returned home, we would have no jobs. This area needed people." [210] China's Public Security Minister also conceded the existence of many problems in arranging employment for "transformed offenders" and urged that "the relevant perfectures and units must proceed from the general situation, strive to overcome all difficulties and actively do a good job of settling criminals so that they can live and work in peace and contentment." [211]

NOTES

Chapter Six

1. For instance, the following laws governing criminal justice were adopted in the 1950s:

(1) Provisional Act for Punishment of Crimes Undermining the National Currency, 1951;

(2) Act for Punishment of Corruption, 1952;

(3) Act for Punishment of Counterrevolutionaries, 1951; and

(4) Security Administration Punishment Act (SAPA), 1957.

Texts of these Acts are in *Gongan Faguei Hubian, 1950–1979* (Collection of Laws and Regulations on Public Security, 1950–1970) *(GAFGHB)* (Beijing: Mass Press, 1980), pp. 67–68, 80–83, 96 and 113–122. English translations of the Acts of counterrevolutionaries and on corruption are available in Jerome A. Cohen, *The Criminal Process in the People's Republic of China, 1949–1963,* (Cambridge, Mass.: Harvard University Press, 1968), pp. 229–302 and 308–311. Counterrevolutionary Act is reproduced in Document 1.

2. See Chapter Two of this book; also Shao-chuan Leng, *Justice in Communist China* (Dobbs Ferry, NY: Oceana, 1967), pp. 99–101; Cohen, *The Criminal Process,* pp. 20–21 and 500–503; Stanley Lubman, "Form and Function in the Chinese Criminal Process," *Columbia Law Review,* Vol. 69, No. 4, 1969, pp. 560–562 and Hungdah Chiu, "Criminal Punishment in Mainland China; A Study of Some Yunnan Province Documents," *Journal of Criminal Law and Criminology,* Vol. 68, No. 3 (1977), pp. 374–398 where several court documents were translated. It is interesting to note that as a departure from the past practice, President Jiang Hua of the Supreme Court said that opinions expressed in newspapers and magazines are useful for academic studies but should not be used as the yardstick to guide the courts in adjudicating criminal cases. *Zhongguo Fazhi Bao* (China's Legal System Paper), Nov. 27, 1981, p. 1.

3. See Harold J. Berman, Susan Cohen, and Malcolm Russell, "A Comparison of the Chinese and Soviet Codes of Criminal Law and Procedure," *Journal of Criminal Law and Criminology,* Vol. 72, No. 1, Nov. 1, 1982, pp. 248–255.

4. Such crimes as cited in *Journal of Criminal Law,* pp. 254–255 are contained in Articles 120, 126, 138, 143, 144, 145, 146, 159, 160, 162, 165, 175, 181 and 182 in the Chinese Criminal Law. Text of China's Criminal Law is in *GAFGHB,* pp. 4–34. English translations are available in the following sources: Jerome A. Cohen, Timothy A. Gelatt, and Florence M. Li, "The Criminal Law of the People's Republic of China," *Journal of Criminal Law and Criminology,* Vol. 27, No. 1, 1982, pp. 138–170; FBIS (Foreign Broadcast Information Service), *Daily Report: The PRC,* July 27, 1979 (Supplement), pp. 33–62; "The Criminal Law of the People's Republic of China" trans. by Wang Chi, *Review of Socialist Law,* Vol. 7, No. 2, 1981, pp. 199–222. See excerpts of this Law in Document 4.

5. Consult comments in He Peng *et al,* eds., *Xingfa Gailun* (An Introductory of the Criminal Law) (Changchun: Jilin People's Press, 1981), pp. 23–28; Quyang Tao *et al,*

eds., *Zhonghua Renmin Gongheguo Xingfa Zhushi* (Annotations on the Criminal Law of the People's Republic of China) (Beijing: Beijing Press, 1980), pp. 5–7.

6. Article 10 of the Criminal Law states: "Any act which endangers state sovereignty and territorial integrity, jeopardizes the regime of the dictatorship of the proletariat, undermines socialist revolution and socialist construction, disrupts public order, encroaches upon the property of the whole people or the property collectively owned by the laboring masses, encroaches the legitimate property owned by private citizens, infringes upon the personal, democratic and other rights of the citizens or any other act which endangers society and is punishable according to law is an offense. However, if the offense is obviously a minor one and its harm is negligible, it shall not be considered a crime." Articles 11–18 treats the questions of criminal responsibility regarding intent, negligence, age, mental patients, drunkedness, handicapped persons, rightful defense, and emergency measures.

7. See Fan Fenglin, "On Fundamental Problems of the Characterization of Crimes," *Faxue Yanjiu* (Studies in Law), No. 4, 1979, pp. 29–33, 41; Cao Zidan, "Questions and Answers on China's Criminal Law," *Beijing Review*, Vol. 23, No. 23, June 9, 1980, pp. 19–20; Criminal Research Group of the Legal Research Institute of the Chinese Academy of Social Sciences, "Lectures on the Criminal Law, (1979)," trans. by D. Cameron *et al, Chinese Law and Government*, Vol. 13, No. 2, 1980, pp. 22–26 (hereinafter "Lectures on the Criminal Law"); Criminal Law and Criminal Procedure Law Teaching and Research Group of the Central Political-Legal Cadre School, *Zhonghua Renmin Gongheguo Xingfa Zongze Jiangyi* (Lectures on the General Principles of the PRC Criminal Law) (Beijing: Mass Press, 1980), pp. 76–80 (hereinafter *Lectures on General Principles*).

8. Part 2, Chapters I–VIII, Articles 90–192.

9. Articles 64–73 of the Soviet Criminal Code. English translations of the Soviet substantive and procedural criminal codes are available in Harold J. Berman and J. Spindler, *Soviet Criminal Law and Procedure: The RSFSR Codes*, (Cambridge, Mass.: Harvard University Press, 1972).

10. Berman *et al*, "A Comparison of the Chinese and Soviet Codes," see above note 3, pp. 252–253.

11. M.J. Meijer, "The New Criminal Law of the People's Republic of China," *Review of Socialist Law*, Vol. 6, No. 2, 1980, pp. 133–134.

12. Liu Rong, "Am I a Counterrevolutionary?" *Minzhu Yu Fazhi* (Democracy and Legal System), No. 2, 1979, p. 39. In one of eight stories written about the Cultural Revolution by a Taiwan-born author, a four-year-old girl is taken from her bed for a nighttime interrogation because she has been heard to chant "Chairman Mao is a rotten egg." Chen Jo-hsi, *The Execution of Major Yin* (Bloomington: Indiana University Press, 1978), pp. 37–66.

13. Anita Chan and Jonathan Unger, eds., "The Case of Li I-che," *Chinese Law and Government*, Vol. 10, No. 3, 1977, pp. 1–112; "Big Character Poster Authors 'Li Yi Zhe' Exonerated," *Beijing Review*, Vol. 22, No. 9, March 2, 1979, pp. 15–16.

14. He Peng *et al*, see above note 5, pp. 183–184; "Lectures on the Criminal Law," see above note 7, pp. 42–45.

15. This reflects the PRC's effort to check the abuse of power by officials. More will be discussed later.

16. The old Marriage Law of 1950 has been replaced by the New Marriage Law, promulgated in 1980. The latter's English text is in *Main Documents of the Third Session of the Fifth National People's Congress of the People's Republic of China* (Beijing: Foreign Languages Press, 1980), pp. 209–224 (hereinafter *3rd Session of NPC*). As its predecessor, the New Marriage Law has a general provision that "persons violating this law shall

be subject to administrative measures or legal sanctions according to law and the circumstances" (Article 34).

17. Articles 28–56. For similar classification of criminal sanctions under Mao, see Cohen, *The Criminal Process*, p. 21.

18. He Peng, *et al*, see above note 5, pp. 122–126; "Lectures on the Criminal Law," pp. 30–32.

19. Article 41 of the Criminal law reads: "A criminal element sentenced to fixed-term imprisonment or life imprisonment shall be sent to a prison or a reform through labor center for executing his sentences. If he is able to work he shall be subject to reform through labor." For a short analysis of Mao's influence in the thought reform program, see Leng, "The Role of Law in the People's Republic of China as Reflecting Mao's Influence," *Journal of Criminal Law and Criminology*, Vol. 68, No. 3, 1977, pp. 11–14.

20. It should be noted that most penalties listed in the PRC's 1951 Act for Punishment of Counterrevolution were capital punishment. For the Act, see *GAFGHB*, pp. 96–99.

21. Ge Ping and Wang Honggu, "On Capital Punishment," *Faxue Yanjiu*, No. 1, 1980, pp. 29–32; *Lectures on General Principles*, pp. 215–219. Similar views on capital punishment were expressed by several Chinese jurists the American Bar Association Delegation talked to in June 1981.

22. This requirement was originally adopted in a NPC resolution on July 15, 1957. Recently, however, implementation of this provision has been temporarily suspended in the drive against serious crimes. For further discussion, see the next section of this chapter.

23. Both Jiang Qing and Zhang Chunqiao, for instance, were sentenced to death with a two-year reprieve by the Special Court on January 25, 1981. *A Great Trial in Chinese History* (Beijing: New World Press, 1981) pp. 128–150. According to the Chinese, the overwhelming majority of those given the death penalty have been successfully reformed at the end of two years to have their sentences reduced to life imprisonment or imprisonment for a fixed term. Ge Ping and Wang Honggu, "On Capital Punishment," see above note 21, p. 32; *Lectures on General Principles*, pp. 218. In answering questions at the briefing session with our Bar group on June 8, 1981, the warden of the Shanghai Municipal Prison also indicated that none of his prisoners with suspended death sentences were ever executed. For a discussion of the PRC's past policy regarding the death penalty and its two-year reprieve, see Cohen, *The Criminal Process*, pp. 342–343; Leng, *Justice in Communist China*, pp. 166–168; *Political Imprisonment in the People's Republic of China* (London: Amnesty International Publications, 1978), pp. 61–69.

24. This phrase appears in Article 4 of the Criminal Procedure Law.

25. For the interesting comments by the Chinese showing a marked departure from the Maoist penal practice, see Luo Ping, "The Principle of Measuring Penalties in China's Criminal Law," *Hongqi* (Red Flag) No. 9, 1979, pp. 71–75; *Lectures on General Principles*, pp. 226–229.

26. See Ding Jianjing, "It Is Unnecessary to Distinguish Between the Two Types of Contradictions in Assessing Offenses and Measuring Penalties," *Minzhu yu Fazhi*, No. 6, 1980, pp. 4–6; Huang Dao *et al*, "The Two Types of Contradictions in Criminal Offenses and the Principle of Acting According to Law," *Minzhu yu Fazhi*, pp. 6–9. In his 1957 speech, Mao prescribed the method of education and persuasion to deal with "contradiction among the people" (nonantagnostic contradictions) and the method of dictatorship to handle "contradictions between the people and the enemy" (antagonistic contradiction). For a discussion of Mao's highly important and yet confusing theory of contradictions, consult Leng, *Justice in Communist China*, pp. 154–157; G.C.

Crockett, "Criminal Justice in China," *Judicature*, Vol. 59, No. 5, 1975, pp. 240, 241–242.

27. Wang Guiwu, "Law Enforcement Must Consider the Overall Situation," *Renmin Ribao*, September 14, 1981, p. 5; Wang Chuansheng, "On Application of Penalty and Its Adapting to the Political Situation," *Faxue Yanjiu*, No. 6, 1981, pp. 1–4; Zheng Lin, "Hitting Hard at the Criminal Activities," *Faxue Yanjiu*, No. 5, 1983, pp. 13–18; Yuan Zuoxi, "Give Full Play to the Deterrent Role of Penalty," *Guangming Ribao* (Enlightenment Daily), Oct. 22, 1983, p. 3. The NPC Standing Committee's decisions of June 1981 and September 1983 will be discussed in the next section.

28. Huang Mingxiu, "Why is it That the Statement of Leniency to Those Who Confess and Severity to Those Who Resist was not Written Into the Criminal Law," *Minzhu Yu Fazhi*, No. 2, 1979, p. 30; Cong Wenhui, "Have a Better Comprehension of the Policy of 'Being Lenient to Those Who Confess Their Crimes and Severe to Those Who Refuse to Confess,' " *Faxue* (Jurisprudence), No. 5, 1982, pp. 19–22.

29. Text of the resolution is in *Renmin Ribao*, March 10, 1982, p. 2. For further discussion, see the following section.

30. Cohen, *The Criminal Justice*, pp. 336–341; Leng, *Justice in Communist China*, pp. 159–161.

31. As expressed by Chinese criminal law professors one the authors interviewed in five law schools during 1979 and 1981. See also Tao Xijin, "Problems in the Study of Criminal Law," *Faxue Yanjiu*, No. 5, 1979, pp. 7–8; Li Yonyi, "On the Stipulation and Analogy of Offenses and Penalties," *Faxue Yanjiu*, No. 5, 1980, pp. 19–24. On the other hand, preference for the analogy principle is voiced in Zhou Mi, "Should Offenses and Penalties be Stipulated or Analogized? " *Faxue Yanjiu*, No. 5, 1980, pp. 25–29. It should be noted that the 1926 Russian Criminal Code incorporated the principle of analogy, which was finally discarded by the Soviets in 1958 as a result of criticisms in the late 1930s. Berman, *et al*, "A Comprehension of the Chinese and Soviet Codes," see above note 3, p. 249.

32. Article 186 reads: "In a serious case where a state functionary divulges important state secrets in violation of laws and regulations for guarding state secrets he shall be sentenced to fixed-term imprisonment for not more than 7 years, detention or deprivation of political rights. If the offender is not a state functionary, he shall be punished according to the seriousness of the case in line with the preceding paragraph."

33. Text of the Act republished in *Renmin Ribao*, April 11, 1980, p. 1. English translation is in FBIS, *Daily Report: PRC*, April 14, 1980, pp. L7–L11 and Document 2.

34. According to a story told to an American reporter, shortly after the Act was reissued, a school called a political study session to go over them. The cadre in charge summarized the message by saying that people should feel free to discuss only that information which had been published in the newspapers. "But what about my name? " a student asked flippantly. "My name has never been in the press. Is it a state secret? " Fox Butterfield, *China: Alive in the Bitter Sea* (New York: Times Books, 1982), pp. 385–386.

35. Liu Rong, "What is the Crime of Leaking State Secrets? " *Guangming Ribao* (Enlightenment Daily), June 19, 1981, p. 3.

36. "Crime of Betraying State Secrets," *Beijing Review*, Vol. 25, No. 20, May 17, 1982, p. 3. See also Michael Weisskopf, "China Holds American As Suspect in Spy Case," *The Washington Post*, June 2, 1982, pp. A1, A13.

37. *The Washington Post*, June 2, 1982, pp. A1, A13; Michael Weisskopf, "China Frees American, Saying She Confessed," *The Washington Post*, June 4, 1982, p. A14.

38. Christopher S. Wren, "China Jails a Hong Kong Editor As A Spy for U.S.," *New York Times*, May 16, 1983, pp. A1, A3; Michael Weisskopf, "China Sentences Prominent Editor As Spy for U.S.," *The Washington Post*, May 16, 1983, pp. A1, A16. The fact that Mr. Lo was released from prison a few months later for his "past merits and current repentence" confirmed the suspicion that his case was a political one used to show the poor state of U.S.—PRC relations. See Luo Bing, "Truth about the Strange Case of Lo Fu," *Cheng Ming* (Contending), No. 10, 1983, pp. 25–26.

39. Frank Ching, "Lawyer Who Worked at American Law Firms Imprisoned in China As Spy for the U.S.," *Asian Wall Street Journal Weekly*, January 23, 1984, p. 3; "China Confirms Jailing of an Ex-U.S. Lawyer," *New York Times*, Feb. 2, 1984, p. A7.

40. See Crockett, "Criminal Justice in China," see above note 26, p. 247; Derrick Bell, "Inside China: Continuity and Social Reform," *Juris Doctor*, Vol. 8, No. 4, 1978, p. 26.

41. "China Posts Crime Rate," *The Washington Post*, August 30, 1980, p. A24.

42. *Renmin Ribao*, September 17, 1980, p. 1.

43. Fox Butterfield, "Peking Bomb Blast is Laid to Ire of Man Kept From Living in City," *New York Times*, November 11, 1980, p. A5.

44. FBIS, *Daily Report: China*, April 23, 1981, p. K1. See also Michael Weisskopf, "Chinese Official Confirms Reports of Labor Unrest," *The Washington Post*, April 30, 1981, p. A30.

45. Michael Weisskopf, "Stem of a Slow Social Boil," *ibid.*, January 17, 1982, p. A17. The taxi driver was tried and sentenced to death on January 30, 1982, and her execution was carried out on February 18, 1982, FBIS, *Daily Report: China*, February 19, 1982, p. K26.

46. Jin Mosheng, "Resolutely Strike at the Lawbreaking, Criminal Activities that Disrupt the Economic Order," *Minzhu yu Fazhi*, No. 5, 1981, p. 38.

47. "Cracking Down on Speculation and Smuggling," *Beijing Review*, Vol. 24, No. 7, February 16, 1981, pp. 5–6.

48. Michael Vink, "Canton's Crackdown on Smuggling Drives," *Asian Wall Street Journal*, December 6, 1980, pp. 1, 5.

49. *Xinhua News Agency*, November 14, 1980.

50. Commentator, "Strike Resolute Blows at Economic Criminals," *Nanfang Ribao* (Southern Daily), June 15, 1980, p. 1.

51. Jay Mathews, "Plagued by Crime, Chinese Increase Use of the Executions," *The Washington Post*, August 5, 1980, p. A13.

52. *The Washington Post*, August 5, 1980, p. A13. This case was well publicized in China. See "Embezzler Sentenced to Death," *Beijing Review*, Vol. 22, No. 45, Nov. 9, 1979, p. 7.

53. FBIS, *Daily Report: PRC*, December 6, 1979, pp. L9–10.

54. "Report on Hebei Ribao's article, June 7, 1981," FBIS, *Daily Report, China*, June 18, 1981. p. R2.

55. Commentator, "Further Tidy Up Social Law and Order," *Sichuan Ribao* (Sichuan Daily), May 25, 1981, p. 1.

56. *Zhongguo Fazhi Bao*, July 31, 1981, p. 1. Besides high officials from Chinese judicial and public security organs, Peng Zhen and Peng Chong, both members of the CCP Central Committee Political Bureau, also attended the forum.

57. See the explanations offered by Wang Hanbing, Vice-Chairman of the Legal Affairs Commission of the NPC Standing Committee, in *Renmin Ribao*, June 11, 1981, p. 1 and also in FBIS, *Daily Report: China*, June 19, 1981, pp. K15–K17.

58. The third one is on strengthening the work of law interpretations. Texts of all three are in *Renmin Ribao*, June 11, 1981, p. 1, translated in FBIS, *Daily Report: China*, June 11, 1981, pp. K3–K5.

59. According to Wang Hanbing, this delegation of authority to the higher courts by the Supreme Court was actually put into practice in 1980 on the basis of a 1979 November decision of the NPC Standing Committee. In this view, since it is hard to make mistakes in handling cases involving murder, rape, robbery, etc. where the facts are generally clear-cut and evidence is solid, to seek approval of the Supreme Court on the death penalty in such cases would only hamper the swift and timely punishment of major criminals under the present conditions. The 1981 resolution in question has temporarily suspended Article 43 of the Criminal Law and Articles 144 and 145 of the Criminal Procedure Law.

60. In a talk with the authors in June 1981, Ma Rongjie, editor of *Studies of Law*, pointed out because of the more complex nature of such crimes as counterrevolution and embezzlement, requirement of the Supreme Court's approval for the death penalty remains unchanged to prevent the miscarriage of justice.

61. Such a provision, Mr. Wang thinks, is not only necessary to the peace and order of the cities but will make it difficult for these persons to commit offenses again.

62. See Zhou Daoluan *et al*, "Deal Heavy and Swift Blows to Serious Criminal Offenders According to Law," *Renmin Ribao*, June 25, 1981, p. 5.

63. "Use the Weapon of Law to Crack Down on Criminal Activities," *Renmin Ribao*, June 22, 1981, p. 1.

64. "Severly and Swiftly Punish Major Criminals," *Jiefang Ribao* (Liberation Daily), June 16, 1981, p. 1.

65. See above notes 62, 63.

66. *Beijing Ribao* (Beijing Daily), June 14, 1981, p. 1; *Renmin Ribao*, June 20, 1981, p. 4; FBIS, *Daily Report: China*, June 22, 1981; pp. 21, R1–R2.

67. *Renmin Ribao*, June 20, 1981, p. 4.

68. *Renmin Ribao*, June 25, 1981, p. 4; *China Daily*, June 26, 1981, p. 3.

69. FBIS, *Daily Report: China*, June 29, 1981, p. S1.

70. *Wenhui Bao* (Cultural Exchange Daily), June 28, 1981, p. 3.

71. *Zhongguo Fazhi Bao*, July 24, 1981, p. 1.

72. This is somewhat confusing. According to Wang Hanbing's explanations regarding the NPC Standing Committee's resolution on approval of the death penalty (see above note 56), death sentences for crimes of murder, robbery and rape would only require the review and approval of a higher People's Court during 1980–1983, unless the latter serves as the court of first instance and the case is appealed to the Supreme People's Court.

73. *Zhongguo Fazhi Bao*, July 17, 1981, p. 1.

74. "Chief Procurator Huang Huoqing's Report to the NPC," *Renmin Ribao*, December 16, 1981, p. 2.

75. "Public Security Improved," *Beijing Review*, Vol. 25, No. 33, August 16, 1982, pp. 6–7.

76. The figures were given by Public Security Minister in an interview in July 1983, UPI, Beijing, August 19, 1983.

77. Zhao Ziyang, "Report of the Work of the Government," *Beijing Review*, Vol. 26, No. 27, July 4, 1983, p. xx.

78. Luo Bing, "Deng Xiaoping's Encounter with Bandits and the Mass Arrests," *Cheng Ming* (Contending), No. 10, 1983, pp. 6–7.

79. "Factual Recording of Killing the 'Two Wangs,'" *Cheng Ming*, p. 13; *Renmin Ribao*, Sept. 19, 1983, p. 4.

80. Luo Bing, see above note 78, pp. 8–9.

81. *Xinhua News Agency*, Aug. 13, 1983; Commentator, "Deal Severe Blows at Criminal Activities," *Renmin Ribao*, Aug. 14, 1983, p. 1.

82. AFP, Beijing, Aug. 23, 1983; Xu Xing, "Mass Arrests and the Rule of Law," *Cheng Ming*, No. 10, 1983, p. 16.

83. For the NPC Standing Committee's "Decision on Severely Punishing Criminals who Gravely Endanger Public Security of the Society" on September 2, 1983, and Wang Hanbin's explanations, see *Renmin Ribao*, Sept. 3, 1983, pp. 1, 4 respectively.

84. *Renmin Ribao*, p. 1.

85. Department of State, *Country Reports on Human Rights Practices for 1983* (Washington, D.C.: US Government Printing Office, 1984), "China," pp. 741–742; Amnesty International, *China: Violations of Human Rights* (London: Amnesty International Publications, 1984), p. 55.

86. *SPEAHRhead*, p. 51; AFP (Agence Française de Presse), Beijing, Nov. 2, 1983.

87. An Zhigno, "Crackdown on Crime," *Beijing Review*, Vol. 26, No. 37, Sept. 12, 1983, p. 4.

88. Notes from the Editor, "On Capital Punishment," *Beijing Review*, Vol. 26, No. 45, Nov. 7, 1983, p. 4.

89. "We Must Severely Crackdown on Criminal Activities," *Renmin Ribao*, Sept. 4, 1983, p. 4; FBIS, *Daily Report: China*, Sept. 12, 1983, p. K8.

90. *Zhongguo Fazhi Bao*, Nov. 18, 1983, p. 1.

91. *Zhongguo Fazhi Bao*, Feb. 12, 1982, p. 1; *Dagong Bao* (L'Impartial), April 4, 1982, p. 1.

92. See Editorial: "Never Allow Smuggling and Tax Evasion to Impair State Interests," *Renmin Ribao*, March 11, 1981, p. 1; Commentator, "Opinion," *China Daily*, February 27, 1982, p. 2; Commentator, "Severe Punishment Should be Imposed on Those Leading Cadres Who Violate Law and Commit Crimes," *Hongqi* (Red Flag), No. 4, 1982, pp. 6–8, 38; "How to Prevent the Abuse of Office and Power for Illegal Economic Activities," *Minzhu Yu Fazhi*, No. 1, 1982, pp. 25–27. For foreign press comments, see Michael Weisskopf, "China Cracks Down on 'Plucking Feathers From a Wild Goose'," *The Washington Post*, January 7, 1982, p. A24.

93. *Renmin Ribao*, March 10, 1982, p. 1; FBIS, *Daily Report: China*, March 10, 1982, pp. K1–K5.

94. "Everyone Should Publicize and Help Implement This Important Resolution to Defend the Socialist System," *Renmin Ribao*, March 10, 1982, p. 1. Also consult Chief Procurator Huang Huoqing's view in answering a *Xinhua* reporter's questions on this resolution, *Zhongguo Fazhi Bao*, April 4, 1982, p. 1.

95. *Zhongguo Fazhi Bao*, April 23, 1982, p. 1.

96. David Bonavia, "Mandarians on the Make," *Far Eastern Economic Review*, Vol. 116, No. 25, June 18, 1982, p. 23.

97. Text of the decision in *Renmin Ribao*, April 14, 1982, pp. 1–2, translated in *FBIS, Daily Report: China*, April 14, 1982, pp. K1–K9. There is a brief report on this decision in "Decision on Combating Economic Crimes," *Beijing Review*, Vol. 25, No. 17, April 26, 1982, pp. 7–9.

98. The decision also stresses that the PRC will continue to uphold the open door policy toward foreign countries and the policy enlivening the domestic economy while carrying out the struggle against criminal activities in the economic field.

99. *Renmin Ribao*, July 27, 1982, pp. 1, 4; FBIS, *Daily Report: China*, July 28, 1982, pp. K4–K9.

100. "Crackdown on Economic Crimes," *Beijing Review*, Vol. 26, No. 33, August 15, 1983, p. 7; *Xinhua News Agency*, July 25, 1983.

101. Stated by Jiang Weng, Deputy Chief Prosecutor of the Supreme People's Procuracy, in an interview. *China Daily*, January 31, 1984, p. 4.

102. Commentator, "It is Imperative to Severely and Expeditiously Punish Economic Criminals According to Law," *Renmin Ribao*, Sept. 15, 1983, pp. 1, 4; *FBIS, Daily Report: China*, Sept. 20, 1983, pp. K4–K6.

103. *Zhongguo Fazhi Bao*, July 31, 1981, p. 1.

104. *Renmin Ribao*, June 26, 1983, p. 2.

105. James P. Sterba, "China Says Its Rising Juvenile Crime Stems From Cultural Revolution," *New York Times*, December 26, 1979, p. A12.

106. Wei Min, "Interviewing Deputy Director of Public Security Bureau," *Beijing Review*, Vol. 24, No. 8, February 23, 1981, p. 22; Zhong Mingguang, "An Important Reason for Juvenile Delinquency: Legal Illiteracy," *Minzhu Yu Fazhi*, No. 8, 1980, p. 6.

107. "Save the Juvenile Delinquents," *Beijing Review*, Vol. 23, No. 9, March 3, 1980, p. 4; information from the author's interviews with Chinese lawyers and law enforcement personnel during November–December 1979 and May–June 1981.

108. "Liaoning Journal Cited on Juvenile Delinquency," FBIS, *Daily Report: China*, July 12, 1982, pp. K18–K19.

109. *China News Analysis*, No. 1232, May 7, 1982, pp. 7–8.

110. "Economic Crime Near the Top," *Yomiuri Shimbun*, April 2, 1982, cited in *Inside China Mainland*, May 1982, pp. 14–15.

111. *Hong Kong Standard*, April 6, 1982, p. 3.

112. *Renmin Ribao*, April 14, 1982, p. 2; FBIS, *Daily Report: China*, April 14, 1982, pp. K14. See Commentator, "A New Party Injunction," *China Daily*, April 23, 1982, p. 4.

113. AFP, Beijing, August 23, 1983.

114. AFP, Beijing, October 21, 1983.

115. *AP*, Beijing, October 12, 1983.

116. See above notes 106 and 107; also Li Shutang, "Strengthen Legal Education for Young People," *Minzhu Yu Fazhi*, No. 8, 1980, pp. 6–7.

117. Wei Min, see above note 106, p. 23; Wang Dexiang, "Some Questions Concerning Our Country's Juvenile Delinquency," *Xinan Zhengfa Xueyuan Xuebao* (Journal of the Southwest Political-Legal Institute), No. 2, 1979, pp. 27–29; Zhai Bugao, "Comment on the Cause and Character of Juvenile Delinquency," *Faxue Yanjiu*, No. 3, 1981, pp. 44.

118. "Use the Weapon of Law to Crack Down on Criminal Activities," *Renmin Ribao*, June 22, 1981, at 1.

119. Wei Min, see above note 106, p. 23.

120. See Butterfield, *China: Alive in the Bitter Sea*, pp. 179–202, Chapter 8, "No Road Out—Youth"; Thomas B. Gold, "China's Youth: Problems and Programs," King-yuh Chang, ed., *The Emerging Teng System: Orientation, Policies, and Implications* (Taipei: Institute of International Relations, 1982), IV-2, pp. 1–24; Mok Bong-ho, *Young Offenders in Contemporary China: Contributing Factors and Related Services* (Hong Kong: Chinese University of Hong Kong, 1983).

121. Wang Dexiang, see above note 117, p. 30; He Peng *et al*, see above note 5, pp. 85–86.

122. It should be noted that in this connection Article 111 of the Criminal Procedure Law provides: "No cases involving crimes committed by minors between the ages of 14 and 16 are heard in public. Generally, cases involving minors between the ages of 16 and 18 are not heard in public." The purpose of this provision, explained by the Chinese, is to protect juvenile offenders from any psychological injury that may damage their health and future growth. Wang Dexiang, see above note 117, pp. 30–31; the Criminal Procedure Teaching and Research Group, Law Department, China People's University, *Zhonghua Renmin Gongheguo Xingshi Susong Fa Jiben Zhishi* (Basic Knowledge

of the Criminal Procedure Law of the People's Republic of China) (Beijing: People's Press, 1980), pp. 31–32.

123. *Zhongguo Fazhi Bao,* July 31, 1981, p. 1.

124. *Beijing Review,* Vol. 25, No. 9, March 3, 1980, p. 4.

125. *Zhongguo Fazhi Bao,* June 19, 1981, p. 2.

126. Wei Min, *supra,* note 106, p. 24; "Juvenile Delinquency," *China News Analysis,* No. 1167, Nov. 9, 1979, pp. 6–7.

127. See Articles 3, 21–24 of the Act for Reform Through Labor (Sept. 7, 1954) in *GAFGHB,* p. 400; "Corrective Centers for Juvenile Offenders," *Faxue Cidan* (Law Dictionary) (Shanghai: Dictionary Press, 1980), p. 77.

128. Yi Chengxin, "Reforming Juvenile Delinquents—A Task for Everything," *China Daily,* June 1, 1983, p. 4.

129. "Reformatory," *Beijing Review,* Vol. 24, No. 8, February 23, 1981, pp. 28–29; Muriel Kessler, "A Chinese Reformatory," *Vesey Street Letter,* Summer, 1981, p. 5; Zhou Zheng, "Save the Teenage Delinquents," *Beijing Review,* Vol. 22, No. 44, Nov. 2, 1979, pp. 18–24; FBIS, *Daily Report: PRC,* Dec. 17, 1979, pp. L12–L13.

130. Liu Zhi, "Notes on the Reform Role of Punishment of China," *Faxue Yanjiu,* No. 4, 1982, pp. 28–29. See also Wu Hengquan, "Persons under Reeducation Through Labor Participate in Democratic Administration," *Minzhu Yu Fazhi,* No. 5, 1982, pp. 25–26.

131. *Minzhu Yu Fazhi,* No. 5, 1982, pp. 25–26; Zhang Ruihong, "What I have Seen and Heard in the Qinhuangdao Reeducation Through Labor Camp," *Minzhu Yu Fazhi,* No. 11, 1981, pp. 5–6; Commentator, "Parental Love Is Needed in Reeducating and Reforming Erring Young People," *Renmin Ribao,* Oct. 15, 1981, p. 1; FBIS, *Daily Report: China,* Oct. 16, 1982, pp. K1–K3.

132. Christopher S. Wren, "China's Black Sheep 'Reeducated' Without Trial," *New York Times,* Aug. 12, 1982, p. A2; "Chinese and Foreign Journalists Visit Beijing's Tuanhe Reeducation through Labor Camp," *Zhongguo Fazhi Bao,* July 16, 1982, p. 1.

133. Liu Zhi, "The Role of Punishment in Reforming Criminals in Our Country," *Guangming Ribao,* Dec. 22, 1981, p. 3; JPRS, 80051, Feb. 8, 1982, pp. 46–47.

134. "Ten Ways to Educate and Reform Young Offenders," *Zhongguo Fazhi Bao,* Oct. 23, 1981; pp. 1–2; Oct. 30, 1981, p. 2; Nov. 6, 1981, 1982, p. 4.

135. Liu Zhi, "Tianjin Approves Five Repentent Youths' Participation in Entrance Examination," *Renmin Ribao,* July 4, 1982, p. 4.

136. "Juvenile Delinquency," see above note 126, p. 7.

137. FBIS, *Daily Report: PRC,* Feb. 7, 1980, p. L1.

138. *Zhongguo Fazhi Bao,* July 31, 1981, p. 1.

139. Wei Min, see above note 106, p. 24.

140. Zhai Bugao, see above note 117, p. 47.

141. *Zhongguo Fazhi Bao,* Aug. 7, 1981, p. 1; July 16, 1982, p. 2.

142. *Renmin Ribao,* April 14, 1982, p. 2.

143. See Zhai Bugao, see above note 117, pp. 44–47; Ji Ling, "Psychological Analysis of the Youths Who Commit Homicide Because of Rejection in Love," *Minzhu Yu Fazhi,* No. 2, 1982, pp. 21–22.

144. *Zhongguo Fazhi Bao,* June 25, 1982, p. 1.

145. Commentator, "Don't Miss the Opportunity to Do A Good Educational Work to Youngsters with Minor Law Infraction," *Zhongguo Fazhi Bao,* Nov. 11, 1983, p. 1.

146. For a discussion of this particular issue consult *Political Imprisonment in the PRC.*

147. *New York Times,* June 6, 1978, p. 1.

148. *Beijing Review,* Vol. 22, Jan. 26, 1979, p. 8.

149. Jiang Hua, "Report of the Work of the Supreme People's Court," *3rd Session of NPC*, see above note 16, p. 121.

150. *Guangming Ribao*, Aug. 5, 1981, p. 1.

151. *FBIS, Daily Report: China*, June 19, 1981, p. R1.

152. Liu was executed on Oct. 22, 1981 while his accomplice was given a suspended death sentence (with a two-year reprieve), according to a report of the *Sichuan Ribao*. Information supplied by Laduquie of Amnesty International.

153. *Renmin Ribao*, Aug. 20, 1982, p. 1.

154. Department of State, see above note 85, p. 743.

155. *A Great Trial in Chinese History*, pp. 128–130.

156. James D. Seymour, ed., *The Fifth Modernization: China's Human Rights Movement, 1978–1979* (Stanfordville, NY: Human Rights Publishing Group, 1980), pp. 1–26; Shaochuan Leng, "Human Rights in Chinese Political Culture," in Kenneth W. Thompson, ed., *The Moral Imperatives of Human Rights* (Washington, DC: University Press of America, 1980), pp. 94–95; Liu Sheng-chi, "The Democratic Movement in Mainland China in Retrospect," *Issues and Studies*, Vol. 17, April 1981, pp. 51–62; June Dreyer, "Limits of the Permissible in China," *Problems of Communism*, Vol. 29, Nov.-Dec. 1980, pp. 53–54, 57. Among the best known underground publications during this period were *Explorations* (Tansuo), *April Fifth Forum* (Siwu Luntan) and *Peking Spring* (Beijing Zhi Chun). For a full list of such publications, see Arlette Laduguie, "The Human Rights Movement," *Index on Censorship*, Vol. 6, February 1980, pp. 24–25; *Dalu Dixia Kanwu Huibian* (Collection of the Mainland Underground Publication) (Taipei: Institute for the Study of Chinese Communist Problems, 1980), Book I.

157. Laduguie, see above note 156, pp. 22–23.

158. *Beijing Ribao*, Dec. 7, 1979, p. 1. One of the authors happened to be in Beijing at that time and visited the Democracy Wall several times to read the posters before they were removed.

159. "Peng Zeng's Report" and "Ye Jianyang's Closing Address," *3rd Session of NPC*, see above note 16, pp. 110–111, 202–203.

160. Lei Jieqiong, "A Painful Lesson," *Beijing Review*, Vol. 23, No. 40, Oct. 6, 1980, p. 28.

161. Zhou Zheng, "Sida: Its Origin," *Beijing Review*, pp. 23–26.

162. Zhang Youyu, "Why 'Sida' Has Been Abolished," *Beijing Review*, pp. 28.

163. Fox Butterfield, "Peking Dissident, in Rare Account, Tells of Political Prisoners' Torture," *New York Times*, May 7, 1979, pp. A1, A10.

164. *Renmin Ribao*, October 17, 1979, p. 4.

165. Hungdah Chiu, "Structural Changes in the Organization and Operation of China's Criminal Justice System," *Review of Socialist Law*, Vol. 7, No. 1, 1981, pp. 63–64. Translated excerpts of Wei's trial transcript are in *New York Times*, Nov. 15, 1979, p. A22.

166. *Renmin Ribao*, Nov. 7, 1979, p. 7 and Nov. 8, 1979, p. 4. Also see interviews with Judge Wu Wenzao and other jurists in FBIS, *Daily Report: PRC*, Nov. 13, 1979, pp. L5–9. On the other hand, people in Hong Kong, even among those sympathetic to Beijing, seemed to feel that Wei's sentence was rather too harsh even if he was guilty as charged. See Tan Xingsheng, "A Talk on News Reports on the Wei Jingsheng Case," *Dongxiang* (Trends), No. 16, Nov. 16, 1979, p. 18; A Da, "It Is Wise to Listen to Both Sides," *Dongxiang*, pp. 18–19.

167. *Xinhua News Agency*, Dec. 24, 1979. A detailed description of Fu's case in Chiu, see above note 139, pp. 65–66.

168. AFP, Beijing, Jan. 28, 1711; FBIS, *Daily Report: PRC*, p. A10.

169. *Ibid*, August 4, 1980, p. L2.

170. Liu's ordeal is described in detail in a 196 page manuscript smuggled out of the labor camp to the hands of foreign journalists. Michael Weisskopf, "A Glimpse of Life in China's Prisons," *The Washington Post*, Sept. 15, 1981, pp. A1, A14. For translation of a shorter version of his alleged manuscript, see "Prison Writings of Dissident Liu Qing Published," JPRS 80461, March 31, 1982, pp. 110–159.

171. "Part 5 of Deng's Speech," *Ming Bao* (Bright Daily), May 5, 1981, p. 13. In carrying out Deng's speech, this Hong Kong paper broke it into six parts. See also *FBIS, Daily Report: China*, May 6, 1981, pp. W1–W3.

172. M. Weisskopf, "China Ends a Fling at Free Thinking," *The Washington Post*, March 23, 1981, pp. A1, A10.

173. Commentary, "Consolidate Stability and Unity in Order to Do a Good Job in Economic Readjustment," *Jiefang Ribao*, Jan. 10, 1981, p. 1; FBIS, *Daily Report: PRC*, Jan. 23, 1981, pp. L10–L14.

174. Ye Zi, "Is There Absolute Freedom of Speech," *Hongqi*, No. 7, 1981, p. 7. Montesquieu is quoted by the writer to show the relationship between counterrevolutionary words and actual deeds.

175. AFP, Beijing, April 20, 1981.

176. AFP, Hong Kong, May 10, 1981: "Le Monde Reports Further Arrests of PRC Dissidents," in *FBIS, Daily Report: China*, May 20, 1981, pp. K2–K3.

177. Department of State, *Country Reports on Human Rights Practices For 1981* (Washington, DC, U.S. Government Printing Office, 1982), "China," p. 566. See also the listing of thirty-four arrested leaders of the China Democratic Movement (CDM) in *SPEAHRhead*, No. 19, Northern Autumn, 1983, pp. 7–12.

178. "The Four Basic Principles Tolerate No Violations—Commenting on the Film Script 'Unrequited Love,'" *Jiefangjun Bao* (Liberation Army Daily), April 20, 1981, p. 1.

179. M. Weisskopf, "China Reviewing Freedom Granted Its Intellectuals," *The Washington Post*, May 7, 1981, p. A36; AP, Beijing, August 10, 1981.

180. "Bai Hua," *Speahrhead*, No. 12/13, Northern Winter-Spring 1982, p. 34. See also Christopher Wren, "China Re-examines Role of the Arts," *New York Times*, Dec. 29, 1981, p. A4.

181. "China: Tale of Two Dengs," *The Economist*, Vol. 290, No. 7327, Feb. 4, 1984, p. 40.

182. AFP, Beijing, May 6, 1981; FBIS, *Daily Report: China*, May 7, 1981, p. K3; AP, Beijing, May 13, 1981. She is, however, now voluntarily on Liu-chang, or long-term residence, in the countryside. See *Speahrhead*, Northern Winter/Spring, 1982, p. 3.

183. See above note 171.

184. Department of State, "China," p. 568. More information in the following section.

185. Department of State, see above note 85, p. 743.

186. Lu Heyun, "An Analysis of All Kinds of Handicaps to the Exposition of Grafts in the Economic Field," *Faxue*, No. 4, 1982, p. 36.

187. *Renmin Ribao*, May 11, 1982, p. 1. See also Commentator, "Party Discipline Must be Strictly Enforced," *Ibid.*

188. *Minzhu Yu Fazhi*, No. 7, 1982, p. 43.

189. Wu Biao, "We Can Never Let Law-Breaking Offenders Subject to Criticism for a Short Period While Enjoying Comforts for a Lifetime," *Minzhu Yu Fazhi*, No. 1, 1982, p. 10.

190. Qiu Xueyao, "The Differences Between Party Discipline, Administrative Discipline, and the Legal Code," *Guangming Ribao*, Dec. 8, 1981, p. 3; JPRS 79954, Jan. 27, 1982, pp. 13–14. The Party's disciplinary sanctions are based on Article 5 of the Party Constitution in *Beijing Review*, Vol. 20, No. 36, Sept. 2, 1977, p. 19. See also

Article 39 of the New Party Constitution of 1982 in *Renmin Ribao*, Sept. 9, 1982, p. 3. The government organs' disciplinary sanctions are based on the Provisional Regulations of the State Council of the PRC Relating to Rewards and Punishments for Personnel of State Administrative Organs (1957) in Cohen, *The Criminal Process*, pp. 193–195.

191. Zeng Longyue, "Links and Differences Between Party Discipline and State Law in Fighting Economic Crimes," *Renmin Ribao*, April 5, 1982, p. 3; FBIS, *Daily Report: China*, April 13, 1982, pp. K1–K2.

192. "Questions and Answers on Party Knowledge" Column: "On Handling the Party Membership of the Communist Party Members who Are Punished in Criminal Cases," *Renmin Ribao*, March 3, 1982, p. 3; FBIS, *Daily Report: China*, March 9, 1982, pp. K13–K14.

193. *Renmin Ribao*, Nov. 30, 1979, p. 1.

194. Text of the SAPA in *GAFGHB*, see above note 1, pp. 113–122, republished in *Renmin Ribao*, Feb. 24, 1980, p. 4.

195. Text of the Decision in *GAFGHB*, pp. 391–392, translated in Cohen, *The Criminal Process*, pp. 249–250. It was republished in *Renmin Ribao*, Feb. 24, 1980, p. 4.

196. Leng, *Justice in Communist China*, pp. 123–124; *Political Imprisonment in the PRC*, pp. 82–83. It should be noted that many "rightists" of the 1950s were detained for reeducation through labor for almost twenty years.

197. Text of the Supplementary Regulations is in *GAFGHB*, p. 391. Also consult Yu Haocheng, "Reeducation Through Labor is an Essential Measure for Strengthening the Legal System and Maintaining Law and Order," *Guangming Ribao*, Dec. 9, 1979, p. 3, translated in FBIS, *Daily Report: PRC*, Dec. 26, 1979, pp. L11–L13; "Differences Between Reeducation Through Labor and Reform Through Labor," *Zhongguo Fazhi Bao*, June 5, 1981, p. 3.

198. *Zhonghua Renmin Gongheguo Guowuyuan Gongbao* (People's Republic of China State Council Gazette), April 16, 1980, pp. 57–58, cited in Timothy A. Gelatt, "The People's Republic of China and the Presumption of Innocence," *Journal of Criminal Law and Criminology*, Vol. 73, No. 1, p. 314.

199. See Yu Haocheng, *Guangming Ribao*. He conceded, however, that "in some places, there has not been much difference in treating people undergoing reeducation through labor and criminals undergoing reform through labor."

200. See above notes 131 and 132.

201. Jay Mathews, "China Revives Labor Camp System," *The Washington Post*, June 1, 1980, pp. A1, A27; Bryan Johnson, "China Dissidents Fall Through Cracks in New Legal Code," *Christian Science Monitor*, June 18, 1980, p. 4; Fox Butterfield, "Hundreds of Thousands Toil in Chinese Labor Camps," *New York Times*, Jan. 3, 1981, pp. 1, 4.

202. Mathews, see above note 201, p. A1.

203. For Liu's personal account, see above note 170.

204. It should be noted that Article 52 of the 1954 Regulations on Reform Through Labor requires the offenders to work for nine to ten or, at most, twelve hours a day. *GAFGHB*, p. 404. A good description of China's corrective institutions up to 1978 is in *Political Imprisonment in the PRC*, Chapters 3–5. Among some personal accounts of China's labor reform institutions are Bao Ruo-Wang and Rudolph Chelminski, *Prisoner of Mao* (New York: McCann and Geoghegan, 1973); "China's Gulag," Seymour, ed., *The Fifth Modernization*, pp. 207–223; Michael Weisskopf, "Ex-Inmate Recalls Life in China's Gulag," *The Washington Post*, Feb. 12, 1982, pp. A1, A44–A45.

205. See Wei Min, "Visiting a Prison," *Beijing Review*, Vol. 24, No. 8, Feb. 23, 1981, pp. 24–28; Shuang Yin, "Behind the Big Wall—What One Sees and Hears in Prison in Beijing," FBIS, *Daily Report: China*, Oct. 22, 1981, pp. K6–K7; "How Beijing

Prison Works—Interview with Prison Warden," *Xhinhua News Agency*, Nov. 11, 1981; Li Binghou, "Visit the Shanghai Municipal Prison," *Minzhu Yu Fazhi*, No. 11, 1981, pp. 7–8.

206. Xu Xinhua, "Victory for the Party's Policy of Transformation—on an interview with Public Security Minister Zhao Cangbi," *FBIS, Daily Report: China*, April 15, 1982, p. K8.

207. See above note 206.

208. Liu Zhi, "Notes on the Reform Role of Punishment of China," see above note 106, p. 29.

209. Butterfield, *China: Alive in the Bitter Sea*, pp. 365–369; interviews with three ex-inmates as well as relatives of several others.

210. Frank Ching, "China's Political Prisoners Help to Develop Frontier," *Asian Wall Street Journal*, June 3, 1982, p. 1.

211. Xu Xinhua, see above note 206, pp. K8–K4.

Conclusion

In the wake of the promulgation of the PRC's new Constitution in December 1982, *China's Legal System Paper*, a publication of China's Justice Ministry, greeted the year of 1983 with an editorial entitled: "Welcome the New Year of Rule of the Country by Law." [1] What a sharp contrast with a 1967 *People's Daily*'s editorial entitled, "In Praise of Lawlessness"! [2]

The discussion in this book has clearly demonstrated that post-Mao China has come a long way to restore the respectability of the jural model of law, to stress rule by law over rule by man, and construct a more equitable and predictable system of criminal justice than ever known in the PRC. There is little doubt that the removal of Mao Zedong from the Chinese political scene, the emergence of Deng Xiaoping and other pragmatic leaders, the nightmare experience the Chinese had with the Cultural Revolution, and the current national imperatives for modernization and development all account for China's turn toward legality.

To be sure, there remain a number of problems and difficulties in the PRC's path to a stable and sound legal order. First of all, China still suffers from the shortage of trained personnel and other resources in the legal field despite some recent progress made in coping with this glaring weakness. Second, both the populace and bureaucracy tend to have an indifferent and skeptical attitude toward law, official publicity campaigns about the legal system notwithstanding. As admitted by an editorial of the *People's Daily*, "The concept of a legal system is rather weak in our country, including among some Party members and even certain responsible Party cadres." [3] In his report to the 12th National Congress of the Communist Party of China on September 1, 1982, Party Secretary-General Hu Yaobang also said, "The problems facing us today are not only a sizable number of non-Party people but also many Party members, including some leading cadres, do not have an adequate understanding of the importance of building the legal system and that laws already enacted are in some cases not fully observed or enforced." [4] Third, the PRC's socialist legality is expected to operate within the limits of the so-called Four Basic Principles: the socialist road, the People's Democratic Dictatorship, the leadership of the Communist Party, and Marxism-Leninism-Mao Zedong Thought. This constraint on all Chinese institutions is explicitly stated in the preamble of what may be considered a liberal Constitution adopted in 1982.[5] Its restrictive implications for individual rights and judicial independence go without saying. Finally, there is always a concern about the stability and continuity of the Chinese leadership and its policies. In view of China's frequent political upheavals and policy shifts in the past, many people understandably cannot help having lingering fears that the pendulum may again swing to the left in the future at the expense of the jural model of law.

On the other hand, current Chinese leaders appear to be aware of these problems and are making conscientious efforts to reassure the public and to educate the bureaucracy. For instance, in Hu Yaobang's report quoted above, he stressed that "Party members should be educated and urged to take the lead in observing the Constitution and laws. The stipulation in the new Party Constitution that 'the Party must conduct its activities within the limits permitted by the Constitution and the laws of the state' embodies a most important principle. It is impermissible for any Party organization or member, from the Central Committee down to the grassroots, to act in contravention of the Constitution and laws." [6] By the same token, Article 5 of the new state Constitution provides: "All state organs, the armed forces, all political parties and public organizations and all enterprises and undertakings must abide by the Constitution and the law . . . No organization or individual may enjoy the privilege of being above the Constitution and the law." [7]

Reporting to the National People's Congress on November 26, 1982, Peng Zhen, Vice-Chairman of the Committee for Revision of the Constitution, made a special point to emphasize the permanent nature of China's new Constitution and legal system by stating that the NPC "assuredly can enact a new Constitution that is distinctly Chinese and meets the needs of our socialist modernization in the new historical period and that will remain valid for a long period of time." [8] This point was elaborated by a *People's Daily* article, which cited Peng's following remarks: "The stable implementation of a constitution depends upon whether its content is correct or not . . . The Constitution formulated this time after summing up both the positive and negative experiences in the past 30-odd years since the founding of the PRC, the serious revision lasting 2 years and 2 months, the discussion of people all over the country, and the examination and approval of the NPC, conform to reality and people's will and interests, hence proving to be a more stable one than those of the past." [9] To dispel the fear of another violent upheaval in the future, Peng was quoted as saying, "The best guarantee is in the fact that the Constitution is mastered by 1 billion people. Through the rigorous tests of the 'Cultural Revolution,' the 1 bilion people have raised their political vigilance and abilities to distinguish things and obtained experience to deal with bad people and deeds. As the power of the Constitution is in the hands of the 1 billion people, it is possible to avoid violent disturbance such as the 'Cultural Revolution.' " [10] Despite Peng's optimistic view on the future of this Constitution, the mechanism embodied in this Constitution to interpret and supervise the enforcement of this Constitution does not seem to warrant such a view. All these functions are, under Article 67, entrusted to a political organ—the Standing Committee of the National People's Congress, and not to an independent judicial organ. This arrangement is similar to the constitutions of the Soviet Union and other Communist countries and none of these countries have taken their constitutions seriously.[11] Whether the present PRC Constitution will be an exception remains to be seen.

In the field of criminal justice, what is being institutionalized in post-Mao China may be called the Chinese variety of socialist justice system with the blending of both Soviet and indigenous experiences. Western influences are also quite evident. As in the case of the Soviet Union, the PRC is using Western forms of law to cement and legitimate political control but has no hesitation to dispense with legal procedures where need arises.[12] In line with the Chinese Li-Fa tradition, Beijing now gives due attention to both jural and societal models of law while continuing to combine punishment with education in its penal policy. For the first time in the PRC history, there are substantive and procedural criminal laws to define criminal acts and their appropriate penalties and to prescribe proper legal standards to guide the sanctioning process. As shown in this book, however, the full implementation of the laws has been handicapped by some objective restraints; official abuses and illegal violation of citizens' rights have continued to occur. The major difference from the past is the considerable determination and candidness manifested by the present leadership to confront the various obstacles in establishing the new justice system in China. From time to time, the press and legal journals have voiced their concern about unlawful or irregular acts on the part of the bureaucracy. In its "Legal Mailbox," for instance, the People's Daily on November 22, 1982 had a column calling for absolute prohibition of illegal arrest and detention by public security organs.[13] One law journal article urged the strict enforcement of the law and the condemnation of continuing the feudal tradition of shielding officials from punishment.[14] Another reminded the Party and government organs that no one is above the law and that law violators must take the consequences.[15] In a letter to a law journal, one reader complained about the practice by a higher court to have direct influence on and interference with a lower court's original decisions on issues of guilt and punishment in criminal cases.[16]

Post-Mao China has abolished the system of "Shuji pian" (approving cases by the secretary), but the continuing assertion of influence in legal affairs by the Party's political-legal committees seems to be limiting the degree of independence allowed to the judiciary. The latest crime suppression campaign is a case in point. As discussed in the preceding chapters, the decision to strike a swift and severe blow at serious criminal activities was first made by the Political-Legal Committee of the CCP Central Committee. It was soon followed by a nationwide crime crackdown in the form of mass arrests and publicized executions. Still later, the fait accompli was legitimized by the Standing Committee of the National People's Congress, which amended the PRC's Criminal Law to sharply increase the number of crimes punishable by death and the Criminal Procedure Law to remove procedural guarantees for certain felons, such as murderers, rapists, and robbers. Intended to "execute one as a warning to one hundred," the harsh anticrime campaign, nonetheless, appears to have "exceeded proper limits to right a wrong" and shaken the fragile foundation of the rule of law even in the eyes of pro-PRC observers.[17]

Despite its apparent problems and shortcomings, the criminal justice system in China today must be considered a vast improvement over the Maoist system of justice in the protection of the individual against state excesses and arbitrary actions. Undoubtedly, the existence of criminal laws, the de-emphasis of class struggle, and the formal commitment to procedural protections and citizens' rights all tend to afford, for the first time in PRC history, the accused a more than window-dressing opportunity to defend himself in criminal proceedings.

One basic limitation on the current development, nevertheless, remains to be the dictates of politics. Both socialist and traditional theories put emphasis on order over freedom, duties over rights, and group interests over individual ones. Consequently, whenever the social order is perceived by the Chinese elites as being threatened, legal niceties are usually set aside. The stern measures used in the crime suppression campaign, the political trials of Wei Jingsheng, Liu Qing, Xu Wenli, Wang Xizhe, He Qin and other dissidents,[18] and the imprisonment of newspaper editors for betraying "state secrets" to foreigners[19] are just a few illustrations. Another inhibiting factor is the roles of the police and other extrajudicial agencies in the sanctioning process. Given China's shortage of legal personnel and traditional preference for informal settlement of disputes and minor infractions, the coexistence of the societal model of law with the resurgent jural model is necessary and probably desirable. But the revival of the police's power to apply a wide range of "administrative" sanctions, including reeducation through labor, can hardly brighten the prospects for legality in the PRC.

All in all, there are stumbling blocks to overcome before China can have the rule of law firmly established. Still, a significant and positive start has indeed been made in this direction by the post-Mao leadership. It is, of course, hazardous to predict China's future development. What seems to be certain is that the PRC needs stable legal institutions to maintain discipline and social order essential to economic modernization.[20] However, in order to enhance the credibility of socialist legality, Beijing will have not only to continue the expansion of legislative and educational programs in the legal field but also to faithfully implement the adopted laws, avoid pursuing short-term goals at the expense of legality, and keep to a minimum the use of extrajudicial measures in the sanctioning process. Certainly, within the broad framework of serving socialism under Party leadership, the Chinese judiciary and procuracy ought to have sufficient functional independence to enforce the law, administer criminal justice, and provide the Chinese with the form of institutional and procedural protections guaranteed by the PRC Constitution.

NOTES

Chapter Seven

1. *Zhongguo Fazhi Bao*, Dec. 31, 1982, p. 1.

2. *Survey of China Mainland Press* (Hong Kong: U.S. Consulate General), No. 3879, Feb. 14, 1967, p. 13.

3. Editorial: "The General Charter for Managing State Affairs and Giving the State Peace and Security in the New Period," *Renmin Ribao*, Dec. 5, 1982, p. 5; also *FBIS, Daily Report: China*, Dec. 6, 1982, pp. K12–K14.

4. Hu Yaobang, "Create a New Situation in All Fields of Socialist Modernization" *Beijing Review*, Vol. 25, Sept. 1, 1982, p. 27.

5. "Constitution of People's Republic of China," *Beijing Review*, December 27, 1982, p. 11.

6. Hu Yaobang, See above note 4. The stipulation he referred to is in the General Programme of the Party Constitution adopted on September 6, 1982. Text of the CCP Constitution is in *Zhongguo Fazhi Bao*, Sept. 17, 1982, pp. 3–4. English text is in *FBIS, Daily Report: China*, Sept. 9, 1982, pp. K1–K19.

7. *Beijing Review*, Vol. 25, Dec. 27, 1982, pp. 12–13. Comments by NPC deputies and Party secretaries all stressed that Party members and organizations should operate

within the framework of the Constitution and the law; *Renmin Ribao*, Dec. 2, 1982, p. 3. See also Editorial in *Renmin Ribao*, Dec. 5, 1982, p. 5.

8. "Report on the Draft of the Revised Constitution of the People's Republic of China," *Renmin Ribao*, Dec. 13, 1982, p. 11.

9. Jing Feng, "All Power Belongs to the People," *Renmin Ribao*, Dec. 7, 1982, p. 7; FBIS, *Daily Report: China*, Dec. 12, 1982, pp. 10–11.

10. Ibid.

11. See Article 121 of the 1977 Soviet Constitution where the Presidium of the Supreme Soviet (equivalent of the Standing Committee of the NPC in the PRC) is entrusted with the function of supervising the implementation of the constitution and interpretation of statutes.

12. David F. Forte, "Western Law and Communist Dictatorship," *Emory Law Journal*, vol. 32, No. 1, Winter 1983, pp. 217–222.

13. *Renmin Ribao*, Nov. 22, 1982, p. 3.

14. Chiu Min, "Develop Democracy and Strengthen the Legal System," *Minzhu Yu Fazhi* (Democracy and Legal System), No. 10, 1982, p. 7.

15. Wang Suwen, Li Buyun and Xu Bing, "On Strengthening Socialist Legal System," *Faxue Yanjiu* (Studies in Law), No. 5, 1982, p. 8.

16. *Minzhu Yu Fazhi*, No. 9. 1982, p. 29.

17. Chou Hui, "Beijing is in the Process of 'Big Sweep,' " *Cheng Ming* (Contending), No. 10, 1983, pp. 11–13; Hsu Hsing, "Mass Arrests and Rule of Law," *Cheng Ming*, pp. 14–16.

18. Wei's and Liu's cases have been discussed elsewhere in the book. As for the trials of Xu, Wang, and He, sources in Hong Kong reported that none of their families were notified in advance about the trials nor was the official record of the verdicts made public (all contrary to the requirements of the Criminal Procedure Law). "Political Trials in China," *Amnesty International Newsletter*, January 1983, Vol. XIII, No. 1., p. 8. See also profiles of Chinese "prisoners of conscience" in Amnesty International, *China: Violations of Human Rights* (London: Amnesty International Publications, 1984), pp. 19–51.

19. Li Guangyi, editor in chief of the *China Finance and Trade Journal*, was sentenced in 1982 to five years imprisonment for allegedly disclosing "details of the proceedings of the plenary session of the 11th Central Committee of the Communist Party of China and contents of the session's confidential documents." Frank Ching, "Official's Punishment Gives Chinese a Message: Don't Talk to Foreigners," *Asian Wall Street Journal Weekly*, April 5, 1982, p. 10. Also mentioned in Chapter Six, and editor-in-chief of a pro-Communist daily in Hong Kong was sentenced in 1983 to ten years in prison on charges of supplying secret information to the U.S.

20. See Stanley B. Lubman, "Emerging Functions of Formal Legal Institutions in China's Modernization," U.S. Congressional Joint Economic Committee, *China Under the Four Modernizations* (Washington, D.C.: U.S. Government Printing Office, 1982), Part 2, pp. 280–289.

II

Documents

Document 1

Act of the People's Republic of China for Punishment of Counterrevolutionaries

(Approved at the 11th Meeting of the Central People's Government Council on February 20, 1951 and Promulgated on February 21, 1951.) (Chinese text in Gongan faqui huibian, pp. 96-99; English translation in Jerome Alan Cohen, The Criminal Process in the People's Republic of China, pp. 299-302.

Article 1. In accordance with the provisions of Article 7 of the Common Program of the Chinese People's Political Consultative Conference, this Act is specifically adopted in order to punish counterrevolutionary criminals, suppress counter-revolutionary activity, and consolidate the people's democratic dictatorship.

Article 2. All counterrevolutionary criminals whose goal is to overthrow the people's democratic regime or to undermine the undertaking of the people's democracy shall be punished in accordance with this Act.

Article 3. Those who collaborate with imperialists to betray their mother country shall be punished by death or life imprisonment.

Article 4. Of those who incite, entice or buy public employees, armed military units, or people's militia units used in the insurrection shall be punished by death or life imprisonment. Others who participate in the inciting, enticing, buying, or insurrection shall be punished by not more than ten years of imprisonment; where the circumstances of their cases are major they shall be punished with increased severity.

Article 5. In a mass, armed uprising, the ringleaders, commanders, and others whose evil crimes are major shall be punished by death. Other active participants shall be punished by not less than five years of imprisonment.

Article 6. Those who engage in any one of the following acts of espionage or of aiding the

enemy shall be punished by death or life imprisonment; where the circumstances of their cases are
relatively minor they shall be punished by not
less than five years of imprisonment:

(1)   Stealing or searching for state secrets
       or supplying intelligence to a domestic
       or foreign enemy;

(2)   Instructing enemy planes or enemy ships
       about bombardment targets;

(3)   Supplying domestic or foreign enemies
       with weapons, ammunition, or other mili-
       tary materials.

Article 7.   Those who participate in organizations of counterrevolutionary secret agents
or spies, and whose cases include any one of the
following circumstances shall be punished by death
or life imprionsment; where the circumstances are
relatively minor they shall be punished by not
less than five years of imprisonment:

(1)   They have been sent by a domestic or
       foreign enemy for [conducting] covert
       activities;

(2)   Since liberation they have organized or
       participated in organizations or coun-
       terrevolutionary secret agents or spies;

(3)   Before liberation they organized or led
       organizations of counterrevolutionary
       secret agents or spies and committed
       other major evil crimes, and since
       liberation their behavior has not es-
       tablished their merit and atoned for
       their crimes;

(4)   Before liberation they participated in
       organizations of counterrevolutionary
       secret agents or spies, and since
       liberation they have continued to par-
       ticipate in counterrevolutionary
       activity;

(5)   After registration with the voluntary
       surrender to the people's government,

they have continued to participate in counterrevolutionary activity;

(6) After being educated and released by the people's government, they have continued to link themselves with counterrevolutionary secret agents and spies or to conduct counterrevolutionary activity.

Article 8. Those who make use of feudal societies to conduct counterrevolutionary activity shall be punished by death or life imprisonment; where the circumstances of their cases are relatively minor they shall be punished by not less than three years of imprisonment.

Article 9. Those who, with a counterrevolutionary purpose, plot or execute any one of the following acts of sabotage or murder shall be punished by death or life imprisonment; where the circumstances of their cases are relatively minor they shall be punished by not less than five years of imprisonment:

(1) Robbing or destroying military facilities, mines, forests, farms, dams, communications, banks, warehouses, safety equipment, or other important public or private property;

(2) Spreading poison, spreading germs, or using other methods that cause major disasters involving people, livestock, or agricultural crops;

(3) Under instructions from a domestic or foreign enemy, disrupting the market or undermining finance;

(4) Attacking, killing, or injuring people or public employees;

(5) Improperly using the name of military or government organs, democratic parties, or groups of people's organizations and forging official documents to engage in counterrevolutionary activity.

Article 10. Those who, with a counterrevolutionary purpose, commit any one of the following acts of provocation or incitement shall be punished by not less than three years of imprisonment; where the circumstances of their cases are major they shall be punished by death or life imprisonment:

(1)   Stirring up the masses to resist or to undermine the enforcement of grain levies, tax levies, public service, military service of the people's government, or other government orders;

(2)   Provoking dissension among the various nationalities, democratic classes, democratic parties and groups, people's organizations or between the people and the government;

(3)   Conducting counterrevolutionary propaganda and agitation and making and spreading rumors.

Article 11.   Those who, with a counterrevolutionary purpose, secretly cross the borders of the state shall be punished by not less than five years of imprisonment life imprisonment, or death.

Article 12.   The organizers and ringleaders of mass prison raids or violent prison breaks shall be punished by death or life imprisonment; other activity participants shall be punished by not less than three years of imprisonment.

Article 13.   Those who harbor or conceal counterrevolutionary criminals shall be punished by not more than ten years of imprisonment; where the circumstances of their cases are major they shall be punished by not less than ten years of imprisonment, life imprisonment, or death.

Article 14.   In any one of the following situations, all those who commit crimes [enumerated] in this Act may, according to the circumstances, be given light punishment, reduced punishment, or may be exempted from punishment:

(1)   They have taken the initiative in going to the people's government and in sincerely and voluntarily surrendering and repenting;

(2)   Before or after they have been exposed or denounced, they have sincerely repented and established their merit and atoned for their crimes;

(3)   They were coerced or deceived by counterrevolutionaries, and their crimes were really involuntary;

(4)   Before liberation their counterrevolutionary crimes were definitely not major, since liberation they have really repented and reformed, and they have severed their links with counterrevolutionary organizations.

Article 15. The punishment of all those who commit several kinds of crimes, except those sentenced to death or life imprisonment, shall, according to the circumstances, be fixed at less than the aggregate punishment [that is possible for all the crimes] but more than the most severe punishment [for any one of those crimes].

Article 16. Those who, with a counterrevolutionary purpose, commit crimes not covered by the provisions of this Act may be given punishments prescribed for crimes [enumerated] in this Act which are comparable to the crimes committed.

Article 17. Those who commit crimes [enumerated] in this Act may be deprived of their political rights, and all or a portion of their property may be confiscated.

Article 18. The provisions of this Act also apply to those who were counterrevolutionary criminals before this Act was put into effect.

Article 19. Anyone has the right to expose or secretly to report counterrevolutionary criminals to the people's government, but no one harboring resentment may make maliciously false accusations.

Article 20. Those who commit crimes [enumerated] in this Act shall, during periods of military control, be tried in accordance with this Act by military courts that are organized by various military district headquarters, military control commissions, or command organs for combatting banditry.

Article 21. This Act shall be put into effect on the day it is approved and promulgated by the Central People's Government Council.

Document 2

Provisional Act on Guarding State Secrets (Excerpts) Passed by the 87th Meeting of the Government Administration Council on June 1, 1951, Approved by the Chairman of the People's Republic of China and Promulgated on June 8, 1951. Republished in Renmin ribao (People's Daily), April 11, 1980, pp. 1, 3. (Translated from Gongan fagui huibian, pp. 472-476.)

Article 1. This Act is specially enacted in order to guard strictly state secrets of the People's Republic of China, prevent domestic and foreign spies, counterrevolutionary elements and destructive elements from gathering intelligence, stealing and selling state secrets and prevent all kinds of personnel from leaking or losing state secrets.

Article 2. State secrets include the following basic categories:

(1)   All national defense and military plans and construction measures;

(2)   Secret information on the authorized strength, destination, actual strength, equipment, stationing, movement and deployment of all armed forces units and on logistics, ordnance construction and so forth;

(3)   Foreign affairs secrets;

(4)   Public security secrets;

(5)   State financial plan, state budget estimate, budget and final accounts and other financial secrets;

(6)   State banking, trade and customs' plans and banking, trade and customs affairs secrets;

(7)   Secret information about railways, transport, postal and telecommunications services;

(8)   Secret information on the country's various economic construction plans and undertakings;

(9)   Secret information on natural resource surveying, geological prospecting, meteorological observation and reporting, geographical surveying and mapping and so forth;

(10) Scientific inventions and discoveries, cultural, educational, public health and medical secrets;

(11) Secret information on legislative, judicial, procuratorial and control affairs;

(12) Secret information on nationalities and Overseas Chinese Affairs;

(13) Internal and personnel secrets;

(14) Files, cipher codes, official seals and all documents, telegrams, letters, data, statistics, figures, charts, books and periodicals concerning state secrets;

(15) All organs, establishments, warehouses, places, and so forth that have something to do with state secrets;

(16) All state affairs which have not yet been decided upon or which have been decided upon but have not yet been made public; and

(17) All other state affairs which should be kept secret.

Article 3. With regard to the various specific matters and categories of state secrets, regulations shall be formulated and promulgated by the Government Administrative Council* of the Central People's Government for state secrets which deal with administrative affairs; and regulations shall be formulated and promulgated by the People's Revolutionary Military Committee of the Central People's Government for state secrets which deal with national defense and military affairs. If secrets must be guarded by a certin locality to meet a specific need, supplemental regulations may be formulated and reported to the next higher level organ for the record. (*Since September 20, 1954 renamed as State Council)

Article 4. Organs for guarding secrets shall be established by the people's government at all levels and all armed forces units to undertake the responsibility for the work of guarding secrets. The general organic rules for these organs shall be formulated separately.

The systems and organizations for guarding state secrets shall be established, in accordance with its own needs, by each democratic party, people's organization, [government] organ, school, factory, enterprises, mine, warehouse and others.

Article 5. All personnel of the people's governments at various levels and each armed forces unit, democratic party, people's organization, [government] organ, school, factory, enterprise, mine, and warehouse and others should strictly guard state secrets and not reveal them. Each and every unit should pay attention to educating its personnel to enhance their self-consciousness and discipline of strictly guarding state secrets. Acting in accordance with actual conditions, each unit shall conduct necessary propaganda and education on guarding state secrets among the masses of people. With regard to the places where secrets must be strictly guarded, the local government may organize the people to guard the secrets and may [ask them] to sign a pact for guarding secrets, which would be implemented through mutual supervision.

Article 6. The personnel in charge of and handling state secrets shall be seriously and strictly examined by the personnel department so that only those who are definitely reliable will be selected for the job.

Article 7. It is necessary to establish a strict control and inspection system to deal with the telegram, documents, data, copying and proofreading of statistics, printing materials and supervision for using [government] seals concerning state secrets as well as receiving and sending, delivering, reading, preserving, disposing and filing of state secret documents and to provide this system with necessary material facilities.

Article 8. Designation of delegates and non-voting delegates to any important meeting shall be decided in accordance with work needs and must be submitted to a specific organ for approval. Personnel who assisted the meeting work shall be strictly examined and subject to education on guarding secrets. The meeting place should be thoroughly covered by security guards. The meeting documents can only be printed with the examination and approval of the personnel in charge and should be returned after the meeting is over unless otherwise approved; there shall be no digesting or copying of the meeting documents; and a file should be kept to indicate which meeting documents are not required to be returned. No one shall take notes [at a meeting] without permission. The situation at a meeting should not be leaked. In case the contents of a meeting are to be relayed, special personnel should be assigned to do the job and the contents to be relayed and the persons to do the relaying must also be specified.

[Articles 9 and 10 omitted]

Article 11. The announcement and report of news, essays and data concerning state policies within the scope of government administration shall be subject to the unified regulations issued by the Government Administration Council of the Central People's Government . . . .

News, essays, data and others publicized by the press and broadcast over radio should not involve state secrets. News agencies, newspaper agencies, broadcasting stations and publishing houses shall establish measures for examining news, essays and data in order to guard secrets.

Article 12. All publications published by units of various government organizations must be approved by the Government Administration Council of the People's Governments of Large Administrative Regions (Military and Administrative Commiteee)* . . . . The above mentioned pulications shall not publish documents containing state secrets and before publication must be examined by the officials in charge of guarding state secrets. (*The Large Administrative Region was abolished after the promulgation of the 1954 Constitution)

Article 13. Any person who commits one of the following acts shall be found guilty of being a counterrevolutionary and punished according to the Act for the Punishment of Counterrevolutionaries:

(1) Selling state secrets to a domestic or foreign enemy;

(2) Deliberately leaking state secrets to a domestic or foreign enemy; or

(3) Selling state secrets to a domestic or foreign unscrupulous merchant.

Article 14. Any person who engages in speculation for profit by using state secrets shall be sent to judicial organs or military courts for punishment according to law.

Article 15. Any person who has leaked out state secrets or lost classified state materials through negligence or oversight shall be punished according to the seriousness of the case.

Article 16. Any person who has distinguished himself in one of the following ways shall be commended or awarded:

(1) Resolutely guarding state secrets by displaying unyielding heroism in the face of the enemy;

(2) In a desperate situation, guarding state secrets in defiance of difficulties and dangers;

(3) Timely reporting to the authorities a case or a person involving the illegal use, selling and stealing of state secrets and thus uncovering the [crime];

(4) Taking timely remedial measures after discovering incidents of losing or leaking state secrets; or

(5) Making marked achievements inconsistently complying with the system of guarding secrets and in promoting other persons to safeguard state secrets.

Article 17. The supervisory organizations of the people's governments at all levels must make their work of supervising the safeguarding of state secrets a constant task.

Article 18. All units shall formulate concrete methods to implement provisions of this Act.

[Article 19 omitted]

Article 20. The Government Administration Council of the Central People's Government has the right to interpret and amend this Act.

Document 3

Arrest and Detention Act of
the People's Republic of China
(Passed by the 6th Meeting of the
Standing Committee of the Fifth National
People's Congress on February 23, 1979)
(Translated from Gongan fagui huibian, pp. 87-89)

Article 1. In accordance with the provisions provided in Articles 18* and 47** of the [1978] Constitution of the People's Republic of China, in order to safeguard the socialist system, maintain social order, punish crime and protect the citizens' freedom of person and the inviolability of their homes, this Act is hereby specially enacted. [*Equivalent to Article 28 of the 1982 Constitution; **Equivalent to Article 37 (freedom of person) and 39 (inviolability of citizens' homes) of the 1982 Constitution]

Article 2. No citizens of the People's Republic of China may be arrested except by the decision of a people's court or with the approval of a people's procuratorate.

Article 3. An offender should be arrested immediately after the principal facts related to the crime have been clearly investigated and he may be sentenced to a prison term or more severe punishment and only where the arrest is necessary, provided that such an arrest is decided upon by a people's court or approved by a people's procuratorate.

If the offender arrested is suffering from a serious illness or is pregnant, or is breast-feeding her own child, that person may be placed on bail waiting for trial or a surveillance can be imposed on that person's residence.

Article 4. The arrest of an offender, as decided upon by a people's court or approved by a people's procuratorate, shall be carried out by a public security organ.

When a public security organ requests the arrest of an offender, it shall be approved by a people's procuratorate.

Article 5. When a public security organ makes an arrest of an offender, it must have an arrest warrant and present it to the person to be arrested. After the arrest, unless in the situation where investigation may be hampered or notification is impossible, the public security organ and the people's procuratorate or the people's court should notify the family of the person under arrest of the reason for the arrest and of the place of detention within twenty-four hours.

Article 6. In any one of the following situations, a public security organ may, in an emergency situation, detain [before it has obtained a warrant] a person in flagrante delicto whose offense justifies an arrest or who is suspected of having committed a major crime:

(1)   [A person who] is preparing to commit a crime, in the process of committing a

crime, or is discovered immediately after committing a crime;

(2)   [A person who] is identified as a criminal by the victim or an eyewitness;

(3)   Where evidence of a crime is found in a person or his residence;

(4)   [A person who] is attempting to commit suicide or to escape, or who is in flight after having committed an offense;

(5)   [A person who] may destroy or fabricate evidence or may collude with others regarding a statement to be made [with respect to a case];

(6)   [A person whose] identity is unknown and is seriously suspected of having committed offenses here and there; or

(7)   [A person who] is in the process of beating, smashing, looting or illegally confiscating and thus seriously undermining the work, production or social order.

Article 7. Any citizen may immediately seize the following offenders and take them to a public security organ, a people's procuracy, or a people's court to be dealt with:

(1)   [A person who] is committing a crime or is discovered immediately after committing a crime.

(2)   [A person who] is wanted in a criminal case.

(3)   [A person who] has escaped from prison.

(4)   [A person who] is being pursued for arrest.

Article 8. If it is necessary to place an offender detained by a public security organ under arrest, the latter should notify the people's procuratorate at the same level, within 3 days after the detention, of the facts related to the detainee's crime and of the evidence. In special cases, the time of detention may be extended for 4 more days. The people's procuratorate should either approve or disapprove the arrest within 3 days after receiving the notification; if the people's procuratorate does not approve an arrest, the public security organ should release the detainee immediately after receiving such notification and issue to him a release certificate.

If a public security organ or a people's procuratorate has not handled the matter in accordance with the provisions of the preceeding paragraph, the detainee or his family has the right to demand his release and the public security organ or the people's procuratorate should immediately release the detainee.

Article 9. In dealing with those offenders who resist arrest or detention, the personnel carrying out the arrest or detention may take proper methods of coercion and may use weapons when necessary.

Article 10. At the time of arrest or detention, in looking for criminal evidence, the public security organ may carry out a search of the offender's body, his property, his residence or other places concerned. If it suspects any other person of hiding the offender or concealing criminal evidence, it may also carry out a search of his body, property, residence or other places concerned. Except for in emergencies, the public security organ should present a search warrant in case of such a search.

In case of a search, a neighbor or any other witness and the person to be searched or members of his family should be present. After the search, a record should be made of the results of the search and of any criminal evidence seized, to be signed by the neighbor or any other witness and by the person searched or members of his family, as well as by the personnel carrying out the search. If the person to be searched or members of his family are in flight or refuse to sign their names, it should be so noted in the record.

Article 11. The people's court, the people's procuratorate and the public security organ, if they deem it necessary, may notify the posts and telecommunications organs to hold the mail and telegram of an offender under arrest or detention.

Article 12. The people's court, the people's procuratorate and the public security organ must carry out interrogation of an offender under arrest or detention within 24 hours after his arrest or detention. If they find that the arrest or detention are unjustified, they should immediately release the detainee and issue to him a release certificate.

Article 13. The people's procuratorate should investigate any responsible personnel who carried out arrests, detentions and searches of citizens in violation of the law. If such illegal acts are carried out for the purpose of framing, taking revenge, corruption, or for some other personal ends, criminal responsibilities should be investigated and ascertained.

Article 14. Provisions of this Act do not apply to the detention of a citizen by a public security organ for the purpose of giving administrative sanction for violation of rules governing security administration rules.* (*See Document 9)

Article 15. This Act shall enter into force on the date of promulgation. Simultaneous with it, the "Arrest and Detention Act of the People's Republic of China" promulgated on December 20, 1954 is hereby abrogated.

Document 4

Criminal Law of the People's Republic of China
(Passed by the Second Plenary Meeting of the
Fifth National People's Congress on July 1, 1979
and entered into force on January 1, 1980)
(Translated from Gongan fagui hubian, pp. 4-33)

Part I -- General Principles

Chapter I.   Guiding Ideology, Function and Scope
of Application

Article 1.   The Criminal Law of the People's
Republic of China is enacted under the guideline
of Marxism-Leninism-Mao Zedong Thought, on the
basis of the Constitution, in accordance with the
policy of combining punishment with leniency and
the concrete experience gained by the people of
all nationalities in our country in exercising the
people's democratic dictatorship, that is, proletarian dictatorship led by the proletariat and
based on the alliance of workers and peasants, and
in carrying out socialist revolution and socialist
construction.

Article 2.   The function of the Criminal Law
of the People's Republic of China is to use
punishment to struggle against all counterrevolutionary and other criminal acts, defend the dictatorship of the proletariat, protect the
socialist property of the whole people and the
property collectively owned by the laboring masses, protect the legitimate property of the private citizens, protect the personal rights, democratic rights and other rights of the citizens,
maintain public order and order in production,
work, teaching, scientific research and the life
of the people and masses and ensure the smooth
progress of the socialist revolution and socialist
construction.

Article 3.   This Law is applicable to offenses committed [by any person] within the territory
of the People's Republic of China except [for
those offenses] specifically provided for by other
laws.

This Law is also applicable to offenses committed [by any person] aboard ships or aircrafts of the People's Republic of China.

If either the commission of an offense or its effect takes place within the territory of the People's Republic of China, the offense shall be considered to be an offense committed within the territory of the People's Republic of China.

Article 4. This Law is applicable to the following offenses committed by citizens of the People's Republic of China outside the territory of the People's Republic of China:

(1)   Counterrevolutionary offenses;

(2)   Counterfeiting of national currency (Article 122) or valuable securities (Article 12);

(3)   Embezzling (Article 155), taking bribes (Article 185) or divulging state secrets (Article 186); and

(4)   Posing as a state functionary to swindle and bluff (Article 166) or forging documents credentials and seals (Article 167).

Article 5. This Law is also applicable to an offense not provided for in the preceding article which is committed by a citizen of the People's Republic of China outside the territory of the People's Republic of China and for which the minimum punishment is imprisonment for not less than three years except if the act is not punishable by law of the place where it is committed.

Article 6. This Law may be applied to a national of a foreign state who has committed an offense against the state or citizen of the People's Republic of China outside the territory of the People's Republic of China and for which the minimum punishment is imprisonment for not less than three years, except if the act is not punishable by law of the place where it was committed.

Article 7. Any offense committed outside the territory of the People's Republic of China which involves criminal responsibility under this Law, even if it has been tried by a foreign state, may still be handled according to this Law. However, if the offender has already been punished in that foreign state, punishment may be entirely excepted or partially mitigated.

Article 8. Questions of criminal responsibility for foreigners who enjoy diplomatic privileges and immunities shall be resolved through diplomatic channels.

Article 9. This Law shall enter into force on January 1, 1980. Acts committed after the founding of the People's Republic of China and before the entry into force of this Law which were not considered as offenses under the law, decrees and policies at that time shall be dealt with according to the law, decrees and policies at that time. Those which were considered offenses under the law, decrees and policies at that time and are punishable according to Section 8 of Chapter IV of the General Principles of this Law shall be punished in accordance with the law, decrees and policies at that time. However, this Law shall be applied if an act is not considered an offense, or if a lighter sentence shall be imposed under this Law.

Chapter II. Offenses

Section 1. Offenses and Criminal Responsibility.

Article 10. Any act which endangers state sovereignty and territorial integrity, jeopardizes the regime of the dictatorship of the proletariat, undermines socialist revolution and socialist construction, disrupts public order, encroaches upon the property of the whole people or the property collectively owned by the laboring masses, encroaches the legitimate property owned by private citizens, infringes upon the personal, democratic and other rights of the citizens or any other act which endangers society and is punishable according to law is an offense. However, if the offense is obviously a minor one and its harm is negligible, it shall not be considered a crime.

Article 11. A person who knows perfectly well that the result of his action would endanger the society and still wishes or let this happen and thus commits a crime is guilty of an intentional offense.

An intentional offense should bear criminal responsibility.

Article 12. A person who should have foreseen that his action would result in endangering the society but has failed to do so due to negligence or has foreseen the danger but gullibly believed he could avoid it is guilty of an unintentional offense.

An unintentional offense should bear criminal responsibility only when the law so prescribes.

Article 13. An action which objectively results in harmful consequences due to irresistible or unforeseeable factors rather than due to intention or negligence is not deemed as commiting an offense.

Article 14. An offender who is above 16 years of age should bear criminal responsibility.

An offender who is between 14 and 16 years of age should bear criminal responsibility if he commits homicide, inflicts serious injury on a person, or commits robbery, arson, repeated theft or other offenses which seriously undermine social order.

An offender who is between 14 and 18 years of age should recieve a lighter or mitigated penalty.

An offender who is exempted from punishment because of not reaching 16 years of age should be required to be disciplined and educated by his parents or guardians. If necessary, he may be taken into custody by the government for upbringing.

Article 15. A mental patient who caused harmful results when in a situation of being unable to understand or control his actions does not bear criminal responsibility. However, his family members or guardians should be instructed to keep close watch over him and give him medical treatment.

A patient of intermittent insanity who committed offenses when he was sane should bear criminal responsibility.

A drunken person who committed offenses should bear criminal responsibility.

Article 16. A deaf-mute person or blind person who commits an offense may receive a lighter or mitigated penalty or may be exempted from punishment.

Article 17. No criminal responsibility shall be incurred for proper self-defense taken to protect the public interest or the personal or other rights of oneself or others from being infringed upon by illegal action.

When a person exceeds the limits of necessity in taking proper self-defense measures and thus causes unnecessary harm, he should bear criminal responsibility. However, the punishment may be mitigated or exempted according to the situation.

Article 18. No criminal responsibility shall be incurred when a person who has no alternative takes emergency measures for averting danger in order to protect the public interests or the personal or other rights of oneself or others from an existing danger.

When a person exceeds the limits of necessity in taking emergency measures for averting danger and thus causes unnecessary harm, he should bear criminal responsibility. However, the punishment may be mitigated or exempted according to the situation.

The provisions in paragraph 1 on protecting oneself from danger are not applicable to a person who is charged with special responsibility in his duty or work.

Section 2. Preparation to Commit a Crime,
           Attempted Crime and Incomplete Crime.

(Articles 19 to 21 omitted)

Section 3. Joint Offense.

(Articles 22 to 26 omitted)

Chapter III. Punishment.

Section 1. Types of Punishment.

Article 27. Punishments are divided into major and supplementary categories.

Article 28. Major punishments are as follows:

(1) Control;

(2) Detention;

(3) Fixed-term imprisonment;

(4) Life imprisonment; and

(5) Death penalty.

Article 29. Supplementary punishments are as follows:

(1) Fines;

(2) Deprivation of political rights; and

(3) Confiscation of property.

In certain cases only a supplementary punishment shall be imposed.

Article 30. Deportation may be applied as an exclusive or supplementary punishment to a foreigner who has committed an offense.

Article 31. Apart from criminal sanctions imposed on the criminal element according to law, if the criminal act results in financial losses to a victim, the offender should also be sentenced to make financial reparation according to the situation.

Article 32. Minor offenses which do not require punishment may be exempted from criminal

sanctions. However, the offender may be repri-
manded or ordered to mend his way, apologize and
pay compensation or be subjected to administrative
disciplinary measures from the department in
charge in accordance with the seriousness of the
case.

Section 2.   Control.

Article 33.   The period of control is not to
be less than three months and not more than two
years.

Control shall be imposed by the people's
court and is to be executed by the public security
organs.

Article 34.   A criminal element sentenced to
control shall observe the following rules during
the period of executing control:

(1)   Observe laws and decrees, submit to mass
      supervision and actively take part in
      collective labor production or work;

(2)   Regularly report their activities to the
      organs executing control; and

(3)   Report to organ executing control for
      approval of change of residence or
      travel.

A criminal element sentenced to control shall
receive equal pay for equal work during the period
of laboring.

Article 35.   When the control period over a
criminal element is over, the organ executing the
control should immediately announce to the person
[under control] and the masses concerned the lift-
ing of control.

Article 36.   The period of control is effective from the date of sentence.   Each day in custody prior to the execution of the sentence is
equivalent to 2 days on the term of sentence.

Section 3.   Detention.

Article 37. The period of detention is from 15 days to 6 months.

Article 38. A criminal element sentenced to detention shall be [detained] by a nearby public security organ.

During the period of detention, the criminal element sentenced to detention may go home 1 to 2 days every month and can be given appropriate remuneration if they participate in laboring.

Article 39. The period of detention is effective from the date of sentence. Each day in custody prior to the sentence is equivalent to 1 day on the term of sentence.

Section 4.   Fixed-Term Imprisonment and Life
             Imprisonment.

Article 40. The period of fixed-term imprisonment is from 6 months to 15 years.

Article 41. A criminal element sentenced to fixed-term imprisonment or life imprisonment shall be sent to a prison or a reform through labor center for executing his sentences. If he is able to work he shall be subject to reform through labor.

Article 42. The period of fixed-term imprisonment is effective from the date of sentence. Each day in custody prior to the execution of the sentence is equivalent to 1 day of imprisonment.

Section 5.   Death Sentence.

Article 43. The death sentence shall be imposed only for the most heinous criminal elements. In case of a criminal element who should be sentenced to death, if immediate execution of the death sentence is not mandatory, two year suspension of execution may be announced with the death sentence and the criminal shall be placed under reform through labor during that period to see if the criminal shows evidence of repentence.

Except for a death sentence rendered by the Supreme People's court, all others shall be submitted to the Supreme People's Court for examination and approval. Suspension of execution of the death sentence may be pronounced or approved by a higher people's court.

Article 44. The death penalty is not applicable to a person under 18 years of age at the time of committing the offense or for a woman pregnant at the time of trial. A person between 16 and 18 years of age who has committed a particularly serious offense may be sentenced to death with the sentence suspended for 2 years.

Article 45. Execution of the death sentence shall be carried out by firing squad.

Article 46. If a criminal shows evidence of repentence during the period of suspension of execution of the death sentence, his punishment shall be commuted to life imprisonment at the end of the two-year period. If he demonstrates definite signs of repentence and performs meritorious services, his sentence shall be commuted to a fixed term imprisonment of no less than fifteen years and no more than twenty years at the end of the two-year period. If he seriously resists reform and the evidence of this is verified, the death sentence shall be carried out with the ruling or approval of the Supreme People's Court.

(Article 47 omitted)

Section 6.   Fine.

(Articles 48 and 49 omitted)

Section 7.   Deprivation of Political Rights.

(Articles 50 to 54 omitted)

Section 8.   Confiscation of Properties.

Article 55. Confiscation of property includes the confiscation of part or all of the personal property of a criminal element.

When confiscating property, the property belonging to the family members of a criminal element or that which they are entitled to must not be confiscated.

Article 56. If the creditors request to use the property to be confiscated for payment of legitimate debts of the criminal element, the request should be referred to a people's court for a decision.

Chapter IV.   The Concrete Application of Punishments.

Section 1.   Measurement of Punishment.

(Articles 57 and 58 omitted)

Article 59. If a criminal element does have the mitigating circumstances provided for in this Law, his imposed sentence should be below the minimum punishment prescribed by law.

If a criminal element does not have the mitigating circumstances provided for in this Law and, according to the concrete situation of the case, the imposition of the minimum punishment prescribed by law is still too severe; then upon the decision of the trial committee of a people's court, he may be sentenced to punishment below minimum punishment prescribed by law.

(Article 60 omitted)

Section 2.   Recidivists.

(Article 61 omitted)

Article 62. A counterrevolutionary element who has served his sentence or been granted pardon shall be dealt with as a recidivist any time he commits any counterrevolutionary offense again.

Section 3.   Voluntary Surrender.

Article 63. An offender who voluntarily surrenders after committing a crime shall be dealt with leniently. A person who commits minor offenses may be given reduced punishment or be exempted from punishment. A person who commits more serious offenses may be given reduced punishment or be exempted from punishment if he produces evidence of meritorious service.

Section 4.   Punishment for Several Crimes at the
             Same Time.

(Articles 64 to 66 omitted)

Section 5.   Probation.

(Articles 67 to 70 omitted)

Section 6.   Reduction of Sentences.

(Articles 71 to 72 omitted)

Section 7.   Parole.

(Articles 73 to 75 omitted)

Section 8.   Prescription.

Article 76.   The period of limitation for
prosecution of offenses is as follows:

(1)   For offenses having a maximum penalty
      prescribed by law of less than 5 years,
      the period of limitation is 5 years;

(2)   For offenses having a maximum penalty
      prescribed by law of less than 10 years,
      the period of limitation is 10 years;

(3)   For offenses having a maximum pealty
      prescribed by law of not less than 10
      years, the period of limitation is 15
      years; and

(4)   For offenses having a maximum penalty
      prescribed by law of life imprisonment
      or the death penalty, the period of
      limitation is 20 years. If it is deemed
      necessary to prosecute after 20 years,
      approval must be obtained from the
      Supreme People's Procuratorate.

Article 77.   An offender who escaped investigation or trial after the adoption of compulsory
measures by the people's court, the people's procuratorate or the public security organ is not
covered by the period of limitation.

(Article 78 omitted)

Chapter V. Other Provisions

Article 79. A person who commits crimes not explicitly defined in the specific parts of the criminal law may be convicted and sentenced, after obtaining the approval of the Supreme People's Court, according to the most similar article in this Law.

(Article 80 to 86 omitted)

Article 87. [Prosecution instituted] upon complaint mentioned in this Law means a case [shall be accepted for consideration of prosecution] upon the complaint of a victim. If the victim is unable to lodge a complaint because of coercion or intimidation, then the people's prosecutorate or the relatives of the victim may also lodge a complaint on his behalf.

(Article 88 omitted)

Article 89. The general principles of this Law are applicable to penal provisions provided in other laws or decrees, except as otherwise provided in other laws.

Part II -- Specific Parts

Chapter I. Counterrevolutionary Offenses.

Article 90. Counterrevolutionary offenses are acts done for the purpose of overthrowing the political power of the dictatorship of the proletariat and the socialist system and endangering the People's Republic of China.

Article 91. A person who colludes with a foreign state and conspires to jeopardize the sovereignty, territorial integrity and security of the motherland shall be sentenced to life imprisonment or fixed-term imprisonment of not less than 10 years.

Article 92. A person who conspires to overthrow the government or split the state shall be sentenced to life imprisonment or fixed-term imprisonment of not less than 10 years.

Article 93. A person who instigates, seduces or bribes any state functionary or any member of the armed forces, the people's police or the militia to defect, turn traitor or rebel shall be sentenced to life imprisonment or fixed-term imprisonment of not less than 10 years.

Article 94. A person who defects to the enemy shall be sentenced to fixed-term imprisonment of not less than 3 and not more than 10 years. In serious cases of defection or in the case of leading a group of persons to defect to the enemy, the guilty person shall be sentenced to fixed-term imprisonment of not less than 10 years or life imprisonment.

A person who leads armed forces, people's police or militia to defect to the enemy shall be sentenced to life imprisonment or fixed-term imprisonment of not less than 10 years.

Article 95. A major culprit of armed rebellious assemblies or other serious offenses shall be sentenced to life imprisonment or fixed-term imprisonment of not less than 10 years. Those taking an active part shall be sentenced to fixed-term imprisonment of not less than 3 and not more than 10 years.

Article 96. A major culprit of gathering a mob to storm prisons and release prisoners or organizing jail-breaks or other serious offenses shall be sentenced to fixed-term imprisonment of not less than 10 years. Those taking an active part shall be sentenced to fixed-term imprisonment of not less than 5 and not more than 10 years.

Article 97. A person who commits espionage or supports the enemy in one of the following manners shall be sentenced to fixed-term imprisonment of no less than 10 years or life imprisonment; in less serious cases, he shall be sentenced to fixed-term imprisonment of not less than 5 and not more than 10 years:

    (1)   Stealing, spying and supplying information to the enemy;

    (2)   Supplying arms or other military materials to the enemy; or

(3)   Joining a secret service or espionage
       organization or receiving orders from
       the enemy.

Article 98. A person who organizes or leads
a counterrevolutionary group shall be sentenced to
fixed-term imprisonment of not less than 5 years.
A person who actively participates in a counterrevolutionary group shall be sentenced to a fixed-
term imprisonment of no more than 5 years, detention, control or deprivation of political rights.

Article 99. A person who organizes or utilizes feudal superstitious beliefs, secret societies or sects to carry out counterrevolutionary
activities shall be sentenced to a fixed-term imprisonment of not less than 5 years. If the
situation is not serious he shall be sentenced to
a fixed-term imprisonment of no more than 5 years,
detention, control or deprivation of political
rights.

Article 100. A person who commits any one of
the following destructive acts for counterrevolutionary purposes shall be sentenced to life imprisonment or fixed-term imprisonment of not less
than 10 years; in less serious cases, he shall be
sentenced to fixed-term imprisonment of not less
than 3 and not more than 10 years:

(1)   Destroying any military installation,
       production facility, telecommunications
       or transportation installation, building
       project and safety installation or other
       public construction and property through
       explosion, arson, flooding, [special
       device] or other means;

(2)   Robbing state archives, military
       materials, factory and mining enter-
       prises, banks, stores, warehouse or
       other public property;

(3)   Highjacking of any ship, aircraft,
       train, streetcar or motorcar;

(4)   Directing the enemy to any bombing or
       shelling target; or

(5) Making, robbing or stealing any gun or ammunition.

Article 101. A person who uses poison, bacteria and other methods to kill or injure people for a counterrevolutionary purpose shall be sentenced to life imprisonment or fixed-term imprisonment of not less than 10 years; in a less serious case, he shall be sentenced to fixed-term imprisonment of not less than 3 and not more than 10 years.

Article 102. A person who commits any of the following acts for a counterrevolutionary purpose shall be sentenced to fixed-term imprisonment of no more than 5 years; if he is the ring leader or his criminal act is serious, he shall be sentenced to fixed-term imprisonment of not less than 5 years:

(1) Inciting the masses to resist or undermine the implementation of the law or decrees of the state; and

(2) Using counterrevolutionary slogans, leaflets, or other means to spread propaganda inciting the overthrow of the regime of the dictatorship of the proletariat and the socialist system.

Article 103. With the exception of Articles 98, 99, and 102, counterrevolutionary offenses provided in this chapter that are seriously endangering the state and the people or the situation of a particularly heinous nature may be given the death sentence.

Article 104. The punishment for offenses in this chapter may also be carried out concurrently with the confiscation of property.

Chapter II. Offenses of Endangering Public Security.

(Articles 105 to 115 omitted)

Chapter III. Offenses of Undermining the
Socialist Economic Order.

Article 116. Apart from confiscation of
smuggled goods and imposition of a fine in accordance with customs laws and regulations, an offender in a serious case shall be sentenced to
fixed-term imprisonment of not more than 3 years
or detention. Confiscation of property may be
imposed   concurrently   with   imprisonment   or
detention.

Article 117. A person who practices speculation and manipulation in violation of financial,
foreign exchange, gold and silver and industrial
and business control laws or regulations, if the
situation is serious, shall be sentenced to fixed-
term imprisonment of no more than 3 years, detention or fined. A fine or confiscation of property
may be imposed concurrently with imprisonment or
detention.

Article 118. A person who engages in smuggling, speculating and profiteering as his regular
profession or in a big way or as a ring leader of
a smuggling, speculating and profiteering group
shall be sentenced to fixed-term imprisonment of
not less than 3 and not more than 10 years. Confiscation of property may be imposed concurrently
with imprisonment.

Article 119. A state functionary who takes
advantage of his position to engage in smuggling,
speculating and profiteering shall be severely
punished.

Article 120. A person who counterfeits or
resells planned supply certificates to make money,
if the case is serious, shall be sentenced to
fixed-term imprisonment of not more than 3 years
or detention or fined. Fines or confiscation of
property may be imposed concurrently with imprisonment or detention.

A person who is a ring leader of the above
offense or in an especially serious case may be
sentenced to fixed-term imprisonment of not less
than 3 and not more than 7 years and confiscation
of property may concurrently be imposed.

Article 121. A directly responsible person who violates tax laws, regulations, evades taxes or refuses to pay a tax, if the case is serious, shall be sentenced to fixed-term imprisonment of not more than 3 years or detention; in addition he shall be required to pay overdue taxes and fines in accordance with tax laws or regulations.

Article 122. A person who counterfeits state currency or transports and sells counterfeited state currency shall be sentenced to fixed-term imprisonment of not less than 3 and not more than 7 years. A fine or confiscation of property may be concurrently imposed with the imprisonment.

A person who is the ring leader of the above offense or in an especially serious case shall be sentenced to fixed-term imprisonment of not less than 7 years or life imprisonment. A confiscation of property may be imposed concurrently with the imprisonment.

Article 123. A person who counterfeits checks, stocks or other valuable securities shall be sentenced to fixed-term imprisonment of not more than 7 years. A fine may be imposed concurrently with the sentence.

(Articles 124 to 130 omitted)

Chapter IV. Offenses of Infringing the Personal Rights or Democratic Rights of the Citizens.

Article 131. The law protects a citizen's personal and democratic rights and other rights against unlawful infringement by any person or organs. A person who is directly responsible for a serious case of unlawful infringement shall be subject to criminal sanction.

(Articles 132 to 135 omitted)

Article 136. It is strictly forbidden to extort a confession by torture. A state functionary who extorts a confession by torture will be sentenced to imprisonment for not more than 3 years or detention. If corporal punishment is used with the result that the person is disabled, he shall be charged with injury and severely punished.

(Article 137 omitted)

Article 138. It is strictly forbidden to bring false charges against the cadres and masses by any means whatsoever. Whoever brings false charges against another person (including a convict in prison) is to be punished according to the nature, seriousness, consequences and measurement of punishment of the falsely accused offense. A state functionary who commits the offense of false charge against another person is to be severely punished.

If a charge is brought by mistake or misinformation with no intention to make a false charge, then paragraph 1 of this article is not applicable.

(Article 139 omitted)

Article 140. A person who forces a female to engage in prostitution shall be sentenced to a fixed-term imprisonment for not less than 3 and no more than 10 years.

Article 141. A person who engages in abduction for purposes of trafficking in human beings shall be sentenced to fixed-term imprisonment for not more than 5 years. In a serious case, the offender shall be sentenced to fixed-term imprisonment for not less than 5 years.

(Artricles 142 to 149 omitted)

Chapter V.   Offenses of Encroaching Upon
                Properties.

(Articles 150 to 154 omitted)

Article 155. A state functionary who takes advantage of his position and power to embezzle public property shall be sentenced to fixed-term imprisonment or detention for not more than 5 years. In a serious case where the amount involved is huge, the offender shall be sentenced to fixed-term imprisonment for not less than 5 years. In an extremely serious case, the offender shall be sentenced to life imprisonment or death.

A person who commits the offense provided in paragraph 1 shall have his property confiscated concurrently or be ordered to return what he has unlawfully taken or pay compensation for it.

A person who is entrusted by a state organ, enterprise, business unit or mass organization to perform public duties and commits the offense provided in paragraph 1 of this article shall be punished according to paragraphs 1 and 2 of this article.

(Article 156 omitted)

Chapter VI. Offenses of Obstructing the Governing of Social Order.

(Articles 157 to 165 omitted)

Article 166. A person who poses himself as a state functionary to bluff or deceive people shall be sentenced to fixed-term imprisonment for not more than 3 years, detention, control, or deprivation of political rights. In a serious case, he shall be sentenced to fixed-term imprisonment for not less than 3 and not more than 10 years.

Article 167. A person who counterfeits, alters, steals, plunders or destroys the documents, certificates or seals of a state organ, enterprise, business unit or mass organization shall be sentenced to fixed-term imprisonment for not more than 3 years, detention, control or deprivation of political rights. In a serious case, he shall be sentenced to fixed-term imprisonment for not less than 3 and not more than 10 years.

(Articles 168 to 178 omitted)

Chapter VII. Offenses Against Marriage or Family.

(Articles 179 to 180 omitted)

Article 181. Anyone who cohabitates with or knowingly marries the spouse of an active military serviceman shall be sentenced to imprisonment for not less than 3 years.

(Articles 182 to 184 omitted)

Chapter VIII. Malfeasance.

Article 185. A state functionary who exploits his office and takes bribes shall be sentenced to fixed-term imprisonment for not more than 5 years or detention. Money or goods received in bribes shall be confiscated and steps taken to recover public funds or property that have been illegally taken away.

A state functionary who commits the offense provided in paragraph 1 and causes serious losses upon the interests of the state or citizens shall be sentenced to fixed-term imprisonment for not less than 5 years.

A person who offers a bribe to a state functionary or acts as a go-between in a bribery case shall be sentenced to fixed-term imprisonment for not more than 3 years or detention.

Article 186. In a serious case where a state functionary divulges important state secrets in violation of laws and regulations for guarding state secrets he shall be sentenced to fixed-term imprisonment for not more than 7 years, detention or deprivation of political rights. If the offender is not a state functionary, he shall be punished according to the seriousness of the case in line with the preceeding paragraph.

(Articles 187 to 192 omitted. Article 192 is the last article.)

Document 5

Decision of the Standing Committee of the National People's Congress on Severely Punishing Criminals Who Gravely Endanger Public Security of the Society (Passed by the Second Meeting of the Standing Committee of the Sixth National People's Congress on September 2, 1983.) (Translation from Renmin ribao, September 3, 1983, p. 1.)

In order to safeguard public security of the society, safeguard the people's lives and property, and guarantee the progress of socialist reconstruction, it is necessary to punish severely criminals who gravely endanger public security of the society, and it is hereby decided:

(1)   The following criminals who gravely endanger public security of the society may be punished more heavily than the severest punishment currently stipulated in the Criminal Law, and may be punished by the death penalty:

A.   The ringleader of a criminal gang or anyone who engages in serious gangster activities with a lethal weapon or whose gangster activities are particularly dangerous;

B.   A person who commits intentional assault and battery and causes severe injury or death to another person in a situation of heinous nature, or does violence and causes injury to state workers or citizens who report, expose and arrest criminals and stop criminal activities;

C.   The ringleader of a group engaging in abduction for purposes of trafficking in human beings or a person who abducts in a particularly serious way;

D.   A person who illegally makes, trades, transports, steals, or robs weapons, ammunition or explosives in a particularly serious way or with serious consequences;

E.   A person who organizes reactionary secret societies or sects and utilizes feudal superstitious beliefs to carry out counterrevolutionary activities and gravely endangers public security of the society;

F.   A person who lures, houses, or forces a female to engage in prostitution and whose case is particularly serious.

(2) A person who passes on methods of committing crimes and whose case is less serious shall be sentenced to imprisonment for not more than 5 years. In a serious case, the offender shall be sentenced to imprisonment for not less than 5 years, and in a particularly serious case, the offender shall be sentenced to life imprisonment or death.

(3) After the promulgation of this decision, it shall be applied to the trials of the above stated criminal cases.

Appendix
Related articles of the Criminal Law

Article 160. A person who incites group fighting, creates disturbances, subjects women to indignities or carries out other gangster activities to disrupt public order and the situation is of heinous nature shall be sentenced to fixed-term imprisonment for not more than 7 years, detention or control.

The ringleader of a criminal gang shall be sentenced to fixed-term imprisonment for not less than 7 years.

Article 134. A person who commits intentional assault and battery to injure another person shall be sentenced to fixed-term imprisonment for not more than 3 years or detention.

A person who commits the aforesaid offense and causes severe injury to another person shall be sentenced to fixed-term imprisonment for not less than 3 years and no more than 7 years; if he causes death to another person, he shall be sentenced to fixed-term imprisonment for not less than 7 years or life imprisonment. Where separate provisions are laid down in this law, such provisions shall be followed.

Article 141. A person who engages in abduction for purposes of trafficking in human beings shall be sentenced to fixed-term imprisonment for not more than 5 years. In a serious case, the offender shall be sentenced to fixed-term imprisonment for not less than 5 years.

Article 112. The illegal making, trading, and transporting of arms and ammunition or the theft or robbery of guns and ammunition from state organs, armed forces, police, or militiamen shall be punishable by fixed-term imprisonment of not more than 7 years. In a serious case, the offender shall be punished by fixed-term imprisonment of not less than 7 years or life imprisonment.

Article 99. A person who organizes or utilizes feudal superstitious beliefs, secret societies or sects to carry out counterrevolutionary activities shall be sentenced to a fixed-term imprisonment of not less than 5 years. If the situation is not serious, he shall be sentenced to a fixed term imprisonment of not more than 5 years, detention, control or deprivation of political rights.

Article 140. A person who forces a female to engage in prostitution shall be sentenced to fixed-term imprisonment for not less than 3 years and no more than 10 years.

Article 169. A person who lures or houses a female and makes her engage in prostitution for the purpose of seeking profits shall be sentenced to fixed-term imprisonment for not more than 5 years, detention or control. In a serious case, the offender shall be sentenced to fixed-term imprisonment for not less than 5 years; concurrently a fine may be imposed or property confiscated.

Document 6

Criminal Procedure Law of the People's Republic of China (Passed by the Second Plenary Meeting of the Fifth National People's Congress on July 1, 1979 and entered into force on January 1, 1980) (Translated from Gongan fagui huibian, pp. 35-65)

Part One -- General Principles

Chapter I. Guiding Ideology, Function and Basic Principles.

Article 1. The Criminal Procedure Law of the People's Republic of China is enacted under the

guideline of Marxism-Leninism-Mao Zedong Thought,
on the basis of the Constitution, in accordance
with the concrete experience gained by the people
of all nationalities in our country in exercising
the people's democratic dictatorship, that is,
proletarian dictatorship led by the proletariat
and based on the alliance of workers and peasants,
and based on the practical necessity of striking
the enemy and protecting the people.

Article 2. The task of the Criminal Procedure Law of the People's Republic of China is to
insure accurate and prompt investigation and establishment of the facts of criminal offenses,
correctly enforce the law, punish the criminals,
protect the innocent from criminal prosecution,
educate citizens to consciously observe the law
and wage an active struggle against criminal offenses in order to uphold the socialist legal system, protect the personal, democratic right and
other rights of citizens and ensure the smooth
progress of the socialist revolution and socialist
reconstruction.

Article 3. The public security organ is in
charge of investigation, detention and preliminary
review of criminal cases. The people's procuratorate approves arrests and conducts procuratorial proceedings (including investigation) and
institutes public prosecution. The people's court
is responsible for adjudicating cases. No other
organ, institution or individual has the right to
exercise such powers.

In handling criminal cases, the people's
court, the people's procuratorate and the public
security organ must strictly observe the relevant
provisions of this and other laws.

Article 4. In handling criminal litigation,
the people's court, the people's procuratorate and
the public security organ must rely on the masses,
base their decisions on facts and take the law as
the yardstick. All citizens are equal in the application of the law. No privilege whatsoever is
permissible before the law.

Article 5. In handling criminal cases, the
people's court, the people's procuratorate and the

public security organ should perform their respective functions while coordinating with and checking each other to guarantee that the law is accurately and effectively enforced.

(Article 6 omitted)

Article 7. In adjudicating cases, the people's courts follow the system under which the court of second instance is the court of last instance.

Article 8. Except as otherwise provided in this Law, the people's court shall conduct its trials in public. The defendant has the right to defense and the people's court has the obligation to guarantee that the defendant is defended.

Article 9. In adjudicating a case, the people's court shall follow the system of having people's assessors in its trial in accordance with this Law.

Article 10. The people's court, the people's procuratorate and the public security organ shall guarantee a person who participated in court proceedings to procedural rights he is entitled to under the law.

In the inquiry and trial of a criminal case involving a person under 18 years of age, his legal representative may be notified to appear in the court.

A participant in court proceedings has the right to file charges against trial, procuratorial and investigative personnel for violation of his citizen's right to legal proceedings or for personal insults.

Article 11. In any one of the following cases no criminal responsibility should be pursued, and if the criminal prosecution has already begun, it should be cancelled, not prosecuted, or the defendant pronounced not guilty:

(1) When the case is obviously a minor one, causing no great harm and should not be deemed as the commission of a criminal offense;

(2)   If the case is beyond the limitation for legal prosecution;

(3)   When there exists an exemption of punishment by decree of special pardon or amnesty;

(4)   In a case which, according to the Criminal Law, can only be accepted for prosecution only if someone files a complaint, but no one has done so, or the complaint has been withdrawn;

(5)   The defendant is deceased; or

(6)   A case which is exempted from the pursuit of criminal responsibility in accordance with other laws or decrees.

Article 12.   The provisions of this Law are applicable to foreigners who have committed offenses and whose criminal responsibility should be pursued.

Foreigners with diplomatic privileges and immunities who have committed offenses and whose criminal responsibility should be pursued shall be settled through diplomatic channels.

Chapter II.   Jurisdiction.

(Article 13 omitted)

Article 14.   The basic-level people's courts have jurisdiction as courts of first instance in ordinary criminal cases, with the exception of those cases which fall under the jurisdiction of higher people's court as stipulated by this law.

Article 15.   Intermediate people's courts have jurisdiction as courts of first instance in the following criminal cases:

(1)   Counterrevolutionary cases;

(2)   Ordinary criminal cases which call for life imprisonment and the death sentence; and

(3)   Cases in which the offenses are committed by foreigners or in which our citizens have encroached upon the legitimate rights of foreigners.

Article 16.   Criminal cases that fall under the jurisdiction of higher people's courts as courts of first instance are major criminal offenses that have a bearing on an entire province (municipality directly under the central government or autonomous region).

Article 17.   Criminal cases that fall under the jurisdiction of the Supreme People's Court as courts of first instance are major criminal offenses that have a bearing on the whole country.

Article 18.   The people's court at a higher level may act as a court of first instance in a criminal case under the jurisdiction of a lower people's court when necessary, and it may also turn over a criminal case under its own jurisdiction as a court of first instance to a lower people's court.   When a lower people's court feels that the seriousness and complexity of a criminal case makes it necessary to be handled by the people's court at a higher level as a court of first instance, it may request permission to transfer the case to the court at the higher level.

(Articles 19 and 20 omitted)

Article 21.   If it is not clear which lower level people's court has jurisdiction over a case, a higher level people's court may make the assignment.   A higher level people's court may also instruct a people's court at a lower level to transfer a case to another people's court for adjudication.

(Article 22 omitted)

Chapter III.   Withdrawal [of Judicial Personnel].

Article 23.   In one of the following circumstances, trial, procuratorial or investigative personnel should withdraw from a case, and a party [to the case] and his legal representative have also the right to ask them to withdraw:

(1)   They are parties to the case or close relatives of the parties of the case;

(2)   They themselves or their close relatives have an interest in the case;

(3)   They are witnesses in, appraisers of, or defense counsel for the case or agents for an incidental civil action; or

(4)   They are otherwise related to the case, which may affect the impartial handling of the case.

Article 24. The withdrawal of adjudicating, procuratorial or investigative personnel from a case shall be determined respectively by the court president, the chief procurator or the person in charge of a public security organ; the withdrawal of the court president shall be determined by the court's adjudicating committee; and the withdrawal of the chief procurator and the person in charge of a public security organ shall be determined by the procuratorial committee of a people's procuratorate at the same level.

Pending the deciding on withdrawal of an investigative personnel, they should not discontinue the investigation of the case.

A party [to a case] may apply for reviewing the decision to reject his application for withdrawal once.

Article 25. The provisions of Articles 23 and 24 shall also apply to clerks, interpreters and appraisers.

Chapter IV. Defense.

Article 26. In addition to exercising the right to defend himself, the accused may entrust the following persons to defend him:

(1)   Lawyers;

(2)   Citizens recommended by a people's organization or unit to which the defendant belongs or others permitted by the people's court; or

(3) Close relatives or guardians of the defendant.

Article 27. In a case in which the public prosecutor appears before the court to conduct public prosecution and the defendant does not entrust anyone to defend his case, the people's court may designate a defense counsel for him.

If a defendant is deaf, mute or has not yet come of age and has not entrusted his case to a defense counsel, the people's court shall appoint a defense counsel for him.

Article 28. The responsibility of a defense counsel is to present, according to the facts and the law, materials and opinions to prove that the defendant is innocent or committed a less severe offense or should receive a mitigated sentence or be exempted from criminal responsibility in order to safeguard the legitimate rights and interests of the defendant.

Article 29. A defense lawyer may request to examine materials pertaining to the case to acquaint himself with the case. He may also meet and correspond with the defendant in custody. Other defense counsels may, with the approval of the people's court, also acquaint themselves with the case and meet and correspond with the defendant.

Article 30. In the process of adjudication, a defendant may discontinue the service of his defense counsel, he may also entrust the defense of his case to another defense counsel.

Chapter V. Evidence.

Article 31. All facts that prove the true situation of a case are evidence. Evidence includes the following six categories:

(1) Material or documentary evidence;

(2) A witness' testimony

(3) A statement by the victim;

(4) A confession, narration, argument and explanation of the defendant;

(5) The conclusion of an appraisal; or

(6) The records of examination and inspection.

The above stated evidence can be used as the basis for reaching a final decision in a case only when they are verified to be true through investigation.

Article 32. The adjudicating, procuratorial and investigative personnel must, in accordance with the legal process, collect various kinds of evidence to prove whether the defendant is guilty or innocent or the degree of seriousness of the offense committed. It is strictly forbidden to extort confession by torture and to collect evidence through duress, enticement, deceit and other illegal means. Conditions shall be guaranteed for citizens who are involved in a case or who have knowledge of the case to furnish fully and objectively evidence. Except in special circumstances, these citizens may be recruited to help in the investigation of the case.

Article 33. The public security organ's request for the approval of an arrest warrant, the people's procuratorate's indictment and the people's court's judgment must be faithful to the truth of the facts. Responsibility shall be pursued for any intentional withholding of the truth of the facts.

Article 34. The people's court, a people's procuratorate, and public security organ have the right to collect or obtain evidence from government organs, enterprises, units of institutions, people's communes, people's organizations and citizens.

Evidences involving state secrets should be kept confidential.

Anyone who forges, withholds or destroys evidence shall be subject to investigation in accordance with the law.

Article 35. In handling judgments on all cases, stress shall be laid on the weight of evidence and on investigation and research, and one should not readily believe confessions. When there is only a confession by the defendant and no other evidence available, the defendant should not be considered guilty or sentenced; when there is no confession by the defendant but there is abundant, reliable evidence against him, the defendant may be considered guilty and so sentenced.

Article 36. The testimony by a witness can be used as evidence in reaching a conclusion on a case only when the witness is questioned and cross-examined in the court by the public prosecutor, the victim, the defendant and the defense counsel, the court listens to the testimony of other witnesses, and verifies it to be true. If the court discovers through investigation that a witness has wilfully committed perjury or withheld evidence, he shall be dealt with in accordance with the law.

Article 37. All those who have knowledge of a case shall have the obligation to be witnesses. Those physically handicapped or mentally-retarded or those who are too young to distinguish right from wrong and express themselves shall not be witnesses.

Chapter VI. Compulsory Measures

[Some articles here are similar to corresponding articles in Document 3. Arrest and Detention Act of the People's Republic of China.]

Article 38. The people's court, people's procuratorate and public security organ may take a defendant into custody, place him on bail while waiting trial or impose surveillance on his residence according to the situation of the case.

A defendant under surveillance on his residence cannot leave the designated area. The order to impose surveillance on the defendant's residence shall be carried out by the local public security station, or by an entrusted people's commune or by the unit to which the defendant belongs.

The order to place a defendant on bail while waiting trial or to impose surveillance on his residence should be cancelled or changed if the situation changes.

Article 39. The arrest of an offender must be either approved by a people's procuratorate or decided by a people's court and is to be carried out by a public security organ.

Article 40. An offender should be arrested according to law if the main facts of the criminal case have been thoroughly investigated and the offender may be at least sentenced to imprisonment, and if such measures as allowing him out on bail while awaiting trial or imposing surveillance on his residence are not sufficient to prevent him from endangering society and there is a necessity for arresting him.

If the arrested offender is suffering from a serious illness or is pregnant, or is breast-feeding her own child, the person may be placed on bail while awaiting trial or be subject to surveillance on that person's residence.

Article 41. [This article is the same as Article 6 of the Arrest and Detention Act except there is no "in an emergency situation" phrase here.]

Article 42. [This article is the same as Article 7 of the Arrest and Detention Act.]

Article 43. In detaining a person, a public security organ must show a detention warrant.

After detention is imposed, the family members of the detainee or the unit to which he belongs should be notified of the reason for detention and the place of custody within 24 hours, except in a case in which such notification would hinder the investigation or in which notification is impossible.

Article 44. A public security organ should interrogate a detainee within 24 hours after the detention. When it is found that the person should not be detained, the detainee should be released immediately and given a release certificate. When it is deemed necessary to make an arrest of a detainee, but sufficient evidence is still lacking, the detainee may be [released] and placed on bail awaiting trial or be subject to surveillance on his residence.

Article 45. When a public security organ requests the arrest of an offender, it should submit a written request with the case file and evidence attached to the people's procuratorate at the same level for review and approval. If necessary, the people's procuratorate may have its personnel participate in the public security organ's discussion of major cases.

Article 46. The chief procurator of a people's procuratorate shall review and approve [the request for arrest submitted by a public security organ]. In major cases, [the request for arrest] should be sent to the procuratorial committee for discussion and decision.

Article 47. Following the review of a request for approval of arrest submitted by a public security organ, the people's procuratorate should decide according to the circumstances whether to approve the arrest, not to approve the arrest or to require a supplementary investigation.

Article 48. When the public security organ considers that a detainee should be placed under arrest, it should, within 3 days after the detention, submit the matter to the people's procuratorate [at the same level] for review and approval. Under special circumstances, the time limit may be extended from 1 to 4 days. After receiving the request for approval of arrest from a public security organ, the people's procuratorate should decide either to approve or disapprove the request within 3 days. If the people's procuratore disapproves the arrest, the public security organ should, upon being notified of the decision of the people's procuratorate, immediately release the detainee and give him a release certificate.

If a public security organ or a people's procuratorate has not handled the matter in accordance with the provisions of the proceeding paragraph, the detainee or his family has the right to demand his release and the public security organ or the people's procuratorate should immediately release the detainee. (Note: This article is similar to Article 8 of the Arrest and Detention Act.)

Article 49. When a public security organ considers the decision of a people's procuratorate on disapproving arrest erroneous, it may request a reconsideration of the decision, but the detainee must be immediately released. If the request for reconsideration is not accepted, the public security organ may submit its request to a higher level people's procuratorate for review. The higher level people's procuratorate should immediately review the matter and decide whether or not to change the decision of the lower level people's procuratorate. The decision shall be communicated to the lower level people's procuratorate and the public security organ for execution.

Article 50. In making an arrest the public security organ must exhibit an arrest warrant.

After an arrest, the family of the arrested person or the unit to which he belongs shall be notified of the reasons for the arrest and the place of detention within 24 hours, except in cases in which such notification might hinder investigation or if notification is not possible.

Article 51. A person arrested by a decision of a people's court, a people's procuratorate or a public security organ with the approval of the people's procuratorate must be interrogated by [the arresting organ] within 24 hours after the arrest. Where it is found that no grounds for such an arrest exists, the arrested person must be immediately released and given a release certificate.

Article 52. In the process of reviewing and approving an arrest, if the people's procuratorate discovers that the public security organ is violating the law in its investigative activities, it should notify the public security organ to correct the [deviation from the law] and the public

security organ shall notify the people's procuratorate of the corrections being made.

Chapter VII. Supplementary Civil Action.

Article 53. If the victim has suffered
material losses as a result of the criminal act of
the defendant, he has the right to file for supplementary civil action in the course of criminal
proceedings.

If the losses are caused to state property or
collective property, the people's procuratorate
may file for supplementary civil action while pursuing the public prosecution.

When necessary, the people's court may place
the defendant's property under legal custody.

Article 54. A supplementary civil action
should be adjudicated together with the same
criminal case. Only in the situation of prevent-
ing excessive delays in an adjudicating of a
criminal case will it be permissible for the supplementary civil action to be continued after the
completion of the adjudication of the criminal
case by the same adjudication organ.

Chapter VIII. Time and Service.

(Articles 55 to 57 omitted)

Chapter 9. Other Provisions.

(Article 58 omitted)

Part II -- Filing a Case, Investigation and
Bringing a Public Prosecution

Chapter I. Filing a Cae.

(Articles 59 to 61 omitted)

Chapter II. Investigation.

Section 1. Interrogating the Defendant.

(Articles 62 to 66 omitted)

Section 2. Interrogating the Witness.

(<u>Articles 67</u> to <u>70</u> omitted)

Section 3.   Inspection and Examination.

(<u>Articles 71</u> to <u>78</u> omitted)

Section 4.   Search.

(<u>Articles 79</u> to <u>83</u> omitted)

Section 5.   Attachment of Material or Documentary
Evidence.

(<u>Articles 84</u> to <u>87</u> omitted)

Section 6.   Appraisal.

(<u>Articles 88</u> to <u>90</u> omitted)

Section 7.   [An Offender] at Large.

(<u>Article 91</u> omitted)

Section 8.   Conclusion of Investigation.

(<u>Articles 92</u> to <u>94</u> omitted)

   Chapter III.   Bringing a Public Prosecution.

(<u>Articles 95 to 104</u> omitted)

Part III. -- Trial

Chapter I.   Organization of Trial

   <u>Article 105</u>.   Adjudication at basic level and
intermediate people's courts of first instance,
except for cases of private prosecution and other
minor criminal cases which may be handled by a
single judge, shall be conducted by a collegiate
chamber composed of one judge and two people's
assessors.

   Adjudication at a higher people's court and
the Supreme People's Court as court of first instance shall be conducted by a collegiate chamber
composed of one to three judges and two to four
people's assessors.

In performing their functions in a people's court, the people's assessors have the same rights as judges.

Cases of appeal or protests of judgments [i.e., a retrial request submitted by a people's procuratorate, see Article 149, paragraph 3] shall be handled by a collegiate chamber of three to five judges.

The president of a people's court or its Division Chief shall designate one judge to be the presiding judge of a collegiate chamber. When the president of a people's court or its Division Chief participates in an adjudication he shall be the presiding judge.

Article 106. When opinions differ at the discussion and comment of a collegiate chamber, the minority shall submit to the majority; but the opinion of the minority should be included in the records. The records of discussion and comment should be signed by members of the collegiate chamber.

Article 107. With respect to an important or difficult case, if the president of a people's court considers it necessary, then the case should be submitted by the president to the adjudicating committee for discussion and decision. The collegiate chamber shall implement the decision of the adjudicating committee.

Chapter II.   Procedure of Adjudication at First Instance.

Section 1.   Cases of Public Prosecution.

(Articles 108 to 125 omitted)

Section 2.   Cases of Private Prosecution.
(Articles 126 to 128 omitted)

Chapter III.   Procedures of Adjudication at Second Instance.

(Articles 129 to 143 omitted)

Chapter IV.   Procedure for Reviewing the Death Sentence.

Article 144. A death sentence shall be approved by the Supreme People's Court.

Article 145. If an intermediate people's court as the court of first instance renders a death sentence and the defendant does not appeal, then the case should, after review by a higher people's court, be reported to the Supreme People's Court for approval. If [in the course of review,] the higher people's court does not approve the death sentence, it may transfer the case to the higher people's court for adjudication or remand the case for retrial.

If a higher people's court as the court of first instance renders a death sentence and the defendant does not appeal or if it renders a death sentence as a court of second instance, the case should be reported to the Supreme People's Court for approval.

Article 146. A death sentence with a two year suspension of execution rendered by an intermediate people's court shall be approved by the higher people's court.

Article 147. The review of a death sentence by the Supreme People's Court or review of a death sentence with a two year suspension of execution shall be conducted by a collegiate chamber of three judges.

Chapter V. Procedure for Supervising Adjuciation.

Article 148. The party [to the litigation], victim and their family members or other citizens may file a complaint against a judgment or ruling which has entered into legal force before a people's court or people's procuratorate. However, the filing of a complaint does not suspend the execution of a judgment or ruling.

Article 149. If the president of a people's court discovers errors in verifying facts or applying law of a judgment or ruling rendered by his court and which has already entered into force, he must submit the case to the adjudicating committee for handling.

When the Supreme People's Court discovers errors in a judgment and ruling rendered by a people's court at any level and which has already entered into force or a higher level people's court discovers errors in a judgment and ruling rendered by a lower level people's court which has entered into force, [either the Supreme People's Court or a higher level people's court] has the right to try the case or instruct the lower level people's court to conduct a retrial.

When the Supreme People's Procuratorate discovers errors in a judgment and ruling rendered by a people's court at any level which has already entered into force or a higher level people's procuratorate discovers errors in a judgment and ruling rendered by a lower level people's court which has already entered into force, it has the right to file a protest against the judgment and ruling in accordance with the procedure for supervising adjudication.

Article 150. The retrial of a case by a people's court in accordance with the procedure of supervising adjudication shall be conducted by a collegiate chamber. If the case is heard by a court of first instance, it shall be adjudicated in accordance with the procedure of courts of first instance and the judgment or ruling may be appealed or subject to protest [by the people's procuratorate]. If the case is of second instance or one transferred to a people's court at a higher level for adjudication, it shall be adjudicated in accordance with the procedures of courts of second instance and the judgment or ruling rendered shall be final.

Part IV. -- Execution

(Articles 151 to 152 omitted)

Article 153. The death sentence rendered and approved by the Supreme People's Court shall be immediately executed and the order for execution shall be signed by the President of the Supreme People's Court.

In the case of a criminal offender sentenced to death but with two years suspension of execution, if during the period of suspension of execution of the death sentence he demonstrates repentance or renders meritorious services for which his sentence should be reduced according to law, the execution organ should submit a written opinion to the ruling of the higher people's court at that area. If the offender's resistance to reform is serious and is verified to be true and he thus should be executed, the higher people's court must report to the Supreme People's Court for approval.

Article 154. After receiving an order from the Supreme People's Court to execute a death sentence, the lower people's court should have the order executed within 7 days. However, if the lower people's court discovers any one of the following circumstances, it should suspend the execution and immediately report to the Supreme Court for a ruling if:

(1) Before execution it discovers that the judgment might be erroneous; or

(2) The criminal is pregnant.

In the situation provided in paragraph 1, if the reason for suspension of execution no longer exists, the lower people's court must report to the Supreme People's Court for the reissuance of an order of the execution of a death sentence to be signed by the President of the Supreme People's Court before it can be executed. In the situation provided in paragraph 2, the lower people's court should report to the Supreme People's Court to change the [death] sentence according to law.

Article 155. Before executing a death sentence, a people's court should notify the people's procuratorate to send its personnel to make an on-site supervision of the execution.

The adjudicating personnel directing the execution should examine and verify the identity of the condemned, ask him if he has any last words or letters and then turn him over to the executioner

for execution. If before the execution it is discovered that there might be a mistake, the execution should be suspended temporarily and a report
of the situation made to the Supreme Court for a
ruling.

The execution of a death sentence should be
announced, but the condemned should not be exposed
to the public.

After execution, the court clerk present at
the spot should make a proper written record. The
people's court executing the sentence should submit a report on the execution situation to the
Supreme People's Court.

After execution, the people's court seeking
the sentence should notify the family of the
condemned.

(Articles 157 to 164 omitted. Article 164 is
the last article.)

Document 7

Decision of Standing Committee of the National
People's Congress on the Procedure to Try Swiftly
Criminals Who Gravely Endanger Public Security of
the Society (Passed by the Second Meeting of the
Standing Committee of the Sixth National People's
Congress on September 2, 1983.) (Translated from
Renmin ribao, September 3, 1983, p. 3.)

In order to punish swiftly and severely
criminals who gravely endanger public security of
the society and to safeguard the interests of the
state and the people, it is hereby decided that:

(1)   Criminals involved in homicide, rape,
robbery, explosion and other activities
that seriously endanger public safety
who warrant the death penalty should be
tried swiftly if the major facts of the
crime are clear, the evidence is conclusive, and they have incurred great public indignation. Their cases shall not
be restricted by the provisions in Article 110 of the Criminal Procedure Law
regarding time limits for the delivery

of the copy of indictment, subpoenas and
notifications.

(2)   The time limit for appeals by criminals
      listed in the foregoing section and for
      the requests for retrial by the people's
      procuratorates is changed to 3 days from
      10 days as stipulated in <u>Article 131</u> of
      the Criminal Procedure Law.

Appendix

Related articles of the Criminal Procedure
Law.

Article 110. After a decision is made to
begin trial proceedings, the people's court should
do the following: . . . .

    (2)   Deliver a copy of the people's procur-
torate's indictment to the defendant at
least 7 days before the opening court
session and inform the accused of his
right to an advocate, or, if necessary,
designate an advocate for the defendant;

    (3)   Notify the people's procuratorate of the
time and place of the court session 3
days before the session;

    (4)   Subpoena the persons concerned and noti-
fy the advocate, witnesses, appraisers
and interpreters, with the subpoenas and
notifications to be delivered at least 3
days before the court session; . . . .

Article 131. An appeal contesting a judgment
should be filed within 10 days, and an appeal contesting a ruling should be filed within 5 days
beginning the second day after the judgment or
ruling in writing has been received.

Document 8

Decision of the Standing Committee of the National
People's Congress on the Exercise by the State
Security Organ [Ministry of State Security] of the
Functions and Powers of Public Security Organs in
Conducting Investigations, Detention, Pretrial
Hearings, an Arrests (Passed by the Second Meeting
of the Standing Committee of the Sixth National
People's Congress on September 2, 1983.)
(Translated from Renmin ribao, September 3, 1983,
p. 3.)

The state security organ [i.e., Ministry of
State Security], established by a decision of the

First Session of the Sixth National People's Congress to assume the function of investigating cases of spies and secret agents originally exercised by the public security organs, is in the nature of a state public security organ; therefore, the state security organ [and its subordinates] may exercise the functions and powers stipulated in the Constitution and laws for public security organs to conduct investigations, detentions, pre-trial hearings and arrests.

Document 9

Act of the People's Republic of China for Security Administration Punishment. (Passed by the 81st Meeting of the Standing Committee of the First National People's Congress on October 22, 1957 and promulgated by the Chairman of the People's Republic of China on October 2, 1957.) (Chinese text in Gongan fagui huibian pp. 113-122; English translation in Jerome Alan Cohen, The Criminal Process in the People's Republic of China, pp. 215, 218-219, 221, 224, 227, 228, 230, 231, 232, 233, 235, 237, 250.)

Article 1. This Act is adopted in keeping with the spirit of the provisions of Article 49, Paragraph 12, and Article 100 of the Constitution of the People's Republic of China.

Article 2. An act that disrupts public order, interferes with public safety, infringes citizens' rights of the person, or damages public or private property violates security administration if the circumstances of the case are minor, if the act does not warrant criminal sanctions, and if it is punishable according to this Act.

Acts that violate security administration, by citizens of the People's Republic of China or by foreigners with the territory of the People's Republic of China, shall be a dealt with according to this Act.

Article 3. Punishments for violation of security administration shall be divided into the following three categories:

(1) Warning.

(2)   Fine: not less than five chiao no more
      than twenty yuan; punishment of in-
      creased severity may not exceed thirty
      yuan. A fine shall be paid within five
      days after decision; one who has not
      paid the fine by the expiration of the
      period shall instead be punished by
      detention.

(3)   Detention: not less than half a day or
      more than ten days; punishment of in-
      creased severity may not exceed fifteen
      days. During detention the detained
      person shall assume the cost of his own
      meals; one who cannot pay the cost of
      his means shall use labor as a sub-
      stitute [for payment].

Article 4. Instruments [used] to commit acts
that violate security adminsitration and which
must be confiscated, shall be confiscated.

Property obtained from acts that violate
security administration shall be confiscated.

With the exception of contraband articles,
the instruments and property mentioned above shall
be returned to the original owner if the original
owner is someone other than the person who violated security administration.

Article 5. A person who commits any one of
the following acts disrupting public order shall
be punished by detention of not more than ten
days, a fine of not more than twenty yuan, or a
warning:

(1)   [Participating] in gang fighting;

(2)   Disrupting order at stations, wharves,
      civilian airports, parks, market places,
      amusement places, exhibitions, athletic
      fields, or other public places, in dis-
      regard of dissuasion;

(3)   Disrupting order in offices of state
      organs, in disregard of dissuasion;

(4) Refusing [to cooperate with] or obstructing state security administration personnel who are performing their duties according to law, but not to such an extent as to constitute violent resistance;

(5) Damaging public notices or seals of state organs that are still in effect;

(6) Defacing scenic or historic places or structures that have commemorative political significance;

(7) Putting up for sale or rent reactionary, obscene, or absurd books, periodicals, picture books, or pictures that have previously been repressed.

(8) Engaging in prostitution or having sexual relations with a woman secretly engaged in prostitution in violation of the government order repressing prostitutes.

Article 6. A person who commits any one of the following acts disrupting public order shall be punished by detention of not more than seven days, a fine of not more than fourteen yuan, or a warning:

(1) Gambling for property, having undergone education without changing;

(2) Engaging in drawing lots, establishing lotteries or other methods of disguised gambling, having undergone education without changing;

(3) Spreading rumors and making trouble to obtain by fraud small amounts of property or to affect production [adversely], having undergone education without changing;

(4) Carving official seals without authorization or forging or altering certificates, where the circumstances of the case are minor;

(5) In printing, casting, or carving enter-
     prises, undertaking to make public seals
     or other certificates, in violation of
     administrative provisions;

(6) Putting up for sale fake drugs to obtain
     by fraud small amounts of money or
     property.

Article 7. A person who commits any one of
the following acts disrupting public order shall
be punished by detention or not more than three
days, a fine of not more than six yuan, or a
warning:

(1) Fishing and hunting in districts where
     fishing and hunting are prohibited, in
     disregard of dissuasion;

(2) Photographing or suveying and mapping in
     districts where photographing and sur-
     veying and mapping are prohibited, in
     disregard of dissuasion;

(3) Passing without authority through dis-
     tricts through which passing is pro-
     hibited, in disregard of dissuasion;

(4) Damaging or unauthorized moving of tem-
     porary surveying markers;

(5) In cities, willfully making loud noises
     that [adversely] affect the work and
     rest of surrounding residents, in dis-
     regard of an order to stop.

Article 8. A person who commits any one of
the following acts interfering with public safety
shall be punished by detention of not more than
seven days, a fine of not more than fourteen yuan,
or a warning:

(1) Digging holes in or placing obstacles on
     railroads or highways in such a way that
     does not make vehicular operation
     dangerous;

(2) Throwing stones, lumps of mud, or other
     similar articles at trains, motor vehi-
     cles, or boats;

(3)   Damaging traffic signs or other traffic safety equipment;

(4)   Damaging street lights;

(5)   Making, storing, transporting, or using explosive or inflammable chemical articles in contravention of safety provisions;

(6)   Making, purchasing, keeping, or using virulent poisons in contravention of safety provisions;

(7)   Violating fire prevention rules, having refused to comply with a request for improvement;

(8)   Damaging fire prevention equipment or fire prevention instruments;

(9)   Transferring without authority public fire prevention equipment for fire prevention instruments to other uses;

(10) Without permission of the local government, burning hillsides or barren fields in such a way that does not create disaster;

(11) Negligently destroying by fire state property, cooperative property, or the property of other persons in a way that does not create serious loss.

Article 9. A person who commits any one of the following acts interfering with public safety shall be punished by detention of not more than five days, a fine of not more than ten yuan, or a waring:

(1)   Without government permission, purchasing or possessing firearms or ammunition for use in athletic activities, or keeping or using such firearms or ammunition in contravention of safety provisions;

(2)   Without government permission, making, purchasing, or possessing firearms for

hunting or opening a workshop for repairing such firearms;

(3) Establishing or using civilian firing ranges in contravention of safety provisions;

(4) Installing or using antennae in contravention of safety provisions;

(5) Creating a danger of personal injury or death by organizing mass assemblies without adopting commensurate safety measures, and not improving the situation after it has been pointed out;

(6) Overloading a ferry, or continuing to use a damaged vessel that is in danger of sinking, in disregard of an admonition to repair it;

(7) Forcing ferry service during a storm or flood that creates a danger of capsizing, in disregard of an order to stop;

(8) Struggling to be first to board a ferry, in disregard of an order to stop, or coercing a ferry pilot to overload in the course of providing ferry service;

(9) Creating the possibility of an incident by selling tickets of admission to public amusement places in excess of their capacity, in disregard of dissuasion;

(10) Not keeping clear entrances, exists, and safety exists of public amusement places during the hours that they are open.

Article 10. A person who commits any one of the following acts infringing citizens' rights of the person shall be punished by detention of not more than ten days or a warning:

(1) Using obscene language and acting indecently with women;

(2) Beating up others;

(3)   Insulting and cursing others, in dis-
      regard of dissuasion;

(4)   Intentionally dirtying the body or
      clothing of others.

Article 11.   A person who commits any one of
the following acts damaging public property or
property of citizens shall be punished by detention of not more than ten days, a fine of not more
than twenty yuan, or a warning:

(1)   Stealing, swindling, or legally ap-
      propriating small amounts of public
      property or the property of others;

(2)   Taking the lead in raising an uproar and
      carrying off small amounts of property
      of an agricultural producers'
      cooperative.

Article 12.   A person who commits any one of
the following acts damaging public property or
property of citizens shall be punished by detention of not more than five days, a fine of not
more than ten yuan, or a warning:

(1)   Injuring livestock in a way that does
      not create serious loss;

(2)   Damaging agricultural crops in the
      fields, melons in melon patches, or
      fruit in orchards, in disregard of
      dissuasion:

(3)   Damaging agricultural implements, small-
      scale water utilization facilties, or
      other production equipment of an
      agricultural producers' cooperative in a
      way that does not create serious loss;

(4)   Cutting down small amounts of bamboo or
      trees belonging to the state, to a
      cooperative, or to another person with-
      out authorization;

(5)   Damaging tree seedlings in a nursery in
      a way that does not create serious loss.

Article 13. A person who commits any one of the following acts violating traffic regulations shall be punished by detention of not more than ten days, a fine of not more than twenty yuan, or a warning:

(1)   Appropriating or lending a vehicle [registration] certificate or a driver's license;

(2)   Driving a motor vehicle without a driver's license;

(3)   Driving a vehicle that is indefective condition or, if a defective condition appears while en route, driving in a manner contrary to regulation;

(4)   Driving an overloaded motor vehicle, speeding, or violating the instructions of traffic signs or signals, in disregard of dissuasion;

(5)   Instructing or coercing personnel who drive vehicles to violate traffic rules;

(6)   Violating traffic rules as pedestrians or as persons who drive vehicles other than motor vehicles, in disregard of dissuasion;

(7)   Obstructing traffic by setting up stalls, piling things or working in the streets, in disregard of an order to stop.

Article 14. A person who commits any one of the following acts violating the regulation of household registration shall be punished by detention of not more than five days, a fine of not more than ten yuan, or a warning:

(1)   Not reporting [matters of] household registration as prescribed [by law];

(2)   Falsely reporting [matters of] household registration;

(3) Altering, transferring, or putting up for loan or sale household registration certificates;

(4) Impersonating another for purposes of household registration.

(5) As a manager of a hotel, not registering guests as prescribed [by law].

Article 15. A person who commits any one of the following acts interfering with public health or the clean appearance of cities shall be punished by detention of not more than three days, a fine of not more than six yuan, or a warning:

(1) Dirtying well water, spring water, or other sources of water used by the public for drinking;

(2) In cities, willfully piling things up, drying things in the sun, or cooking articles with a foul odor, in disregard of an order to stop;

(3) Dumping rubbish or filth in the street, throwing away the carcasses of animals there, or urinating or defecating anywhere in the street;

(4) Willfully smearing, carving up or painting on structures, or pasting advertisements or items of propaganda at places other than those assigned, in disregard of dissuasion;

(5) Intentionally damaging flowers, grass, or trees in parks or on the sides of streets.

Article 16. Cases of violation of security administration shall be under the jurisdiction of city and county public security organs.

Article 17. Security administration punishments shall be decided upon by city and county public security bureaus and public security subbureaus; warnings may be decided upon by public security stations.

In rural villages detention of not more than five days may be decided upon by public security stations; in places where there are no public security stations, administrative village (town) people's councils may be entrusted to decide upon warnings and upon detentions of not more than five days. In order to deal with the specific circumstances in rural villages, public security stations and administrative village (town) people's councils may impose labor instead of detention.

Article 18. Procedures for the imposition of security administration punishments:

(1)   A summons shall be used to summon persons who have violated security administration; persons who are in the act of volating security administration may be summoned orally on the spot.

(2)   A record must be made of acts that violate security administration, and the person who violated security administration must sign it; if there are witnesses, the witnesses shall also sign their names.

(3)   A decision to impose security administration punishment must be written and given to the person who violated security administration.

(4)   If a person who has violated security administration does not accept the decision made by a public security subbureau or a public security station, he may file a petition for review within forty-eight hours; the organ that originally decided the case shall, within twenty-four hours, send the petition for review, together with the written decision, to the public security organ of the next higher level; within five days of its receipt of the petition for review the public security organ of the next higher level shall make the final decision. If the decision of the administrative village (town) people's council is not accepted, the county

public security bureau shall receive the petition for review.

(5) If a person who has violated security administration does not accept the decision made by a city or county public security bureau, he may file a petition for review within forty-eight hours; within five days of its receipt of the petition for review the city or county public security bureau shall reinvestigate and make the final decision.

(6) In remote mountainous districts, where communications are difficult, when the organ that originally decided the case or the organ that accepted the petition for review actually has no way to send the petition for review or to make the final decision in accordance with the times prescribed by Paragraphs 4 and 5, it need not observe the prescribed time limitations, but it is required to make a notation in the written decision of the time by which the prescribed time was exceeded and the reason therefor.

(7) Execution of the original decision shall be temporarily suspended from the time a person who violates security administration files his petition for review. If a person who has violated security administration has no fixed local residence, execution of the original decision can be temporarily suspended only after he finds a guarantor or pays a given amount of guarantee money.

Article 19. Persons who commit acts that violate security administration shall be exempt from punishment if after three months they have not been pursued [for responsibility].

The period specified in the previous paragraph shall be calculated from the day on which the acts that violate security administration occur. If acts that violate security administration are of a successive or continuing nature, calculation shall begin with the day on which the acts terminate.

Security administration punishment shall not be executed if, after three months from the day of decision, it has not yet been executed.

Article 20. Persons who commit acts that violate security administration shall be punished lightly or shall be exempted from punishment in any one of the following situations:

(1) Actual lack of understanding of the rules of security administration;

(2) Coercion by another;

(3) Spontaneous confession or sincere admission or error.

Article 21. Persons who commit acts that violate security administration shall be punished severely or shall be given punishment of increased severity in any one of the following situations:

(1) The consequences are relatively serious;

(2) Repeated punishment fails to change the violator;

(3) The violator sifts the blame to another person;

(4) The violator refuses to respond to a summons for interrogation or evades punishment.

Article 22. Where one person commits two or more kinds of acts that violate security administration, the punishments shall be determined separately but shall be combined in one decision. However, the combined [period of] detention may not exceed fifteen days, and the combined fine may not exceed thirty yuan. When detention and a fine are imposed at the same time, they shall be executed at the same time.

When two or more kinds of results arise from one act, punishment shall be [determined] on the basis of the most serious kind of result.

When a person successively commits the same kind of act that violates security administration,

he shall be punished severely or shall be given
punishment of increased severity.

Article 23. When two or more persons jointly
commit acts that violate security administration,
they shall be punished separately.

One who incites or coerces another to violate
security administration shall be given the punishment prescribed for the acts incited or coerced.

Article 24. When acts that violate security
administration by an organ, organization, school,
enterprise, or cooperative actually arise from
orders of that unit's responsible executive ad-
ministrator, the responsible executive administra-
tor shall be punished.

Article 25. No punishment shall be given to
one who violates security administration due to an
irresistible cause.

Article 26. No punishment shall be given for
acts that violate security administration by persons who have not reached the age of thirteen;
acts that violate security administration by persons who have reached the age of thirteen but who
have not reached the age of eighteen shall be
punished lightly. However, the heads of their
families or their guardians shall be ordered to
discipline them more strictly. If this kind of
act arises from overindulgence by the head of the
family or guardian, the head of the family or
guardian shall be punished, but punishment shall
be limited to a warning or a fine.

Article 27. No punishment shall be given to
a mentally ill person who violates security administration at a time when he is unable to understand the nature of or to control his own acts;
the head of his family or his guardian shall be
ordered to watch over him more strictly and to
give him medical care. If the family head or
guardian actually has the ability to watch over
him but does not and he causes a violation of
security administration, the family head or guardian shall be punished, but punishment shall be
limited to a warning or a fine.

Article 28. One who violates security administration while in a state of intoxication shall be punished after his state of intoxication has passed.

When, during the state of intoxication, there is danger to the person of the one who is intoxicated or a threat to the safety of the surroundings, the intoxicated person shall be restrained until he recovers sobriety.

Article 29. If a violation of security administration creates loss or injury, the violator shall pay compensation or assume the medical expenses; if the person who causes the loss or injury has not reached eighteen years of age or is mentally ill, the head of his family or his guardian shall be responsible for paying compensation or assuming the medical expenses.

Article 30. After their punishment [under this Act] has been completed, persons who are habitual loafers, who do not engage in proper employment and who repeatedly violate security administration may be sent to organs of reeducation through labor if they require such reeducation.

Article 31. Acts which violate security administration but which are not enumerated in this Act may, by comparison with the most similar [acts enumerated in the] clauses of Articles 5 to 15 of this Act, be punished by city or county public security bureaus. However, such action shall be subject to the approval of the city or county people's council.

Article 32. Apart from Articles 5 to 15, all provisions of this Act shall be applicable to other rules of security administration that prescribe security administration punishments except, however, where laws and decrees have [made] separate provisions.

Document 10

Decision of the State Council Relating to Problems
of Reeducation Through Labor. (Approved by the
78th Meeting of the Standing Committee of the
National People's Congress on August 1, 1957 and
promulgated by the State Council on August 3,
1957.)   (Chinese text in Gongan fagui huibian, pp.
391-392; English translation in Jerome Alan Cohen,
The Criminal Process in the People's Republic of
China, pp. 249-250.)

On the basis of the provisions of Article 100
of the Constitution of the People's Republic of
China, the following Decision with respect to
problems of reeducation through labor is made in
order to reform into self-supporting new persons
those persons with the capacity to labor who loaf,
who violate law and discipline, or who do not engage in proper employment, and in order further to
preserve public order and to benefit socialist
construction:

1. The following kinds of persons shall be
provided shelter and their reeducation through
labor shall be carried out:

   (1) Those who do not engage in proper em-
        ployment, those who behave like hooli-
        gans, and those who, although they
        steal, swindle, or engage in other such
        acts, are not pursued for criminal
        responsibility, who violate security
        administration and whom repeated educa-
        tion fails to change;

   (2) Those counterrevolutionaries and an-
        tisocialist reactionaries who, because
        their crimes are minor, are not pursued
        for criminal responsibility, who receive
        the sanction of expulsion from an organ,
        organization, enterprise, school, or
        other such unit and who are without a
        way of earning a livelihood;

   (3) Those persons who have the capacity to
        labor but who for a long period refuse
        to labor or who destroy discipline and
        interfere with public order, and who

[thus] receive the sanction of expulsion from an organ, organization, enterprise, school, or other such unit and who have no way of earning a livelihood:

(4) Those who do not obey work assignments or arrangements for getting them employment or for transferring them to other employment, or those who do not accept the admonition to engage in labor and production, who ceaselessly and unreasonably make trouble and interfere with public affairs and whom repeated education fails to change.

2. Reeducation through labor is a measure of a coercive nature for carrying out the education and reform of persons receiving. It is also a method of arranging for their getting employment.

Persons who receive reeducation through labor shall be paid an appropriate salary in accordance with the results of their labor. Moreover, in the exercise of discretion a part of their salary may be deducted in order to provide for the maintenance expenses of their family members or to serve as a reserve fund that will enable them to have a family and an occupation.

During the period of reeducation through labor, persons who receive it must observe the discipline prescribed by organs of reeducation through labor. Those who violate this discipline shall receive administrative sanctions. Those who violate the law and commit crimes shall be dealt with in accordance with law.

As for the aspect of administering education, the guideline of combining labor and production with political education shall be adopted. Moreover, discipline and a system shall be prescribed for them to observe in order to help them establish [in their minds] the concepts of patriotic observance of law and of the glory of labor, learn labor and production skills, and cultivate the habit of loving labor, so that they become self-supporting laborers who participate in socialist construction.

3.   If a person must be reeducated through labor, the application for reeducation through labor must be made by a civil affairs or a public security department; by the organ, organization, enterprise, school, or other such unit in which he is located; or by the head of his family or his guardian. The application shall be submitted to the people's council of the province, autonomous region, or city directly under the central authority, or to an organ that has been authorized by them, for approval.

4.   If during the period of reeducation through labor a person who receives it behaves well and has the conditions for getting employment, he may, with the approval of the organ of reeducation through labor, separately [independently] get employment. If the unit, head of the family, or guardian that originally made the application for the person's reeducation through labor asks to take him back so that it can assume responsibility for disciplining him, the organ of reeducation through labor may also, giving consideration to the circumstances, approve the request.

5.   Organs of reeducation through labor shall be established at the level of the province, autonomous region, and city directly under the central authority and shall be established [at lower levels] with the approval of the people's council of the province, autonomous region, or city directly under the central authority. Civil affairs departments and public security departments shall jointly be responsible for leading and administering the work of organs of reeducation through labor.

Document 11

Supplementary Regulations Issued by the State Council on Reeducation Through Labor (Approved by the Twelfth Meeting of the Standing Committee of the Fifth National People's Congress on November 29, 1979) (Promulgated for Entry into Force on November 29, 1979 by the State Council) (Translated from Gongan fagui huibian, p. 393.)

In order to implement thoroughly in an even better way the State Council's Decision on the

Question of Reeducation through Labor approved by the 78th Meeting of the First National People's Congress on August 1, 1957, the following supplementary regulations are hereby issued:

(1) Administrative committees for reeducation through labor shall be formed by the people's governments of provinces, autonomous regions, municipalities directly under the central government and of big and medium-sized cities. These committees shall consist of responsible persons of civil administration, public security and labor departments who will guide and take charge of the work of reeducation through labor.

(2) Those people in big and medium-sized cities who need to be reeducation through labor shall be accepted for reeducation through labor. The persons who need to be rehabilitated through labor shall be examined and approved by the administrative committees for reeducation through labor of the provinces, autonomous regions, municipalities directly under the central government and of big and medium-sized cities.

(3) The period of reeducation through labor shall range from 1 to 3 years. It may be extended for one more year, if necessary. Festivals and Sundays shall be rest days.

(4) After their release, those who have undergone reeducation through labor shall not be discriminated against in opportunity for employment and schooling. No discrimination against the families and children of those receiving reeducation through labor shall be permitted.

(5) People's procuratorates shall exercise supervision over the activities of organs for reeducation through labor.

Document 12

Act of the People's Republic of China for Reform
Through Labor. (Passed by the 22nd Meeting of the
Government Administration Council on August 26,
1954 and promulgated by the Government
Administration Council on September 17, 1954.)
(Excerpts) (Chinese text in Gongan fagui huibian,
pp. 397-409; English translation in Jerome Alan
Cohen, The Criminal Process in the People's
Republic of China, pp. 365-368, 374-375, 376-377,
589-595, 619-621, 634.)

Chapter I. General Principles

Article 1. In accordance with the provisions
of Article 7 of the Common Program of the Chinese
People's Political Consultative Conference, this
Act is adopted specially in order to punish all
counterrevolutionary and other criminal offenders
and to compel them to reform themselves through
labor and become new persons.

Article 2. Organs of reform through labor of
the People's Republic of China are instruments of
the people's democratic dictatorship and are organs for enforcement of punishment and reform of
all counterrevolutionary and other criminal
offenders.

Article 3. With respect to reform through
labor of offenders, those whose cases have already
been adjudged shall, in accordance with the nature
of the crime and the seriousness of the crime and
punishment, be held in prisons and reform through
labor discipline groups individually established
to handle the different types of offenders.

Detention houses shall be established in order to hold offenders whose cases have not been
adjudged.

Juvenile rehabilitation houses shall be established in order to conduct educational reform
for juvenile offenders.

Article 4. Organs of reform through labor
shall implement the guidelines of combining
punishment and control with thought reform and of

combining labor and production with political education when putting into effect reform through labor of all counterrevolutionary and other criminals.

Article 5. When holding all counterrevolutionary and other criminal offenders, organs of reform through labor shall effect strict control and must not be apathetic or relax their vigilance. Mistreatment and corporal punishment shall be strictly prohibited.

Article 6. Organs of reform through labor shall be led by people's public security organs, shall be supervised by people's procuratorial offices of the various levels, and, in matters relating to judicial business, shall be guided by people's courts of the various levels.

Article 7. The work of organs of reform through labor in holding the educating offenders whose cases are being investigated and adjudicated shall accord with the work of investigaiton and adjudication.

Chapter II. Organs of Reform Through Labor

Section 1. Detention Houses

Article 8. Detention houses shall be mainly [used] for confining in custody offenders whose cases have not been adjudged.

Criminals who have been sentenced to two years or less of imprisonment and whom it is inconvenient to send to reform through labor discipline groups for execution of sentence, may be held by detention houses.

Article 9. Detention houses shall be responsible for being informed about the circumstances of offenders whose cases have not been adjudged. Where the circumstances of the case are major, offenders whose cases have not been adjudged shall be kept in solitary confinement and those who are involved in the same case or in related cases shall be isolated [from one another] in order to meet the needs of investigation and adjudication organs in quickly closing the case.

Offenders whose cases have not been adjudged shall be organized to engage in appropriate labor under conditions that do not hinder investigation or adjudication.

Offenders whose cases have already been adjudged and who are being held in a detention house on behalf of another [institution] shall be kept in custody separately from those whose cases have not been adjudged. They should be compelled to engage in labor production and political education should be conducted toward them.

Article 10. If offenders whose cases have not been adjudged and who are confined to custody in detention houses are then sentenced to control or to labor service [outside of prison] but are exempted from imprisonment, they shall, on the basis of a judgment determined by a people's court, be sent back to their original place of residence or to the department where they originally worked, and the sentence shall be executed by the local people's government of that place or by the department where they originally worked.

Article 11. Detention houses shall be established with the central government, the province, the city, the special district and the county as units, and shall be under the jurisdiction of people's public security organs of the various levels.

Detention houses of [different] units that are located in the same place may be merged with consideration to local circumstances.

When necessary, detention houses may be established by public security subbureaus of city-administered districts in cities directly under the central authority and in provincial capitals.

Article 12. Detention houses shall each have a director, one or two deputy directors, and a number of staff members and guards.

Section 2. Prisons

Article 13. Prisons shall be [used] primarily for holding counterrevolutionary offenders and other important criminal offenders whose cases have already been adjudged, who have been given suspended death sentences or life imprisonment, and for whom the execution of sentence by labor outside of prison would be inappropriate.

Article 14. Prison [authorities] shall strictly control offenders and also guard them closely. When necessary, offenders may be placed in solitary confinement. Under the principle of strict control and distinguishing the different circumstances of offenders, prison [authorities] shall put into effect compulsory labor and education.

Article 15. Provinces and cities shall establish prisons on the basis of actual needs, and they shall be under the jurisdiction of provincial and city people's public security organs.

Article 16. Prisons shall each have one warden and one or two deputy wardens and shall establish discipline, production, general affairs, and other such work departments under them.

Section 3.   Reform Through Labor Discipline
              Groups.

Article 17. Reform through labor discipline groups shall hold counterrevolutionary offenders and other criminal offenders whose cases have already been adjudged and for whom labor outisde of prison is appropriate.

Article 18. Reform through labor discipline groups shall organize offenders for planned participation in agriculture, industry, construction work, and other such production and shall combine labor and production and conduct political education.

Article 19. Provinces and cities shall establish reform through labor discipline groups on the basis of actual needs, and they shall be under the jurisdiction of provincial and city people's public security organs.

Article 20. Reform through labor discipline groups may establish platoons, companies, battalions, regiments, and corps, depending on the number of offenders and the needs of production. These groups shall each have a leader and a number of assistant leaders and, in accordance with the actual needs of discipline and production work, may establish work departments.

Section 4.   Houses of Discipline for Juvenile Offenders.

Article 21. Houses of discipline for juvenile offenders shall discipline juvenile offenders who are over the age of thirteen but who have not reached the age of eighteen.

Article 22. In educating juvenile offenders houses of discipline shall emphasize political education, education in the new morality, and education in basic culture and production skills. Moreover, they shall make juvenile offenders engage in light labor under circumstances that show concern for their physical development.

Article 23. Houses of discipline for juvenile offenders shall be established on the basis of the need for them, with provinces and cities as units, and shall be under the jurisdiction of provincial and city people's public security organs.

Article 24. Houses of discipline for juvenile offenders shall each have a director and one or two deputy directors, and they may arrange for a number of discipline officers in accordance with the needs of the work.

Chapter 3.   Reform Through Labor and Reform Through Education

Article 25. In order to make compulsory labor gradually approach voluntary labor and thereby attain the goal of reforming offenders into new persons, reform through labor must be combined with political and ideological education.

Article 26. In order to expose the essence of crime, to eliminate criminal thoughts, and to establish new concepts of morality, collective classes, individual conversations, assigned study of documents, organized discussions, and other such methods shall be regularly and systematically used to educate offenders about admitting their guilt and observing the law, about current political events, about labor and production, and about culture.

Offenders may be organized to engage in appropriate athletic and cultural recreation and in examination and discussion of their lives, their labor, and their study.

Article 27. Attention shall be paid to cultivation of the production skills and labor habits of offenders. During reform through labor attention shall be paid to the full utilization of technical skills of offenders who have them.

Article 28. Production contests may be conducted among offenders in order to raise production efficiency and to promote in offenders a positive attitude toward reform through labor.

Article 29. In order to examine the circumstances of the reform of offenders a card file system shall be established for them. Moreover, there shall be special persons to administer this system and to record at any time the circumstances of the offenders' observance of discipline and their behavior with respect to labor and study. Evaluations shall be made periodically.

Chapter IV. Production Through Reform Through Labor

(Articles 30 to 35 omitted.)

Chapter V. System for Regulating Offenders

Section 1. Commitment

Article 36. The commitment of offenders to custody shall require a written judgment, a written order for execution [of sentence], or a warrant for commitment to custody. Without the above-mentioned documents, commitment to custody shall not be permitted. If the material recorded in the above-mentioned documents is discovered to be not in conformity with the actual circumstances or is incomplete, it shall be explained or supplemented by the organ that originally sent the offender into custody.

Article 37. A health examination shall be given to offenders who are committed to custody. Except for major counterrevolutionary offenders and other offenders whose criminal acts are major, commitment to custody shall not be permitted in any one of the following situations:

(1) Mental illness or acute or malignant contagious disease;

(2) Serious illness that may endanger he life of the offender while he is being held in custody;

(3) Pregnancy or childbirth six months or less before the time of commitment.

Offenders who under the preceding items may not be committed to custody shall, after the organ that originally ordered their commitment to custody has considered the situation, be sent to a hospital, turned over to a guardian, or put in another appropriate place.

Article 38. For offenders who are committed to custody there shall be established, on the basis of the actual circumstances, multiple occupancy cells, single occupancy cells, women's cells, cells for the sick, and other such cells for holding offenders on an individual basis. There shall be female guards in places where female offenders are held.

Article 39. Female offenders shall not be permitted to bring their infants into prison with them. As for infants whom the offenders really cannot give to another for care, civil affairs departments of local state administrative organs shall entrust them to residents, orphanages, or nurseries. Necessary expenditures shall be paid out of social relief funds.

Article 40. A thorough examination shall be made of offenders who are committed to custody. Contraband articles shall be sent to the people's court for confiscation. Articles which are not of daily use shall be kept on the offenders' behalf; a receipt shall be given to them and the articles shall be returned at the time of their release. But when they have a proper use for them, the offenders may be permitted to use the articles. If materials are discovered that contribute to investigation and adjudication, they shall be sent to the organs in charge of investigation and adjudication.

Female offenders shall be examined by female guards.

Article 41. The name, sex, age, race, place of origin, address, [social] origin, occupation, cultural level, special abilities, type of crime, term of imprisonment, health circumstances, family circumstances, the people's court that determined judgment, etc., of an offender who is committed to custody shall be recorded item by item in his status identification booklet. When necessary a photograph may be glued in.

Article 42. When investigation or adjudication has not yet been concluded and the commitment to custody of an offender whose case has not been adjudged already exceeds the legally prescribed limit, the detention house shall promptly notify the organ that sent the offender into custody to deal with the case quickly.

Article 43. As for an offender whose case has already been adjudged and who is being held by an organ of reform through labor [while serving his sentence], if that organ discovers reliable material sufficient to alter [the assessment of] the facts of the case, it shall immediately send the material to the original adjudication organ or to the people's court of the place in which the organ of reform through labor is located to serve as the basis for adjudicating the case anew.

Section 2. Guarding

Article 44. The people's public security armed units have exclusive responsibility for the armed guarding of offenders. Organs of reform through labor shall exercise professional leadership over the armed units performing that task.

Article 45. Areas around prison cells, areas around places where offenders work and relax, and routes by which they come and go shall be closely guarded. Except for armed guard units and discipline personnel, no person who enters prison cells and places where offenders work and relax shall be permitted to carry weapons.

Article 46. When there is a possibility of escape, violence, or other dangerous acts on the part of offenders, upon special instructions from investigation organs or with the approval of the responsible office of organs of reform through labor, instruments of restraint may be used. But when the above-mentioned situation is eliminated, they shall be immediately removed.

Article 47. When all other methods have been used and have proved incapable of checking the situation, organs of reform through labor and armed guard units may use weapons when they encounter any one of the following situations:

(1)   A mass riot by offender;

(2)   An escaping ofender disregards an order to stop or resists arrest;

(3)   An offender possesses a deadly weapon or dangerous object, is in the process of committing a deadly act or destroying something, and disregards an order to stop or offers resistance;

(4)   Someone takes an offender away by force or [otherwise] helps an offender to escape and disregards an order to stop;

(5)   An offender forcibly seizes a guard's weapon. Every use of weapons shall be reported in detail for the examination of the people's public security organ in charge and the people's procuratorial organ.

If organs of reform through labor and armed guard units erroneously use weapons and such erroneous use constitutes a criminal act, they shall be held criminally responsible.

Article 48. When organs of reform through labor and armed guard units encounter natural disasters and accidents, they shall strive to rescue offenders and strengthen their guard.

Article 49. Organs of reform through labor shall conduct an inspection of offenders and prison cells daily. Every week or fortnight they shall conduct a major inspection.

Section 3. Daily Life

Article 50. Standards for the clothing and food of offenders shall be imposed according to uniform provisions, and unauthorized reduction and appropriation shall be strictly prohibited.

In administering the food of offenders, they [the authorities] shall within the standards of supply, strive for variety and improvement. Moreover, they shall show concern for the habits of offenders from minority nationality groups.

Article 51. Supply stations may be established in reform through labor camps on the basis of actual needs in order to supply offenders with supplementary and articles of daily use.

Article 52. The time for actual labor for offenders generally shall be fixed at nine to ten hours each day. With seasonal production it may not exceed twelve hours. The time for sleep generally shall be fixed at eight hours. The time for study may be fixed in accordance with concrete circumstances, but it shall not be permissible to average less than one hour a day. Sleep and study periods for juvenile offenders shall be appropriately extended. Offenders who do not participate in labor should have one to two hours a day of outdoor activities.

A day of rest for offenders shall generally be fixed at once every fortnight, for juvenile offenders once every week.

Article 53. In accordance with the size of their unit, organs of reform through labor shall establish medical dispensaries, hospitals, and other such institutions for medical treatment, and they shall have necessary medical equipment. But detention houses in counties (cities) that have few offenders may use the county hospital as a medical institution.

Attention must constantly be paid to seeing that offenders bathe, have haircuts, wash their clothes, use disinfectants, guard against contagious diseases, and take other such measures for cleanliness and sanitation.

Article 54. When an offender dies, a medical evaluation shall be made, and it shall be examined by the local people's court. Moreover, members of the offender's family and the organ that took him into custody shall be notified.

Article 55. The expenses for offenders' medical, health, education, physical exercises, instruments for cultural activities and recreation and others shall be defrayed by the organs of reform through labor according to the standard [set by the government] and practical need.

Section 4. Receiving Visits and Correspondence

Article 56. Offenders shall not be permitted to receive visits from family members more than twice a month, and each visit may not exceed thirty minutes. In special circumstances, with the approval of a responsible officer of the organ of reform through labor, it [the time] may be appropriately extended. When receiving visits, use of secret languages or foreign languages shall be prohibited. When offenders from foreign countries receive visits from family members, there shall be an interpreter present.

Before receiving visits from family members, offenders whose cases have not been adjudged shall secure the approval of the organ that originally sent them into custody or of the adjudication organ.

Article 57. Articles of daily use of people's currency given to offenders by famiy members shall be carefully examined by organs of reform through labor, and the sending in of all unnecessary articles shall be prohibited. Organs of reform through labor shall register people's currency sent by members of offenders' families, keep it on their behalf, and issue a receipt to the offenders. When offenders have a proper use for the money, it may be given to them.

Article 58. Mail sent and received by offenders whose cases have not been adjudged shall be examined by the organ that originally sent them into custody or by the adjudication organ, or an organ of reform through labor may be authorized to make the examination. If situations of collusion regarding the [presentation of] circumstances of a case or of hindering education and reform are discovered, it [the mail involved] shall be held back.

Article 59. In special circumstances an offender's receipt of visits and receipt of articles sent by family members and the sending and receipt of mail, etc., may all be further limited or stopped.

Section 5. Obtaining a Guarantor

Article 60. When an offender is in any one of the following situations, he may be permitted to obtain a guarantor and serve his sentence outside of prison, but this must first be reviewed and approved by the people's public security organ in charge, and the people's public security organ at the place in which the offender is located must be notified to place him under supervision. The period that the offender is outside of prison [during his term of imprisonment] is counted as within his term of imprisonment.

(1) Except for an offender whose crime is heinous, one who is seriously ill and for whom it is necessary to obtain a guarantor and seek medical treatment outside of prison;

(2) One who is fifty-five years of age or is physically disabled, whose term of imprisonment is five years or less and who has lost the capacity to endanger society.

The provisions of Paragraph 1 above also apply to offenders whose cases have not been adjudged, but the matter must first be submitted for the approval of the organ that sent them into custody, and the people's public security organ at their place of residence must be notified to place them under supervision.

Section 6. Release

Article 61. Offenders shall be released on the basis of the following circumstances:

(1) Their term of imprisonment has expired;

(2) Investigation or adjudication organs notify the organs of reform through labor that they [the offenders] should be released;

(3) Conditional release [is ordered].

Offenders who should be released shall be given a certificate of release by organs of reform through labor and shall be released on time. Before their release an evaluation shall be made, and the conclusion shall be recorded in the certificate of release. Organs of reform through labor shall give released offenders funds for travel expenses for their return home. Members of families of those who have fallen seriously ill shall be notified in advance to come to meet them.

Article 62. All offenders, when their terms of imprisonment have expired and they are about to be released, may voluntarily remain in their group and get work, or if they have no home to which to return and no employment to get or if it is possible to place them in sparsely inhabited districts, organs of reform through labor shall then organize them for labor and get them employment. Methods for this shall be covered by separately issued provisions.

Chapter VI. Supervision and Governing Committee

(Articles 63 to 66 omitted.)

Chapter VII. Rewards and Punishments

Article 67. In order to enable offenders to establish their merit and atone for their crimes,

a reward and punishment system with clearly defined rewards and punishments shall be put into
effect.

Article 68. Offenders in any one of the following situations may, on the basis of different
behavior, be given a commendation, material reward, merit mark, reduction of sentence, conditional release, or other such reward:

(1)   They habitually observe discipline, dil-
       igently study, and really demonstrate
       that they have repented and reformed;

(2)   They dissuade other offenders from un-
       lawful conduct, or information given by
       them denouncing counterrevolutionary
       organizations and activity inside or
       outside prisons is confirmed through
       investigation;

(3)   They actively labor and fulfill or over-
       fulfill production tasks;

(4)   They have special accomplishments in
       conserving raw materials and taking care
       of public property;

(5)   They diligently study technical skills
       and specifically demonstrate inventive-
       ness, creativity, or [ability in] teach-
       ing their own technical skills to
       others;

(6)   They eliminate disasters or major inci-
       dents and avoid loss [to the people];

(7)   They engage in other acts that are
       beneficial to the people and the state.

Article 69. In any one of the following
situations offenders may, on the basis of the different circumstances of each case, be given warning, demerit, confinement to quarters or other
such punishment:

(1)   They hinder the reform of other
       offenders;

(2) They do not take care of or they damage instruments of production;

(3) They are lazy or deliberately work slowly;

(4) They engage in other acts that violate the rules of administration.

Article 70. The rewards and punishments prescribed in Articles 68 and 69 shall be announced and given after review and approval by a responsible officer of the organ of reform through labor. But, for reduction of sentence or conditional release, a recommendation of the organ of reform through labor must be submitted to the people's public security organ in charge for review and then sent to the local provincial or city people's court for approval, announcement and execution.

Article 71. On the basis of the seriousness of the circumstances of each case, organs of reform through labor shall [decide whether to] recommend that the local people's court sentence, in accordance with law, offenders who commit any one of the following crimes while they are being held by those organs:

(1) Rioting or committing deadly acts or inciting others to commit deadly acts;

(2) Escaping or organizing escapes;

(3) Destroying construction work or important public property;

(4) Openly resisting labor despite repeated education;

(5) Engaging in other acts that seriously violate the law.

Article 72. When major conterrevolutionary offenders, habitual robbers, habitual thieves, and other offenders who, during the period of their reform through labor, do not labor actively but repeatedly violate prison rules, and the facts prove that they still have not reformed and that

there is a real possibility that they will continue to endanger the security of society after
release, before their term of imprisonment expires
organs of reform through labor may submit to the
people's security organ in charge the suggestion
that their reform through labor be continued;
after the suggestion is reviewed by the public
security organ and after the offenders are sentenced by the local people's court in accordance
with law, their reform through labor shall be
continued.

Article 73. If, after they receive punishment, offenders really demonstrate that they have
reformed and that they repent, their punishment
may be reduced or terminated, according to the
degree of their reform and repentance.

Chapter VIII. Expenses

(Articles 74 to 75 omitted.)

Chapter IX. Supplementary Regulations

(Articles 76 to 77 omitted.)

Document 13

Provisional Measures for Dealing with the Release
of Reform Through Labor Criminals at the
Expiration of Their Term of Imprisonment and for
Placing Them an Getting Them Employed. (Approved
by the 22nd Meeting of the Government
Administration Council on August 26, 1954 and
promulgated by the Government Administration
Council on September 7, 1954.) (Chinese text in
Gongan fagui huibian, pp. 410-411; English
translation in Jerome Alan Cohen, Criminal Process
in the People's Republic of China, pp. 634-635.)

Article 1. These measures are adopted on the
basis of the provisions of Article 62 of the Act
of the People's Republic of China for Reform
Through Labor in order to implement the policy of
reform through labor, consolidate the security of
society, and resolve the offenders' problem of
getting employment after expiration of their term
of imprisonment.

Article 2. Organs of reform through labor may retain, place, and get employment for offenders whose term of imprisonment has already expired and who are in any one of the following circumstances:

(1) They themselves desire to remain in the group and get employment, and they are needed for reform through labor production;

(2) They have no home to which to return and no employment to get;

(3) They are criminals who have undergone reform through labor in sparsely inhabited districts and, after expiration of their term of imprisonment, they are needed to stay with settlers, have a family, and have an occupation there.

Article 3. Organs of reform through labor shall, three months before expiration of the term of imprisonment of an offender who meets any one of the conditions prescribed in Article 2 (2)-(3) of these measures, submit their opinion to the people's public security organ in charge for review and approval in order to facilitate retaining, placing, and getting him employment after expiration of his term of imprisonment.

Article 4. For all persons who are retained and placed and who have obtained employment, on the day of expiration of their release announced and, in accordance with the original judgment, they shall have their political rights restored or shall continue to be deprived of them.

Article 5. Methods for placing and getting employment for offenders who are released upon expiration of their term of imprisonment:

(1) Those whose reform through labor was relatively good, who have production skills, and are needed by enterprises and departments for social production, may be encouraged to get their own employment or, under conditions where it

is possible, may be introduced to employment by organs of reform through labor and departments of labor;

(2)   Offenders may be placed and may get employment within reform through labor discipline groups, and their salary may be fixed in accordance with their labor conditions and skills;

(3)   Some land on or near a reform through labor farm may be set aside for organizing collective production and establishing new villages.

Article 6. The establishment of new villages shall be jointly planned by provincial organs of reform through labor and civil affairs departments of the same level.

Article 7. When all those whose term of imprisonment has expired are placed and have obtained employment in sparsely inhabited districts, and they are able to support themselves through production, civil affairs departments may use settlement measures to assist them in receiving members of their families, having a family, and having an occupation there.

Article 8. In reform through labor units in factories, mines, enterprises, construction groups, and units with relatively small-scale production, with the exception of cases that are dealt with by those units in accordance with measures prescribed by Article 5(1)-(2), if after the term of imprisonment of offenders has expired there is no way of dealing with them, provincial, city, or central organs of reform through labor shall transfer them to other assigned reform through labor production units or new villages for placement.

Article 9. These measures shall be implemented after the approval by the Government Administrative Council of the Central People's Government. (This article was translated by Hungdah Chiu.)

Document 14

Provisional Act on Lawyers of the People's
Republic of China (Passed by the 15th Meeting of
the Standing Committee of the Fifth National
People's Congress on August 26, 1980.) (Translated
from <u>Zhongguo baike nianjian 1981</u> (China
Encyclopaedic Yearbook 1981), Beijing: China Great
Encyclopaedia Publisher, 1982, pp. 190-191.)

Chapter I. The Functions and Rights of Lawyers

<u>Article 1</u>. Lawyers are the state's legal
workers and function to give legal assistance to
the state organs, units of enterprises and institutions, social groups, the people's communes,
and the citizens in order to ensure the correct
implementation of law and safeguard the interests
of the state, the collectives and the legitimate
rights and interests of citizens.

<u>Article 2</u>. The major services of lawyers
are:

   (1) to accept the invitation of the state
       organs, units of enterprises and in-
       stitutions, social groups, and the peo-
       ple's communes to act as their legal
       advisers;

   (2) to accept a litigant's entrustment to
       serve as an agent in a civil case;

   (3) to accept a defendant's entrustment or
       the assignment of a people's court to
       serve as a defense counsel in a criminal
       case, to accept the entrustment of a
       party who initiates a private prosecu-
       tion and to accept the entrustment of an
       injured party or that of his close rela-
       tives in a public prosecution, to serve
       as an agent in litigation.

   (4) to accept the entrustment of the party
       in a nonlitigious matter to give legal
       assistance or act as an agent to par-
       ticipate in mediation and arbitration
       activities;

> (5) to answer questions on law and to draft documents for litigation and other documents related to legal matters.

Lawyers must through their entire professional activities propagate the socialist legal system.

Article 3. In carrying out their professional activities, lawyers must act on the basis of facts, take law as their criterion, and be loyal to the interests of socialist causes and the people.

In carrying out their duties according to law, lawyers are protected by the law of the state. There shall be no interference by any unit or individual.

Article 4. Acting as legal advisers, lawyers are responsible for giving advice on legal questions pertaining to the activities of the inviting unit, drafting and examining legal documents, acting as agents in litigation, mediation, or arbitration activities for the inviting unit, and safeguarding its legitimate rights and interests.

Article 5. Acting as agents in litigious and nonlitigious matters, lawyers are responsible for safeguarding the legitimate rights and interests of their clients within the authority of their entrustments.

The acts in litigation and the juristic acts of lawyers within the scope of their entrustments have the same effect as those of their clients themselves.

Article 6. Acting as defense counsel in criminal cases, lawyers are responsible for safeguarding the legitimate rights and interests of the defendant on the basis of facts and law.

If in the opinion of a lawyer a defendant is not telling the truth relating to the facts of his case, the lawyer has the right to refuse to serve as his defense counsel.

Article 7. Lawyers participating in litigious activities have the right, according to the relevant regulations, to examine and to read the materials relevant to their cases and to make inquiry to relevant units and individuals. Lawyers serving as defense counsel in criminal cases may visit and correspond with the defendant in custody.

The relevant units and individuals have the duty to support the lawyers in carrying out the preceding activities.

When lawyers come into contact with state secrets and personal secrets of individuals in carying out their professional activities, they have the duty to keep those secrets.

Chapter II. The Qualifications of Lawyers

Article 8. Citizens who cherish the People's Republic of China, support the socialist system, have the right to vote and to be elected and with the following qualifications are eligible to be lawyers after having been evaluated and found to be qualified:

    (1) those who graduated with a law major from institutions of higher learning and have engaged for 2 or more years in judicial work, teaching of law, or legal research;

    (2) those who have received training in a law major and have worked as judges of the people's courts or procurators of the people's procuratorates;

    (3) those who have received higher education, have done 3 or more years of economic, scientific, technological or other work, are proficient in their fields and in the laws and decrees related to their fields, have gone through training in a law major and are suitable to engage in lawyers' work;

    (4) those who posess the same level of legal knowledge as listed in items No. 1 or No. 2 of this article, have the cultural level of [graduates] of institutions of

higher learning, and are suitable to engage in lawyers' work.

Article 9. To be qualified as a lawyers, [a person must submit his application] to the judicial department (or bureau) of a province, autonomous region, or municipality under the direct control of the central government for evaluation and approval. [If approved, he shall] be issued a lawyer's certificate, which shall be reported to the Ministry of Justice of the People's Republic of China for record. If the Ministry of Justice finds the evaluation and approval to be improper, it shall notify the judicial department (or bureau) to make a reevaluation.

Article 10. Those who have acquired the qualifications of a lawyer but are unable to leave their posts may serve as part-time lawyers. The units to which the part-time lawyers are attached shall give them support.

Active personnel of the people's courts, people's procuratorates and people's security organs are not allowed to serve as part-time lawyers.

Article 11. Those who have graduated with a law major from institutions of higher learning or have received training in a law major may serve as apprentice lawyers after having been evaluated and approved by the judicial departments (or bureaus) or provinces, autonomous regions, or municipalities under the direct control of the central government.

The training period for apprentice lawyers is 2 years. Upon completion of the apprenticeship period, apprentice lawyers are entitled to be qualified as lawyers in accordance with the procedure provided in Article 9 of this Act; those who do not meet the requirement of the evaluation may extend their apprenticeship period.

Article 12. Lawyers who are seriously incompetent may have their qualifications for lawyers cancelled by the decision of the judicial department (or bureau) of the provinces, autonomous regions or municipalities under the direct control of the central government and with the approval of the Ministry of Justice.

Article 13. The organs for lawyers in performing their functions are the legal advisers
offices.

The legal advisers offices are institutional
units under the organizational leadership and
operational supervision of the state judicial administrative organs.

Article 14. Legal advisers offices are established at the county, municipality, and
municipal district levels. When necessary, specialized legal advisers offices can be established
with the approval of the Ministry of Justice.

Legal advisers offices are not subordinate to
each other.

Article 15. The principal functions of a
legal advisers office are to lead lawyers to
develop professionally and to organize lawyers to
study politics and professional legal knowledge as
well as to sum up and exchange their experience as
lawyers.

Article 16. A legal advisers office shall
have one director and may have deputy director(s)
as necessary. The director and deputy director(s)
shall be elected by the lawyers in that office;
such elections shall be approved by the judicial
departments (or bureaus) of provinces, autonomous
regions, and municipalities under the direct control of the central government. They are elected
for a term of 3 years and are eligible for
reelection.

The director and the deputy director(s) of a
legal advisers office shall lead the work of the
office and must also carry out lawyers' work.

Article 17. When lawyers conduct their business, their entrustments shall be accepted and
service fees shall be collected by their legal
advisers office on a unified basis.

In distributing work to lawyers, the legal
advisers office shall try to assign the lawyers
named by clients as far as practical conditions
permit.

Article 18. A legal advisers office may assign lawyers to carry out professional activities in other localities and local legal advisers offices should provide them with assistance.

Article 19. Lawyers' associations shall be established to protect the legitimate rights and interests of lawyers, to exchange work experience, and to promote lawyers' work and contacts between legal workers both at home and abroad.

Lawyers' associations are social organizations and their organizational charter shall be formulated and adopted by the lawyers' associations.

Chapter IV. Supplementary Articles

Article 20. The provisions governing the standards for the title of lawyers and for rewarding and disciplining lawyers as well as the measures for the service fees for lawyers shall be separately formulated and adopted by the Ministry of Justice.

Article 21. This Act shall enter into force on 1 January 1982.

Document 15

Decision of the Standing Committee of the National People's Congress on the Question of the Validity of the Laws and Decrees Enacted Since the Founding of the People's Republic of China
(Passed by the Twelfth Meeting of the Standing Committee of the Fifth National People's Congress on November 29, 1979.)
(Translated from Gongan fagui huibian, pp. 447-448.)

In order to strengthen and perfect the socialist legal system and to safeguard the smooth progress of the socialist modernization reconstruction, in accordance with the spirit of the resolution on the validity of the People's Republic of China's existing laws and decrees adopted by the First Meeting of the First National People's Congress in 1954, it is hereby decided: Laws and decrees enacted or approved by the former

Central People's Government since the founding of
the People's Republic of China on October 1, 1949
and the laws and decrees enacted or approved by
the National People's Congress and its Standing
Committee since the enactment of the Constitution
of the People's Republic of China on September 20,
1954, shall remain in effect except for those
which are in conflict with the constitution or
laws enacted by the Fifth National People's Congress and the decrees enacted by the Standing Committee of the Fifth National People's Congress.

Document 16

Constitution of the People's Republic of China
(Excerpts)
(Adopted on December 4, 1982 by the Fifth National
People's Congress of the People's Republic of
China at Its Fifth Session)
(translated in Beijing Revew, Vol. 25, No. 52
(December 27, 1982), pp. 10, 11, 12, 13, 16-18,
19, 20, 21, 28-29.)

Preamble

. . .

Both the victory of China's new-democratic
revolution and the successes of its socialist
cause have been achieved by the Chinese people of
all nationalities under the leadership of the Communist Party of China and the guidance of Marxism-
Leninism and Mao Zedong Thought, and by upholding
truth, correcting errors and overcoming numerous
difficulties and hardships. The basic task of the
nation in the years to come is to concentrate its
effort on socialist modernization. Under the
leadership of the Communist Party of China and the
guidance of Marxism-Leninism and Mao Zedong
Thought, the Chinese people of all nationalities
will continue to adhere to the people's democratic
dictatorship and follow the socialist road,
steadily improve socialist institutions, develop
socialist democracy, improve the socialist legal
system and work hard and self-reliantly to modern-
ize industry, agriculture, national defence and
science and technology step by step to turn China
into a socialist country with a high level of culture and democracy.

The exploiting classes as such have been eliminated in our country. However, class struggle will continue to exist within certain limits for a long time to come. The Chinese people must fight against those forces and elements, both at home and abroad, that are hostile to China's socialist system and try to undermine it.

Taiwan is part of the sacred territory of the People's Republic of China. It is the lofty duty of the entire Chinese people, including our compatriots in Taiwan, to accomplish the great task of reunifying the motherland.

. . .

This Constitution affirms the achievements of the struggles of the Chinese people of all nationalities and defines the basic system and basic tasks of the state in legal form; it is the fundamental law of the state and has supreme legal authority. The people of all nationalities, all state organs, the armed forces, all political parties and public organizations and all enterprises and undertakings in the country must take the Constitution as the basic norm of conduct, and they have the duty to uphold the dignity of the Constitution and ensure its implementation.

Chapter I.   General Principles.

Article 1.   The People's Republic of China is a socialist state under the people's democratic dictatorship led by the working class and based on the alliance of workers and peasants.

The socialist system is the basic system of the People's Republic of China. Sabotage of the socialist system by any organization or individual is prohibited.

Article 2.   All power in the People's Republic of China belongs to the people.

The organs through which the people exercise state power are the National People's Congress and the local people's congresses at different levels.

The people administer state affairs and manage economic, cultural and social affairs through various channels and in various ways in accordance with the law.

Article 3. The state organs of the People's Republic of China apply the principle of democratic centralism.

The National People's Congress and the local people's congresses at different levels are instituted through democratic election. They are responsible to the people and subject to their supervision.

All administrative, judicial and procuratorial organs of the state are created by the people's congresses to which they are responsible and under whose supervision they operate.

The division of functions and powers between the central and local state organs is guided by the principle of giving full play to the initiative and enthusiasm of the local authorities under the unified leadership of the central authorities.

. . .

Article 5. The state upholds the uniformity and dignity of the socialist legal system.

No law or administrative or local rules and regulations shall contravene the Constitution.

All state organs, the armed forces, all political parties and public organizations and all enterprises and undertakings must abide by the Constitution and the law. All acts in violation of the Constitution and the law must be looked into.

No organization or individual may enjoy the privilege of being above the Constitution and the law.

. . .

Chapter II. The Fundamental Rights and Duties of Citizens.

Article 33. All persons holding the nationality of the People's Republic of China are citizens of the People's Republic of China.

All citizens of the People's Republic of China are equal before the law.

Every citizen enjoys the rights and at the same time must perform the duties prescribed by the Constitution and the law.

Article 34. All citizens of the People's Republic of China who have reached the age of 18 have the right to vote and stand for election, regardless of nationality, race, sex, occupation, family background, religious belief, education, property status, or length of residence, except persons deprived of political rights according to law.

Article 35. Citizens of the People's Republic of China enjoy freedom of speech, of the press, of assembly, of association, of procession and of demonstration.

Article 36. Citizens of the People's Republic of China enjoy freedom of religious belief.

No state organ, public organization or individual may compel citizens to believe in, or not to believe in, any religion; nor may they discriminate against citizens who believe in, or do not believe in, any religion.

The state protects normal religious activities. No one may make use of religion to engage in activities that disrupt public order, impair the health of citizens or interfere with the educational system of the state.

Religious bodies and religious affairs are not subject to any foreign domination.

Article 37. The freedom of person of citizens of the People's Republic of China is inviolable.

No citizen may be arrested except with the approval or by decision of a people's procuratorate or by decision of a people's court, and arrests must be made by a public security organ.

Unlawful deprivation or restriction of citizens' freedom of person by detention or other means is prohibited; and unlawful search of the person of citizens is prohibited.

Article 38. The personal dignity of citizens of the People's Republic of China is inviolable. Insult, libel, false charge or frame-up directed against citizens by any means is prohibited.

Article 39. The home of citizens of the People's Republic of China is inviolable. Unlawful search of, or intrusion into, a citizen's home is prohibited.

Article 40. The freedom and privacy of correspondence of citizens of the People's Republic of China are protected by law. No organization or individual may, on any ground, infringe upon the freedom and privacy of citizens' correspondence except in cases where, to meet the needs of state security or of investigation into criminal offences, public security or procuratorial organs are permitted to censor correspondence in accordance with procedures prescribed by law.

Article 41. Citizens of the People's Republic of China have the right to criticize and make suggestions to any state organ or functionary. Citizens have the right to make to relevant state organs complaints and charges against, or exposures of, violation of the law or dereliction of duty by any state organ or functionary; but fabrication or distortion of facts with the intention of libel or frame-up is prohibited.

In case of complaints, charges or exposures made by citizens, the state organ concerned must deal with them in a responsible manner after ascertaining the facts. No one may suppress such complaints, charges and exposures, or retaliate against the citizens making them.

Citizens who have suffered losses through infringement of their civic rights by any state organ or functionary have the right to compensation in accordance with the law.

Article 42. Citizens of the People's Republic of China have the right as well as the duty to work.

Using various channels, the state creates conditions for employment, strengthens labour protection, improves working conditions and, on the basis of expanded production, increases remuneration for work and social benefits.

Work is the glorious duty of every ablebodied citizen. All working people in state enterprises and in urban and rural economic collectives shoud perform their tasks with an attitude consonant with their status as masters of the country. The state promotes socialist labour emulation, and commends and rewards model and advanced workers. The state encourages citizens to take part in voluntary labour.

The state provides necessary vocational training to citizens before they are employed.

Article 43. Working people in the People's Republic of China have the right to rest.

The state expands facilities for rest and recuperation of working people, and prescribed working hours and vacations for workers and staff.

Article 44. The state prescribes by law the system of retirement for workers and staff in enterprises and undertakings and for functionaries of organs of state. The livelihood of retired personnel is ensured by the state and society.

Article 45. Citizens of the People's Republic of China have the right to material assistance from the state and society when they are old, ill or disabled. The state develops the social insurance, social relief and medical and health services that are required to enable citizens to enjoy this right.

The state and society ensure the livelihood of disabled members of the armed forces, provide pensions to the families of martyrs and give preferential treatment to the families of military personnel.

The state and society help make arrangements for the work, livelihood and education of the blind, deaf-mute and other handicapped citizens.

Article 46. Citizens of the People's Republic of China have the duty as well as the right to receive education.

The state promotes the all-round moral, intellectual and physical development of children and young people.

Article 47. Citizens of the People's Republic of China have the freedom to engage in scientific research, literary and artistic creation and other cultural pursuits. The state encourages and assists creative endeavours conducive to the interests of the people that are made by citizens engaged in education, science, technology, literature, art and other cultural work.

Article 48. Women in the People's Republic of China enjoy equal rights with men in all spheres of life, political, economic, cultural and social, including family life.

The state protects the rights and interests of women, applies the principle of equal pay for equal work for men and women alike and trains and selects cadres from among women.

Article 49. Marriage, the family and mother and child are protected by the state.

Both husband and wife have the duty to practice family planning.

Parents have the duty to rear and educate their minor children, and children who have come of age have the duty to support and assist their parents.

Violation of the freedom of marriage is prohibited. Maltreatment of old people, women and children is prohibited.

Article 50. The People's Republic of China protects the legitimate rights and interests of Chinese nationals residing abroad and protects the lawful rights and interests of returned overseas Chinese and of the family members of Chinese nationals residing abroad.

Article 51. The exercise by citizens of the People's Republic of China of their freedoms and rights may not infringe upon the interests of the state, of society and of the collective, or upon the lawful freedoms and rights of other citizens.

Article 52. It is the duty of citizens of the People's Republic of China to safeguard the unity of the country and the unity of all its nationalities.

Article 53. Citizens of the People's Republic of China must abide by the Constitution and the law, keep state secrets, protect public property and observe labour discipline and public order and respect social ethics.

Article 54. It is the duty of citizens of the People's Republic of China to safeguard the security, honour and interests of the motherland; they must not commit acts detrimental to the security, honour and interests of the motherland.

Article 55. It is the sacred obligation of every citizen of the People's Republic of China to defend the motherland and resist aggression.

It is the honourable duty of citizens of the People's Republic of China to perform military service and join the militia in accordance with the law.

Article 56. It is the duty of citizens of the People's Republic of China to pay taxes in accordance with the law.

Chapter III. The Structure of the State.

Section 1. The National People's Congress

Article 57. The National People's Congress of the People's Republic of China is the highest organ of state power. Its permanent body is the

Standing Committee of the National People's
Congress.

Article 58. The National People's Congress
and its Standing Committee exercise the legislative power of the state.

Article 62. The National People's Congress
exercises the following functions and powers:

(1)   to amend the Constitution;

(2)   to supervise the enforcement of the
      Constitution;

(3)   to enact and amend basic statutes con-
      cerning criminal offences, civil af-
      fairs, the state organs and other
      matters;

                    . . .

(7)   to elect the President of the Supreme
      People's Court;

(8)   to elect the Procurator-General of the
      Supreme People's Procuratorate;

(11) to alter or annul inappropriate deci-
      sions of the Standing Committee of the
      National People's Congress;

                    . . .

Article 63. The National People's Congress
has the power to recall or remove from office the
following persons:

                    . . .

(4)   the President of the Supreme People's
      Court; and

(5)   The Procurator-General of the Supreme
      People's Procuratorate.

Article 64. Amendments to the Constitution
are to be proposed by the Standing Committee of
the National People's Congress or by more than
one-fifth of the deputies to the National People's

Congress and adopted by a majority vote of more than two-thirds of all the deputies to the Congress.

Statutes and resolutions are adopted by a majority vote of more than one half of all the deputies to the National People's Congress.

Article 67. The Standing Committee of the National People's Congress exercises the following functions and powers:

(1)   to interpret the Constitution and supervise its enforcement;

(2)   to enact and amend statutes with the exception of those which should be enacted by the National People's Congress;

(3)   To enact, when the National People's Congress is not in session, partial supplements and amendments to statutes enacted by the National People's Congress provided that they do not contravene the basic principles of these statutes;

(4)   to interpret statutes;

. . .

(6)   to supervise the work of the State Council, the Central Military Commission, the Supreme People's Court and the Supreme People's Procuratorate;

(7)   to annul those administrative rules and regulations, decisions or orders of the State Council that contravene the Constitution or the statutes;

(8)   to annul those local regulations or decisions of the organs of state power of provinces, autonomous regions and municipalities directly under the Central Government that contravene the Constitution, the statutes or the administrative rules and regulations;

. . .

(11) to appoint and remove the Vice-Presidents and judges of the Supreme People's Court, members of its Judicial Committee and the President of the Military Court at the suggestion of the President of the Supreme Peoples' Court;

(12) to appoint and remove the Deputy Procurators-General and procurators of the Supreme People's Procuratorate, members of its Procuratorial Committee and the Chief Procurator of the Military Procuratorate at the request of the Procurator-General of the Supreme People's Procuratorate, and to approve the appointment and removal of the chief procurators of the people's procuratorates of provinces, autonomous regions and municipalities directly under the Central Government.

. . .

(17) to decide on the granting of special pardons;

. . .

(20) to decide on the enforcement of martial law through the country or in particular provinces, autonomous regions or municipalities directly under the Central Government; and

. . .

Article 74. No deputy to the National People's Congress may be arrested or placed on criminal trial without the consent of the Presidium of the current session of the National People's Congress or, when the National People's Congress is not in session, without the consent of its Standing Committee.

Article 75. Deputies to the National People's Congress may not be called to legal account for their speeches or votes at its meetings.

. . .

Section VII.   The People's Courts and the People's
              Procuratorates

   Article 123.   The people's courts in the People's Republic of China are the judicial organs of the state.

   Article 124.   The People's Republic of China establishes the Supreme People's Court and the local people's courts at different levels, military courts and other special people's courts.

   The term of office of the President of the Supreme People's Court is the same as that of the National People's Congress: he shall serve no more than two consecutive terms.

   The organization of people's courts is prescribed by law.

   Article 125.   All cases handled by the people's courts, except for those involving special circumstances as specified by law, shall be heard in public.   The accused has the right of defense.

   Article 126.   The people's courts shall, in accordance with the law, exercise judicial power independently and are not subject to interference by administrative organs, public organizations* or individuals.   (*The Chinese original here is "Shehui tuanti," which should be translated in English as "social organization."   The discrepancy in translation here is significant as "social organizations" do not include the Communist Party of China, while the term "public organizations" might include the Party.

   Article 127.   The Supreme People's Court is the highest judicial organ.

   The Supreme People's Court supervises the administration of justice by the local people's courts at different levels and by the special people's courts; people's courts at higher levels supervise the administration of justice by those at lower levels.

   Article 128.   The Supreme People's Court is responsible to the National People's Congress and its Standing Committee.   Local people's courts at

different levels are responsible to the organs of
state power which created them.

Article 129. The people's procuratorates of
the People's Republic of China are state organs
for legal supervision.

Article 130. The People's Republic of China
establishes the Supreme People's Procuratorate and
the local people's procuratorates at different
levels, military procuratorates and other special
people's procuratorates.

The terms of office of the Procurator-General
of the Supreme People's Procuratorate is the same
as that of the National People's Congress; he
shall serve no more than two consecutive terms.

The organization of people's procuratorates
is prescribed by law.

Article 131. People's procuratorates shall,
in accordance with the law, exercise procuratorial
power independently and are not subject to interference by administrative organs, public organizations* or individuals. (*See note following Article 126.)

Article 132. The Supreme People's Procuratorate is the highest procuratorial organ.

The Supreme People's Procuratorate directs
the work of the local people's procuratorates at
different levels and of the special people's procuratorates; people's procuratorates at higher
levels direct the work of those at lower levels.

Article 133. The Supreme People's Procuratorate is responsible to the National People's
Congress and its Standing Committee. Local people's procuratorates at different levels are
responsible to the organs of state power at the
corresponding levels which created them and to the
people's procuratorates at the higher level.

Article 134. Citizens of all nationalities
have the right to use the spoken and written languages of their own nationalities in court proceedings. The people's courts and people's procuratorates should provide translation for any

party to the court proceedings who is not familiar with the spoken or written languages in common use in the locality.

In an area where people of a minority nationality live in a compact community or where a number of nationalities live together, hearings should be conducted in the language or languages in common use in the locality; indictments, judgments, notices and other documents should be written, according to actual needs, in the language or languages in common use in the locality.

Article 135. The people's courts, people's procuratorates and public security organs shall, in handling criminal cases, divide their functions, each taking responsibility for its own work, and they shall coordinate their efforts and check each other to ensure correct and effective enforcement of law.

(Article 138 is the last Article)

III

Glossary, Tables, Bibliography

Glossary

act	tiaoli 条例
adjudicating Committee	shenpan weiyuan hui 审判委员会
adjudication supervision	shenpan jiandu 审判监督
appeal	shangsu 上诉
approving cases by the secretary	shuji pian 书记批案
arrest	daibu 逮捕
arrest warrant	daibuzheng 逮捕证
arson	fanghuo 放火
associate chief judge	fu tingzhang 副庭长
autonomous region	zizhi qu 自治区
basic people's court	jiceng renmin fayuan 基层人民法院
beating, smashing and looting	da, za, qiang 打砸抢
bigamy	chonghun 重婚
bribery	huilu 贿赂
capital punishment	sixing 死刑
chief judge	tingzhang 庭长
civil law	minfa 民法
civil procedure law	minshi susongfa 民事诉讼法

class enemy	jieji diren 阶级敌人
collection	hubian 汇编
collegiate system	heyizhi 合议制
communique	gongbao 公报
confession	kougong 口供
confiscation of property	moshou caichan 没收财产
contract	hetong 合同
contradiction	maodun 矛盾
control	guanzhi 管制
corruption	tanwo 贪污
constitution	xianfa 宪法
counterfeiting	weizou 伪造
counterrevolutionary	fangeming 反革命
court	fayuan 法院
crime	zui 罪
criminal law	xingfa 刑法
criminal procedure law	xingshi susong fa 刑事诉讼法
damaging precious [Mao's] picture	huihuai baoxiang 毁坏宝象
death sentence	sixing 死刑
deceit	qipian 欺骗
defense	bianhu 辩护
democracy	minzhu 民主
department of law	falu xi 法律系
deprivation of political rights	boduo zhengzhi quanli 剥夺政治权利
dereliction of duty	duzhi 渎职
detention	juliu 拘留
detention	juyi 拘役
dictatorship of the proletariat	wuchan jieji zhuanzheng 无产阶级专政

disrupting the regulation of social order	fanghai shehuizhuyi guanli zhixu 妨害社会主义管理秩序
division	ting 庭
divulging of state secrets	xielu guojia jimi 泄露国家机密
draft	caoan 草案
embezzlement of public funds	tanwu gonggong caiwu 贪污公共财物
encroachment	qinfan 侵犯
endangering public security	weihai gonggong anquan 危害公共安全
enticement	yinyou 引诱
evidence	zhengju 证据
extortion	lesuo 勒索
fine	fajin 罚金
four basic principles	sida jiben yuanze 四大基本原则
four big rights	sida 四大
gang of four	siren bang 四人帮
higher people's court	gaoji renmin fayuan 高级人民法院
homicide	sharen 杀人
imprisonment for a fixed term	youqi tuxing 有期徒刑
imprisonment for life	wuqi tuxing 无期徒刑
inflicting injury	shanghai 伤害
intermediate people's court	zhongji renmin fayuan 中级人民法院
investigation	zhencha 侦查
judge	shenpanyuan 审判员
judgment	panjue 判决
judicial independence	sifa duli 司法独立
judicial work	sifa gongzuo 司法工作
landlord	dizhu 地主
lawyer	lushi 律师

legal history	fazhishi 法制史
legal system	fazhi 法制
leniency to those who confess and severity to those who resist	tanbai congkuan kangju congyan 坦白从宽，抗拒从严
life imprisonment	[see imprisonment for life]
Mao Zedong thought	Mao Zedong sixiang 毛泽东思想
marriage law	hunyinfa 婚姻法
Marxism and Leninism	Malie Zhuyi 马列主义
mediation committee	tiaojie weiyuanhui 调解委员会
ministry of justice	sifa bu 司法部
municipality directly under the central government	zhixiashi 直辖市
organic law	zuzhifa 组织法
party discipline	dangji 党纪
people's assessor	renmin peishenyuan 人民陪审员
people's congress	renmin daibiao dahui 人民代表大会
people's democratic dictatorship	renmin minzhu zhuanzheng 人民民主专政
personal rights	renshen quanli 人身权利
plundering	qiangduo 抢夺
police	jingcha 警察
political power	zhengquan 政权
political-legal institute	zhengfa xueyuan 政法学院
political-legal secretary	zhengfa shuji 政法书记
preparatory examination	yushen 预审
presumption of innocence	wuzui tuiding 无罪推定
procuracy	jiancha 检察
procuratorate	jianchayuan 检察院

production brigade   shengchandui
                             生产队

property   caichan
                             财产

prostitution   maiyin
                             卖淫

protest   kangsu
                             抗诉

Provisional Act on Guarding   baoshou guojia jimi
  State Secrets   zhanxing tiaoli
                             保守国家机密暂行条例

public prosecution   gongsu
                             公诉

public security organ   gongan jiguan
                             公安机关

rape   qiangjian
                             强奸

recidivist   leifan
                             累犯

reeducation through labor   laodong jiaoyang
(Note: also translated as   劳动教养
"rehabilitation through labor")

reform through labor   laodong gaizao
                             劳动改造

regulation   faguei
                             法规

residents' committee   jumin weiyuanhui
                             居民委员会

retrial   zaishen
                             再审

rich peasant   funong
                             富农

rightist   youpai fenzi
                             右派份子

robbery   qiangjie
                             抢劫

search warrant   souchazheng
                             搜查证

Security Administration   zhian guanli chufa taoli
  Punishment Act   治安管理处罚条例

security defense committee   zhian baowei weiyuanhui
                             治安保卫委员会

sida   [see four big rights]

six articles of public security gongan liutiao
                             公安六条

smuggling   zousi
                             走私

socialist road   shehuizhuyi luxian
                             社会主义路线

speculation   touji daoba
                             投机倒把

standing committee   changwu weiyuanhui
                             常务委员会

State Council   guowuyuan
国务院

state functionaries   guojia gongzuo renyuan
国家工作人员

Supreme People's Court   zuigao renmin fayuan
最高人民法院

swindling   guanpian
惯骗

taking the facts as the basis
and law as the criterion   yi shishi wei genju, yi falu
wei zhunsheng
以事实为根据，以法律为准绳

tax evasion   toushui
偷税

theft   dauqie
盗窃

there must be laws for people
to follow, these laws must be
observed, their enforcement
must be strict and lawbreakers
must be dealt with   youfa keyi, youfa biyi, zhifa
biyan, weifa bijiu
有法可依，有法必依，执法必严，
违法必究

threat   weixie
威胁

to extort confessions by torture   xingxun bigong
刑讯逼供

undermining the socialist
economic order   pohuai shehuizhuyi jingji zhixu
破坏社会主义经济秩序

unjust verdict   yuanan
冤案

viciously attacking socialism   edu gongji shehuizhuyi
恶毒攻击社会主义

voluntary surrender   zishou
自首

withdrawal   huibi
回避

wrong verdict   cuoan
错案

Table 1. Number of Laws and Decrees Enacted or Ratified by the Plenary Meeting of the First Session of the Chinese People's Political Consultative Conference and the Central People's Government (September 1949—September 15, 1954).[1]

Types of Laws[2] or Decrees	sub-division[3]	Year					
		1949	1950	1951	1952	1953	1954
Constitutional Law and Organic Law for State Agencies	Constitutional Law	4	0	0	0	0	0
	Highest State Organs and Adm. Organs	4	1	1	2	2	1
Election		0	0	0	0	3	0
Organization of Central State Organs	People's Courts	1[4]	1[6]	1	0	0	0
	People's procuratorates	1[5]	0	2	0	0	0
Local State Organs and Adm. Organs		3	0	1	4	0	3
Appointments and Removal of State Organ Personnels		0	1	1	0	0	0
Politics and Law	Land Reform	0	2	0	0	0	0
	Suppression of counter-revolutionaries	0	0	1	0	0	0
	3-Anti and 5 Anti	0	0	0	1	0	0
	Marriage and Family	0	1	0	0	0	0
	Keeping State Secret	0	0	1	0	0	0
National Defense	People's Armed Work	0	0	0	1	0	0
Finance		1	1	0	0	0	0
Labor		0	1	0	0	0	0
National Minorities		0	0	1	2	0	0
Foreign Affairs		0	0	1	0	0	0
TOTAL		14	8	10	10	5	4

Table 1. Continued

1. Political-Legal Section of the Office of the Standing Committee of the National People's Congress and the Legal Office of the Legal System Committee of the Standing Committee of the National People's Congress), editors, *Zhongguo renmin zhengzhi xieshang huiyi diyijie quanti huiyi, zhong yang renmin zhengfu, diyi zhi sijie quanguo renmin daibiao dahui ji qi changwu weiyuanhui zhiding hezhe pizhun de falu, faling he qita wenjian mulu* (List of laws, decrees and other documents enacted or ratified by the plenary meeting of the first session of the Chinese People's Political Consultative Conference, Central People's Government, first to fourth session of the National People's Congress and its Standing Committee) (September 1949—October 1977). Beijing: Qunzhong chubanshe, 1980), pp. 3–23. Hereinafter referred to as *List of Laws and Decrees between 1949-1977*.
2. Classification made by the authors to make it consistent with Table 2.
3. Classification used in *List of Laws and Decrees between 1949-1977*, pp. 3–23.
4. Provisional Organic Act for the Supreme People's Court of the People's Republic of China, no date was given in *List of Laws and Decrees between 1949-1977*, p. 11, but the authors believed that this law was enacted in 1949.
5. Provisional Organic Act for the Supreme People's Procuratorate of the People's Republic of China, no date was given in *List of Laws and Decrees between 1949-1977*, p. 12, but the authors believed that this law was enacted in 1949.
6. General Rules on the Organization of People's Tribunal, July 20, 1950, it was mistakenly listed under the category of Land Reform in *List of Laws and Decrees between 1949-1977*, p. 14.

Table 2. Number of Laws, Decrees and Other Documents Adopted or Ratified by the 1st, 2nd, 3rd and 4th National People's Congress (NPC) or its Standing Committee (September 16, 1954—October 1977)

Type of Laws Decrees and Documents Adopted	1954	1955	1956	1957	1958	1959	1960	1961	1962	1963	1964	1965	1966	1967-74	1975	1976	1977	Total for each type
Constitutional and Organic Law for State Agencies	6	2	1	0	0	0	0	0	0	0	0	0	0	0	1	0	0	10
NPC Election, Activities and Meetings	0	10	5	6	4	5	1	4	2	5	4	0	0	0	0	0	1	47
Organization of Central State Organs	2	3	3	1	5	3	2	2	2	4	3	3	0	0	0	0	0	33
Organization of Local State Organs	3	5	2	2	1	0	0	0	0	0	0	0	0	0	0	0	0	13
Delimitation of Administrative Area	0	2	0	2	1	1	0	0	0	0	0	0	0	0	0	0	0	6
Election, Appointment, Removal, Punishment, and Award for State Personnel	9	3	2	6	4	9	1	0	3	1	0	0	0	0	2	1	0	41
National Economic Planning, Budget and Financial Statement	0	4	2	1	2	2	1	0	0	2	1	0	0	0	0	0	0	15
National Defense	0	10	0	1	1	0	0	0	1	1	0	2	0	0	0	0	0	16
Politics and Law	3	2	7	11	6	1	2	1	0	3	3	0	1	0	1	0	0	41
Finance	1	1	3	5	8	0	0	0	0	0	0	0	0	0	0	0	0	18
Industry and Commerce	0	0	0	4	0	0	0	0	0	2	0	0	0	0	0	0	0	6
Agriculture	0	2	4	2	3	0	2	0	0	0	0	0	0	0	0	0	0	13

Table 2. Continued

Type of Laws Decrees and Documents Adopted	1954	1955	1956	1957	1958	1959	1960	1961	1962	1963	1964	1965	1966	1967-74	1975	1976	1977	Total for each type
Labor	0	0	0	8	2	0	0	0	0	0	0	0	0	0	0	0	0	10
Culture, Education and Health	0	1	0	1	2	0	0	0	0	0	0	0	0	0	0	0	0	4
National Minorities Affairs	0	3	15	14	18	22	0	0	2	2	15	6	6	0	0	0	0	103
Overseas Chinese Affairs	0	1	0	4	0	0	0	0	0	0	0	0	0	0	0	0	0	5
International Affairs	3	14	17	17	15	20	31	24	14	8	11	9	0	0	0	1	0	184
Items on Agenda, Press Communique, Speech of Foreign Guests and Other (Publication) omitted. Reports of Work [of government]	3	16	18	23	7	17	20	6	30	17	21	5	0	0	4	1	2	190
Total	30	79	79	108	79	80	60	37	54	45	58	25	7	0	8	3	3	755
Total if excluding Reports of Work	27	63	61	85	72	63	40	31	24	28	37	20	7	0	4	2	1	565
Total if excluding International Affairs and Reports of Work	24	49	44	68	57	43	9	7	10	20	26	11	7	0	4	1	1	381
Total if excluding National Minorities Affairs, International Affairs and Reports of Work	24	46	29	54	39	21	9	7	8	13	11	5	1	0	4	1	1	278

Source: List of Laws, Decrees and Other Documents Adopted by CPPCC and NPC . . . (see complete citation in Table 1, note 1), pp. 27–217.

Table 3. Chart on Number of Laws, Decrees and Other Documents Adopted By Chinese People's Political Consultative Conference (1949–1954) and National People's Congress or Its Standing Committee (1954–1977)

Year

49 50 51 52 53 54 55 56 57 58 59 60 61 62 63 64 65 66 67 68 69 70 71 72 73 74 75 76 77

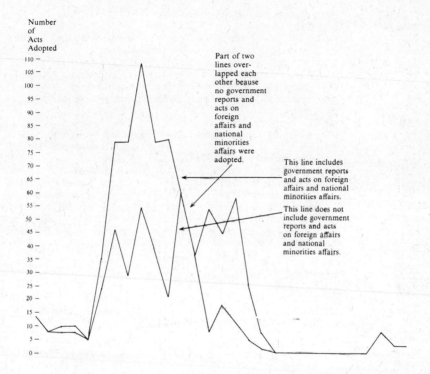

Number
of
Acts
Adopted

110 —
105 —
100 —
95 —
90 —
85 —
80 —
75 —
70 —
65 —
60 —
55 —
50 —
45 —
40 —
35 —
30 —
25 —
20 —
15 —
10 —
5 —
0 —

Part of two lines over-lapped each other beause no government reports and acts on foreign affairs and national minorities affairs were adopted.

This line includes government reports and acts on foreign affairs and national minorities affairs.

This line does not include government reports and acts on foreign affairs and national minorities affairs.

Table 4. Selected Titles on Important Laws, Regulations, Resolutions, and Decisions Relating to the Legal System and Criminal Justice Promulgated between 1978–1983

(The asterisk (*) indicates complete or partial translation appears in the documentary section of this book.)

1978

3/5	Constitution (Amendment)

1979

2/23	Forestry Law (Trial Implementation)
2/23	*Arrest and Detention Act (Amendment)
7/1	(1) Organic Law of the Local People's Congress and Local People's Government at Various Levels (Amendment)
	(2) Electoral Law for the National People's Congress and the Local People's Congress at Various Levels (Amendment)
	(3) Organic Law of the People's Courts (Amendment)
	(4) Organic Law of the People's Procuratorates (Amendment)
	*(5) Criminal Law
	*(6) Criminal Procedure Law
	(7) Law on the Joint Ventures Using Chinese and Foreign Investment
	(8) Resolution of the National People's Congress on Amending Certain Provisions in the Constitution
9/16	Environmental Protection Law (Trial Implementation)
11/29	*(1) Decision of the Standing Committee of the National People's Congress on the Question of Validity of the Laws and Decrees Enacted Since the Founding of the People's Republic of China
	*(2) Supplementary Regulations on Reeducation Through Labor (Promulgated by the State Council and approved by the Standing Committee of the National People's Congress)

1980

8/26	*Provisional Act on Lawyers
9/10	(1) Nationality Law
	(2) Marriage Law (Amendment)
	(3) Resolution of the National People's Congress on Amending Article 45 of the Constitution

1981

6/10	(1) Provisional Act on Punishing Dereliction of Duties of Military Personnel
	(2) Resolution of the Standing Committee of the National People's Congress on Strengthening the Work of Interpretation of Laws
	(3) Decision of the Standing Committee of the National People's Congress on the Question of Approving Death Sentences
	(4) Decision of the Standing Committee on the National People's Congress on Handling Reform Through Labor Criminals or Reeducation through Labor Personnel Who Have Escaped or Committed Criminal Offenses Again
12/13	(1) Economic Contract Law
	(2) Joint Venture Income Tax Laws

1982

3/8	(1) Decision of the Standing Committee of the National People's Congress on Severely Punishing Criminals Who Have Severely Undermined the Economy
	(2) Civil Procedure Law (Trial Implementation)
4/13	Act on Public Notary (Issued by the State Council)
8/23	(1) Maritime Environmental Protection Law
	(2) Trademark Law

Table 4. Continued

11/19	(1) Law on the Protection of Cultural Materials
	(2) Food Sanitation Law (Trial Implementation)
12/4	Constitution (Amendment)
12/10	(1) Organic Law of the National People's Congress
	(2) Organic Law of the State Council
	(3) Organic Law of the Local People's Congress and the Local People's Government at Various Levels (Amendment)
	(4) Electoral Law for the National People's Congress and the Local People's Congress at Various Levels (Amendment)

1983

3/12	Provisional Regulations on Control of Some Cutting Tools (Promulgated by the Ministry of Public Security with the Approval of the State Council)
9/2	*(1) Decision of the Standing Committee of the National People's Congress on Severely Punishing Criminals Who Gravely Endanger Public Security of the Society (1983)
	*(2) Decision of the Standing Committee of the National People's Congress on the Procedure to Swiftly Try Criminals Who Gravely Endanger Public Security of the Society (1983).
	(3) Decision of the Standing Committee on the Revision of the Organic Law of the People's Courts
	(4) Decision of the Standing Committee of the National People's Congress on the Revision of the Organic Law of the People's Procuratorates
	*(5) Decision of the Standing Committee of the National People's Congress on the Exercise by the State Security Organ [Ministry of State Security] of the Functions and Powers of Public Security Organs in Conducting Investigations, Detentions, Pretrial Hearings, and Arrests (1983).
	(6) Law on the Safety of Maritime Traffic
9/20	Regulations on the Implementation of the Law on Joint Ventures Using Chinese and Foreign Investment (promulgated by the State Council)

Selected Bibliography

Articles or news items in *Foreign Broadcast Information Service (FBIS), China* and *Zhongguo Fazhi Bao* (China's Legal System Paper) and some short articles in various newspapers and *Beijing Review* are not included. OPRSCAS is the abbreviation for the *Occasional Papers/Reprints Series in Contemporary Asian Studies,* edited by Hungdah Chiu of the University of Maryland School of Law at Baltimore.

Chinese newspapers and journals titles are translated as follows:

Beijing Ribao	Peking Daily
Faxue	Jurisprudence
Faxue Yanjiu	Studies in Law
Guangming Ribao	Enlightenment Daily
Hongqi	Red Flag
Jiefang Ribao	Liberation Daily
Minzhu Yu Fazhi	Democracy and Legal System
Nanfang Ribao	Southern Daily
Renmin Ribao	People's Daily
Sichuan Ribao	Sichuan Daily
Xinan Zhengfa Xueyuan Xuebao	Journal of the Southwest Political-Legal Institute
Zhengfa Yanjiu	Political-Legal Research

"Advance in the Direction of Strengthening Socialist Democracy and the Legal System," *Hongqi,* No. 3, 1981, pp. 14–15.

Amnesty International, *China: Violations of Human Rights, Prisoners of Conscience & the Death Penalty in the People's Republic of China,* London: Amnesty International Publications, 1984.

Bao Rue-wang (Jean Pasqualini) and Rudolph Chelminski, *Prisoner of Mao,* New York: Coward, McCann & Geoghegan, Inc., 1973.

Bell, Derrick, "Inside China: Continuity and Social Reform," *Juris Doctor,* Vol. 8, No. 4, April 1978, pp. 23–26, 31.

Berman, Harold, Susan Cohen, and Malcolm Russell, "A Comparison of the Chinese and Soviet Codes of Criminal Law and Procedure," *Journal of Criminal Law and Criminology*, Vol. 73, No. 1, Spring 1982, pp. 238–258.

Bernstein, Richard, " 'Gang of 4' Trial Dramatic But Case Far From Proved," *The Washington Star*, December 14, 1980, p. A11.

Bernstein, Thomas P., *Up to the Mountains and Down to the Village*, New Haven: Yale University Press, 1977.

Butterfield, Fox, *China, Alive in the Bitter Sea*, New York: Times Books, 1982.

———, "Chinese Said to Torture African Student in Sex Inquiry," *New York Times*, June 1, 1980, p. 3.

———, "Hundreds of Thousands Toil in Chinese Labor Camps," *New York Times*, January 3, 1981, pp. 1, 4.

———, "Leading Chinese Dissident Gets 15-Year Prison Term," *New York Times*, October 17, 1979, p. A3.

———, "Peking Bomb Blast is Laid to Ire of Man Kept From Living in City," *New York Times*, November 11, 1980, p. A5.

———, "Peking Dissident, in Rare Account, Tells of Political Prisoners' Torture," *New York Times*, May 7, 1979, pp. A1, A10.

———, "Revenge Seems to Outweigh Justice at Chinese Trial," *New York Times*, December 6, 1980, p. 2.

Campbell, Colin, "To Shame Its Felons, China Puts Them on Parade," *New York Times*, September 16, 1983, p. A2.

Canton *Fan Peng-Lo Heixian* (Anti-Peng and Lo's Black Line), No. 2, July 1968; English translation in *Selections from China Mainland Magazine*, Hong Kong: U.S. Consulate-General, No. 625, September 3, 1968, pp. 23–28.

Cao Zidan, "Questions and Answers on China's Criminal Law," *Beijing Review*, Vol. 23, No. 25, June 9, 1980, pp. 19–20.

Cen Ying, ed., *Zhongquo Dalu Zuian Xiaoshuoxuan* (A Selection of Chinese Mainland Crime Stories), Hong Kong: Tongjun Publishers, n.d., Preface, October 1980.

Chan, Anita and Jonathan eds., "The Case of Li I-che," in *Chinese Law and Government*, Vol. 10, No. 3, 1977, pp. 3–112.

Chen Chunlong, et al., *Falu Zhishi Wenda* (Questions and Answers in Legal Knowledge), Beijing: Beijing Publishing House, 1979.

Chen Guangzhong, "The Principle of Presumption of Innocence Should be Critically Assimilated," *Faxu Yanjiu*, No. 4, 1980, pp. 34–36.

Chen, Hefu, ed., *Zhongguo Xianfa Leibian* (Classified Collection of Chinese Constitutions), Beijing: Chinese Sciences Publisher, 1980.

Chen Jo-hsi, *The Execution of Mayor Yin*, Bloomington, Indiana: Indiana University Press, 1978.

Chen Lang, "Flies and Tigers," *Minzhu Yu Fazhi*, No. 4, 1982, p. 5.

Chen, Shouyi, "A Review of New China's Research in Law During the Past Thirty Years," *Faxue Yanjiu*, No. 1, 1980, pp. 1–10.

Chen, Shouyi, Liu Shengping and Zhao Shenjiang, "Thirty Years of the Building Up of Our Legal System," *Faxue Yanjiu*, No. 4, 1979, pp. 1–5.

Chen Weidian and Zhou Xinning, "Strengthen the Legal System, Ensure Stability and Unity," *Faxue Yanjiu*, No. 1, 1980, pp. 35–36.

Chen Yiyun and Kong Qingyum, "On Capital Punishment," *Remin Ribao*, February 25, 1980, p. 3.

"China Confirms Jailing of an Ex-U.S. Lawyer," *New York Times*, February 2, 1984, p. A7.

"China Post Crime Rate," *The Washington Post*, August 30, 1980, p. A24.

"China's Leaders Said to be Split on the Sentencing of Jiang Qing," *New York Times*, January 11, 1981, p. 7.

Ching, Frank, "China's Political Prisoners Help to Develop Frontier," *Asian Wall Street Journal*, June 3, 1982, p. 1.

———, "Chinese Nationwide Mull Their New Constitution," *Asian Wall Street Journal*, June 24, 1982, p. 6.

———, "Lawyer Who Worked at American Firms Imprisoned in China as Spy for the U.S.," *Asian Wall Street Journal Weekly*, January 23, 1984, p. 3.

———, "Official's Punishment Gives Chinese a Message: Don't Talk to Foreigners," *Asian Wall Street Journal Weekly*, April 5, 1982, p. 10.

———, "Robes of Justice Sit Uneasily on Gang of Four Judges," *The Asian Wall Street Journal*, November 28, 1980, p. 4.

Chiu, Hungdah, "Certain Legal Aspects of the Recent Peking Trials of the 'Gang of Four' and Others," in James C. Hsiung, ed., *Symposium: The Trial of the "Gang of Four" and Its Implication in China*, OPRSCAS, No. 3–1981 (40), pp. 27–39 and also published in *Chengchi Law Review*, Vol. 22, 1980, pp. 191–201 and *Asian Thought & Society*, Vol. 6, No. 16, April 1981, pp. 54–62.

———, "Certain Problems in Recent Law Reform in the People's Republic of China," in *Comparative Law Yearbook*, Vol. 3 (1979), Alphen aan den Rijn, The Netherlands: Sijthoff & Noordhoff, 1980, pp. 1–31, reprinted in OPRSCAS, No. 5–1980 (34).

———, "China's New Legal System," *Current History*, Vol. 79, No. 458, September 1980, pp. 29–32, 44.

———, *Chinese Law and Justice: Trends Over Three Decades*, OPRSCAS, No. 7–1982 (52).

———, "Criminal Punishment in Mainland China: A Study of Some Yunnan Province Documents," *Journal of Criminal Law & Criminology*, Vol. 68, 1977, pp. 374–398, reprinted with addition of Chinese text of documents in OPRSCAS, No. 6–1978 (18).

———, "The Judicial System Under the New PRC Constitution," in Michael Lindsay, ed., *The New Constitution of Communist China*, Taipei: Institute of International Relations, 1976, pp. 63–121.

———, "The Judiciary in Post-Cultural Revolution China," *Proceedings of the Fifth Sino-American Conference on Mainland China*, Taipei: Institute of International Relations, 1976, pp. 95–121.

———, "Social Disorder in Peking After the 1976 Earthquake as Revealed by a Chinese Legal Document," *Review of Socialist Law*, Vol. 5, 1979, pp. 5–16, reprinted with addition of Chinese text of the document in OPRSCAS No. 2–1979 (23).

————, "Socialist Legalism: Reform and Continuity in Post-Mao People's Republic of China," *Issues & Studies*, Vol. 17, No. 11, November 1981, pp. 45–75, reprinted in OPRSCAS No. 1–1982 (46).

————, "Structural Changes in the Organization and the Operation of China's Criminal Justice System," *Review of Socialist Law*, Vol. 7, 1981, pp. 53–72.

Cohen, Jerome Alan, "China's Changing Constitution," *The China Quarterly*, No. 76, December 1978, pp. 794–841.

————, "The Chinese Communist Party and 'Judicial Independence': 1949–1959," *Harvard Law Review*, Vol. 82, March 1969, pp. 967–1006.

————, *The Criminal Process in the People's Republic of China, 1949–1963: An Introduction*, Cambridge, Mass.: Harvard University Press, 1968.

————, "Is There Law in China?," *International Trade Law Journal*, Vol. 5 (1979), pp. 73–91.

————, "Rebuilding China's Shattered Legal System," *Asia*, November/ December 1983, p. 49.

————, "Reflections on the Criminal Process in China," *Journal of Criminal Law and Criminology*, Vol. 68, No. 3, September 1977, pp. 323–355.

————, "Will China Have a Formal Legal System? " *American Bar Association Journal*, Vol. 64, 1978, pp. 1510–1515.

Cohen, Jerome Alan, T.A. Gelatt and F.M. Li, translators, "The Criminal Law in the People's Republic of China," *Journal of Criminal Law and Criminology*, Vol. 73, No. 1, Spring 1982, pp. 136–203.

Commentator, "Further Tidy Up Social Law and Order," *Sichuan Ribao*, May 25, 1981, p. 1.

Commentator, "Parental Love is Needed in Educating and Reforming Erring Young People," *Renmin Ribao*, October 15, 1981, p. 1.

Commentator, "Severe Punishment Should be Imposed on Those Leading Cadres Who Violated the Law and Committed Crimes," *Hongqi*, No. 4, 1982, pp. 6–8, 38.

Commentator, "Strike Resolute Blows at Economic Criminals," *Nanfang Ribao*, June 15, 1980, p. 1.

Commentator, "Warn Those Cadres' Children and Younger Brothers Who Violate the Law and Commit Crimes," *Renmin Ribao*, August 9, 1980, p. 4.

Compilation Section of Lectures on Criminal Procedural Law of China People's University. *Xingshi susong fa jiangyi* (Lectures on Criminal Procedure Law). Beijing: China People's University Press, 1981.

Cong Wenhui, "Have a Better Comprehension of the Policy of 'Being Lenient to Those Who Confess Their Crimes and Severe to Those Who Refuse to Confess,' " *Faxue*, No. 5, 1982, pp. 19–20.

"Continue to Reverse Unjust and Erroneous Verdicts Based on False Charges," *Guangming Ribao*, June 28, 1979, p. 1.

"Cracking Down on Speculation and Smuggling," *Beijing Review*, Vol. 24, No. 7, February 16, 1981, pp. 5–6.

"Crime of Betraying State Secrets," *Beijing Review*, Vol. 25, No. 20, May 17, 1982, p. 3.

"The Criminal Law," *China News Analysis*, No. 1160, August 3, 1979, pp. 6–8.

Criminal Law and Criminal Procedure Law Teaching and Research Group of the Central Political-Legal Cadre School, *Zhonghua Renmin Gongheguo Xinfa Zhongzhe Jiangyi* (Lectures on the General Principles of the PRC Criminal Law), Beijing: Mass Press, 1980.

The Criminal Law and the Criminal Procedure Law of the People's Republic of China, Beijing: Foreign Languages Press, 1984.

Criminal Procedure Teaching and Research Group, Law Department, China People's University, *Zhonghua Renmin Gonghequo Xinshi Susong Fa Jiben Zhishi* (Basic Knowledge of the Criminal Procedure Law of the People's Republic of China), Beijing: People's Press, 1980.

Criminal Research Group of the Legal Research Institute [Institute of Law] of the Chinese Academy of Social Sciences," Lectures on the Criminal Law, (1979)," translated by D. Cameron, et al., in *Chinese Law and Government*, Vol. 13, No. 2, Summer 1980, pp. 3–112.

Crocket, George W. Jr., "Criminal Justice in China," *Judicature*, Vol. 59, No. 5, December 1975, pp. 239–247.

Cui Min, "How Should We Interpret 'Everyone is Equal Before the Law,' " *Renmin Ribao*, July 24, 1979, p. 3.

"Decision on Combating Economic Crimes," *Beijing Review*, Vol. 25, No. 17, April 26, 1982, pp. 7–9.

Department of State, *Country Report on Human Rights Practices for 1983*, "China" Washington, D.C.: U.S. Government Printing Office, 1984, pp. 740–755.

Ding Jianjing, "It is Unnecessary to Distinguish Between the Two Types of Contradictions in Assessing Offenses and Measuring Penalties," *Minzhu Yu Fazhi*, No. 6, 1980, pp. 4–6.

Documents of the First Session of the First National People's Congress of the People's Republic of China, Peking: Foreign Languages Press, 1955.

Documents of the First Session of the Fifth National People's Congress of the People's Republic of China, Beijing: Foreign Languages Press, 1978.

Dong, Biwu, *Lun Shehui Zhuyi Minzhu Yu Fazhi* (On Socialist Democracy and the Legal System), Beijing: People's Press, 1979.

Dreyer, June Teufel, "Limits of the Permissible in China," *Problems of Communism*, Vol. 29, Nov.-Dec. 1980, pp. 48–65.

"Economic Crimes Near the Top," *Yomiuri Shimbun*, April 2, 1982, translated in *Inside China Mainland*, May 1982, pp. 14–15.

Edwards, Randle, "Reflections on Crime and Punishment in China, with Appended Sentencing Documents," *Columbia Journal of Transnational Law*, Vol. 18 (1977), pp. 45–103 Documents co-translated with Hungdah Chiu, reprinted with Chinese texts of documents in OPRSCAS, No. 8–1977.

Eighth National Congress of the Communist Party of China, Vol. 1, Documents, Peking: Foreign Languages Press, 1956.

Eliasoph, Ellen R. and Susan Grueneberg, "Law on Display in China," *The China Quarterly*, No. 88, December 1981, pp. 669–685.

"Embezzler Sentenced to Death, *Beijing Review*, Vol. 22, No. 45, November 9, 1979, p. 7.

Fan Fenglin, "On Fundamental Problems of the Characterization of Crimes," *Faxue Yanjiu*, No. 4, 1979, pp. 29–33, 41.

Faxue Cidan (Law Dictionary), Shanghai: Dictionary Press, 1980.

Fazhi Yu Renzhi Wenti Taolun Ji (Collection of Discussions on the Question of Rule by Law and Rule by Man), Beijing: Mass Press, 1981.

Forte, David F., "Western Law and Communist Dictatorship," *Emory Law Journal*, Vol. 32, No. 1 (Winter 1983), pp. 135–235.

Foster, Frances Hoar, "Codification in Post-Mao China," *American Journal of Comparative Law*, Vol. 30 (1982), pp. 395–428.

Gao Minxuan, ed., *Xinfa Xue* (The Science of Criminal Law), Beijing: Law Press, 1981.

Ge Ping and Wang Honggu, "On Capital Punishment," *Faxue Yanjiu*, No. 1, 1980, pp. 29–32, 44.

Gelatt, Timothy A., "The People's Republic of China and the Presumption of Innocence," *Journal of Criminal Law and Criminology*, Vol. 73, No. 1, Spring 1982, pp. 259–316.

Gelatt, Timothy A. and Frederick E. Snyder, "Legal Education in China: Training for a New Era," *China Law Reporter*, Vol. 1, No. 2, 1980, pp. 41–60.

Gold, Thomas B., "China's Youth: Problems and Programs," in King-yuh Chang, ed., *The Emerging Teng System: Orientation, Policy & Implication*, Taipei: Institute of International Relations, 1982, pp. IV-2, 1–24.

A Great Trial in Chinese History, Beijing: New World Press, 1981.

Griffin, Patricia E., *The Chinese Communist Treatment of Counterrevolutionaries: 1924–1949*, Princeton, N.J.: Princeton University Press, 1976.

Gu Fangping, "The Great Victory of the Policy of Reforming Criminals," *Zhengfa Yanjiu*, No. 6, 1959, pp. 35–37.

Hazard, John N., *Communists and Their Law*, Chicago: University of Chicago Press, 1969.

He Bian, "China's Lawyers," *Beijing Review*, Vol. 25, No. 23, June 7, 1982, pp. 14–17.

He Bingsong, "On the Democratic Principal of China's Criminal Law," *Faxue Yanjiu*, No. 4, 1980, pp. 22–27.

He Peng, Gao Ge and Jin Kai, eds., *Xinfa Gailun* (An Introductory of the Criminal Law), Changchun: Jilin People's Press, 1981.

"High Officials' Sons Punished," *Beijing Review*, Vol. 23, No. 35, September 1, 1980, pp. 7–8.

"Hong Kong 'Compatriots' Missing in China," *Asian Wall Street Journal Weekly*, October 11, 1982, pp. 4, 17.

"How to Prevent the Abuse of Office and Power for Illegal Economic Activities," [This includes six short articles and one report on several publicly announced court judgements], *Minzhu Yu Fazhi*, No. 1, 1982, pp. 6–10.

Hsia Tao-tai, "Legal Developments in the PRC Since the Purge of the Gang of Four," *Review of Socialist Law*, Vol. 5, 1979, pp. 109–130.

Hsia, Tao-tai and Charlotte Hambley, "The Lawyer's Law: An Introduction," *China Law Reporter*, Vol. 1, No. 4, Fall 1981, pp. 213–221.

Hsia, Tao-tai and Kathryn A. Haun, *The Re-Emergence of the Procuratorial System in the People's Republic of China*, Washington, D.C.: Library of Congress, 1978.

Hsin Fei [Xin Fei in Pinyin], "Test for the Chinese Communist Legal System," *Chung-pao Yueh-k'an* [Zhongbao Yuekan in Pinyin; Center News Monthly], No. 46, November 1983, pp. 54–56.

Hsiung, James C., ed., with contributions by H. Lyman Miller, Hungdah Chiu, and Lillian Craig Harris, *Symposium: The Trial of the "Gang of Four" and Its Implication in China*, OPRSCAS No. 3–1981 (40).

Hu Sheng, "On the Revision of the Constitution," *Beijing Review*, Vol. 25, No. 18, May 3, 1982, pp. 15–18.

Huang Dao, Wang Gangxiang and Jin Zitong, "The Two Types of Contradictions in Criminal Offenses and the Principle of Acting According to Law," *Minzhu Yu Fazhi*, No. 6, 1980, pp. 6–10.

Huang Mingxiu, "Why is it that the Statement of Leniency to Those Who Confess and Severity to Those Who Resist Was Not Written into the Criminal Law," *Minzhu Yu Fazhi*, No. 2, 1979, p. 30.

Huang Yifeng, "Drafting Economic Laws and Regulations Is An Urgent Task in the Current Drive to Realize the Four Modernizations," *Minzhu Yu Fazhi*, No. 8, 1980, pp. 8–9.

Hung Xiang, "On Expanding Research into International Law," *Faxue Yanjiu*, No. 2, 1980, pp. 9–11.

Ji Ling, "Psychological Analysis of the Youths Who Commit Homicide Because of Rejection in Love," *Minzhu Yu Fazhi*, No. 2, 1982, pp. 21–22.

Jianmin falu cidian (Concise law dictionary), Hubei Province: Hubei People's Press, 1982.

Jin Mosheng, "Resolutely Strike at the Lawbreaking, Criminal Activities that Disrupt the Economic Order," *Minzhu Yu Fazhi*, No. 5, 1981, p. 38.

Johnson, Bryan, "China Dissidents Fall Through Cracks in New Legal Code," *Christian Science Monitor*, June 18, 1980, p. 4.

Jones, William C., "The Criminal Law of the People's Republic of China," *Review of Socialist Law*, Vol. 6, No. 4, December 1980, pp. 405–423.

———, "On the Campaign Trial in China," *Review of Socialist Law*, Vol. 5, No. 4, December 1979, pp. 457–462.

———, "A Possible Model for the Criminal Trial in the People's Republic of China," *American Journal of Comparative Law*, Vol. 2, 1976, pp. 229–245.

"Juvenile Delinquency," *China News Analysis*, No. 1167, November 9, 1979, pp. 6–7.

Kaminski, Gerd, "International Law: A Robust Plant Among the Hundred Flowers of China's Law Reform," *Asian Thought and Society*, Vol. VII, March 1982, pp. 3–17.

Keith, Ronald C., "Transcript of Discussions with Wu Daying and Zhang Zhonglin Concerning Legal Change and Civil Rights," *The China Quarterly*, No. 81, March 1980, pp. 111–121.

Kelsen, Hans, *The Communist Theory of Law*, London: Stevens & Sons, 1955.

Kim, Hyung I., *Fundamental Legal Concepts of China and the West: A Comparative Study*, Port Washington, N.Y.: Kennikat Press, 1981.

Laduguie, Arlette, "The Human Rights Movement," *Index on Censorship*, Vol. 6, February 1980, pp. 24–25.

Lamb, Franklin P., "An Interview with Chinese Legal Officials," *The China Quarterly*, No. 66, June 1976, pp. 323–325.

Lan Chuanbu, *Sanshi Nianlai Woguo Fagui Yange Gaikuang* (Survey of the Development of the Laws and Regulations of Our Country in the Last Thirty Years), Beijing: Mass Press, 1980.

Law Annual Report of China 1982/3, Hong Kong: Kingsway International Publications, Ltd., October 1982.

"Legal Studies of America in China," *China Exchange News*, Vol. 11, No. 3, September 1983, pp. 6–12.

Leng, Shao-chuan, "Crime and Punishment in Post-Mao China," *China Law Reporter*, Vol. II, No. 1, Spring 1982, pp. 5–33.

―――, "Criminal Justice in Post-Mao China," *The China Quarterly*, No. 87, September 1981, pp. 440–469.

―――, "Human Rights in Chinese Political Culture," Kenneth W. Thompson, ed., *The Moral Imperative of Human Rights*, Washington, D.C.: University Press of America, 1980.

―――, *Justice in Communist China*, Dobbs Ferry, New York: Oceana, 1967.

―――, "The Role of Law in the People's Republic of China as Reflecting Mao Tse-tung's Influence," *Journal of Criminal Law and Criminology*, Vol. 68, No. 3, 1977, pp. 356–73, reprinted in OPRSCAS, No. 5–1978 (17).

Leys, Simon, *Broken Images*, New York: St. Martins Press, 1980.

Li Binghou, "Visit the Shanghai Municipal Prison," *Minzhu Yu Fazhi*, No. 11, 1981, pp. 7–8.

Li Buyun, "On the Scientific Character of the Concept of Rule by Law," *Faxue Yanjiu*, No. 1, 1982, pp. 6–11.

Li Guangcan, *Woguo Gongmin Di Jiben Quanli He Yiwu* (The Fundamental Rights and Duties of the Citizens of Our Country), Beijing: People's Press, 1956.

Li Maoguan, "Citizens' Freedom and the Law," *Faxue Yanjiu*, No. 2, 1981, pp. 5–8.

Li Shutang, "Strengthen Legal Education for Young People," *Minzhu Yu Fazhi*, No. 8, 1980, pp. 6–7.

Li, Victor H., "Reflections on the Current Drive Toward Greater Legalization in China," *Georgia Journal of International and Comparative Law*, Vol. 10, 1980, pp. 221–232.

―――, "The Role of Law in Communist China," *The China Quarterly*, No. 44, October-December 1970, pp. 66–111.

Li Yonyi, "On the Stipulation and Analogy of Offenses and Penalties," *Faxue Yanjiu*, No. 5, 1980, pp. 19–24.

Liang Heng and Judith Shapiro, *Son of the Revolution*, New York: Alfred A. Knopf, 1983.

Liao Junchang, "Independent Adjudication and Approving Cases by the Secretary," *Xinan Zhengfa Xueyuan Xuebao*, No. 1, May 1979 pp. 6–9.

Liao Zengyun, "View on the Principle of Presumption of Innocence," *Faxue Yanjiu*, No. 5, 1980, pp. 32–34.

Li Rong, "What is the Crime of Leaking State Secrets? " *Guangming Ribao*, June 19, 1981, p. 3.

Lindsay, Michael, ed., *The New Constitution of Communist China*, Taipei: Institute of International Relations, 1976.

Lin Guoding, "The Criminal Advocacy of Lawyers," *Faxue Yanjiu*, No. 5, 1981, pp. 21–23.

Liu Guangming, "The People's Courts Administer Justice Independently, Subject only to the Law," *Faxue Yanjiu*, No. 3, 1979, pp. 29–32.

Liu Sheng-chi, "The Democratic Movement in Mainland China in Retrospect," *Issues and Studies*, Vol. 17, No. 4, April 1981, pp. 51–62.

Liu Zhi, "Notes on the Reform Role of Punishment of China," *Faxue Yanjiu*, No. 4, 1982, pp. 28–29,

———, "The Role of Punishment in Reforming Criminals in Our Country," *Guangming Ribao*, December 22, 1981, p. 3.

Lu Heyun, "An Analysis of All Kinds of Handicaps to the Exposition of Grafts in the Economic Field," *Faxue*, No. 4, 1982, p. 36.

Lu Ming, "Big Cases and Little People," *Minzhu Yu Fazhi*, No. 3, 1982, pp. 25–26.

Luo Bing, "Truth About the Strange Case of Lo Fu," *Cheng Ming* (Contending), No. 10, 1983, pp. 25–26.

Luo Ping, "The Principle of Measuring Penalty in China's Criminal Law," *Hongqi*, No. 9, 1979, pp. 71–75.

Luo Ting, "The Prisoner Condemned to Die is Still Alive," *Cheng Ming* [Hong Kong, *Zhengming* in Pinyin], No. 57, July 1982, pp. 73–74.

Lubman, Stanley, "Emerging Functions of Formal Legal Institutions in China's Modernization," U.S. Congressional Joint Economic Committee, *China Under the Four Modernizations*, Washington, D.C.: Government Printing Office, 1982, Part 2, pp. 235–289.

———, "Form and Function in the Chinese Criminal Process," *Columbia Law Review*, Vol. 69, No. 4, April 1969, pp. 535–575.

———, "New Development in Law in the People's Republic of China," *Northwestern Journal of International Law & Business*, Vol. 1 (1979), pp. 122–133.

Ma Jian, "Three Crickets and Eighteen Years' Imprisonment," *Minzhu Yu Fazhi*, No. 10, 1980, p. 38.

Ma Rongjie, "Which is Superior, the 'Official' or the Law? " *Renmin Ribao*, July 29, 1981, p. 5.

MacDonald, R.S.J., "Legal Education in China Today," *Dalhousie Law Journal*, Vol. 6, 1980, pp. 313–337.

Main Documents of the Second Session of the Fifth National People's Congress of the People's Republic of China, Beijing: Foreign Languages Press, 1979.

Main Documents of the Third Session of the Fifth National People's Republic of China, Beijing: Foreign Languages Press, 1980.

Mathews, Jay, "China Revives Labor Camp System," *The Washington Post*, June 1, 1980, pp. A1, A27.

————, "Plagued by Crime, Chinese Increase Use of the Executions," *The Washington Post*, August 5, 1980, p. A13.

Mathews, Jay and Linda, *One Billion, A China Chronicle*, New York: Random House, 1983.

Meijar, M.J., "The New Criminal Law of the People's Republic of China," *Review of Socialist Law*, Vol. 6, No. 2, 1980, pp. 125–140.

"Ministry of State Security Established," *Beijing Review*, Vol. 26, No. 27, July 4, 1983, p. 6.

Mok Bong-ho, *Young Offenders in Contemporary China: Contributing Factors and Related Services*, Hong Kong: The Chinese University of Hong Kong, December 1983.

Mosher, Steven W., *Broken Earth, The Rural Chinese*, New York: The Free Press, 1982.

"Oil Rig Accident Sternly Dealt With," *Beijing Review*, Vol. 23, No. 36, September 8, 1980, pp. 7–8.

Pan Nianzhi and Qi Naikuan, "On 'Everyone is Equal Before the Law,'" *Guangming Ribao*, February 9, 1980, p. 3.

"Party Discipline Should Not Replace State Law," *Jiefang Ribao*, October 7, 1980, p. 3.

Peng Zhen, "Explanation on the Draft of the revised Constitution of the PRC," *Beijing Review*, Vol. 25, No. 19, May 10, 1982, pp. 18–26.

————, "Explanation on Seven Laws," *Beijing Review*, Vol. 22, No. 29, July 20, 1979, pp. 8–16.

————, "Report on the Draft of the Revised Constitution of the People's Republic of China," *Beijing Review*, Vol. 25, No. 50, December 13, 1982, pp. 9–23.

————, "Several Questions on the Socialist Legal System," *Hongqi*, No. 11, 1979, pp. 3–7.

"The People's Verdict—Wei Jingsheng's Appeal Rejected," *Beijing Review*, Vol. 22, No. 46, November 16, 1979, pp. 15–16.

Pfennig, Werner, "Political Aspects of Modernization and Judicial Reform in the PRC," *Journal of Chinese Studies*, Vol. 1, No. 1, February 1984, pp. 79–103.

Policy and Law Research Office of the Ministry of Public Security, ed., *Gongan Fagui Huibian, 1950–79* (Collection of Laws and Regulations on Public Security, 1950–79), Beijing: Mass Press, 1980.

Political Imprisonment in the People's Republic of China, London: Amnesty International, 1978.

Political-Legal Section of the Office of the Standing Committee of the National People's Congress and the Legal Office of the Legal System Committee of the Standing Committee of the National People's Congress, eds., *Zhongguo remin zhengzhi xieshang huiyi diyijie quanti huiyi, zhongyang renmin zhengfu, diyi zhi sijie guanguo renmin daibiao dahui ji qi changwu weiyuanhui zhiding hezhe pizhen de falu, falin he qita wenjian mulu* (List of laws, decrees and other documents enacted or ratified by the plenary meeting of the first session of the Chinese People's Political Consultative Conference, Central People's Government, first to fourth session of the

National People's Congress and Its Standing Committee) September 1949–October 1977, Beijing: Mass Press, 1980.

"Principal Legal Journals in China," *China Exchange News*, Vol. 11, No. 3, September 1983, p. 12.

"Prospect and Retrospect: China's Socialist Legal System," *Beijing Review*, Vol. 22, No. 2, January 12, 1979, pp. 25–30.

Qiu Xueyao, "The Differences Between Party Discipline, Administrative Discipline; and the Legal Code," *Guangming Ribao*, December 8, 1981, p. 3.

Quyang Tao and Zhang Shengzu, eds., *Zhonghua Renmin Gongheguo Xinfa Zhushi* (Annotations on the Criminal Law of the People's Republic of China), Beijing: Beijing Press, 1980.

Ramundo, Bernard P., *The Soviet Legal System: A Primer*, Chicago: American Bar Association, 1971.

Rickett, W. Allyn and Adele Rickett, *Prisoners of Liberation*, New York: Cameron Associates, 1957.

Ruge, Gerd, "An Interview with Chinese Legal Officials," *The China Quarterly*, No. 61, March 1975, pp. 118–126.

"Senior Cadres Support Sentences on Their Criminal Sons," *Beijing Review*, Vol. 25, No. 20, May 17, 1982, p. 5.

"Severely and Swiftly Punish Major Criminals," *Jiefang Ribao*, June 16, 1981, p. 1.

Seymour, James D., ed., *The Fifth Modernization: China's Human Rights Movement, 1978–1979*, Stanfordville, N.Y.: Human Rights Publishing Group, 1980.

"Shanghai Publicizes the Legal System," *Beijing Review*, Vol. 26, No. 3, August 15, 1983, pp. 22–24.

Snow, Edgar, *The Other Side of the River*, New York: Random House, 1962.

Special Group Assisting the Handling of Cases from the Southwest Political-Legal Institute, "Looking at Some Existing Problems in Judicial Work from the Practice of Handling Cases," *Xinan Zhengfa Xueyuan Xuebao*, No. 1, May 1979, pp. 26–30.

Stahnke, Arthur, "The Background and Evolution of Party Policy on the Drafting of Legal Codes in Communist China," *American Journal of Comparative Law*, Vol. 15, 1967, pp. 506–525.

Sterba, James P., "China Says Its Rising Juvenile Crime Stems from Cultural Revolution," *New York Times*, December 26, 1979, p. A12.

―――, "Former Chinese Leaders Given Long Prison Terms," *New York Times*, January 26, 1981, p. A3.

"Strengthen Legal System and Democracy," *Beijing Review*, Vol. 22, No. 27, July 6, 1979, pp. 32–36.

Sun Yinji and Feng Caijin, *Lushi Jiben Zhishi* (Basic Knowledge about Lawyers), Beijing: Mass Press, 1980.

"Suppression of Criminality," *China News Analysis*, No. 1215, September 11, 1981, pp. 2–3.

Talu Dixia Kanwu Huibian (Collection of the Mainland Underground Publication), Taipei: Institute for the Study of Chinese Communist Problems, 1980–1981, 5 Vols.

Tao, Lung-sheng, "Politics and Law Enforcement in China: 1949–1970," *American Journal of Comparative Law*, Vol. 22, No. 4, Fall 1974, pp. 713–756.

Tao Mao and Li Baoyue, "The Principle of 'Not Increasing Sentences on Appeal' Should Not be Negated," *Minzhu Yu Fazhi*, No. 2, 1980, pp. 25–26.

Tao Xijin, "Problems in the Study of Criminal Law," *Faxue Yanjiu*, No. 5, 1979, pp. 1–8.

Teaching and Research Office of the Beijing Political-Legal Institute, *Zhonghua Renmin Gonghequo Xinshi Susong Fa Jianghua* (Lectures on the Criminal Procedure Law of the People's Republic of China), Beijing: Mass Press, 1979.

Teaching and Research Office for Criminal Law of the Central Political-Legal Cadres' School, *Lectures on the General Principles of Criminal Law of the People's Republic of China* (Peking: Law Press, 1957), translated by Joint Publication Research Service (JPRS), No. 13331, 1962.

Tian Yun, "The Police and the People," *Beijing Review*, Vol. 26, No. 21, May 23, 1983, pp. 22–27.

"Use of the Weapon of Law to Crack Down on Criminal Activities," *Renmin Ribao*, June 22, 1981, p. 1.

Vink, Michael, "Canton's Crackdown on Smuggling Drives," *Asian Wall Street Journal*, December 6, 1980, pp. 1, 5.

Wang Bingxin, "Exploration on the Principle of Presumption of Innocence," *Xinan Zhengfa Xueyuen Xuebao*, No. 1, 1979, pp. 10–15.

Wu Biao, "We Can Never Let Law-Breaking Offenders Subject to Criticism for a Short Period While Enjoying Comforts for a Lifetime," *Minzhu Yu Fazhi*, No. 1, 1982, p. 10.

Wang Chi, "The Criminal Law of the People's Republic of China," *Review of Socialist Law*, Vol. 7, No. 2, 1981, pp. 199–222.

Wang Chuansheng, "On Application of Penalty and Its Adapting to the Political Situation," *Faxue Yanjiu*, No. 6, 1981, pp. 1–4.

Wang Dexiang, "Some Questions Concerning Our Country's Juvenile Delinquency," *Xinan Zhengfa Xueyuan Xuebao*, No. 2, 1979, pp. 27–31.

Wang Guiwu, "Law Enforcement Must Consider the Overall Situation," *Renmin Ribao*, September 14, 1981, p. 5.

———, "Upholding Four Basic Principles: Continuously Emancipating Our Minds," *Faxue Yanjiu*, No. 2, 1979, pp. 21–23.

Wang Rouwang, "Jokes Should Not Be Considered as 'Law,' " *Minzhu Yu Fazhi*, No. 1, 1980, pp. 25–27.

Wang Shunhua, "Why Is It Necessary to Strictly Ban Torture in Extracting Confessions?" *Guangming Ribao*, March 19, 1980, p. 3.

———, *Woguo xingshi susong zhong di jiancha jiquan* (The Procuratorial Organ in Our Country's Criminal Litigation), Beijing: Mass Press, 1982.

Wang Suwen, Li Buyun and Xu Bing, "On Strengthening Socialist Legal System," *Faxue Yanjiu*, No. 5, 1982, pp. 1–8.

"Wei Jingsheng Sentenced," *Beijing Review*, Vol. 22, No. 43, October 26, 1979, pp. 6–7.

Wei Remin, "Be Cautious! Be Cautious!," *Minzhu Yu Fazhi*, No. 11, 1980, p. 27.

Wei Min, "Interviewing Deputy Director of Public Security Bureau," *Beijing Review*, Vol. 24, No. 8, February 23, 1981, pp. 22–24.

Weisskopf, Michael, "China Cracks Down on 'Plucking Feathers From a Wild Goose,'" *The Washington Post*, January 7, 1982, p. A24.

———, "China Ends a Fling at Free Thinking," *The Washington Post*, March 23, 1981, pp. A1, A10.

———, "China Holds American As Suspect in Spy Case," *The Washington Post*, June 2, 1982, pp. A1, A13.

———, "China Reviewing Freedom Granted Its Intellectuals," *The Washington Post*, May 7, 1981, p. A36.

———, "China Sentences Prominent Editor As Spy for U.S.," *The Washington Post*, May 16, 1983, pp. A1, A16.

———, "Ex-Inmate Recalls Life in China's Gulag," *The Washington Post*, February 12, 1982, pp. A1, A44–A45.

———, "A Glimpse of Life in China's Prisons," *The Washington Post*, September 15, 1981, pp. A1, A14.

———, "Mao's Wife Spared, Gets Life in Prison," *The Washington Post*, January 26, 1983, p. A26.

White Book on Forced Labour and Concentration Camp in the People's Republic of China, 2 Vols., Paris: Commission Internationale Contre Le Regime Concentrationnaise, 1957.

Wren, Christopher S., "China's Black Sheep 'Reeducated' Without Trial," *New York Times*, August 12, 1982, p. A2.

———, "China Jails a Hong Kong Editor As a Spy for U.S.," *New York Times*, May 16, 1983, pp. A1, A3.

———, "Peking to Create New Security Unit," *New York Times*, June 7, 1983, p. A11.

Wu Hengquan, "Persons Under Reeducation Through Labor Participate in Democratic Administration," *Minzhu Yu Fazhi*, No. 5, 1982, pp. 25–26.

Xie Wen, "Class Struggle and the Principal Contradiction in Socialist Society," *Hongqi*, No. 20, 1981, pp. 26–31, 6.

Xiao Yongging and others, "Subjects and Methods of Research on the History of the Legal System," *Faxue Yanjiu*, No. 5, 1979, pp. 17–20.

Yang Kedian, "Correctly Implement the Principle of Independent Adjudication," *Guangming Ribao*, July 17, 1981, p. 3.

Ye Chuangu, "How Do the Lawyers Carry On Their Task of Defense Amidst the Drive to Mete Out Severe and Swift Punishment to Current Major Offenders?" *Minzhu Yu Fazhi*, No. 8, 1981, pp. 10–11.

Ye Zi, "Is There Absolute Freedom of Speech," *Hongqi*, No. 7, 1981, pp. 31–35.

Yu Haocheng, "The 'Offense of Malicious Attack' and 'Six Articles of Public Security,'" *Minzhu Yu Fazhi*, No. 1, 1979, pp. 36–37.

———, "Party Committees Should Not Continue Reviewing and Approving Cases," *Beijing Ribao*, January 23, 1981, p. 3.

————, "Rehabilitation Through Labor is an Essential Measure for Strengthening the Legal System and Maintaining Law and Order," *Guangming Ribao*, December 9, 1979, p. 3.

Yu Zhi, "Presumption of Innocence Cannot Serve as a Guiding Concept in Criminal Procedure—A Discussion with Comrade Lan Chuanbu," *Minzhu Yu Fazhi*, No. 3, 1980, pp. 20–21.

Yuan Xiaofan, "On the Equality of the Application of Law," *Faxue Yanjiu*, No. 2, 1980,, pp. 23–26.

Zeng Longyao, "Upholding the Principle of Mutual Coordination and Restriction by the Public Security Organs, Procuratorial Organs and People's Courts," *Faxue Yanjiu*, No. 1, 1979, pp. 42–45.

Zeng Longyue, "Links and Differences Between Party Discipline and State Law in Fighting Economic Crimes," *Renmin Ribao*, April 5, 1982, p. 3.

Zhai Bugao, "Comment on the Cause and Character of Juvenile Delinquency," *Faxue Yanjiu*, No. 3, 1981, pp. 44–47.

Zhang Ruihong, "What I have Seen and Heard in the Qinhuangdao Rehabilitation Through Labor Camp," *Minzhu Yu Fazhi*, No. 11, 1981, pp. 5–6.

Zhang Shangzhou, "New Development of Socialist Democracy and the Legal System," *Renmin Ribao*, May 11, 1982, p. 5.

Zhang Zhiye, "How Do China's Lawyers Work?" *Beijing Review*, Vol. 26, No. 23, June 6, 1983, pp. 19–27.

————, "Legislative and Judicial Work in China," *Beijing Review*, Vol. 26, No. 33, August 15, 1983, pp. 19–22.

Zhang Youyu, "On the Revision of the Constitution of China," *Faxue Yanjiu*, No. 3, 1982, pp. 1–9.

————, "Revolution and the Legal System," *Minzhu Yu Fazhi*, No, 7, 1981, pp. 5–7.

Zhang Zipei, "Analysis of the Principle of 'Presumption of Innocence,'" *Faxue Yanjiu*, No. 3, 1980, pp. 30–33.

Zhao Cangbi, "Strengthen the Concept of the Legal System and Act Strictly According to the Law," *Hongqi*, No. 8, 1979, pp. 40–45.

Zheng Lin, "Hitting Hard at the Criminal Activities," *Faxue Yanjiu*, No. 5, 1983, pp. 13–18.

Zhongguo Baike Nianjian, 1980 (Chinese Encyclopedia Yearbook, 1980), Beijing: Chinese Encyclopedia Press, 1981.

————, *1981*, Beijing: 1982.

————, *1982*, Beijing: 1983.

Zhonghua Renmin Gongheguo Fagui Huibian (Collection of Laws and Regulations of the People's Republic of China), 13 Vols., Beijing: Law Press, 1956–1965.

Zhong Minguang, "An Important Reason for Juvenile Delinquency: Legal Illiteracy," *Minzhu Yu Fazhi*, No. 8, 1980, pp. 6–7.

Zhongyang Renmin Zhengfu Faling Huibian (Collection of Laws and Decree of the Central People's Government), 7 Vols., Beijing: People's Press, 1950–1955.

Zhou Daoluan, et al., "Deal Heavy and Swift Blows to Serious Criminal Offenders According to Law," *Renmin Ribao*, June 25, 1981, p. 5.

Zhou Xinmin, "Law Is a Sharp Weapon of Class Struggle," *Renmin Ribao*, October 28, 1964, p. 2.

Zhou Zheng, "Save the Teenage Delinquents," *Beijing Review*, Vol. 22, No. 44, November 2, 1979, pp. 18–21.

Zhuang Huichen, "On Public Trial," *Faxue Yanjiu*, No. 5, 1980, pp. 35–38.

Index

Act for Punishment of Corruption, 12, 85

Act for Punishment of Counterrevolutionaries, 12, 26, 147

Act on Academic Degrees, 45

Act on Arrest and Detention, 77, 85, 87, 89

Adjudication (judicial) Committee (of a people's court), 63, 66, 73, 80, 129

adjudication supervision, 108, 109

administration of justice, 8, 23, 38

administrative discipline, 151

administrative sanctions, 21, 123, 152, 172

alimony claims, 75

American Bar Association, 37, 75, 95

Amnesty International, 137

analogous application of penal provisions, 8, 26, 129, 147

Andrei Y. Vishinsky, on definition of law, 9

antagonistic contradiction, 10, 157

anticrime campaign, 111, 112, 136, 137, 145, 171

antigovernment protests, 148

Anti-Rightist Campaign, 16, 22, 97, 104, 149

antisocial conduct, 152

antisocialist reactionaries, 27, 152

appeal and review of cases, 108–111, 121

appraisal, 91

apprehension, 88

April 5 Forum, 148, 149

arbitrary actions, 171

arbitrary arrest, or detention, 12, 14, 20, 78, 150

arbitration, 73

armed coup, 96

armed forces, 129

armed robbery, 132

arrest, 87, 88, 114, 115; formal arrest, 148; illegal arrest, 170; indiscriminate arrest, 12

arson, 10, 110, 123, 127, 134, 142

assault, 141

Austrian judicial institutions, 51

autonomous counties, 63

autonomous regions, 64, 133, 135

bad elements, 12, 21

Bai Hua, author of *Unrequited Love*, 149

Bao Ruo-wang, author of *Prisoner of Man*, 17, 24

Bartek, appealed his sentence, 24

Basic People's Courts, 14, 64

Beidaihe, gang attacked on Deng Xiaoping's motorcade, 136

Beijing, 75, 85, 89, 90, 95, 103, 112, 130, 131, 132, 134, 136, 138, 142, 144, 146, 147, 148, 149, 153, 154, 170, 172

Beijing Daily, 101

Beijing Institute of Foreign Trade, 90

Beijing Law Society, 49

Beijing Municipal Bureau of Public Security, 144

Beijing Municipal Higher People's Court, 147

Beijing Municipal Intermediate People's Court, 134, 147

Beijing Municipal Reformatory, 143

Beijing Political-Legal Institute, 47

Beijing Railroad Station, 131

Beijing Review, 12, 36, 94, 130, 137

Beijing University, 47, 48, 90